Georg Simmel

ON INDIVIDUALITY

AND SOCIAL FORMS

THE HERITAGE OF SOCIOLOGY

A Series Edited by Morris Janowitz

Georg Simmel

ON INDIVIDUALITY
AND SOCIAL FORMS

Selected Writings

Edited and with an Introduction by

DONALD N. LEVINE

THE UNIVERSITY OF CHICAGO PRESS

CHICAGO AND LONDON

The University of Chicago Press, Chicago 60637
The University of Chicago Press, Ltd., London

ISBN: 0-226-75775-7 (clothbound); 0-226-75776-5 (paperbound)
Library of Congress Catalog Card Number: 78-157146

Contents

v

Acknowledgments

FOR HELPFUL COMMENTS on the introductory essay I am greatly indebted to Robert K. Merton and Lewis A. Coser. Mrs. Robert Redfield kindly provided materials for the section on Robert E. Park. Guenther Roth graciously made available a copy of the unpublished manuscript by Max Weber which is cited in the essay.

A belated word of gratitude is due to Everett C. Hughes, whose seminar on Simmel in the mid-1950s helped confirm a young graduate student's interest.

Introduction

Simmel as Innovator

OF THOSE who created the intellectual capital used to launch the enterprise of professional sociology, Georg Simmel was perhaps the most original and fecund. In search of a subject matter for sociology that would distinguish it from all other social sciences and humanistic disciplines, he charted a new field for discovery and proceeded to explore a world of novel topics in works that have guided and anticipated the thinking of generations of sociologists. Such distinctive concepts of contemporary sociology as social distance, marginality, urbanism as a way of life, role-playing, social behavior as exchange, conflict as an integrating process, dyadic encounter, circular interaction, reference groups as perspectives, and sociological ambivalence embody ideas which Simmel adumbrated more than six decades ago. These and kindred ideas represent only a fraction of Simmel's total intellectual output, which also included lasting contributions to aesthetics, ethics, epistemology, metaphysics, and intellectual history.

The period in which Simmel's mature works appeared was one of great cultural ferment. Central Europe from the turn of the century to World War I witnessed the birth of psychoanalysis, relativity theory, logical positivism, phenomenology, atonal music, and several milestones of literature and humanistic scholarship. Berlin of the period was a congenial setting for the cultivated style of life and thought which Simmel followed. Born there in 1858, he remained to study at the University of Berlin, where he subsequently spent most of his academic career lecturing. He moved, to Strasbourg, only at the age of fifty-six, four years before his death.

Despite his record of achievement, Simmel's position in the intellectual world of his time was notably ambiguous. Although his works were hailed by some of the foremost of his contemporaries, he was rejected by most of his professional colleagues in philosophy and the social sciences with an often malicious passion. Although groups of all persuasions vigorously discussed his writings in the cafés frequented by German university students, no students chose to follow him as an academic master. On close terms with a number of cultural luminaries—his friends and correspondents included Stefan George, Rainer Maria Rilke, Auguste Rodin, Edmund Husserl, Martin Buber, Albert Schweitzer, Ernst Troeltsch, Max and Marianne Weber—he has been described as the loneliest figure of them all.

MARGINALITY Simmel's extraordinary originality may well be connected with his position as a relatively isolated thinker. He was, indeed, a "stranger" in the academy. The stylistic manifestations of a marginal position are striking in his written work. Neither in Simmel's text nor in annotations does one find acknowledgment of scholarly predecessors or contemporaries. He speaks for himself, along with the immortal dead. What is more, Simmel deliberately shied away from recruiting disciples to carry on his kinds of inquiry. The contrast with his contemporary Emile Durkheim—who drew heavily and explicitly from a century of sociological predecessors, wrote copious footnotes, employed research assistants, founded and edited a sociological journal, and encouraged a school of younger men to carry on his work—could scarcely be more conspicuous.

The institutional manifestation of Simmel's marginality was his failure to be granted full academic accreditation until the twilight of his life, and that in an unsatisfying appointment as professor at the University of Strasbourg in 1914. The victim of expressed anti-Semitism, pedantic aversions to his unprofessional style, and persisting biases against sociology in the German academy, Simmel spent nearly all of his career writing and lecturing at the University of Berlin without the benefit of a regular faculty appointment.

This exclusion from the German academic establishment doubtless reinforced the unscholarly aspects of Simmel's style, as Lewis Coser has skillfully argued.[1] Yet there is evidence that Simmel was disposed toward academic nonconformity from an early age. The evidence includes a graphological analysis of samples of Simmel's handwriting, which reports that "already at 22 years Simmel's writing shows an unusually personalized character. . . . He begins his own way at this time. This appears especially clearly in the fact that he employs two kinds of script: an academically correct one and one that is significantly individualized."[2] The first dissertation Simmel submitted was rejected by his professors for being too speculative, aphoristic, and stylistically careless. He was advised by Professor Zeller not to publish that study (on ethnomusicology) unless he cleared up a number of faults, but apparently he proceeded to do so without making the indicated corrections.[3] During his trial colloquium at Berlin in 1884, Simmel showed a conspicuous disregard for academic etiquette.[4] His habit of omitting scholarly references was well established by the time of his first sociological publication: Simmel's is the only entry in the 1890–91 volume of Schmoller's *Jahrbuch* without footnotes.

A less superficial aspect of Simmel's nonconformity was the disjointed, seemingly haphazard manner in which he presented his ideas. Rarely did he submit to the discipline required for system-

---

[1]   "Georg Simmel's Style of Work," *American Journal of Sociology* 63 (May 1958) : 635–41. Reprinted as "The Stranger in the Academy," in *Georg Simmel*, ed. Lewis Coser (Prentice-Hall, 1965).

[2]   *Buch des Dankes an Georg Simmel*, ed. Kurt Gassen and Michael Landmann (Berlin: Duncker & Humblot, 1958), p. 35.

[3]   See Georg Simmel, *The Conflict in Modern Culture and Other Essays*, trans. K. Peter Etzkorn (New York: Teachers College Press, 1968), p. 128.

[4]   Simmel bluntly rebuked Professor Zeller when the latter asserted that the soul was located in a certain brain lobe, for which rudeness, according to Simmel family tradition, his admittance to the status of *Privatdozent* was delayed nearly a year. Cf. Gassen and Landmann, *Buch des Dankes*, p. 21. A similar anecdote is reported in Rudolph Weingartner, *Experience and Culture: The Philosophy of Georg Simmel* (Middletown, Conn.: Wesleyan University Press, 1960), p. 4, n. 1.

atic exposition of a body of knowledge. This trait, however, reflected neither laziness, indifference to his audience, nor arbitrary willfulness. Simmel was indefatigable in exploring the labyrinths of complex analysis. Concern for his reading audience is shown by the frequency with which he revised his writings for second and third editions. His lectures were prepared and delivered with exquisite care; he was reputedly one of the most brilliant lecturers of his generation. Indeed, some of the very disjointedness for which he has been faulted reflects the skill of the teacher, concerned more at times to engage and provoke his students through unusual illustrations and the disclosure of unexpected relationships than with relentlessly pressing forward a narrow train of thought.

INDIVIDUALITY Beyond this, it must be noted that Simmel maintained a studied ambivalence toward the canons and claims of "objective" scholarship. He believed that the ultimate justification for scholarship lies in the materials it provides for the cultivation of educated individuals. "The great epochs which have pursued a Kulturpolitik," he pointedly observed, "have always focussed their attention on the subjective factor—on the *education* of *individuals*."[5] Because of Simmel's belief in the primacy of "subjective culture" over "objective culture," to use his own terms, he is not so anxious to work out a fully articulated, coherent exposition of all his basic ideas and their interrelations. However serious he may be about a particular subject matter, he is less concerned with attaining scientific closure in the sense of an exhaustive, rigorously demonstrated, and consensually validated set of propositions than in speaking whatever truth he can about it in relation to his intellectual needs at any given time. The disclaimer which he used to justify the fragmentary nature of his magnum opus *Soziologie* holds good for nearly everything he wrote: "The individual can attain closure here only in the subjective sense that he communicates everything that he has been able to see."[6]

[5]   "Die Zukunft unserer Kultur" (1909). Reprinted in Georg Simmel, *Brücke und Tür*, ed. M. Landmann and M. Susman (Stuttgart: Koehler, 1957), p. 97; italics in original.
[6]   *Soziologie* (Leipzig: Duncker & Humblot, 1908), p. 17, n. 1.

Philosophical conviction, therefore, as well as temperament combined with situational factors caused Simmel to follow the path of an academic loner. He pursued no less than he described and extolled the ideal of authentic individuality. "One cannot categorize Simmel among the general intellectual currents of the time," wrote Dean Hampe of Heidelberg in 1908, "he has always gone his own way."[7] The originality and fecundity of Simmel's thought are clearly grounded in the courage and stubbornness—one should probably even say "grace"—with which he pursued his own ideas and insights, exploring the unknown. His life illustrated a point which he articulated in his essay on the stranger: that the absence of firm social ties promotes intellectual freedom.

Simmel's devotion to the principle of individuality notwithstanding, scholarship remains in many respects an inexorably communal enterprise. In a famous passage inscribed in his diary at the end of his life he wrote: "I know that I shall die without intellectual heirs, and that is as it should be. My legacy will be like cash, distributed to many heirs, each transforming his part into use according to *his* nature—a use which will no longer reveal its indebtedness to this heritage." It is time now, a half-century after his death, to take stock of the capital Simmel created, to trace the indebtedness of Simmel's many heirs, to identify reserves from his legacy which have not yet been tapped.

PRODUCTIVITY   The full list of Simmel's known publications includes some two dozen books and well over two hundred articles. The scatter of topics therein and the haphazard order in which they appear present a continuing challenge for those who dare to intuit within this carnival a constancy of intellectual effort.

Yet constancy is undeniably there. From his student days until the end of his life, Simmel's creativity was continuously exercised along three discernible lines. One was a search for the origins, essences, and destinies of cultural forms—music, painting, drama, science, philosophy, history, ethics, and religion—this in a series of essays that begin his doctoral study on music, published in 1882,

7   Gassen and Landmann, *Buch des Dankes*, p. 25.

and culminate with chapter 2 of *Lebensanschauung* in 1918. In a second series, from the monograph *Über sociale Differenzierung* in 1890 to the *Fundamental Problems of Sociology* in 1917, he explored with recurring enthusiasm the origins and structural properties of diverse social forms. Finally, from the early sketches of Goethe and Michelangelo in the late 1880s to the magisterial chapter on the metaphysics of individuality, again in *Lebens-anschauung*, he was concerned with the formal properties of fulfilled personality.

This is not to say that Simmel's ideas did not significantly change over the years. One can, in fact, readily distinguish three periods of his intellectual development. In the early 1890s, when he published *Über sociale Differenzierung* and the two-volume *Einleitung in die Moralwissenschaft*, his thinking was influenced by the social Darwinism of the time. In the middle period he was primarily concerned with working out the implications of a neo-Kantian position for the analysis of social and cultural forms. In his last years, under the influence of Bergson, but with renewed interest in Goethe, Hegel, Schopenhauer, and Nietzsche as well, he was chiefly concerned with developing a philosophy of life.[8] Through the vicissitudes of these periods, however, there is a continuous effort to deepen and expand an interpretation of the basic nature of cultural forms, social forms, and forms of individuality.

Despite occasional illuminating moments of overlap, these three sets of inquiries were never related in any coherent way. In particular, it should be noted that the framework which Simmel constructed for the science of sociology explicitly restricted the

---

[8]   For a sketch of the phases of Simmel's intellectual career, see Paul Honigsheim, "The Time and Thought of the Young Simmel," in *Georg Simmel, 1858–1918*, ed. Kurt H. Wolff (Columbus: Ohio State University Press, 1948 [reprinted as Georg Simmel et al., *Essays on Sociology, Philosophy and Aesthetics* (New York: Harper Torchbooks, n.d.), hereinafter referred to as *Essays*]), pp. 167–74. For an unusually sensitive interpretation of the philosophical influences on Simmel, see Margarete Susman, *Die geistige Gestalt Georg Simmels* (Tübingen: J. C. B. Mohr, 1959).

attention of this discipline to the study of *social* forms.[9] Thus, although Simmel was one of the first to articulate and observe a clear distinction between the realms of social structure and culture, his sociological framework stood to oppose efforts to integrate the two in an overarching conception of sociocultural systems. It will, however, become apparent that his modes of analyzing social and cultural forms, although carried out independently of one another, are essentially similar.

Form in Culture and Personality

The starting point of Simmel's theory of culture, as indeed of all his thought, is the distinction between form and content. Contents are those aspects of existence which are determined in themselves, but as such contain neither structure nor the possibility of being apprehended by us in their immediacy. Forms are the synthesizing principles which select elements from the raw stuff of experience and shape them into determinate unities. In this respect forms are identical with Kant's a priori categories of cognition; but they differ from the latter in two important respects. They inform not only the cognitive realm, but any and all dimensions of human experience. And they are not fixed and immutable, but emerge, develop, and perhaps disappear over time.

[9]   This largely accounts for the fact that in the United States, at least, Simmel has been known almost exclusively as a student of social relations. Inasmuch as his ideas were imported into American thought by sociologists who followed the focus on social forms, and since his work on culture was mostly carried out under a rubric to which American sociologists have tended to be allergic, that of philosophy, it was natural for them to project a lopsided view of Simmel's intellectual profile.

Simmel's writings on culture are less richly developed and less obviously interconnected than are his studies on social forms—perhaps another reason for their relative neglect. Still, they offer much that is pertinent to contemporary cultural analysis. Here we can only broadly sketch some of their principal ideas. A more detailed account may be found in the excellent exegesis of Simmel's philosophy by Rudolph Weingartner, *Experience and Culture.*

Forms emerge to shape contents when the undifferentiated unity of immediate experience is ruptured by some sort of stress. The experiencing self divides into a self-conscious subject and a confronted object, defined in some mode—cognitive, aesthetic, evaluative—according to the nature of the originating situation. The forms which come into being at this stage are fragmentary and preliminary in character—what Weingartner has aptly called "proto-culture"—for they are bound by the pragmatic interests and adaptive exigencies of the immediate situation. Thus, protomusic arises when people feel a need to express unusually strong emotions, such as anger, joy, or religious-mystical feelings. Frustrated by the limitations of mere language, they begin to reshape verbal sounds by adding rhythm and then melody.[10] Protoscience arises to solve various problems connected with mastery of the environment. At the stage of protoculture one has just as big and just as little a fund of formed objects as are needed for carrying out one's practical activities: just enough culture, but no more.

As soon as elements of protoculture have been created for specific practical reasons, they take on an existence of their own. While still rooted in subjective purposes, they become objectified. They need not be continuously reinvented, and the more successful of them accumulate to form a tradition. When that happens, a second level of cultural development is possible. Sooner or later the forms can be liberated from their connection with practical purposes and become objects of cultivation in their own right. They become autonomous, in that men become devoted to them not for some practical advantage but for their own sake. The structural potential within each set of forms can then be drawn out. Thus, the rhythmic and melodic variations of sound initially formed to aid human communication become transformed into music composed and played according to intrinsic canons. Knowledge of the heavens needed to grow crops or sail the seas becomes transformed into the science of astronomy. Moral regulations designed to regulate human relationships become transformed into autonomous

[10] See Etzkorn (trans.), *Conflict in Modern Culture*, pp. 100–106.

ethical principles. This is the movement from protoforms to objective forms.

Beyond any particular realization of objective culture, moreover, there is a third level of cultural formation which Simmel refers to as that of "worlds."[11] Each of the main types of formative capacity of the human spirit is able to shape the *totality* of contents into a self-contained, irreducible world of experience. The so-called real world consists of that complex of representations needed for us to act adaptively in accord with the psychobiological requirements of our species. Historically it develops first, but it does not thereby have any special ontological claims. Equally valid as ways of organizing all the contents of life are the worlds of art, of theoretical knowledge, of values, of religion, and so on. Worlds come into being over time through the interaction of specific ways of experiencing—the practical, the aesthetic, the scientific, the religious—with various kinds of contents. Although in principle any given content can be constructed as an element in any world, some contents lend themselves more readily than others to becoming part of certain worlds. Thus, three areas of life experience particularly lend themselves to being "transposed into the religious key"—man's relation to the forces of nature, to fate, and to his fellow humans.[12] But each world exists as a sovereign form, urging those who are at all responsive to its claims to translate more and more of the contents of the cosmos into its domain.

The energy inherent in life to create forms that transcend life is a force toward cultural diversity, not unity. In radical contrast to Comte and Marx, who envisioned the goal of evolution to be the production of a homogeneous culture for one humanity, Simmel saw the generation of increasingly specialized cultural products ordered in fundamentally discrete and incommensurable worlds. The gods who rule these worlds are not at war with one another—any more than colors and sounds are in basic conflict—but each

11   *Lebensanschauung* (Munich and Leipzig: Duncker & Humblot, 1918), chap. 2.
12   See *The Sociology of Religion*, trans. Curt Rosenthal (New York: Wisdom Library, 1959).

tries to move human accomplishment closer to the universal implementation of its basic principle.

The formal elaboration of a given body of culture may proceed, however, in either of two directions. These depend on the relationship between cultural forms and the self. To understand this choice properly we must first digress for a brief consideration of Simmel's theory of personality.

Simmel's approach to the study of personality is structural; it is based, again, on the distinction between form and content.[13] For the most part he is concerned not with the instinctual or experiential bases of specific dispositions, skills, or habits,[14] but rather with how out of the multiplicity of psychic contents a unified personality is formed. Simmel refers to that which gives form to the multiplicity of contents distributed around the periphery of personality as its central core or ego.

Just as concrete cultural products are only finite and imperfect realizations of the ideality of some "world," so individual persons are only limited realizations of their ideal selves—ideal not in the sense of what they should be according to some external criteria, but ideal in the sense of a projection of the actual tendencies and syntheses manifested in each individual's own existence. The attainment of individuality is thus not a matter of arbitrary subjectivity, but rather a movement toward the realization of a determinate objective form.

In the course of reflecting on this topic over many years, Simmel produced a number of profound questions and observations: the different forms in which individuality may be attained;[15] the

[13]   See D. Levine, "Some Key Problems in Simmel's Work," in Coser, *Georg Simmel*, pp. 97–98.

[14]   A notable exception to this is Simmel's discussion of the primary drives of hostility and sympathy. See chapter 6 below.

[15]   See chapters 15–17 below; also, "Individual and Society in Eighteenth- and Nineteenth-Century Views of Life," in *The Sociology of Georg Simmel*, ed., trans., and with an introduction by Kurt H. Wolff (Glencoe, Ill.: Free Press, 1950), pp. 58–84; "Individualismus," in *Brücke und Tür*, pp. 251–59.

social conditions which favor the attainment of individuality;[16] the individualities manifested in outstanding historic personalities, like Rembrandt, Goethe, and Nietzsche; and the ethical implications of living in accord with directives that are rooted in the totality of one's unique individual life.[17]

We are concerned here with only one aspect of this vast topic: the relation between individuality and objective culture. In the sense in which Simmel himself prefers to use the term, culture refers to the cultivation of individuals through the agency of external forms which have been objectified in the course of history. Objective culture refers to only one side of this process—to the complex of ideal and actualized products. The other side—the extent to which individuals assimilate and make use of these products for their personal growth—is the domain of subjective culture.

The importance of subjective culture derives from the fact that man, unlike any other creature known to us, carries within himself the need to be "cultivated." Cultivation is the process of developing a state of being in a creature which (1) would not come about naturally, but (2) for which it has a natural propensity, (3) by utilizing objects external to it. Plants and animals can be cultivated, but the impulse to do so stems from outside their beings. By contrast, the obligation and capacity for full cultivation are inseparably bound up with the human soul. This process involves much more than the mere assimilation of a number of diverse cultural contents; above all, it requires that these contents be relevant to and integrated into the central core of personality. Culture, in the proper (i.e., subjective) sense of the term, exists only in the presence of the self-development of a psychic center, provided that this self-development relies on external, objective means.

With respect to both the direction and the scale in which cultural contents are treated, the growth of objective culture differs radically from that of subjective culture. Objective culture grows

16   See chapters 18–21 below; also, "The Web of Group-Affiliations," in *Conflict and The Web of Group-Affiliations*, trans. Kurt H. Wolff and Reinhard Bendix (Glencoe, Ill.: Free Press, 1955).
17   "Das individuelle Gesetz," in *Lebensanschauung*, chap. 4.

according to its own immanent logic; subjective culture grows according to the logic of the unfolding personality. Mastery of, say, an ethical argument, a botanical monograph, and the Schönberg quartets would be indicated by and subordinated to the form of one's emerging individuality in the latter case; in the former, to the developmental needs of the disciplines of ethics, botany, and music.

From the many contents which offer themselves as means for individual development, the self selects circumspectly. Its receptive capacity is limited by the degree of unity and closure it has already attained as well as by the limitations of time and energy of each individual life. The development of objective culture, on the other hand, knows no such limits. It can draw on the contributions of numberless individuals over many generations. "There is no reason why it should not be multiplied in the direction of the infinite, why book should not be added to book, work of art to work of art, or invention to invention. The form of objectivity as such possesses a boundless capacity for fulfillment."[18] Of the tension which exists between these two modalities of culture, we shall have more to say below.

The Intellectual Disciplines

The established intellectual disciplines, then, are in Simmel's view the products of a great cultural transformation. They all have their origins in the needs and interests of practical life. At some point they become liberated from praxis, objectified, and developed autonomously as realms of pure cognitive culture. Without all the turmoil displayed by Max Weber and members of the *Verein für Sozialpolitik* in trying to hammer out a justification for keeping scientific judgments separate from value judgments, Simmel coolly asserts the reality and validity of pursuing cognitive culture for its own sake. He thus concludes his classic analysis of the tumult of the modern metropolis with Spinozan calm: "It is

[18]   "On the Concept and Tragedy of Culture," in Etzkorn (trans.), *Conflict in Modern Culture*, p. 44.

our task not to complain or to condone but only to understand."[19]

PHILOSOPHY Simmel himself was more or less continuously engaged in trying to come to terms with three of these disciplines: philosophy, history, and sociology. For Simmel, philosophy is the intellectual effort to make sense of the totality of things. It does this by extrapolating some particular cognitive set, representing one of the great *typical* orientations of the human mind, to interpret the entire world. From a mere sum of fragments philosophy forms a unified whole. Philosophy operates at such a level of abstraction—at such a distance from things—that it does not matter if the general propositions it asserts are contradicted by data obtained from a position much nearer to things.[20]

In relation to any empirical discipline, philosophy has two tasks, one prior and one posterior to the work of that discipline. The first task is to deal with the basic concepts and presuppositions which underlie concrete research—questions that cannot be handled in research itself because inquiry is based on them. The other task involves the speculative rounding out of the results of research and the effort to integrate them into a total picture of things by connecting them with ideas that lie beyond direct experience and objectively verifiable knowledge. These tasks are the provinces, respectively, of the epistemology and the metaphysics of the particular discipline. Social philosophy, therefore, deals on the one hand with questions concerning the principles and methods of the social sciences, and on the other with such questions as whether the development of social systems is analogous in any respects to the evolution of other kinds of systems, and whether the chief value of society lies in the functions of social life itself, the creation of objective culture, or the ethical qualities it nurtures in the individual.[21]

19   In practice, however, Simmel's sociology does not altogether avoid a certain suggestive moralism, chiefly in praise of individuality.
20   See "The Nature of Philosophy," in *Essays*, pp. 282–309. See also Weingartner, *Experience and Culture*, chap. 3.
21   Simmel wavered concerning where he thought social philosophy should be located. In 1908 he was content to leave it as a branch of philos-

HISTORY   The area of social philosophy to which Simmel devoted the most attention—in six different publications issued between 1892 and 1918—was that concerning the basic
concepts and presuppositions of historical inquiry.[22] Along with
Dilthey, Rickert, and Croce, he was one of the originators of the
modern, critical conception of the philosophy of history.

Simmel continues the critique of the positivist view of historiography initiated by Dilthey and Windelband but pushes it in
quite new directions. Unlike Dilthey, he maintains that what is
distinctive about history is not its subject matter, human experience, for man can be apprehended with equal validity through the
perspectives of many different worlds. Unlike Windelband (and
later Rickert), he maintains that the distinctive perspective of history is not its focus on unique, concrete events, but rather that
history is an entirely special way of constructing reality: it, too,
offers a form for the whole world.

In contrast to the other world-forms, history does not shape raw
contents, but rather gives additional form to contents that have
already been shaped in human experience. History is that way of
ordering the world that *selects* certain contents from among all
those that have been formed through experience and recombines
them into continuous series, in such a way as to gain understanding (*Verstehen*) of events *that have been located in time in terms
of their future.* The act of selection is crucial, Simmel tirelessly asserts; there is no such thing as relating history "as it really was."
The principles of selection are based on some particular province
of experience, like politics, art, technology, or fashions, and cer-

---

ophy; in 1917 he tried to make it a branch of sociology. See "The Problem of Sociology," in *Essays*, pp. 333–35; and Wolff, *Sociology of Georg
Simmel*, pp. 23–25.
[22]   Chapter 1, below, is the introduction to *Probleme der Geschichtsphilosophie*, 3d ed. Each of the first two editions was significantly different. In addition, Simmel published three late papers on this subject: "Das
Problem der historischen Zeit," "Die historische Formung," and "Vom
Wesen des historischen Verstehens." For a fuller exposition of Simmel's
thought on the philosophy of history, see Weingartner, *Experience and
Culture*, chap. 2.

tain qualities of events such as typicality, unusualness, and significance.

Because of Simmel's dogmatic pluralism he is led to assert that
history forms a world of its own, self-contained and incommensurable. Criteria from the world of science are therefore irrelevant.
This leads, Weingartner has argued, to a needlessly subjectivistic
conception of history, in which the only criteria of adequacy are
those which refer to the *coherence* with which past events are
linked up with subsequent events in a continuous series. This radical separation of history from sociology is what makes Simmel's
sociology so different from that of Max Weber.

At the level of protoculture, the discipline of history is rooted
and prefigured in two common, indeed, indispensable activities of
everyday life. The act of historical *Verstehen* draws on, and arises
from, the capacity for empathic understanding by means of which
we relate to our neighbors: "The understanding of Saint Paul and
Louis XIV is essentially the same as is the understanding of a
personal acquaintance."[23] Practical life depends, moreover, on the
selective reconstruction of past events in relation to their implications for present circumstances. It is the categories of mutual understanding and interpretation of significant past experience in
everyday life which are differentiated and refined to become the
concepts and methods of disciplinary history.

SOCIOLOGY   The roots of sociology are somewhere else.
They derive from the ascendancy of the masses over the interests
of individuals during the nineteenth century. As the lower classes
grew in importance and forced the attention of the upper classes,
the phenomenon of class itself—a societal formation—came into
focus. The consequence of this growing awareness of social *classes*,
whose properties lie not in the constitutions of individuals but in
their *social* constitutions, was the perception that *all* individual
phenomena are determined by innumerable influences stemming

[23]   "Vom Wesen des historischen Verstehens," in *Brücke und Tür*,
p. 60. A related point is expressed in the epigram, made famous by Max
Weber, but apparently originating with Simmel, that "one does not need to
be Caesar to understand him."

from their human environments. This idea was then projected backward: past society came to appear "as the substance which formed individual existence, as the sea creates waves."[24]

The practical power gained by social classes thus served to stimulate the growth of sociology as a science of everything that takes place in society: in other words, as the science of everything human. Yet a field so broadly and vaguely conceived does not meet the requirements for becoming an autonomous branch of objective scientific culture. Every science rests upon a conception which permits the abstraction of specified qualities and functions and the methodical observation of their occurrence in concrete things. Primitive (e.g., Comtian) sociology—sociology as the all-inclusive human discipline, as the queen of sciences—offers a name and an omnibus category, but that is not enough. Nevertheless, the basic insight from which primitive sociology proceeds—the insight that man in all aspects of his being and activity is determined by the fact of living in interaction with other men—may lead to a conception that could establish sociology as an independent and clearly delimited objective science.

Simmel proceeds to develop that conception, to help make sociology autonomous, by applying the distinction between forms and contents to the social realm. "Contents" take on a special meaning here: they are the needs, drives, and purposes which lead individuals to enter into continuing association with one another. Forms are the synthesizing processes by which individuals combine into supraindividual unities, stable or transient, solidary or antagonistic, as the case may be. The task of sociology properly objectified is studying the forms of human sociality.

Form in Society and History

To ground a major scholarly discipline upon so precarious a basis as the distinction between form and content may seem arbitrary or capricious, but in doing this Simmel finds ample serious precedent. Grammar studies the pure forms of language, abstracted

[24] *Soziologie*, p. 2.

from the linguistic contents through which these forms come to life. Logic and epistemology study the pure forms of knowing, abstracted from the multitude of cognitions of particular things. Geometry studies pure spatial forms, abstracted from the physical objects which embody them. Sociology as the science of social forms relates to the special sciences which deal with the various contents of social life, such as economic activity, sexual behavior, education, law, or religion, much as geometry relates to the various physical sciences. The great difference between the two is that spatial forms, though only approximated in physical objects, can be isolated, absolutely identified and logically derived in geometric thought, whereas, owing to the fluctuations and complexities of social life, the status of the forms of social interaction which sociology abstracts is more ambiguous. In general, however, sociology may be regarded as the geometry of social forms.

Analogies to the three levels at which cultural forms exist are discriminated in Simmel's theory of society, but the meaning of the concepts employed and the significance of the different levels have been altered. Corresponding to the forms of protoculture are the forms of elementary social behavior, to the study of which Simmel's own sociological investigations are largely devoted. Individuals enter into interaction with one another for the sake of certain purposes or to satisfy certain emotional needs—for instrumental or for expressive reasons, to use more contemporary terms. Such interactions originate in, and remain close to, the practical needs of daily life. The spontaneous processes through which persons interact constitute the "microscopic-molecular" processes of social life:

That people look at one another and are jealous of one another; that they exchange letters and have dinner together; that apart from all tangible interests they strike one another as pleasant or unpleasant; that gratitude for altruistic acts makes for inseparable union; that one asks another to point out a certain street; that people dress and adorn themselves for each other—these are a few casually chosen illustrations from the whole range of relations that play between one person and another. They may be momentary or permanent, conscious or unconscious, ephemeral or of grave consequence, but they incessantly tie men together. At each moment such threads are spun, dropped, taken up again, displaced by others, interwoven with others. . . . They explain all the toughness and elasticity, all the colorfulness and consistency of social life, which is so striking and yet so mysterious.[25]

The protoforms of social life thus assume an interest and importance which Simmel reserves for objectified forms in the area of culture.

Social forms gain autonomy from the momentary impulses and pressing demands of the life process in two ways. They become combined and hypostatized into larger, institutionalized structures (*Gebilde*). These more visible, solid structures—states, labor unions, priesthoods, family structures, military organizations, communities—represent an objectification of social forms. But it is an objectification that remains closely tied to praxis. Their counterpart in the domain of culture would be the forms of institutionalized technology and any other established traditions of developed protoculture—customary wisdom as contrasted with trial-and-error wisdom.

The other mode by which social forms become autonomous corresponds precisely to the transformation of accumulated protoculture into the pure forms of objective culture. That is, there emerge certain forms of interaction which are realized not for some practical purpose but for the sake of the forms themselves. These are the "play" forms of sociality. Devoid of pragmatic content, they exist for those moments when we wish to participate in the "world" of society as an end in itself. Instead of the serious pursuit of erotic objectives, one can play at it in the form of coquetry.[26] Instead of the serious competitive pursuit of economic or political goals, one can play at aggressive competition through sports and games.[27] Instead of the serious performance of social roles in daily life, one can playact, or watch others play at imagined roles in the theater.[28] The form of sociability, moreover, exists as the arche-

---

[25]   "The Problem of Sociology," in *Essays*, pp. 327–28.
[26]   "Die Koketterie," in *Philosophische Kultur* (Leipzig: Alfred Kroner, 1919), pp. 95–115.
[27]   See chapter 6 below.
[28]   See "Zur Philosophie des Schauspielers," in *Fragmente und Aufsätze* (Munich: Drei Masken, 1923).

typal play form of all human sociality.[29] In all these modes of inter-action, the emphasis is on *good form*.

As the foregoing implies, the concept of society is analogous, strictly speaking, not to the concept of culture in general but to one of the world-forming cultural categories like religion, art, or science. Society exists as one of the ways in which all experience can potentially be organized.[30] A given number of individuals, there-fore, *can be society to a greater or lesser degree*, just as a given number of sounds can be music to a greater or lesser degree. Society as a form presents the ideality of a world awaiting actualiza-tion in history.[31]

The conceptual scaffolding of Simmel's sociology, then, con-sists of four types or levels of forms: (1) the forms of elementary social interaction; (2) institutionalized structures; (3) autono-mous "play" forms; and (4) the generic form of society itself. Each of these, we have seen, has its counterpart in Simmel's theory of culture.

SOCIOLOGY AND CULTURE   The agenda which Sim-mel provides for sociology is largely confined to the intrinsic analy-sis of social forms. Sociologists are directed to identify and classify the different forms of social interaction; to analyze their subtypes; to study the conditions under which they emerge, develop, flour-

---

[29]   See chapter 9 below.

[30]   Like any cultural category, the concept of society can be used in either a concrete or an abstract sense. Music, for example, can refer either to a set of actual compositions or performances, or else—abstractly—to the general form by which sounds are organized in rhythmic and melodic patterns for aesthetic effects. In its concrete sense, society designates a complex of societalized individuals, an empirical network of human rela-tionships operative at a given time and place. In the abstract sense of the term, society denotes the totality of those relational forms through which individuals become part of such a network. (Simmel uses the contrast be-tween a material sphere and the geometric form of the sphere to illustrate this distinction.) It is the abstract general concept which subsumes all the particular forms of sociality.

[31]   This is, ironically, very close to a central conception of Comte, who spoke of progress as the growth of order and described this in terms of an absolute increase in the amount of sociality.

ish, and dissolve; and to investigate their structural properties.[32] Although Simmel tended to follow this agenda, focusing on the analysis of social forms in his sociology and reserving the analysis of cultural forms for his philosophy, a rigid separation between social and cultural facts can in no way be justified by Simmel's principles. Simmel frequently calls attention to the ambiguity, and flexibility, of his fundamental distinction: it is an essential tenet of his philosophy that what is form in one context can be content in another. In the perspective of sociology, cultural forms are social contents. Simmel is therefore being entirely consistent when he states the rationale for a sociology of culture: "The facts of . . . religion . . . law, culture styles, language, and innumerable others can be analyzed by asking how they may be understood, not as individual achievements or in their objective significance, but as products and developments of society."[33] Conversely, the *content* of a particular social interaction "often if not always has a decisive effect on the way [the interaction] is formed."[34] In other words, that a number of persons assemble to play music may cause them to organize themselves differently from when they come together to worship or carry out scientific research.

Simmel's occasional excursions into the areas where society and culture interpenetrate include some of the most imaginative, and most neglected, pages of his work. Here we can only call attention to them in a schematic fashion.

1. Social forms provide contents which lend themselves particularly well to the elaboration of certain cultural forms. Faith in another person prefigures the faith elaborated in the symbolism of religion. The playing of social roles prefigures the art of the dramatic actor.

2. Social forms create conditions which affect the nature of certain cultural products. Thus, expansion of the societal base of interaction creates the social conditions for universalistic cognitive and ethical conceptions such as the norm of logical consistency

[32] See chapter 3 below.
[33] Wolff, *Sociology of Georg Simmel*, p. 18.
[34] *Soziologie*, p. 10.

and the principle of justice.[35] The types of exchange and the quantity of interaction which characterize modern urban life create a need for distance from things, expressed in certain cultural styles such as symbolism,[36] and account for the cultural lability of the metropolis.[37]

3. Orientation to certain cultural forms creates a disposition to prefer social forms which are parallel in structure. Thus, a preference for symmetry in art favors a taste for the planned symmetry of social forms, as under socialism.[38]

SOCIOLOGY AND HISTORY   One of the branches of culture—history—has an especially interesting relationship to sociology, by virtue of the peculiar status of these two disciplines in Simmel's system. Whereas philosophy, art, religion, ethics, and natural science bring their distinctive categories to the totality of contents and shape them according to their respective principles, it is the nature of both history and sociology that they deal with contents which have already been given form. Both of them study the already formed contents of human experience, and there is no reason why they cannot study the *same* formed contents. This is why the separation of disciplines proposed by Windelband—between sciences of the unique (idiographic) and sciences of the general (nomothetic)—makes no sense to Simmel. In contemporary terms he would say that interchange at the boundaries between sociology and history yields two profitable enterprises, social history and historical sociology.

When the forms of social interaction are examined with respect to their occurrence in a specific time and place and their subsequent development in a specific group, they are being studied in the perspective and for the benefit of history. This would constitute social history for Simmel, an enterprise parallel to the histories of

35   "Sur quelques relations de la pensée theorique avec les intérêts pratique," *Revue de métaphysique et de la morale*, 4 (1896) : 160–78.
36   "Sociological Aesthetics," in Etzkorn (trans.), *Conflict in Modern Culture*, pp. 77–80.
37   *Philosophie des Geldes*, chap. 6.
38   "Sociological Aesthetics," pp. 68–76.

other formed contents like religion and technology. The development of friendship in fifth-century B.C. Athens, the growth of trade unions in the nineteenth-century United States, the relationship between primogeniture and the rise of sports in seventeenth-century England—these are illustrative of possible topics for social history as (implicitly) conceived by Simmel.

Conversely, the facts accumulated in diverse kinds of history provide invaluable material for the *sociological* study of social forms. They do so in three ways. First, to determine the origins and structural properties of any social form one must look at its realization in a great variety of contents. One can learn something about competition, for example, from a great many fields—economic history, history of art, history of religion, and so on. After looking at a variety of actual instances of competition one can then abstract the common structural features from these cases, in order to determine what competition is as a pure form of human behavior. (There are certain forms, moreover—like that of hereditary office—which are found only in specific periods.)

Forms like competition are recurrent social processes. Other forms which Simmel writes about are more complex in that they involve structural changes over time. These may be called forms of development, or developmental patterns.[39] Thus Simmel writes, for example, that

the process of development of almost all [political] parties shows the same form: during the initial period dominated by its basic idea . . . the party is, on the one hand, small, and on the other hand, marked by decisiveness and compactness. These qualities tend to disappear as the party increases in size and expands its program.[40]

By definition, the only way to examine diachronic forms of this sort is to compare a number of continuous series which historians have reconstructed.

[39]   See D. Levine, "Some Key Problems in Simmel's Work," in Coser, *Georg Simmel*, pp. 98–104.
[40]   *Über sociale Differenzierung*, in *Staats- und socialwissenschaftliche Forschungen*, ed. Gustav Schmoller, vol. 10 (Leipzig: Duncker & Humblot, 1890), p. 22.

In addition to these two kinds of problems within the field of "pure," or formal, sociology, there is a third kind of problem which Simmel identified late in his life and assigned to an area he called "general sociology." The problem defined here is to study "the whole of historical life insofar as it is formed societally."[41] Simmel's discussion of this area is obscure, but it seems that what he has in mind would include sociologies like those of Toynbee or Sorokin, or inductive generalizations about social evolution—in short, comparative macroscopic social history.

Principles and Method

Enough has been said to indicate that not only is Simmel's sociology more than a varied assortment of perceptive insights by a talented man, as has often been asserted—not only does his sociology form a coherent and continuously developed system of ideas—but it also forms an integral part of the larger body of ideas which was his life's work as a whole. In this section we shall focus directly on some of the aspects of Simmel's thought which create its underlying unity.

UNITY OF METHOD   Whether he is examining a social process or a developmental pattern, a world of culture or a philosophic system, a historic individual or a personality type, the logic of Simmel's inquiry is the same. His method is to select some bounded, finite phenomenon from the world of flux; to examine the multiplicity of elements which compose it; and to ascertain the cause of their coherence by disclosing its form. Secondarily, he investigates the origins of this form and its structural implications.

The *results* of Simmelian inquiry are therefore a series of discrete analyses. They do not lend themselves to being integrated through a single interpretative scheme, whether an overarching dialectical conception of the total social-historical process or a theoretical system constructed of universally applicable analytic categories. This is what produces the appearance (and in the sense

41   Wolff, *Sociology of Georg Simmel*, p. 22. See also pp. 16–21.

here specified, the reality) of disunity in Simmel's work. It suffers from the "type atomism" for which Talcott Parsons has criticized the work of Max Weber even more than does Weber's work.[42]

At the same time Simmel's method has certain distinct advantages. It has the advantage of remaining close to both the interests of the knower and the stubborn realities of the known. It does not force all phenomena together into a general scheme nor does it molest them with arbitrary or rigid categories; at the same time it avoids mindless empiricism by providing a context of meanings for sets of observations. It enhances discovery.

Four basic presuppositions underlie all of Simmel's analyses of culture, society, and personality. These may be identified as the principles of form, reciprocity, distance, and dualism.[43] We shall articulate them here, again comparing his sociology with his philosophy of culture.

Form. The world consists of innumerable contents which are given determinate identity, structure, and meaning through the imposition of forms which man has created in the course of his experience. We have seen how this principle generates the basic conceptual tools used by Simmel in constructing his theories of culture and social structure. It may suffice here to call attention to one of the passages where he explicitly advocates the primacy of this analytic distinction.

There is perhaps no necessity of thought which is so hard to cast off as the analysis of things into content and form, even though this analysis has neither logical force nor the force of sensibly given data. In countless modifications, under this and other names, this division cuts across our image of the world. It is one of the organizers and flexible instruments with which the mind gives structure to the mass of all that is a mass which, in its immediate unity, is structureless.[44]

---

[42]   "Introduction," Max Weber, *The Theory of Social and Economic Organization*, trans. R. A. Henderson and T. Parsons, ed. T. Parsons (New York: Oxford University Press, 1947), p. 15. See also Parsons, *The Structure of Social Action* (Glencoe, Ill.: Free Press, 1949), p. 716.

[43]   An earlier formulation of this interpretation appears in D. Levine, "The Structure of Simmel's Social Thought," in *Essays*, esp. pp. 19–24.

[44]   "On the Nature of Philosophy," in *Essays*, p. 288. See also Weingartner, "Form and Content in Simmel's Philosophy of Life," ibid., pp. 33–60.

Reciprocity. No thing or event has a fixed, intrinsic meaning; its meaning only emerges through interaction with other things or events. This is equally true of the particular items within any cultural system, of the individual's relationship to any given piece of culture, and of the individual's actions in society.

A fundamental circularity is involved in all cultural systems. No legal precept is valid in itself, but only in relation to other legal precepts.[45] A line has no intrinsic length; it can be measured only by comparing it with another line. The validity of any scientific or philosophic proposition depends on its relation to another proposition, the validity of which ultimately depends on the first.[46] The experience of cultural products, moreover, must be understood in terms of the individual's interaction with them. Cultural traditions attain true value in life only if they are balanced to a certain extent by a creative power stemming from the individual. For example, when looking at a portrait, the viewer is involved in

a kind of interaction: the bodily appearance, by virtue of its aesthetic unification, evokes the idea of a soul in the mind of the viewer, and this idea in turn works back upon the picture to give it additional unity, firmness, reciprocal justification of features.[47]

It is through applying the principle of reciprocity that Simmel manages to sidestep the age-old controversy between sociological realism and nominalism: whether society is an entity with a character and properties of its own or whether society is merely a name for the aggregation of a multiplicity of individual actions. Simmel rejects both views, arguing on the one hand that the idea of a societal substance, of an independent collective entity (*Volksseinheit*), does not correspond to anything that can be observed.[48] The place where all societal events occur is within the minds of individuals. On the other hand, there is a way of looking at those psychic events that is not psychological, but that is able to perceive the synthetic *realities* of processes and relations through

45   *Philosophie des Geldes*, p. 66.
46   Ibid., p. 68.
47   "Das Problem des Porträts," in *Zur Philosophie der Kunst*, ed. Gertrud Simmel (Potsdam: Kiepenheuer Verlag, 1922), pp. 102–3.
48   *Über sociale Differenzierung*, p. 14.

which individuals act upon and with one another. Reciprocal influence is the reality to which the term society corresponds.

The degree of reciprocity among individuals or groups is one variable Simmel uses for distinguishing social forms. It is of the essence of certain forms that they entail complete reciprocity—economic exchange,[49] personal adornment,[50] and crowd behavior[51] are examples. In other forms the reciprocity may be more or less symmetrical. In some cases a relationship gives the appearance of being wholly one-way—power, for example—but closer inspection reveals that in some measure ego is being influenced by, as well as influencing, alter. When the last trace of reciprocity in a relationship has disappeared, it no longer exists as a social fact; society, in Simmel's sense, has ceased to be.

Distance. The properties of forms and the meanings of things are a function of the relative distances between individuals and other individuals or things.

Cultural forms arise, it may be recalled, when the unity of immediate experience is disrupted and a distance is interposed between subject and object. Thereafter, cultural forms serve not only to enable the self to experience objects in characteristic modes but also to stand at a characteristic distance from that object. One of the respects in which worlds, and various forms within the same world, differ from one another is how near or how far they bring objects to the individual.

It is characteristic of the worlds of philosophy and art to present the outlines of things at a much greater distance than do the worlds of science and praxis.[52] Among the sciences, different disciplines look at things from different distances. It is wrong to think that a more detailed view of something is thereby "truer" than a more distant view. All we can say is that "a view gained at any distance whatsoever has its own justification." Each distance has its own correct picture and its own margin for error.[53] Differences

[49]   See chapter 5 below.
[50]   "Adornment," in Wolff, *Sociology of Georg Simmel*, pp. 338–44.
[51]   *Über sociale Differenzierung*, p. 80.
[52]   "The Nature of Philosophy," in *Essays*, pp. 305–9.
[53]   Wolff, *Sociology of Georg Simmel*, pp. 7–8.

among artistic styles, such as naturalism and symbolism, can be interpreted as a function of different distances they produce between us and phenomena.[54] Religion offers a point that transcends all the contrasts of psychic experience and toward which they all converge.[55]

All social forms are defined to some extent in terms of the dimension of interpersonal distance. Some forms, like conflict, bring distant people into close contact. Others, like secrecy, increase the distance between people. Some forms organize gradations of vertical distance, whereas others are forms for organizing horizontal distances. Forms like the stranger and fashion entail distinctive combinations of both nearness and distance. Simmel's sociology also includes a pioneering analysis of the effects of variations in physical distance on social relations.[56]

Dualism. The world can best be understood in terms of conflicts and contrasts between opposed categories. It was Simmel's repeatedly expressed view that the condition for the existence of any aspect of life is the coexistence of a diametrically opposed element. Sometimes these opposed qualities or tendencies are seen as stemming from an originally undifferentiated unity; sometimes they are seen as joined together, so that a form is defined as a synthesis of opposites or as a midpoint between them; sometimes they are seen as varying inversely with one another. Often they are presented as only apparent contrasts, polarized dimensions of what is actually a more encompassing unity.[57]

54 "Sociological Aesthetics," in Etzkorn (trans.), *Conflict in Modern Culture*, p. 77 ff.
55 "Die Gegensatze des Lebens und der Religion," *Das freie Wort* (Frankfurt/Main), 4, Nr. 8 (1904/5) : 307.
56 "Der Raum und die räumlichen Ordnungen der Gesellschaft," chapter 9 of *Soziologie*. The major part of this chapter has never been translated. The essay "The Stranger" (chapter 10 in this volume) is an excerpt from it.
57 Thus, "Good and evil are certainly mutually exclusive in a relative sense; but perhaps in an absolute, divine sense, existence is simply good, in a way that contains both the relative good and the relative evil. Certainly intellectual progress and intellectual stagnation are in irreconcilable opposition; but perhaps the overall intellectual process is one of

The opposition between subject and object forms the fundamental constitutive dualism in the realm of culture. This is so in two respects. Insofar as subjects are creators of cultural objects, they stand opposed to the latter as agents of the progressive forces of life confronted by fixed, objectified products detached from the continuity of life. The needs and impulses which give birth to culture are highly unstable. They shift emphasis and direction from one moment to the next. No sooner has a form been objectified than it seems in some measure constricting or inappropriate to the vital processes which called it into being. From this tension arise the dynamics of culture history, a result of "the deep contradiction between life's eternal flux and the objective validity and authenticity of the forms through which it proceeds."

Subjects are not, however, merely anonymous bearers of the ongoing stream of species life. They are also more or less active centers of a drive toward individuality. As such, they are consumers of cultural objects in accord with the needs of their developing subjective culture. As we have seen, this type of investment in cultural objects stands opposed to the type of investment required for promoting the systematization of objective culture for its own sake. The dualism of subjective culture and objective culture is, like the dualism of cultural objects and life process, inherent in the existence of culture.

The dualisms inherent in social forms stem both from man's ambivalent instinctual dispositions and from society's need to have some ratio of discordant to harmonious tendencies in order to attain a determinate shape. Publicity and privacy, conformity and individuation, antagonism and solidarity, compliance and rebelliousness, freedom and constraint are some of the many specific sociological dualisms which Simmel finds compresent in social in-

---

absolute progress, in which the empirically progressive factor is something relative and that which we call stagnation is also an element of progress. And so perhaps life and death, though they seem to exclude one another logically and physically, may be only relative contrasts, encompassed by life in its absolute sense, which grounds and transcends the reciprocal confrontation and mutual determination of life and death." *Rembrandt* (Leipzig: Kurt Wolff, 1916), p. 92.

teraction and utilizes to analyze the structure of various social forms.

Image of Man

In the course of his varied analyses Simmel develops a number of substantive points—now implicitly, now overtly—which together provide a distinctive and penetrating interpretation of human experience. Simmel sees human experience as endlessly creative, multiply fragmented, inexorably conflictual, and most meaningful when in the service of individuality.

CREATIVITY   Simmel heartily endorses Kant's view that the human mind is not a passive receptor of external stimuli: "Cognitive representations of things are not poured into us like nuts in a sack."[58] But for Simmel, the mind not only is active in that it brings its own categories to make cognition possible, it is involved in creating those categories and refining them and seeking out new areas in which to apply them. The most rudimentary act of conscious adaptation involves a creative forming of the elements of protoculture. The transformation of protoculture into the forms of autonomous objective culture involves a massive creative effort, sustained over generations, of an order that one might compare to what some economists describe in speaking of a "takeoff" into self-sustaining economic growth. And the diverse worlds—science, art, religion, philosophy, ethics, perhaps others as yet unborn—exist as beacons constantly drawing man onward to new reaches of creativity.

This stress on creativity may help to account for what is one of the peculiarities of Simmel's choice of topics as a sociologist: his neglect of the institutionalized structures. Simmel prefers not to consider man as a passive being who is molded and constrained by imposing, established institutions. His concern is not how a society or large social organization functions, but mainly how individual needs and goals create the very forms of sociality in spontaneous

58   "The Nature of Philosophy," in *Essays*, p. 290.

interaction. The prerequisites of society are identified not in a formidable array of social systemic requirements, but in the mental categories which individuals must have in order to enter into association with one another.[59]

FRAGMENTATION   Despite all his creative capacities, man rarely if ever experiences wholeness in his life. The nature of culture, society, and personality is such that the most he attains are fragments of things. The separate and incommensurable worlds of culture make competing claims on his attention. It may be given to a few to devote themselves wholly to a single world, but for most men Simmel's observation holds: "We are constantly circulating over a number of different planes, each of which presents the world-totality according to a different formula; but from each our life takes only a fragment along at any given time."[60]

The structure of social interaction displays a comparable plurality of claims on the individual. Individuals usually belong to a number of different groups; the person is caught in the intersection of their crosscutting interests and expectations. Even within a single relationship, moreover, the individual will not find his experience shaped within a single form. A person may relate to another primarily through one particular form, say, competition; but other forms are invariably involved in their experience—secrecy; domination; gratitude, possibly; mutual exploitation, perhaps; sociability on occasion.

It is true that having access to a plurality of cultural forms and participating in a plurality of membership groups makes it easier for a person to express his individuality more fully. But wholeness in this endeavor is no less futile than in extraindividual realms. Not only are we all fragments, Simmel observes, of the general cultural and social types we embody, but "we are also fragments of the type which only we ourselves are."[61]

---

[59]   See chapter 2 below.
[60]   *Lebensanschauung*, p. 37.
[61]   Ibid., p. 79.

C O N F L I C T   From the foregoing, as from the discussion of Simmel's principled dualism, it should be clear that Simmel sees human experience as permeated by innumerable conflicts. From this it might seem that his view of life is starkly and utterly pessimistic. What such a conclusion overlooks is that the inevitable conflicts Simmel identifies are not all of a piece. Some are tonic and constructive; others, though costly and painful, are historically productive. Only in certain determinate areas are conflicts inescapably tragic.

Within the realms of culture and society, conflict is tonic and constructive. The different worlds of culture are not really antagonistic to one another; they conflict only insofar as they compete for attention and resources. The irreconcilable differences among them are the source of the greatest richness and profundity in life. Similarly, the conflicts among individuals and between different formal principles are the preconditions for a determinate structure in society. They give society texture, durability, and resilience. The desire for a social world of perfect harmony is thus fundamentally misguided.

A more serious sort of conflict obtains *between* the ongoing process of life, on the one hand, and the various social and cultural forms which it generates, on the other. Once created, forms are rigid. They are incapable of adapting to the continuous oscillations of subjective need. The conflict between established forms and vital needs produces a perpetual tension, a tension which is nevertheless the source of the dialectical development or replacement of social structures and cultural forms throughout history.

In modern culture, this kind of conflict has reached a particularly serious point, a hitherto unexperienced level of intensity. Owing to the modern tendency to idealize the life process as such, as well as the difficulty of assimilating the rapidly changing products of objective culture, a reaction has set in. No longer is merely this or that particular set of forms under attack. The very principle of form as such has been thrown into disrepute. This observation leads Simmel to raise the question whether modern man is living in a protracted transitional stage, in which the normal processes of cultural obsolescence and reconstruction are simply drawn out over a much longer period, or whether this period represents a more radical departure—to an era where formlessness itself will be the dominant form of life.[62]

In either case, some new formal principle will be established. Life must create forms through which to proceed just as surely as it must oppose every given form sooner or later. This dual necessity, far from constituting a tragic condition, provides the very basis on which life attains its unitary character as self-transcendence: "Life as immediately experienced is precisely the unity of being formed and that reaching out beyond form which manifests itself at any single moment as destruction of the given current form."[63]

Simmel reserves the term "tragic" primarily to qualify two types of conflict, both of which involve some lesion of the boundaries of formed individuality.[64] He names them the tragedy of culture and the sociological tragedy. Noting that a relationship is called tragic when destructive forces directed against some being are called forth by the very nature of that being itself, Simmel sees the existence of individuality attacked and threatened by the very forms which individual creativity has produced—objective culture and sociality.

The forms of sociality are created by individuals to satisfy their wants, but the successful enactment of sociality among a large number of individuals greatly endangers the individual's integrity. This is because social interaction rests on a base of shared qualities and understandings that make reciprocal responsiveness

[62]   See chapter 24 below.
[63]   See chapter 23 below.
[64]   Simmel also speaks (in his essay "Über die Liebe") of an "overtone of the tragic" which adheres to every great love because although the instinctual basis of love is connected with the life of the species, the pure experience of love is self-contained, an end in itself—opposed to the purposiveness involved in the continuation of the species and the procreation of third parties.

For a broader and more extended interpretation of Simmel's treatment of the concept of tragedy, see Isadora Bauer, *Die Tragik in der Existenz des modernen Menschen bei G. Simmel* (Berlin: Duncker & Humblot, 1962).

possible. As sociality is expanded to include more and more individuals, the qualities which can serve as the basis for interaction become reduced in number and lowered in quality—to what must be, by definition, a lowest common denominator. Therefore, the more refined and developed a man's individuality, the less likely is he to be able to interact meaningfully with others. Insofar as he does so, it is on the basis of primitive levels of human functioning and sensibility. This difference between the individual and collective levels accounts for the fact that "the necessity to oblige the masses, or even habitually to expose oneself to them, easily corrupts the character. It pulls the individual down to a level with all and sundry."[65] The conflict between the forms of individuality and sociality is self-generated and inescapable; it constitutes the "sociological tragedy."

A more profound tragedy exists in the conflict between individuality and cultural forms. The very concept of culture depicts the self as creating objectified forms which it must reintegrate in order to develop but whose logic places the self in jeopardy. To subordinate one's personal growth to the requirements of a boundless stretch of cultural materials is to betray one's individuality; in following that path, the self "loses itself either in a dead end alley or in an emptiness of its innermost and most individual life." Yet to abandon those requirements is an equally serious betrayal. One does injustice thereby not only to the claims of autonomous cultural forms but moreover, because self-cultivation entails mastery of the relevant objective culture, to the claims of individual self-development as well. "The situation is tragic: even in its first moments of existence, culture carries something within itself which, as if by an intrinsic fate, is determined to block, to burden, to obscure and divide its innermost purpose, the transition of the soul from its incomplete to its complete state."[66]

In the modern period, owing to the complex division of labor and a highly developed money economy, this tragedy has been ex-

---

65   Wolff, *Sociology of Georg Simmel*, p. 31 ff.
66   "On the Concept and Tragedy of Culture," in Etzkorn (trans.), *Conflict in Modern Culture*, p. 46.

perienced in a most acute form. Modern facilities and organization have made possible an unparalleled development of autonomous, objective culture. This has greatly magnified the distance between subject and object. On the one hand, specialized cultural production goes on with little or no consideration of the "cultural" value of its objects. On the other,

the typically problematic situation of modern man comes into being: his sense of being surrounded by an innumerable number of cultural elements which are neither meaningless to him nor, in the final analysis, meaningful. In their mass they depress him, since he is not capable of assimilating them all, nor can he simply reject them, since after all they do belong *potentially* within the sphere of his cultural development.[67]

Man stands to become alienated from the most advanced products of his creative spirit.

INDIVIDUALITY   Simmel's devotion to the principle of individuality is expressed in a number of ways: in his reserving the stature of tragedy for only those conflicts in which one of the parties is the principle of individuality, as we have just seen; in his repeated assertion that the cultivation of individuals is the ultimate goal and justification for all forms of objective culture; in his inspired accounts of the forms of individuality and his expressed hope that "the ideas of free personality as such and of unique personality as such are not the last words of individualism—that, rather, the unforeseeable work of mankind will produce ever more numerous and varied forms with which the human personality will affirm itself and prove the worth of its existence."[68]

There are three points at which Simmel's treatment of some social phenomenon differs from that of its cultural counterpart, and each of these represents the differential implications of the principle of individuality for those two different worlds. One concerns the fragmentary character of life. For Simmel, the fragmentation of social life is liberating and gratifying, whereas the fragmenta-

[67]   Ibid., p. 44.
[68]   See chapter 15 below.

tion of man's experience of culture is frustrating. This is because social fragmentation promotes the conditions for developing individuality, whereas cultural fragmentation both hinders and assists man's self-development.

Similarly, Simmel's attitude toward social evolution is much more positive than his attitude toward cultural evolution. In his various attempts to deal with the long-term secular trends of societal development, the end product is always a high degree of individuation. Because of the opposition between objective culture and individuality, however, the most advanced manifestations of cultural development are tragically conflictual.

Finally, in his analysis of the forms themselves, we have noted that Simmel concentrates on the *protoforms* of society but on the *objectified forms* of culture. The former permits him to remain close to the level of individual experience and creativity, the latter permits him to focus on the great products of the free human spirit. In social life, a comparable freedom exists only in the realm of the autonomous play forms of sociality, which accounts for the seemingly disproportionate interest Simmel shows in them—forms of association in which the dominant note is a feeling of personal liberation.

Impact on Contemporaries

The unifying aspects of Simmel's thought which we have tried to identify have not been apparent to previous readers of Simmel. It is an open question to what extent Simmel was conscious of all of them himself. In any case, he communicated his ideas in fragments—fragments whose glitter was so seductive that they disinclined the beholder to look beyond for systematic connections.

In spite of his fragmentalism, his marginality, and his inferior academic status, Simmel's impact on his academic contemporaries was immediate and far-reaching. This was particularly true of his sociological writings. "There is no doubt that Simmel, thanks to his extensive and many-sided knowledge and the penetrating energy of his thought, is the only man capable of lifting sociology from the level of mere data collecting and general reflection to the rank of a truly philosophical undertaking"—thus the academic dean at Heidelberg.[69]

Clearly, Simmel's attempt to provide a more rigorous basis for the sociological enterprise met a felt intellectual need. His first major programmatic statement, *Das Problem der Soziologie*, published in Schmoller's *Jahrbuch* in 1894, was published in French the same year, in English in 1895, and in Italian, Polish, and Russian shortly after. By 1909 Simmel was being referred to in the standard reference work in the social sciences in Germany as "the most important German sociologist."[70] The following year, at the first meeting of the German Sociological Society in Frankfurt, Simmel was given the honor of presenting the opening paper. In 1915 the faculty at Heidelberg, still trying vainly to recruit Simmel, recommended him to the ministry in the following terms:

Simmel's major service is without doubt the transformation and provision of completely new foundations for the social sciences. . . . He has established anew the discipline of sociology, which hitherto has been the arena for arbitrariness and personal amateurism or else for a rigid positivism. He has drawn its boundaries, determined its method, created its concepts and, above all, brilliantly laid its psychological foundations.[71]

Simmel's writings in sociology and social philosophy were familiar to the most energetic minds in sociology throughout the formative years of the modern discipline. Although Durkheim and Weber seem not to have taken each other's work into account, both of them were well acquainted with Simmel. Durkheim found Simmel's effort to redefine the boundaries of sociology "subtle and ingenious,"[72] and saw to it that Simmel's essay on the persistence of social groups was published in the first volume of *L'année sociologique*. Although on methodological grounds Durkheim and his followers went on to reject Simmel's conception of sociology, the

[69]   Gassen and Landmann, *Buch des Dankes*, p. 25.
[70]   Cited in Heinz Mauss, "Simmel in German Sociology," in *Essays*, p. 186.
[71]   Gassen and Landmann, *Buch des Dankes*, p. 32.
[72]   "Sociology and Its Scientific Field," in Coser, *Georg Simmel*, p. 48.

writings of Simmel continued to stimulate a small number of French sociologists, most notably Celestin Bouglé.

The influence of Simmel on Max Weber and other German sociologists was more direct and enduring. During the critical years of intellectual gestation preceding publication of his essay on the Protestant Ethic, Weber was led to some of his most fundamental methodological ideas and substantive insights from Simmel's writings. In the judgment of their gifted young contemporary György Lukacs, Weber's achievement in the sociology of culture "was possible only on the foundation created by Simmel."[73] From Simmel's *Probleme der Geschichtsphilosophie* Weber drew solutions to some of the methodological dilemmas which vexed the previous generation of German scholars—the synthesis of positivism and neo-Kantian idealism, and the articulation of a methodology of *Verstehen* and ideal types. In *Philosophie des Geldes* Weber found a model for sociological analysis that was both penetrating and restrained, and a provocative interpretation of the all-pervasive effects of rationalization in modern society and culture. Later Weber's treatment of social relationships in *Wirtschaft und Gesellschaft* would incorporate some concepts from Simmel's analyses of the forms of social interaction.[74]

Weber found it deeply regrettable that Simmel's works had never been the subject of a systematic, coherent critical study. He began to write such a critique himself around 1908, but did not complete the project because he was anxious to promote an academic appointment for Simmel at Heidelberg and did not want to publish anything that might be construed to Simmel's disadvantage. Of Weber's contemplated essay an introductory fragment has been preserved at the Max Weber Institute in Munich. It begins with a frank expression of Weber's profound ambivalence toward Simmel's thinking:

In evaluating the work of Georg Simmel one's responses prove to be highly contradictory. On the one hand, one is bound to react to

[73]   Gassen and Landmann, *Buch des Dankes*, p. 175.
[74]   For further comments on Simmel's influence on Weber, see the essays by F. H. Tenbruck and Heinz Maus in *Essays*.

Simmel's works from a point of view that is overwhelmingly antagonistic. In particular, crucial aspects of his methodology are unaccept-
able. His substantive results must with unusual frequency be regarded
with reservations, and not seldom they must be rejected outright. In
addition, his mode of exposition strikes one at times as strange, and
often it is at the very least uncongenial.

On the other hand, one finds oneself absolutely compelled to affirm
that this mode of exposition is simply brilliant and, what is more important, attains results that are intrinsic to it and not to be attained
by any imitator. Indeed, nearly every one of his works abounds in important new theoretical ideas and the most subtle observations. Almost
every one of them belongs to those books in which not only the valid
findings, but even the false ones, contain a wealth of stimulation for
one's own further thought, in comparison with which the majority of
even the most estimable accomplishments of other scholars often appear to exude a peculiar odor of scantiness and poverty. The same
holds true of his epistemological and methodological foundations and,
again, doubly so just where they are perhaps ultimately not tenable.
All together, then, Simmel, even when he is on the wrong path, fully
deserves his reputation as one of the foremost of thinkers, a first-rate
stimulator of academic youth and academic colleagues (insofar as the
spirit of the latter is not too dull or their vanity and/or bad conscience
too lively to let themselves be "stimulated" by a man of fifty years who
has not advanced beyond the position of Extraordinarius [associate
professor] and thus quite obviously belongs to the ranks of the "unsuccessful").

Weber goes on to observe that many of Simmel's colleagues in
philosophy and the social sciences expressed inexplicable animosity toward Simmel's ideas, an animosity which Weber traced in
part to Simmel's tendency to utilize far-ranging analogies in his
mode of argument. But he adds that:

This is not the place to inquire whether Simmel's colleagues in
philosophy, upon finding difficult logical and other philosophical problems being utilized by Simmel as "analogies" to illustrate totally
heterogeneous subject matters, do not find in this procedure, which
certainly often strikes one as "playful," a legitimation for not occupying themselves with him seriously—without regard to the question
whether Simmel for his part attains his goals through this usage. Because Simmel's ultimate *interests* are directed to metaphysical prob-

lems, to the *"meaning"* of life, and because these interests are so very noticeable in his treatment of technical substantive questions, it is all too easy to overlook the fact that he has withal probably contributed more to the advancement of the technical substantive concerns of his discipline, even if at times this is more in the nature of a "by-product," than a considerable number of professors of philosophy of the quality that is becoming customary today put together.

Weber's interest in value-orientations, institutionalization, and questions of historical causation issued in sociology of a quite different stamp from that of Simmel. Other German sociologists followed Simmel's lead more directly. Reviewing Simmel's *Soziologie* in 1910, Leopold von Wiese declared that to a certain extent "I am ready to consider his way as correct, and to see in his sociology a significant advance over all past attempts." He added that the science of the forms of association needed certain guiding ideas if it were to develop beyond fragments of analysis into a unified theory.[75] A decade later von Wiese began to provide those guiding ideas himself, both in his editorial supervision of the *Kölner Vierteljahrshefte für Sozialwissenschaft* and in his own development of an axiomatic sociology, in which more than 650 different forms of social relationship were identified and classified according to a few basic analytic variables.[76]

Von Wiese's project was only the most elaborate and conspicuous example of the widespread reliance on Simmel in German sociology of the 1920s. The work of the ethnologist Alfred Vierkandt took a new turn in 1923 with his promulgation of a social theory founded on analysis of the protoforms and established forms of sociality.[77] At the same time Theodor Litt used Simmel's conception of the triad as a building block for a general theory of social structures.[78] In the great synthetic works of German sociology of the time—the volumes of Franz Oppenheimer, Hans Freyer, and

75 Coser, *Georg Simmel*, p. 55.
76 Leopold von Wiese and Howard Becker, *Systematic Sociology* (New York: Wiley, 1932).
77 *Gesellschaftslehre* (Stuttgart: F. Enke, 1923).
78 *Individuum und Gemeinschaft*, 2d comp. rev. ed. (Berlin: B. G. Teubner, 1924).

Ernst Troeltsch—Simmel's ideas were accorded serious and appreciative attention. Those who took serious exception to his whole approach to sociology, men like Eduard Spranger and Othmar Spann, nevertheless felt obliged to engage in criticism against him. Although Albion Small may have exaggerated in calling the whole sociological movement in post-War Germany neo-Simmelian,[79] it is clear that Simmel's ideas enjoyed a privileged position in German sociology, until sociology in general and Simmel's books in particular were suppressed by the Nazis.

In the United States it was Small who, though not a follower of Simmel, was responsible for introducing Simmel when sociology was becoming established in the academy.[80] In his book on the origins of American sociology, Small pointed to the diffusion of ideas from German universities as the decisive factor affecting the rise of sociology in the United States.[81] Small's own career was a notable case in point: he studied at Berlin and Leipzig from 1879 to 1881 and remained in touch with developments in German social science thereafter. Small was thus poised to appreciate Simmel's work as soon as it appeared. He corresponded with Simmel and spoke with him directly during subsequent trips to Europe.

Small felt that Simmel's conception of sociology was unduly restricting—that sociology should be concerned with social control, functional problems, social dynamics, and value orientations as well as with the analysis of social forms. He did consider the study of social forms an important *part* of the field, and felt that in this area Simmel was "without a rival." Even more, Small applauded the spirit of Simmel's effort to give sociology a firm methodological foundation. So it was that shortly after Small founded the *American Journal of Sociology* in 1895 he began a program of publishing papers by Simmel—a total of fifteen entries between volumes 2

[79]   *American Journal of Sociology* 30: 352, 31: 86, 87.
[80]   Albion Small was founding chairman of the world's first department of sociology—at the University of Chicago in 1892. The accreditation of sociology at Chicago had a decisive impact on the acceptance of the subject in other American universities. See A. Small, "Fifty Years of Sociology in the United States," *American Journal of Sociology* 21: 763 ff.
[81]   *Origins of Sociology* (Chicago: University of Chicago Press, 1924).

and 16, most translated by Small himself. Despite his continued opposition to Simmel's definition of the field, Small thought that Simmel remained underappreciated as he watched the growth of American sociology. Feeling that his efforts to win a serious hearing for Simmel's ideas had been in vain, Small expressed one last "devout hope" in the year before he died that American sociologists would show themselves wise enough to familiarize themselves with Simmel's social theory.[82]

Simmel and Park

In spite of Small's valiant efforts (and those of his contemporary in political science, Arthur Bentley), Simmel would probably have been forgotten in American sociology were it not for the intervention of the man who eventually succeeded Small as the dominant figure in the Chicago department, Robert Ezra Park. Park's experience deserves especially close attention because the way Park related to Simmel decisively affected the degree and manner in which Simmel was subsequently integrated into American sociology.

While an undergraduate at the University of Michigan, Park came under the influence of John Dewey and developed an interest in the empirical study of social facts and in the phenomena of communication and public opinion. After college Park carried out Dewey's "assignment" to study the nature and social functions of the newspaper by working as a journalist. A decade later, Park returned to academic study because he was "interested in communication and collective behavior and wanted to know what the universities had to say about it."[83] His experience at Harvard, where he took an M.A. in philosophy and psychology under James, Munsterberg, and Royce, was stimulating but not wholly satisfying,

[82] Review of Spykman, *The Social Theory of Georg Simmel*, in *American Journal of Sociology* 31: 84–87. See also Small's reviews of *Soziologie*, in *American Journal of Sociology* 14: 544, and of the *Kölner Vierteljahrsheft*, in *American Journal of Sociology* 27: 92.

[83] Robert Park, unpublished autobiographical statement, February 1929.

so he went to Germany to study European contributions to collective psychology and social philosophy more intensively.

Thus it was that, at the mature age of thirty-five, primed with both philosophical training and a rich fund of worldly experience, Robert Park came to listen to the lectures of Georg Simmel during the winter semester 1899/1900 at Humboldt University in Berlin. "It was," as Everett Hughes has written, "his only formal instruction in sociology—instruction that influenced him and the course of American sociology deeply."[84] In an autobiographical essay written three decades later Park recalled: "It was from Simmel that I *finally gained a point of view for the study of the newspaper and society*."[85]

Soon after, Park left Berlin to study with Windelband at Strasbourg and, subsequently, Heidelberg. He carried with him the impact of Simmel's teaching. The dissertation which Park submitted to Windelband in 1904 was in large measure a chapter in Simmel's formal sociology.[86] The expressed aim of *Masse und Publikum* is to articulate precisely the essential characteristics of two basic forms (*Grundformen*) of social interaction, the crowd and the public. It follows Simmel further by distinguishing between the effort to describe these forms, which is sociological, and the effort to explain them by analyzing them into their elements, which is social psychological. In the substantive analysis of these forms, moreover, Park draws on Simmel at a number of points.[87]

---

[84]   Everett C. Hughes, "Robert Park," *New Society*, 31 Dec. 1964, p. 18.

[85]   Park, autobiographical statement, February 1929. Italics mine.

[86]   *Masse und Publikum: Eine methodologische und soziologische Untersuchung* (Bern: Lack & Grunau, 1904), p. 4.

[87]   In seeking to conceptualize the public as a social form in which individuals take differing positions with respect to bodies of fact which they possess in common, Park draws on Simmel's notion of exchange as a basic and distinguishing form of interaction, whereby one places oneself so as to take the point of view of the other, but acts in a contrary direction (p. 56). In a similar vein he draws on Simmel's ideas about social differentiation to refute the conception of society as resting purely on like-mindedness and to assert the crucial place of opposition and competition in the general form of the public (pp. 69–70). Elsewhere, he alludes to Simmel when seeking support for the proposition that crowds diminish the intellectual powers of an individual and heighten his emotionality (pp. 7–8).

In 1914 Park began his career as an academic sociologist at Chicago. In this position he gave renewed currency to Simmel's ideas. In the list of readings assembled by Park and his junior colleague, Ernest Burgess, for a basic course in sociology—published in 1921 as materials in their highly influential textbook—ten selections by Simmel were included. This was many more than were included from any other author.[88] Moreover, the frame of reference used to organize the readings was largely Simmelian in conception. Park's impressions of Simmel became part of local lore for generations of Chicago graduate students, some of whom issued his notes from the lectures he heard by Simmel in Berlin as the first publication of their Society for Social Research. In personal communications Park frequently named Simmel and Durkheim (in that order) as the greatest sociologists, and at one point he asserted that "Simmel has written the most profound and stimulating book in sociology, in my opinion, that has ever been written."[89] What is most important, moreover, in his own work Park utilized Simmel's ideas more productively than did any other sociologist, at least before the 1950s.

For all his admiration of Simmel, Park's intellectual relationship to his mentor was not one of discipleship. Although Park's attitude toward Simmel was not, like Durkheim's, one of principled rejection, or even, like Small's, one of aloof appreciation, neither was it like that of Park's German contemporaries—von Wiese, Vierkandt, Litt—who sought to construct systematic social theory on Simmelian foundations. Park relied closely on Simmel, but in his own eclectic fashion. Thanks to Park, Simmel's ideas were given new life by being translated into a more accessible idiom, at the same time that they were being weakened as a basis for a general analytic theory.

There are certain sets of ideas which Park appears to have ex-

---

[88]   *Introduction to the Science of Sociology* (Chicago: University of Chicago Press, 1921). Compared to ten selections by Simmel, there were two each by Durkheim, Hobhouse, and Spencer; three by Le Bon; and none by Tarde or Weber. In addition, there are thirty-three references to Simmel cited in the index, compared with twenty-three each for Durkheim and Le Bon, thirteen for Hobhouse, and three for Weber.

[89]   Cited by Hugh D. Duncan in *Essays*, p. 116, n. 5.

plicitly derived from Simmel: (*a*) that sociology should describe
the ideal types of forms of social interaction abstracted from their
contents; (*b*) that this effort should include accounts of the emergence of these forms (Park's "natural histories") and be sensitive
to the oscillation between established form and spontaneous
process; (*c*) the idea of social distance, and its use in analyzing the
position of social types epitomized by the stranger (Park's "marginal man"); (*d*) the idea of continuing reciprocal stimulation
(Park's "circular interaction"); and (*e*) a set of ideas concerning
conflict: the oscillation between conflict and accommodation; the
relation between out-group hostilities and in-group morale; the
ways in which group antagonisms provide a basis for stabilizing
social structure. More important in the present discussion, however, is the fact that in two significant respects Park changed the
character of some of Simmel's key ideas. He altered Simmel's definition of what constitutes a social fact, and he shifted the main
referent of interaction from that of *trans*action to that of *concerted*
action.

Both of these changes reflect the complementary influences on
Park of Sumner and Durkheim. These men considered moral regulation the most essential aspect of social life. Simmel, in contrast,
had depicted norms as a phenomenon of secondary interest, a mere
side effect of social interaction.[90] Already in his dissertation Park
sought to synthesize these two viewpoints, concluding that human
groups have two distinct traits, a set of interaction processes *and* a
general will manifested subjectively in conscience and objectively
in the mores. In later work Park came to express this distinction
in terms of two types of interaction, one that is normatively regu-

[90]   "The members of a credit union are certainly subject to definite
regulation of their contributions and withdrawals . . . but that is only a limiting condition. The positive sociological principle is the reciprocally extended help. . . . A social party doubtless presumes a large number of
external regulations of the behavior of its participants. But there is a
party, according to its meaning and vital principle . . . only when there
is reciprocal pleasing, stimulating, cheering." "Zur Methodik der Sozialwissenschaft," *Jahrbuch für Gesetzgebung, Verwaltung, und Volkswirt-
schaft im deutschen Reich* 20 (1896) : 227–37.

lated and one that is not. The latter, based on competition in the struggle for existence and directly parallel with similar processes in plant and animal communities, constitutes what Park called the biotic or the ecological order. In human groups, its effects were always modified by interaction processes which make up the *moral or social* order. Social control, then, became "the central fact and the central problem of society,"[91] not the normatively indifferent fact of human association, as with Simmel.

The bearers of moral or social order, moreover, are organized collectivities. Following Simmel, Park sees collectivities not as substantive entities but as networks of interaction. Crowds are made up of persons interacting through milling, sects through the interstimulation of unrest, racial groups through the communication of shared grievances, publics through the circulation of news. Through their various processes of communication, collectivities attain some consensus regarding values and goals. Concerted action is thus the dynamic aspect of moral order and social control. Sociology must therefore be "the science of collective behavior," not, as for Simmel, the science of the forms of association pure and simple.

This subtle shift of definition was not inconsequential. It had three methodological implications which shaped the character of sociology as practiced by Park and his students and distinguished their work from that of Simmel. (1) Its empirical focus was on types of concrete collectivities rather than on the empirical referents of analytically abstracted types of social interaction.[92] (2) Its explanatory focus was on how these types of collectivity come into being, persist, and change, rather than on the structural implications of a particular kind of form. (3) By relegating competition and conflict to the sphere of the presocial, or subsocial, it led to an identification of sociality with consensus, rather than a conception of all *social* facts as inherently based on fundamental dualisms. In sum, Park's sociology was concrete, dynamic, and oriented to social

91   Park and Burgess, *Introduction to the Science of Society*, p. 42.
92   In his contributions to human ecology, however, Park maintained an interest in such analytic abstractions when developing concepts like invasion, succession, and dominance.

consensus, whereas Simmel's was abstract, structural, and oriented to sociological dualism.[93]

Repercussions

The peculiar transmutation of Simmel's thought in the work of Park may provide a point of departure for explaining the vicissitudes of Simmel's career in American sociology during the half-century since his death. In tracing this story four phases may be discerned.

PARK AND HIS STUDENTS   It seems that for each of the topics Park wished to pursue, an apppropriate vehicle appeared in the form of one or more of his students.[94] In connection with topics specifically suggested by Simmel, there were three such instances.

Drawing on Simmel's discussions of social distance, Park formulated this concept more precisely[95] and encouraged Emory Bogardus to construct a number of indexes purporting to measure social distance, expressed in terms of degrees of intimacy with

[93]   It is perhaps worth noting that I have described a central tendency in Park's thinking, not every detail of it. He does not entirely ignore transaction, particularly in his treatment of personality; but "concerted action" is the key theme of his programmatic statements and of his own work in the 1920s. I am not saying, moreover, that Park ignores the *phenomenon* of conflict; far from it. He was deeply interested in phenomena like social movements and revolutions. My point is that he sees conflict as technically pre- or extrasocial. It is a source of disruption or of constructive change in the social order, but not constitutive of society as such.

[94]   This was due to a number of factors: Park's own generosity as a teacher; the advanced age at which he began work as a productive scholar; and exceptionally favorable conditions for graduate study at Chicago in the 1920s which provided a supply of able students on which he could draw. On this last point, see Robert E. L. Faris, *Chicago Sociology, 1920–1932* (San Francisco: Chandler, 1967).

[95]   Park and Burgess, *Introduction to the Science of Society*, pp. 282–86; Park, "The Concept of Social Distance," *Journal of Applied Sociology* 8 (1924) : 339–44.

which members of various ethnic groups preferred to associate with one another.[96] (Work in a similar vein was subsequently carried out by J. L. Moreno in his sociometrics of associational preferences in small groups—through which Simmel's appeal for a geometry of social relations was first realized in graphic form.)[97] Similarly, drawing on Simmel's ideas about the stranger, Park articulated his conception of the marginal man and stimulated Everett Stonequist to write his dissertation on that topic.[98] Earlier, two other of Park's students had studied specific types of social isolation, the hotel resident and the hobo.[99] The literature inspired by Park's revitalization of Simmel's essay on the stranger subsequently grew enormously.[100]

Finally, Park was probably led to some of his ideas on the individuating aspects of urban life by Simmel's essay "The Metropolis and Mental Life" and related writings, an interest elaborated with particular distinction by two of his students, Louis Wirth and Robert Redfield. In the course of the sixty-seven-page bibliographical essay on the city prepared by Wirth for the volume on the city written by Park, Burgess, and MacKenzie, Wirth de-

[96]   "Social Distance and Its Origins," *Journal of Applied Sociology* 9 (1925): 216–26, 299–308. See also Bogardus, *Social Distance* (Los Angeles, 1959).
[97]   Jacob L. Moreno, *Who Shall Survive?* (1934), rev. and enl. ed. (Beacon, N.Y.: Beacon House, 1953). Moreno names Simmel as the first of the sociologists to have theorized about interpersonal relations (p. xxxi) and to have conceptualized "certain aspects of sociometry" (p. 15).
[98]   "The Marginal Man: A Study in the Subjective Aspects of Cultural Conflict" (doctoral dis., 1930). *The Marginal Man* (New York: Scribner's, 1937).
[99]   Horman Hayner, "The Sociology of Hotel Life" (1923; book published in 1936 as *Hotel Life*). Nels Anderson, *The Hobo* (M.A. thesis, 1925; published by the University of Chicago Press in 1923).
[100]   To name but a few out of dozens: A. Schuetz, "The Stranger," *American Journal of Sociology* 49 (1944); Everett C. Hughes, "Social Change and Status Protest: An Essay on the Marginal Man," *Phylon* 10 (1946); Donald Wray, "Marginal Men of Industry: The Foremen," *American Journal of Sociology* 54 (1949); Julie Meyer, "The Stranger and the City," *American Journal of Sociology* 56 (1951).

scribes Simmel's essay as "the most important single article on the city from the sociological standpoint,"[101] and used its ideas freely in his own important essay a dozen years later, "Urbanism as a Way of Life."[102]

It is notable that all these extensions of Simmel's ideas by Park's students—in their studies of social distance, social isolation, and individuation in the metropolis—deal with social *relationships*, not with social *process*. In Park's scheme, the study of social processes was usurped, as we have seen, by the rather non-Simmelian concerns about the dynamics of collectivities and the natural histories of their growth. Given an established social order, however, one could study social relationships either as representing stable patterns of social accommodation or in terms of relative distance from a presumed social consensus.

THE PARSONIAN SYNTHESIS The net effect of Park's adaptation of Simmel, then, was to revive and transmit selected ideas concerning social relationships but to undermine the possibility of using Simmel as a point of departure for building a sociological frame of reference. With the publication of Talcott Parsons's *Structure of Social Action* in 1937, the eclipse of Simmel was virtually total. Through an extended treatment of Durkheim, Pareto, and Weber, this work adumbrated the principles of a theory of social action that could dispense with the kind of transactional analysis advocated by Simmel.

Two points must be clarified in order to explain the impact of Parsons's opus on the fate of Simmel: why it achieved such an eminent position in the literature, and why it was able to dispense with Simmel.

One reason for its eminence, of course, is intrinsic. *The Structure of Social Action* was an impressive piece of scholarship (and remains so, even though its interpretations and conclusions are not always beyond dispute.) But the commanding position it assumed

101 *The City* (Chicago: University of Chicago Press, 1925), p. 219.
102 *American Journal of Sociology* 44: 1–24. See also Robert Redfield, *The Folk Culture of Yucatan* (Chicago: University of Chicago Press, 1939).

in American social theory was also due to certain extrinsic factors. One was that the crucially important theories of Durkheim and Weber had not yet been integrated into the mainstream of American sociology even to the limited extent that Simmel's had been. A second factor was that by the mid-1930s, American sociology had worked itself into a theoretical vacuum. Not since Cooley's *Social Organization* in 1909 had there been a major creative synthesis in American social theory. The growing edge of American sociology lay in the refinement of research methodologies. Park and Burgess had asserted in 1921 that the period of debate about fundamental assumptions in sociology was over, that it was being replaced by a period of "investigation and research."[103] Sociologists subsequently became much more excited about their research procedures than about the depth, coherence, or implications of their ideas. Park's students were mainly exercised over the demands of doing natural histories, community studies, urban surveys, and field interviewing. The students of Ogburn and many of the faculty at Columbia were caught up with the possibilities of statistical analysis. What slack remained was taken up by renewed interest in social problems and reforms. Only at Harvard, first with Pitirim Sorokin (who was summarily hostile toward Simmel, as toward so many others) and then Parsons himself, was a sustained effort made to innovate in a rigorous, systematic way in a social theory that was continuous with the great works in the tradition.

A third factor contributing to the success of Parsons's book was that it articulated a paradigm which was broadly congruent with the orientations of most American sociologists. The emphasis on shared values and normative constraints represented what many felt was the sociologist's mission to save the world from the naive utilitarian assumptions about homo economicus.

How Parsons's grand synthesis could dispense with Simmel is a complex question which we cannot treat in detail here. Virtually all the principles developed by Parsons are at variance with the

[103]   Illustrative of this shift is the fact that the bibliography following Park's introduction to the reader contains twenty-five items on "methods of sociological investigation," only fifteen items representing various schools of social theory.

previously discussed principles of Simmel.[104] The main thing to note here is that Parsons in many ways follows the same logic as Park did. Although Parsons starts with "action," Park with "interaction," both find the central sociological problem to be that of explaining concerted action. Once one defines the phenomenon of consensually maintained moral restraints as the essential ingredient of social order, one can dispense with looking at social order, as Simmel had, as the complex resultant of a great number of variously shaped transactions.

COUNTERPOINT　In the years following World War II, the Parsonian paradigm gained ascendancy in American social theory, now buttressed by a much more differentiated terminology for dealing with types of shared values and their institutional implications. By the late 1950s, however, a decided revival of interest in Simmelian sociology had set in. Just as Parsons's earlier an-

---

[104] This is a central conclusion of Donald N. Levine, "Simmel and Parsons: Two Approaches to the Study of Society," Ph.D. diss., University of Chicago, 1957. Some of the principal differences between these two theoretical approaches can be summarized schematically as follows:

	Simmel	*Parsons*
Central analytic abstraction	Forms of interaction	Social systems
Main dimension for sociological description	Distance between individuals and groups	Institutionalized value-orientations and norms
Methodology of description	Dualistic (both/and)	Unique determination (either/or)
Approach to sociological explanation	Analysis of structural implications and effects	Analysis of functional needs, resources, and strains
Conception of social conflict	Constitutive of social order	Disruptive of social order; source of change
Conception of relations between personality, society, and culture	Three distinct ways of organizing the contents of human experience	Independently variable but interpenetrating systems of action
Scientific objective	Determination of types	Empirical-theoretical system

nouncement concerning the death of Spencer had proved premature, so now his omission of Simmel from the mainstream of modern social theory began to prove unviable.

This revival was associated with three developments in contemporary sociology. One was the interest in codifying the structural properties of small groups, an enterprise in which scholars of such widely varying styles as Theodore Mills, Robert Merton, and Erving Goffman have drawn heavily on Simmel.[105] A second was a burgeoning of interest in the study of social conflict, in which Lewis Coser's codification of Simmel's propositions about conflict played a catalytic role.[106] The third was the effort to develop a general analytic theory based on the principle of social exchange, initiated with great éclat by George Homans.[107]

What all three developments had in common was an effort to deal with social relations in terms of spontaneous transactions rather than in terms of shared values and norms. Complementing the Parsonian approach, they restored to systematic social theory that bifocal awareness expressed by Park's doctoral distinction between interaction process and general will. In the terms of a later formulation of the Parsonian framework, they dealt with society as a set of *conditions* where Parsons had dealt with it mainly as a set of *controls*.[108]

TODAY "As many of us have discovered in our excur-

[105] Theodore M. Mills, "The Coalition Pattern in Three-Person Groups," *American Sociological Review* 19 (1954):657–67; idem, "Some Hypotheses on Small Groups from Simmel," *American Journal of Sociology* 63 (1958): 642–50; Robert K. Merton, "Continuities in the Theory of Reference Groups and Social Structure," in *Social Theory and Social Structure*, rev. and enl. ed. (Glencoe, Ill.: Free Press, 1957), pp. 281–386; Erving Goffman, *Behavior in Public Places* (New York: Free Press, 1963).
[106] *The Functions of Social Conflict* (Glencoe, Ill.: Free Press, 1956) ; see also his *Continuities in the Study of Social Conflict* (New York: Free Press, 1967).
[107] "Social Behavior as Exchange," *American Journal of Sociology* 63 (1958): 597–606; *Social Behaviour: Its Elementary Forms* (New York: Harcourt, Brace, 1961).
[108] Talcott Parsons, *Societies: Evolutionary and Comparative Perspectives* (New York: Prentice-Hall, 1966), p. 28.

sions into sociological theory, the figure of Simmel often appears toward the end of the journey. We greet him with dismay as well as respect, for he is coming back from a point we are still struggling to reach."[109] This is not only so for Simmel the prophet of symbolic interactionism, as the author of those words would have it; it is equally true for efforts going on in many diverse reaches of current sociology.

Simmel's presence is palpable in such diverse places as Cartwright and Harary's literal construction of a geometry of social relationships through the utilization of linear graphs;[110] Edwin O. Laumann's measurement of subjective and objective social distances in personal relations in urban settings;[111] Peter M. Blau's elaboration of a general theory of social exchange;[112] Ralf Dahrendorf's continuing reformulation of a theory of conflict in modern society;[113] Walter Buckley's efforts to construct sociological models based on cybernetics, and information and communication theories;[114] Barry Schwartz's essays on the gift and the social psychology of privacy;[115] Robert K. Merton's and Elinor Barber's formalization of the concept of sociological ambivalence;[116] Peter L. Berger's analysis of worlds of experience and consciousness;[117]

[109]   Hugh D. Duncan, "Simmel's Image of Society," in *Essays*, p. 108.
[110]   "Structural Balance," *Psychological Review* 63 (1956) : 277–93.
[111]   *Prestige and Association in an Urban Community* (Indianapolis, Ind.: Bobbs-Merrill, 1966).
[112]   *Exchange and Power in Social Life* (New York: Wiley, 1964).
[113]   *Class and Class Conflict in Industrial Society* (Stanford: Stanford University Press, 1959) ; *Conflict after Class* (London: Longmans, 1967).
[114]   Walter Buckley, *Sociology and Modern Systems Theory* (New York: Prentice-Hall, 1967).
[115]   "The Social Psychology of the Gift," *American Journal of Sociology* 73 (1967): 1–11; "The Social Psychology of Privacy," *American Journal of Sociology* 73 (1968) : 741–52.
[116]   "Sociological Ambivalence," in *Sociological Theory, Values, and Sociological Change*, ed. E. A. Tiryakian (New York: Free Press, 1963), pp. 91–120.
[117]   *Invitation to Sociology: A Humanistic Perspective* (New York: Doubleday Anchor Books, 1963), chaps. 2 and 3; Berger and Luckmann, *The Social Construction of Reality* (Garden City, N.Y.: Doubleday, 1966).

the work on sociability by David Riesman, Jeanne Watson, and Robert J. Potter;[118] and Theodore Caplow's explorations of triadic structures.[119]

The list of current creative applications of his ideas is not, I think, the full measure of Simmel's legacy. We may just be getting to a point where we can take certain other parts of that legacy seriously—the bases of the contemporary revolt against forms, for example, and the character of the quest for new forms of individuality. Other parts we may not yet be ready for—the isomorphism between social forms and symbolic forms; the aesthetic dimension of sociality; the measurement of ambivalence. Still more we are barely acquainted with. Much work remains to bring our level of critical understanding of Simmel up to the point already attained with regard to Durkheim and Weber. Beyond all particulars, Simmel's image of society may provide a continuing challenge to conceptions of social facts and social order which lay *primary* emphasis on systemic requirements and normative constraints, offering the counterparadigm of a fluctuating field of self-regulating transactions—an alternative which stresses the phenomenology of individual experience and the dimension of distance in social relations.

Simmel paid a high price for his nonconformity. He has been damned with many epithets—amateur, exhibitionist, relativist, "merely" talented, coquettish, empty, aimless. Although his nonconformity was professionally offensive as well as personally costly, it was tied to a fight for individuality and an intellectual achievement, neither of which has been exhausted more than half a century later. It is the editor's hope that the selections in this volume will exhibit more than a little of the trenchancy and richness of his work.

[118]   Jeanne Watson, "A Formal Analysis of Sociable Interaction," *Sociometry* 21 (1958) : 269–80; David Riesman, Robert J. Potter, and Jeanne Watson, "Sociability, Permissiveness, and Equality," *Psychiatry* 23 (1960) : 323–40.
[119]   *Two Against One: Coalitions in Triads* (Englewood Cliffs, N.J.: Prentice-Hall, 1968).

Selections in This Volume

The plan for a complete German edition of Simmel's works projects fourteen thick volumes.[120] The equivalent of only about one of those volumes has hitherto been translated into English. In preparing the present volume I have therefore tried to add as much as possible to the total amount of Simmel's writings available in English translation, as well as to present at least a partially representative sample of his work and to provide some points of departure for readers who wish to integrate some of Simmel's diverse and far-flung essays.

ON THE TRANSLATIONS   Half the selections in this book are fresh translations. The principal contribution they make to the list of Simmel's sociological writings available in English is the translation of the lengthy chapter 10 of *Soziologie*, which is presented here in chapters 4, 14, and 18. Other new translations include three selections from *Philosophie des Geldes* (5, 8, and 12), the introduction to *Probleme der Geschichtsphilosophie* (1), chapter 1 of *Lebensanschauung* (23), and three essays—"Das Individuum und die Freiheit," "Vom Wesen der Kultur," and the *Exkurs* "Der platonische und der moderne Eros" from "Über die Liebe" (15, 16, and 17).

Two of the translations prepared for this volume are new translations of writings that have previously appeared in English: the essay on the stranger (chapter 10), and the essay on exchange (chapter 5). The latter appeared as "A Chapter in the Philosophy of Value" in volume 5 of the *American Journal of Sociology*. It was a highly unreliable translation of a manuscript which Simmel subsequently revised twice before its publication in the edition of *Philosophie des Geldes* on which the present translation is based.

Of the new translations, chapters 1, 4, 5, 10, 17, and 23 were prepared by Donald N. Levine. The others were done by Richard P. Albares and Roberta Ash under the supervision of Donald N.

[120]   See Horst Muller, "Plan einer Gesamtausgabe der Werke Georg Simmels," in Gassen and Landmann, *Buch des Dankes*, pp. 60–63.

Levine—chapters 14, 15, and 18 by Mr. Albares and chapters 8, 12, and 16 by Mrs. Ash. Of the published translations which have been reprinted, chapters 2, 3, 6, 7, 21, and 22 were made by Kurt H. Wolff; chapter 9 by Everett C. Hughes; chapter 11 by Claire Jacobson; chapter 13 by David Kettler; chapter 20 by Edward A. Shils; and chapter 24 by K. Peter Etzkorn. Several of the previously published translations have been abridged in this volume, and where possible obvious errors have been corrected. In most of the longer chapters, section headings have been supplied by the translators.

ON THE SELECTIONS In the chapters which follow, strictly sociological essays have been supplemented by selected philosophical writings in order to provide more insight into the unity and scope of Simmel's thought.

The selections in part I illustrate the four main ways in which Simmel adapted the Kantian idea of a priori forms of understanding. Chapter 1 represents the first major adaptation Simmel made, namely, to the province of historical knowledge. The type of form involved here is that of a general category of cultural orientation. In chapter 2 the referent of the forms shifts from the realm of knowledge to that of being. In this place Simmel asks what forms of orientation—what cognitive sets, as it were—an individual must have in order to be able to relate to others. In chapter 3 the forms in question are patterns which relate two or more individuals. It is these forms which Simmel considers to be the proper object of study for the discipline of sociology. In chapter 4, finally, Simmel returns to a consideration of forms as cognitive categories. Here, however, his concern is not with varieties of cultural orientation—like historical understanding, philosophy, or science—but with subject matter: What are the basic alternative categories in terms of which the various contents of human experience can be organized?

Part II contains illustrations of Simmel's analyses of forms of interaction—the program advocated in chapter 3. The first of these, on "exchange," is drawn from *Philosophie des Geldes*, Simmel's book on the meaning of money and the nature of a society dominated by money. I have included it not only to show how Simmel anticipated current theories of social exchange but chiefly because the paradigm of exchange it articulates remains so suggestive for further thinking in this area. In chapters 5, 6, and 7, moreover, values, norms, and conscience, respectively, are depicted as by-products of interaction—a perspective that affords a stimulating contrast to those which depict them as *bases* of action systems. The imaginative reader will learn much about Simmel's sociology, and about social process, by thoughtfully comparing his analyses of exchange, conflict, domination, prostitution, and sociability.

Simmel approached the interpretation of what we might call "social types" in two ways. On the one hand, he analyzed types in terms of the characteristics of a particular position in an interactional structure. Sociologists may speak, he suggested, not only of the process of competition, but of the characteristics of a competitor; not only of coquetry, but of the nature of a coquette. This approach is illustrated by the first two readings of part III, on the stranger and the poor.

On the other hand, Simmel was fond of portraying certain human types in terms of the general category of orientation to the world they embodied. Just as all the contents of the world can be defined in terms of the category of science, or religion, or love, so one can speak of the man of science, the religious man, or the erotic man—individuals whose experience is dominated by one of the forms of orientation. This approach is illustrated by the last three readings of part III, on the miser and the spendthrift, the adventurer, and the nobility.

The theme of individuality, which informs nearly all of Simmel's work, is focused on directly in the next two sections. Part IV consists of some of Simmel's analyses of the philosophical bases of individuality: analyses of eighteenth- and nineteenth-century conceptions of individuality and their relation to the idea of freedom, the kind of individual perfection entailed in the concept of subjective culture, and the place of individuality in the modern idea of love. The selections in part V consider the effect on individuality of such sociological variables as the size of the group, the money economy, the vicissitudes of fashion, and the hierarchical organization of social relations.

The eternal conflict between established form and the needs of the ongoing life process forms the topic for part VI. This theme above all others preoccupied Simmel during his last years. It is examined here in three areas—in social relations, metaphysics, and modern cultures—analyses which anticipate our contemporary concerns with the opposition between structure and antistructure.

I. Philosophy of the Social Sciences

1

HOW IS HISTORY POSSIBLE?

1905

How DOES THE raw material of immediate experience come
to be the theoretical structure which we call history? The transformation in question is of a more radical sort than common sense
usually assumes. To demonstrate this is to develop a critique of historical realism—of the view that the science of history should provide a mirror image of the past "as it really was." Such a view
commits no less an error than does realism in art, which pretends
to copy reality without being aware how thoroughly this act of
"copying" in fact stylizes the contents of reality.

In the cognition of nature, the formative influence of the human mind is generally recognized. For history this influence is
less easily perceived because the material of history is mind itself.
When the human mind creates history, the independent character
of the categories it uses and the way they mold the materials are
less apparent than in natural science. What we must determine—
not in detail, but as a matter of principle—is the a priori dimension of historical knowledge. Over against historical realism, which
sees historiography as merely reproducing events, at most with
some quantitative condensation, we must show the justification of
asking, in the Kantian sense, How is history possible?

The answer Kant gave to *his* question—How is nature possible?—is of value for a philosophy of life. Its value has to do with

---

From Georg Simmel, *Die Probleme der Geschichtsphilosophie*, 3d, enl. ed.
(Leipzig: Duncker & Humblot, 1907), pp. vii–ix. Translated by Donald N.
Levine.

the freedom the ego has won, thanks to Kant, over against nature. Inasmuch as the ego produces nature as its conception, and the general laws constitutive of nature are nothing other than the forms of our mind, natural existence has been subordinated to the sovereign ego. Not, to be sure, to the ego's arbitrariness and idiosyncratic vicissitudes, but to its *being* and the imperatives of that being—imperatives which do not stem from norms external to the ego, but make up its very life.

Kant's answer provides release from one of the two oppressions which threaten modern man, nature and history. Both appear to stifle the free, self-possessed personality: the former, because its mechanicism subjects the soul to the same blind forces as the falling stone and the sprouting stalk; the latter, because it makes of the soul a mere point of intersection of social threads spinning through history and reduces its whole creativity to a matter of administering the inheritance of the race. The imprisonment of our empirical existence by nature has, since Kant, been counteracted by the autonomy of mind: the picture of nature in our consciousness, the conceptualization of her forces and of what she can be for the soul, is the achievement of the soul itself.

Now, however, nature's shackles on the ego, sprung by the mind, have turned into an enchainment by mind itself. Although the necessity and superior might which history exerts upon individual personality may appear in the guise of freedom, since this history is of the human mind, in truth history—as something given, as a reality, a suprapersonal power—represents no less an oppression of the ego by an external agency. The temptation to regard as freedom what in reality is bondage through something alien is just more subtly at work here, since in this case what binds us is of the same essential substance as ourselves.

The liberation from naturalism which Kant achieved must now be won from historicism. Perhaps the same critique of knowledge will be successful: that here, too, the mind forms the picture of *psychic existence* which we call history in sovereign wise, through categories which inhere in the knower alone. Man, as something known, is made by nature and history; but man, as knower, makes nature and history.

That form in which all psychic reality comes to consciousness, which emerges as the history of every ego, is itself a product of the creative ego. Mind becomes aware of itself in the stream of becoming, but mind has already marked out the banks and currents of that stream and thereby made it into "history." The investigations which follow serve the general objective of preserving the freedom of the human spirit—that is, form-giving creativity—over against historicism in the same way that Kant did with respect to naturalism.

2

HOW IS SOCIETY POSSIBLE?

1908

KANT ASKED and answered the fundamental question of his philosophy, "How is nature possible?" He could do so only because nature for him was nothing but the representation of nature. It was so not merely in the sense that "the world is my representation" and that we can therefore speak of nature too as only a content of consciousness, but also in the sense that what we call nature is the special way in which the mind assembles, orders, and shapes sense perceptions. These given perceptions of color, taste, tone, temperature, resistance, and smell pass through our consciousness in the accidental sequence of our subjective experience. In themselves, they are not yet nature. They rather become nature, and they do so through the activity of the mind which combines them into objects and series of objects, into substances and attributes, and into causal connections. In their immediate givenness, Kant held, the elements of the world do not have the interdependence which alone makes them intelligible as the unity of nature's laws. It is this interdependence which transforms the world fragments—in themselves incoherent and unstructured—into nature. . . .

It is very suggestive to treat as an analogous matter the ques-

Reprinted from "How is Society Possible?", translated by Kurt H. Wolff, in *Georg Simmel, 1858–1918: A Collection of Essays, with Translations and a Bibliography*, edited by Kurt H. Wolff. Copyright 1959 by the Ohio State University Press. All rights reserved. Originally published in German as "Exkurs über das Problem: Wie ist Gesellschaft möglich?", in *Soziologie: Untersuchungen über die Formen der Vergesellschaftung* (Munich and Leipzig: Duncker & Humblot, 1908).

tion of the aprioristic conditions under which society is possible. Here, also, we find individual elements. In a certain sense, they too, like sense perceptions, stay forever isolated from one another. They, likewise, are synthesized into the unity of society only by means of a conscious process which correlates the individual existence of the single element with that of the other, and which does so in certain forms and according to certain rules. However, there is a decisive difference between the unity of a society and the unity of nature. It is this: In the Kantian view (which we follow here), the unity of nature emerges in the observing subject exclusively; it is produced exclusively by him in the sense materials, and on the basis of sense materials, which are in themselves heterogeneous. By contrast, the unity of society needs no observer. It is directly realized by its own elements because these elements are themselves conscious and synthesizing units.

Kant's axiom that connection, since it is the exclusive product of the subject, cannot inhere in things themselves, does not apply here. For societal connection immediately occurs in the "things," that is, the individuals. As a synthesis, it too, of course, remains something purely psychological. It has no parallels with spatial things and their interaction. Societal unification needs no factors outside its own component elements, the individuals. Each of them exercises the function which the psychic energy of the observer exercises in regard to external nature: the consciousness of constituting with the others a unity is actually all there is to this unity. This does not mean, of course, that each member of a society is conscious of such an abstract notion of unity. It means that he is absorbed in innumerable, specific relations and in the feeling and the knowledge of determining others and of being determined by them. On the other hand, it should be noted that it is quite possible for an observing outsider to perform an additional synthesis of the persons making up the society. The synthesis would proceed as if these persons were spatial elements, but it is based only upon the observer himself. The determination of which aspect of the *externally* observable is to be comprehended as a unity depends not only on the immediate and strictly objective content of the observable but also upon the categories and the cognitive requirements of the subjective psyche. Again, however, society, by contrast, is the objective unit which needs no outside observer. . . .

Owing to these circumstances, the question of how society is possible implies a methodology which is wholly different from that for the question of how nature is possible. The latter question is answered by the forms of cognition, through which the subject synthesizes the given elements into nature. By contrast, the former is answered by the conditions which reside a priori in the elements themselves, through which they combine, in reality, into the synthesis, society. In a certain sense, the entire content of this book [*Soziologie*], as it is developed on the basis of the principle enunciated, is the beginning of the answer to this question. For it inquires into the processes—those which, ultimately, take place in the individuals themselves—that condition the existence of the individuals as society. It investigates these processes, not as antecedent causes of this result, but as part of the synthesis to which we give the inclusive name of "society."

But the question of how society is possible must be understood in a still more fundamental sense. I said that, in the case of nature, the achieving of the synthetic unity is a function of the observing mind, whereas, in the case of society, that function is an aspect of society itself. To be sure, consciousness of the abstract principle that he is forming society is not present in the individual. Nevertheless, every individual knows that the other is tied to him—however much this knowledge of the other as fellow sociate, this grasp of the whole complex as society, is usually realized only on the basis of particular, concrete contents. Perhaps, however, this is not different from the "unity of cognition." As far as our conscious processes are concerned, we proceed by arranging one concrete content alongside another, and we are distinctly conscious of the unity itself only in rare and later abstractions. The questions, then, are these: What, quite generally and a priori, is the basis or presupposition of the fact that particular, concrete processes in the individual consciousness are actually processes of sociation? Which elements in them account for the fact that (to put it abstractly) their achievement is the production of a societal unit out of individuals?

The sociological apriorities envisaged are likely to have the same twofold significance as those which make nature possible. On the one hand, they more or less completely determine the actual processes of sociation[1] as functions or energies of psychological processes. On the other hand, they are the ideational, logical presuppositions for the perfect society (which is perhaps never realized in this perfection, however). We find a parallel in the law of causation. On the one hand, it inheres and is effective in the actual processes of cognition. On the other hand, it constitutes truth as the ideal system of perfect cognition. And it does so irrespective of whether or not this truth obtains in the temporal and relatively accidental psychological dynamics in which causation actually operates—irrespective, that is, of the greater or lesser degree to which the actual, consciously held truth approximates the ideally valid truth. . . .

(1) The picture of another man that a man gains through personal contact with him is based on certain distortions. These are not simple mistakes resulting from incomplete experience, defective vision, or sympathetic or antipathetic prejudices. They are fundamental changes in the quality of the actual object perceived, and they are of two types. We see the other person generalized, in some measure. This is so, perhaps, because we cannot fully represent to ourselves an individuality which deviates from our own. Any re-creation of a person is determined by one's similarity to him. To be sure, similarity is by no means the only condition of psychological insight, for dissimilarity, too, seems required in order to gain distance and objectivity. In addition, aside from the question of similarity or dissimilarity, an intellectual capacity is needed. Nevertheless, *perfect* cognition presupposes perfect identity. It seems, however, that every individual has in himself a core of individuality which cannot be re-created by anybody else whose core differs qualitatively from his own. And the challenge to re-create is logically incompatible with psychological distance

---

1   *Vergesellschaftung.* For a discussion of this translation of the term, see *The Sociology of Georg Simmel*, p. lxiii. Elsewhere in the present volume other translators at times use the words "sociality" or "association."—ED.

and objective judgment which are also bases for representing another. We cannot know completely the individuality of another.

All relations among men are determined by the varying degrees of this incompleteness. Whatever the cause of this incompleteness, its consequence is a generalization of the psychological picture that we have of another, a generalization that results in a blurring of contours which adds a relation to other pictures to the uniqueness of this one. We conceive of each man—and this is a fact which has a specific effect upon our practical behavior toward him—as being the human type which is suggested by his individuality. We think of him in terms not only of his singularity but also in terms of a general category. This category, of course, does not fully cover him, nor does he fully cover it. It is this peculiarly incomplete coincidence which distinguishes the relation between a human category and a human singularity from the relation which usually exists between a general concept and the particular instance it covers. In order to know a man, we see him not in terms of his pure individuality, but carried, lifted up or lowered, by the general type under which we classify him. Even when this transformation from the singular to the typical is so imperceptible that we cannot recognize it immediately; even when all the ordinary characterological concepts such as "moral" or "immoral," "free" or "unfree," "lordly" or "slavish," and so on, clearly appear inadequate, we privately persist in labeling a man according to an unverbalized type, a type which does not coincide with his pure, individual being.

This leads to a further step. It is precisely because of the utter uniqueness of any given personality that we form a picture which is not identical with its reality but which at the same time does not coincide with a general type. The picture we form is the one the personality would show if the individual were truly himself, so to speak, if he realized, toward a good or toward a bad side, for better or worse, his ideal possibility, the possibility which lies in every individual. All of us are fragments, not only of general man, but also of ourselves. We are outlines not only of the types "man," "good," "bad," and the like but also of the individuality and uniqueness of ourselves. Although this individuality cannot, on principle, be identified by any name, it surrounds our perceptible reality as if traced in ideal lines. It is supplemented by the other's view of us, which results in something that we never are purely and wholly. It is impossible for this view to see anything but juxtaposed fragments, which nevertheless are all that really exist. However, just as we compensate for a blind spot in our field of vision so that we are no longer aware of it, so a fragmentary structure is transformed by another's view into the completeness of an individuality. The practice of life urges us to make the picture of a man only from the real pieces that we empirically know of him, but it is precisely the practice of life which is based on those modifications and supplementations, on the transformation of the given fragments into the generality of a type and into the completeness of the ideal personality.

In practice, this fundamental process is only rarely carried to completion. Nevertheless, within an existing society it operates as the a priori condition of additional interactions that arise among individuals. Every member of a group which is held together by some common occupation or interest sees every other member not just empirically, but on the basis of an aprioric principle which the group imposes on every one of its participants. Among officers, church members, employees, scholars, or members of a family, every member regards the other with the unquestioned assumption that he is a member of "my group." Such assumptions arise from some common basis of life. By virtue of it, people look at one another as if through a veil. This veil does not simply hide the peculiarity of the person; it gives it a new form. Its purely individual, real nature and its group nature fuse into a new, autonomous phenomenon. We see the other not simply as an individual but as a colleague or comrade or fellow party member—in short, as a cohabitant of the same specific world. And this inevitable, quite automatic assumption is one of the means by which one's personality and reality assume, in the imagination of another, the quality and form required by sociability.

Evidently, this is true also of the relations of members who belong to different groups. The civilian who meets an officer cannot free himself from his knowledge of the fact that this individual is an officer. And although his officership may be a part of this particular individuality, it is certainly not so stereotypical as the civilian's prejudicial image would have it. And the same goes for the Protestant in regard to the Catholic, the businessman in regard to the bureaucrat, the layman in regard to the priest, and so on. In all these cases, reality is veiled by social generalization, which, in a highly differentiated society, makes discovering it altogether impossible. Man distorts the picture of another. He both detracts and supplements, since generalization is always both less and more than individuality is. The distortions derive from all these a priori, operative categories: from the individual's type as man, from the idea of his perfection, and from the general society to which he belongs. Beyond all of these, there is, as a heuristic principle of knowledge, the idea of his real, unconditionally individual nature. It seems as if only the apprehension of this nature could furnish the basis for an entirely correct relation to him. But the very alterations and new formations which preclude this ideal knowledge of him are, actually, the conditions which make possible the sort of relations we call social. The phenomenon recalls Kant's conception of the categories: they form immediate data into new objects, but they alone make the given world into a knowable world.

(2) There is another category under which the individual views himself and others and which transforms all of them into empirical society. This category may be suggested by the proposition that every element of a group is not only a societal part but, in addition, something else. However trivial it may seem, this fact nevertheless operates as a social a priori. For that part of the individual which is, as it were, not turned toward society and is not absorbed by it, does not simply lie beside its socially relevant part without having a relation to it. It is not simply something outside society to which society, willingly or unwillingly, submits. Rather, the fact that in certain respects the individual is not an element of society constitutes the positive condition for the possibility that in other respects he is: the way in which he is sociated is determined or codetermined by the way in which he is not. The chapters of this book discuss, among other things, several types whose

essential sociological significance lies in the very fact that in some fashion or other they are excluded from society (for which their existence, nevertheless, is important). Such types are the stranger, the enemy, the criminal, even the pauper. But this peculiar relationship to society not only holds for such generalized types as these but, albeit with innumerable modifications, for any individual whatever. The proposition is not invalidated by the fact that at every moment we are confronted, as it were, by relations which directly or indirectly determine the content of every moment: for the social environment does not surround all of the individual. We know of the bureaucrat that he is not only a bureaucrat, of the businessman that he is not only a businessman, of the officer that he is not only an officer. This extrasocial nature—a man's temperament, fate, interests, worth as a personality—gives a certain nuance to the picture formed by all who meet him. It intermixes his social picture with non-social imponderables—however little they may change his dominant activities as a bureaucrat or businessman or officer.

Man's interactions would be quite different if he appeared to others only as what he is in his relevant societal category, as the mere exponent of a social role momentarily ascribed to him. Actually, individuals, as well as occupations and social situations, are differentiated according to how much of the non-social element they possess or allow along with their social content. On this basis, they may be arranged in a continuum. One pole of the continuum is represented by an individual in love or friendship. What this individual preserves for himself after all the developments and activities devoted to the friend or beloved are taken care of is almost nothing. In his case, there is only a single life that can be viewed or lived from two sides, as it were: from the inside, from the *terminus a quo* of the subject and in the direction of the beloved, and from the *terminus ad quem*, by which, too, this life is covered without residue. A very different tendency is illustrated by the formally identical phenomenon of the Catholic priest, where the clerical function entirely supersedes and absorbs his individual existence. In the first of these two extreme subtypes, the non-social element, which exists in addition to the social, disappears, because its content has completely vanished in the individual's turning toward another person. In the second case, it disappears because the corresponding type of content itself has completely disappeared.

The opposite pole of the continuum is found in certain phenomena characteristic of modern culture with its money economy. Here the individual, inasmuch as he produces, buys, sells, and in general performs anything, approaches the ideal of absolute objectivity. Except in the highest leading positions, the individual life and the tone of the total personality is removed from the social action. Individuals are merely engaged in an exchange of performance and counter-performance that takes place according to objective norms—and everything that does not belong to this pure objectivity has actually disappeared from it. The personality itself, with its specific coloration, irrationality, and inner life, has completely absorbed the non-social element and, in a neat separation, has left to the social activities only those energies which are specifically appropriate for them.

Actually, social individuals move between these two extremes. They do so in such a way that the energies and characteristics which are directed back toward the individual have significance at the same time for the actions and attitudes which are directed toward another. There is an extreme case, namely, the notion that this social activity or mood is something separate from the rest of the personality, that the personality's non-social existence and significance do not enter into social relations. Clearly, even this notion, however, has its effect upon the attitude which the subject holding it adopts toward others and upon the attitude which others adopt toward him. The a priori of empirical social life consists of the fact that life is not entirely social. The reservation of a part of our personalities so as to prevent this part from entering into interaction has an effect upon our interactions which is twofold. In the first place, through general psychological processes it has its effect upon the social structure of the individual. In the second place, the formal fact itself, the part that exists outside the individual, affects this structure.

A society is, therefore, a structure which consists of beings who stand inside and outside of it at the same time. This fact forms the basis for one of the most important sociological phenomena, namely, that between a society and its component individuals a relation may exist as if between two parties. In fact, to the degree that it is more open or more latent, this relation, perhaps, always does exist. Society shows possibly the most conscious, certainly the most general, elaboration of a fundamental form of general life. This is that the individual can never stay within a unit which he does not at the same time stay outside of, that he is not incorporated into any order without also confronting it. This form is revealed in the most transcendent and general as well as in the most singular and accidental contexts. The religious man feels himself fully seized by the divine, as if he were merely a pulse-beat of its life. His own substance is given over unreservedly, if not in a mystical, undifferentiated fusion, to that of the absolute. But in spite of this, in order to give this fusion any significance whatever, he must preserve some sort of self-existence, some sort of personal counter, a differentiated ego, for whom the absorption in this divine all-being is a never ending task. It is a process that neither would be possible metaphysically, nor could be felt religiously, if it did not start from the existence of the individual: to be one with God is conditioned in its very significance by being other than God.

We do not have to adduce this experience of the transcendental. The same form of life is expressed in the idea that man's relation to nature is as a part of the totality of nature, an idea which the human mind has vindicated throughout its history. We view ourselves as incorporated into nature, as one of its products, as an equal of all other natural products, as a point which the stuffs and forces of nature reach and leave just as they circulate through flowing water and a blossoming plant. Yet we have the feeling of being independent and separate from all these entanglements and relationships, a feeling that is designated by the logically uncertain concept "freedom." We have a feeling that we represent a counter and contrast to this process, whose elements we nevertheless are. The most radical formulation of this feeling is found in the proposition that nature is merely a human imagination. In this formulation, nature, with all its undeniable autonomy and hard reality is made part of the individual self, although this self, with all its freedom and separate existence and contrast to "mere" nature, is nevertheless a link in it. In its most general form, the very essence of the relation between nature and man is that man comprises nature in spite of the fact that it is independent and very often hostile; that which is, according to man's innermost life-feeling, outside of him, must necessarily be his medium and element.

This formula is no less valid in regard to the relation between individuals and the groups to which they are socially tied or, if these groups are subsumed under the over-all concept or feeling of sociation, in regard to the relation among individuals in general. On the one hand, we see ourselves as products of society. The physiological succession of our ancestors, their adaptations and peculiarities, the traditions of their work and knowledge and belief —the whole spirit of the past as it is crystallized in objective forms determines the pattern and content of our lives. The question has even been raised as to whether the individual is anything more than a vessel in which elements existing before him are mixed in varying measures. For even if these elements ultimately are produced by the individual himself, his contribution is only minimal; only as individuals converge in species and society do the factors arise whose synthesis results in any discernible degree of individuality. On the other hand, we see ourselves as members of society. In this capacity we depend on it. By our life and its meaning and purpose, we are as inextricably woven into society, as a synchronic, coexisting phenomenon, as we are, as products, into diachronic, successive society.

In our capacity as natural objects we have no self-existence. The circulation of natural forces passes through us as through completely self-less structures, and our equality before the laws of nature resolves our existence without residue into a mere example of the necessity of these laws. Analogously, as social beings we do not live around any autonomous core. Rather, at any given moment, we consist of interactions with others. We are thus comparable to a physical body which consists merely of the sum of numerous sense impressions and does not have its own existence. Yet we feel that this social diffusion does not entirely dissolve our personalities. We feel this, not only because of the reservations already mentioned, that is, because of particular contents whose significance and development inhere exclusively in the individual and find no room whatever in the social sphere; nor only because the unifying center, the individual phenomenon, in the formation of social contents is not itself social (just as the artistic form, though composed of color spots on canvas, cannot be derived from the chemical nature of the colors); but also because, although it may be possible to explain the whole content of life completely in terms of social antecedents and interactions, this content must also be considered under the category of the individual life, as the individual's experience, as something exclusively oriented toward the individual. The two—social and individual—are only two different categories under which the same content is subsumed, just as the same plant may be considered from the standpoint of its biological development or its practical uses or its aesthetic significance. In the same way, the standpoint from which the life of the individual is conceived and structured may be taken from within as well as from without the individual. With all its socially derivable contents, a total life may be interpreted as the centripetally directed fate of its bearer as legitimately as—with all the elements that are reserved for the individual—it may be conceived of as the product and component of social life.

We thus see how the fact of sociation puts the individual into the dual position which I discussed in the beginning: The individual is contained in sociation and, at the same time, finds himself confronted by it. He is both a link in the organism of sociation and an autonomous organic whole; he exists both for society and for himself. The essence and deepest significance of the specific sociological a priori which is founded on this phenomenon is this: The "within" and the "without" between individual and society are not two unrelated definitions but define together the fully homogeneous position of man as a social animal. His existence, if we analyze its contents, is not only partly social and partly individual, but also belongs to the fundamental, decisive, and irreducible category of a unity which we cannot designate other than as the synthesis or simultaneity of two logically contradictory characterizations of man—the characterization which is based on his function as a member, as a product and content of society; and the opposing characterization which is based on his functions as an autonomous being, and which views his life from its own center and for its own sake. Society consists not only of beings that are partially non-sociated, as we saw earlier, but also of beings which, on the one hand, feel themselves to be complete social entities, and, on the other hand—and without thereby changing their content at all—complete personal entities. And we do not deal here with two unrelated, alternative standpoints such as we adopt, for instance, when we look at an object in regard to either its weight or its color; for we are dealing with two elements that together form the unit we call the social being, that is, with a synthetic category. The phenomenon parallels the concept of causation. It, too, is an a priori unit, in spite of the fact that it covers two elements which are heterogeneous in content, cause and effect. We do perform the synthesis "social being." We are capable of constructing the notion of society from the very idea of beings, each of whom may feel himself as the *terminus a quo* and the *terminus ad quem* of his developments and destinies and qualities. And we do construct this concept of society, which is built up from that of the potentially autonomous individual, as the *terminus a quo* and the *terminus ad quem* of the individual's very life and fate. This capacity constitutes an a priori of empirical society. It makes possible the form of society as we know it.

(3) Society is a structure composed of unequal elements. The "equality" toward which democratic or socialistic efforts are directed—and which they partly attain—is actually an equivalence of people, functions, or positions. Equality in people is impossible because of their different natures, life contents, and destinies. On the other hand, the equality of everybody with everybody else in an enslaved mass, such as we find in the great oriental despotisms, applies only to certain specific aspects of existence—political or economic aspects, for example—never to the total personality. For innate qualities, personal relations, and decisive experiences inevi-

tably make for some sort of uniqueness and irreplaceability in both the individual's self-evaluation and his interactions with others.

Society may be conceived as a purely objective system of contents and actions connected by space, time, concepts, and values. In such a scheme, personality, the articulation of the ego (in which, nevertheless, the dynamics of society is located) may be ignored. However, the elements of this system are heterogeneous. Every action and quality within it is individual and is irrevocably located in its specific place. Society appears as a cosmos whose complex nature and direction are unlimited, but in which every single point can be fixed and can develop only in a particular way because otherwise the structure of the whole would change. What has been said of the structure of the world in general—that not a single grain of sand could have a shape different from what it has or be in a position different from its actual position without first conditioning the alteration by a change of the whole and without entailing such a change in the whole—is true of the structure of society, or society considered as a web of qualitatively differentiated phenomena.

This image of general society finds a small-scale analogy (infinitely simplified and stylized) in bureaucracy. A bureaucracy consists of a certain order of positions, of a predetermined system of functions. It exists as an ideal structure, irrespective of the particular occupants of these positions. Every new entrant finds within it a clearly defined place which has waited for him, so to speak, and to which his individual talents must be suited. In society at large, what here is a conscious, systematic determination of functions is a deeply entangled play and counterplay of them. Positions within society are not planned by a constructive will but can be grasped only through an analysis of the creativity and experience of the component individuals. Empirical, historical society is therefore vastly different from a bureaucracy because of its irrational and imperfect elements. From certain value standpoints, some of these elements must be condemned. Nevertheless, the phenomenological structure of society is the sum of the objective existences and actions of its elements and the interrelations among these existences and actions. It is a system of elements each of which occupies an individual place, a co-ordination of functions and function-centers which have objective and social significance, although they are not always valuable. Purely personal and creative aspects of the ego, its impulses and reflexes, have no place in this system. To put it otherwise: The life of society (considered not psychologically but phenomenologically, that is, exclusively in regard to its social contents) takes its course as if each of its elements were predestined for its particular place in it. In spite of all discrepancies between it and ideal standards, social life exists as if all of its elements found themselves interrelated with one another in such a manner that each of them, because of its very individuality, depends on all others and all others depend on it.

We are thus in a position to see the a priori which we must now discuss. This a priori provides the individual with the basis for, and offers the "possibility" of, his being a member of a society. An individual is directed toward a certain place within his social milieu by his very quality. This place which ideally belongs to him actually exists. Here we have the precondition of the individual's social life. It may be called the general value of individuality. It is independent both of its development into a clear, consciously formed conception and of its realization in the empirical life-process. In the same way, the apriority of causality as a determining precondition of cognition depends neither on its conscious formulation in specific concepts nor on the behavior of reality, as we grasp it psychologically, in accord or discord with it. For our cognition is based on the premise of a pre-established harmony that exists between our psychological energies, however individualized they may be, and external, objective existence. This existence always remains immediate, no matter how many attempts there have been to show, metaphysically or psychologically, that it is the intellect's own product. In a similar fashion, social life presupposes an unquestionable harmony between the individual and society as a whole. This harmony, of course, does not preclude violent ethical and eudaemonistic dissonances. If social reality were determined by this presupposition of harmony alone, without the interference of other factors, it would result in the perfect society. It would be perfect, however, not in the sense of ethical or eudaemonistic perfection, but of conceptual perfection; it would be not the *perfect* society but the perfect *society*. The a priori of the individual's social existence is the fundamental correlation between his life and the society that surrounds him, the integrative function and necessity of his specific character, as it is determined by his personal life, to the life of the whole. In so far as he does not realize this a priori or does not find it realized in society, the individual is not sociated and society is not the perfect system of interactions called for by its definition.

This situation is shown with particular sharpness in the phenomenon of vocation. Antiquity, to be sure, did not know this concept in its connotation of personal differentiation in a society articulated by a division of labor. But even antiquity knew its root, the idea that socially effective action is the unified expression of the inner qualification of the individual, the idea that by functioning in society the wholeness and permanence of subjectivity becomes practically objective. Yet in antiquity this relationship was exemplified by contents that were much less heterogeneous than they are today. Its principle is expressed in the Aristotelian axiom that some individuals are by nature destined to slavery; others, to domination. The more highly developed concept of vocation refers to a particular phenomenon: On the one hand, society within itself produces and offers to the individual a place which—however different in content and delimitation it may be from other places—can be filled by many individuals, and which is, for this reason, something anonymous, as it were. On the other hand, this place, in spite of its general character, is nevertheless taken by the individual on the basis of an inner calling, a qualification felt to be intimately personal. For such a thing as vocation to be possible, there must exist that harmony, whatever its origin, between the structure and development of society, and individual qualities and impulses. It is this general premise that constitutes the ultimate basis of the idea that for every personality there exist a position and a function in society to which he is called and which he must seek and find.

Empirical society becomes possible because of the a priori that finds its most obvious expression in the concept of vocation. Never-theless, like the other a prioris thus far discussed, it cannot be designated by a simple slogan like those which it is possible to use for the Kantian categories. The processes of consciousness which formulate sociation—notions such as the unity of the many, the reciprocal determination of the individuals, the significance of the individual for the totality of the others and vice versa—presup-pose something fundamental which finds expression in practice although we are not aware of it in its abstractness. The presupposi-tion is that individuality finds its place in the structure of general-ity and, furthermore, that in spite of the unpredictable character of individuality, this structure is laid out, as it were, for individ-uality and its functions. The nexus by which each social element (each individual) is interwoven with the life and activities of every other, and by which the external framework of society is produced, is a causal nexus. But it is transformed into a teleological nexus as soon as it is considered from the perspective of the ele-ments that carry and produce it—individuals. For they feel them-selves to be egos whose behavior grows out of autonomous, self-determined personalities. The objective totality yields to the indi-viduals that confront it from without, as it were; it offers a place to their subjectively determined life-processes, which thereby, in their very individuality, become necessary links in the life of the whole. It is the dual nexus which supplies the individual consciousness with a fundamental category and thus transforms it into a social element.

3

THE PROBLEM OF SOCIOLOGY

1908

Society exists where a number of individuals enter into
interaction. This interaction always arises on the basis of certain
drives or for the sake of certain purposes. Erotic, religious, or
merely associative impulses; and purposes of defense, attack, play,
gain, aid, or instruction—these and countless others cause man
to live with other men, to act for them, with them, against them,
and thus to correlate his condition with theirs. In brief, he influences and is influenced by them. The significance of these interactions among men lies in the fact that it is because of them that
the individuals, in whom these driving impulses and purposes are
lodged, form a unity, that is, a society. For unity in the empirical
sense of the word is nothing but the interaction of elements. An
organic body is a unity because its organs maintain a more intimate exchange of their energies with each other than with any
other organism; a state is a unity because its citizens show similar
mutual effects. In fact, the whole world could not be called one if
each of its parts did not somehow influence every other part, or,
if at any one point the reciprocity of effects, however indirect it
may be, were cut off.

This unity, or sociation, may be of very different degrees, according to the kind and the intimacy of the interaction which obtains. Sociation ranges all the way from the momentary getting together for a walk to the founding of a family, from relations maintained "until further notice" to membership in a state, from the temporary aggregation of hotel guests to the intimate bond of a medieval guild. I designate as the content—the materials, so to speak—of sociation everything that is present in individuals (the immediately concrete loci of all historical reality)—drive, interest, purpose, inclination, psychic state, movement—everything that is present in them in such a way as to engender or mediate effects upon others or to receive such effects. In themselves, these materials which fill life, these motivations which propel it, are not social. Strictly speaking, neither hunger nor love, work nor religiosity, technology nor the functions and results of intelligence, are social. They are factors in sociation only when they transform the mere aggregation of isolated individuals into specific forms of being with and for one another, forms that are subsumed under the general concept of interaction. Sociation is the form (realized in innumerably different ways) in which individuals grow together into a unity and within which their interests are realized. And it is on the basis of their interests—sensuous or ideal, momentary or lasting, conscious or unconscious, causal or teleological—that individuals form such unities.

In any given social phenomenon, content and societal form constitute one reality. A social form severed from all content can no more attain existence than a spatial form can exist without a material whose form it is. Any social phenomenon or process is composed of two elements which in reality are inseparable: on the one hand, an interest, a purpose, or a motive; on the other, a form or mode of interaction among individuals through which, or in the shape of which, that content attains social reality.

It is evident that that which constitutes society in every current sense of the term is identical with the kinds of interaction discussed. A collection of human beings does not become a society because each of them has an objectively determined or subjectively impelling life-content. It becomes a society only when the vitality of these contents attains the form of reciprocal influence; only when one individual has an effect, immediate or mediate, upon another, is mere spatial aggregation or temporal succession transformed into society. If, therefore, there is to be a science whose subject matter is society and nothing else, it must exclusively investigate these interactions, these kinds and forms of sociation. For everything else found within "society" and realized through it and within its framework is not itself society. It is merely a content that develops or is developed by this form of coexistence, and it produces the real phenomenon called "society" in the broader and more customary sense of the term only in conjunction with this form. To separate, by scientific abstraction, these two factors of form and content which are in reality inseparably united; to detach by analysis the forms of interaction or sociation from their contents (through which alone these forms become social forms); and to bring them together systematically under a consistent scientific viewpoint—this seems to me the basis for the only, as well as the entire, possibility of a special science of society as such. Only such a science can actually treat the facts that go under the name of sociohistorical reality upon the plane of the purely social.

Abstractions alone produce science out of the complexity or the unity of reality. Yet however urgently such abstractions may be demanded by the needs of cognition itself, they also require some sort of justification of their relation to the structure of the objective world. For only some functional relation to actuality can save one from sterile inquiries or from the haphazard formulation of scientific concepts. Certainly, naïve naturalism errs in assuming that the given itself contains the analytic or synthetic arrangements through which it becomes the content of a science. Nevertheless, the characteristics of the given are more or less susceptible to such arrangements. An analogy may help here. A portrait fundamentally transforms the natural human appearance, but one face is better suited than another to such a transformation into something radically alien. Remembering this helps us to appraise the greater or lesser appropriateness of various scientific problems and methods. The right to subject sociohistorical phenomena to an analysis in terms of form and content (and to synthesize the forms) rests upon two conditions which must be verified on a factual basis. On the one hand, we must demonstrate that the same form of sociation can be observed in quite dissimilar contents and in connection with quite dissimilar purposes. On the other hand, we must show that the content is realized in using quite dissimilar forms of sociation as its medium or vehicle. A parallel is found in the fact that the same geometric forms may be observed in the most heterogeneous materials and that the same material occurs in the most heterogeneous spatial forms. Similar relations obtain between logical forms and the material contents of cognition.

Both of these conditions are undeniable facts. We do find that the same form of interaction obtains among individuals in societal groups that are the most unlike imaginable in purpose and significance. Superiority, subordination, competition, division of labor, formation of parties, representation, inner solidarity coupled with exclusiveness toward the outside, and innumerable similar features are found in the state as well as in a religious community, in a band of conspirators as in an economic association, in an art school as in a family. However diverse the interests that give rise to these sociations, the forms in which the interests are realized are identical. On the other hand, the identical interest may take on form in very different sociations. Economic interest is realized both in competition and in the planned organization of producers, in isolation from other groups and in fusion with them. Although the religious contents of life remain identical, at one time they demand an unregulated, at another time a centralized, form of community. The interests upon which the relations between the sexes are based are satisfied by an almost endless variety of family forms. The educational interest may lead to a liberal or to a despotic relation between teacher and pupil, to individualistic interaction between them, or to a more collectivistic type of interaction between the teacher and the totality of his pupils. Hence, not only may the form in which the most widely different contents are realized be identical, but a content too may persist while its medium—the interactions of the individuals—moves in a variety of forms. We see, then, that the analysis in terms of form and content transforms the facts—which in their immediacy present form and content as an indissoluble unity of social life—in such a way as to furnish the legitimation of the sociological problem. This problem demands that the pure forms of sociation be identified, ordered systematically, explained psychologically, and studied from the standpoint of their historical development. . . .

This conception of society implies a further proposition: A given number of individuals may be a society to a greater or a smaller degree. With each formation of parties, with each joining for common tasks or in a common feeling or way of thinking, with each articulation of the distribution of positions of submission and domination, with each common meal, with each self-adornment for others—with every growth of new synthesizing phenomena such as these, the same group becomes "more society" than it was before. There is no such thing as society "as such"; that is, there is no society in the sense that it is the condition for the emergence of all these particular phenomena. For there is no such thing as interaction "as such"—there are only specific kinds of interaction. And it is with their emergence that society too emerges, for they are neither the cause nor the consequence of society but are, themselves, society. The fact that an extraordinary multitude and variety of interactions operate at any one moment has given a seemingly autonomous historical reality to the general concept of society. Perhaps it is this hypostatization of a mere abstraction that is the reason for the peculiar vagueness and uncertainty involved in the concept of society and in the customary treatises in general sociology. We are here reminded of the fact that not much headway was made in formulating a concept of "life" as long as it was conceived of as an immediately real and homogeneous phenomenon. The science of life did not establish itself on a firm basis until it investigated specific processes within organisms—processes whose sum or web life is; not until, in other words, it recognized that life consists of these particular processes.

Only if we follow the conception here outlined can we grasp what in "society" really *is* society. Similarly, it is only geometry that determines what the spatiality of things in space really is. Sociology, the discipline that deals with the purely social aspects of man (who, of course, can be an object of scientific inquiry in innumerable other respects), is related to the other special sciences of man as geometry is related to the physicochemical sciences. Geometry studies the forms through which any material becomes an empirical body, and these forms as such exist, of course, in abstraction only, precisely like the forms of sociation. Both geometry and sociology leave to other sciences the investigation of the contents realized in the forms, that is, the total phenomena whose forms they explore.

It is hardly necessary to point out that this analogy with geometry does not go beyond the clarification of the fundamental problem of sociology. It was only in attempting this clarification that we made use of this analogy. Above all, geometry has the advantage of having at its disposal extremely simple structures into which it can resolve the more complicated figures. Geometry can construe the whole range of possible formations from a relatively few fundamental definitions. Not even a remotely similar resolution into simple elements is to be hoped for in the foreseeable future as regards the forms of sociation. Sociological forms, if they are to be even approximately definite, can apply only to a limited range of phenomena. Even if we say, for instance, that superordination and subordination are forms found in almost every human sociation, we gain very little from this general knowledge. What is needed is the study of specific kinds of superordination and subordination, and of the specific forms in which they are realized. Through such a study, of course, these forms would lose in applicability what they would gain in definiteness.

In our day, we are used to asking of every science whether it is devoted to the discovery of timelessly valid laws or to the presentation and conceptualization of real, unique historical processes. Generally, this alternative ignores innumerable intermediate phenomena dealt with in the actual practice of science. It is irrelevant to our conception of the problem of sociology because this conception renders a choice between the two answers unnecessary. For, on the one hand, in sociology the object abstracted from reality may be examined in regard to laws entirely inhering in the objective nature of the elements. These laws must be sharply distinguished from any spatiotemporal realization; they are valid whether the historical actualities enforce them once or a thousand times. On the other hand, the forms of sociation may be examined, with equal validity, in regard to their occurrence at specific places and at specific times, and in regard to their historical development in specific groups. In this latter case, ascertaining them would be in the service of history, so to speak; in the former case, it would provide material for the induction of timeless uniformities. About competition, for instance, we learn something from a great many fields—political science, economics, history of religion, history of art, and so on. The point is to ascertain from all the facts what competition is as a pure form of human behavior; under what circumstances it emerges and develops; how it is modified by the particular character of its object; by what contemporaneous formal and material features of a society it is increased or reduced; and how competition between individuals differs from that between groups. In short, we must ascertain what competition is as a form of relation among individuals. This form may involve all sorts of contents. But in spite of the great variety of these contents, the form maintains its own identity and proves that it belongs to a sphere which is governed by its own laws and which may legitimately be abstracted from other spheres or from total reality. What we are suggesting, in brief, is that similar elements be singled out of the complex phenomena so as to secure a cross-section, whereby dissimilar elements—in our case the contents—reciprocally paralyze each other, as it were.

We have to proceed in this fashion with respect to all the great situations and interactions that form society—the formation of parties; imitation; the formation of classes and circles; secondary subdivisions; the embodiment of types of social interaction in special structures of an objective, personal, or ideal nature; the growth and the role of hierarchies; the representation of groups by individuals; the bearing of common hostility on the inner solidarity of the group. In addition to such major problems, there are others which no less regularly involve the form of the group and which are either more specialized or more complex than these. Among the more specialized questions, there are those such as the significance of the non-partisan, the role of the poor as organic members of society, the numerical determination of group elements, and the phenomena of *primus inter pares* and *tertius gaudens*. Among more complex processes are the intersection of various social circles in the individual; the special significance of the secret for the formation of groups; the modification of the character of groups by a membership composed of individuals who belong together geographically, or by the addition of elements who do not; and innumerable other processes.

In this whole discussion, as I have already indicated, I waive the question of whether there ever occurs an *absolute* identity of forms along with a difference in content. The *approximate* identity that forms exhibit under materially dissimilar circumstances (and vice versa) is enough to conceive, in principle, of an affirmative answer to this question. The fact that absolute identity is not actually realized shows the difference between historical-psychological and geometrical phenomena. Historical-psychological processes, in their fluctuations and complexities, can never be completely rationalized. Geometry, by contrast, does have the power to isolate absolutely pure forms out of their material realizations. It should always be remembered that this identity of the kinds of interaction in the face of the simultaneously existing variety of human or objective material (and vice versa) is nothing primarily but a device to make and legitimate the scientific discrimination between form and content in the treatment of empirical phenomena. Methodologically speaking, this discrimination would be required even if the actual constellations did not call for the inductive procedure of crystallizing the like out of the unlike. In the same way, the geometrical abstraction of the spatial form of a body would be justified even if a body with such a particular form occurred only once empirically.

It cannot be denied, however, that this discussion suggests a difficulty in methodology. For instance, toward the end of the Middle Ages, extended trade relations forced certain guild masters to employ apprentices and to adopt new ways of obtaining materials and attracting customers. All of this was inconsistent with traditional guild principles, according to which every master was to have the same living as every other. Through these innovations, every master sought to place himself outside this traditional narrow unity. Now, what about the purely sociological form which is abstracted from the special content of this whole process? The process seems to indicate that the expansion of the circle with which the individual is connected through his actions is accompanied by a greater articulation of individuality, an expansion of the freedom of the individual, and a greater differentiation of the members of the circle. Yet, as far as I can see, there is no sure method of distilling this sociological significance out of our complex fact which is, after all, real only along with all its contents. In other words, there is no sure method for answering the question of what purely sociological configurations and what specific interactions of individuals (irrespective of the interests and impulses residing in the individual, and of purely objective conditions) are involved in the historical process. On the contrary, all this can be interpreted in more than one way and, furthermore, the historical facts that attest to reality of the specific sociological forms must be presented in their material totality. In brief, there is no means of teaching and, under certain conditions, even of performing, the analysis of form and content into sociological elements. The case is comparable to the proof of a geometrical theorem by means of figures drawn in the unavoidably accidental and crude way of all drawings. The mathematician can feel quite safe in assuming that, in spite of the imperfect drawing, the concept of the ideal geometrical figure is known and understood, and that it is regarded as the essential significance of the chalk or ink marks. The sociologist, however, may not make the corresponding assumption; the isolation of truly pure sociation out of the complex total phenomenon cannot be forced by logical means.

Here we must take upon ourselves the odium of talking about intuitive procedures (however far these are removed from speculative, metaphysical intuition). We admit that we are discussing a particular viewpoint that helps to make the distinction between form and content. This viewpoint, for the time being, can be conveyed only by means of examples. Only much later may it be possible to grasp it by methods that are fully conceptualized and are sure guides to research. The difficulty is increased by two factors. Not only is there no perfectly clear technique for applying the fundamental sociological concept itself (that is, the concept of sociation), but, in addition, where this concept can be effectively applied, there are still many elements in the phenomena to be studied whose subsumption under the concept or form and content remains arbitrary. There will be contrary opinions, for instance, concerning the extent to which the phenomenon of the poor is a matter of form or content; the extent to which it is a result of formal relations within the group, a result which is determined by general currents and shifts that are the necessary outcome of contacts among human beings; or the extent to which poverty is to be regarded as a merely material characteristic of certain individuals, a characteristic that must be studied exclusively from the viewpoint of economic interests (that is, as regards its content)....[2]

To this extent, any history or description of a social situation is an exercise of psychological knowledge. But it is of extreme methodological relevance—even of decisive importance—to the principles of human studies in general to note that the scientific treatment of psychic data is not thereby automatically psychological. Even where we constantly use psychological rules and knowledge, even where the explanation of every single fact is possible only psychologically (as is true in sociology), the sense and intent of our activities do not have to be psychological. They do not have to aim, that is, at an understanding of the law of the psychic process itself (which, to be sure, has its content), but can aim rather at this content and its configurations. There is only a difference in degree between the studies of man and the sciences of external nature. After all, the natural sciences too, inasmuch as they are phenomena of the intellectual life, have their locus in the mind. The discovery of every astronomical or chemical truth, as well as the rethinking of each of them, is an event occurring in consciousness, an event which a perfect psychology could deduce without residue from physical conditions and developments alone. The procedure followed by the natural sciences in choosing the con-

[2]   Simmel's development of the former interpretation of poverty appears as chapter 11 below.—ED.

tents and interrelations of psychological processes—rather than the processes themselves—for their subject matter is similar to the procedure which determines the significance of a painting from its aesthetic relevance and from its place in the history of art, rather than from the physical oscillations which produce its colors and which constitute and carry its whole, actual existence. There is always one reality and we cannot grasp it scientifically in its immediacy and wholeness but must consider it from a number of different viewpoints and thereby make it into a plurality of mutually independent scientific subject matters. This applies, too, to those psychological phenomena whose contents fail to combine into an autonomous spatial world and which are not strikingly set apart from their psychic reality. Language, for instance, is certainly constructed out of psychological forces and for psychological purposes. But its forms and laws are treated by the science of linguistics with complete neglect of the realization (a realization which alone is given) that this is the object; they are treated exclusively through the presentation and analysis of the construction of the content and the forms that result from it.

The facts of sociation offer a similar picture. That people influence one another—that an individual does something, suffers something, shows his existence or his development because there are others who express themselves, act, or feel—is, of course, a psychological phenomenon. And the only way to grasp the historical emergence of each particular instance of this general phenomenon is to re-create it psychologically, to construct plausible psychological series, to interpret the externally observable by means of psychological categories. Yet from the particular scientific viewpoint conceived by the notion of sociation, this psychological phenomenon as such may be entirely ignored, and attention may be focused rather upon tracing, analyzing, and connecting its contents. Suppose, for example, that it is noted that the relation of a stronger to a weaker individual, which has the form of *primus inter pares*, tends to lead to a possession of absolute power by the stronger party and a gradual elimination of any elements of equality. This, in terms of historical reality, is certainly a psychological process. Yet from the sociological viewpoint, we are interested only in such questions as: How do the various phases of super-ordination and subordination follow one another? To what extent is superordination in a given relation compatible with co-ordination in other relations? How much superordination is required in the initial phase of the relation to destroy co-ordination completely? Has combination or co-operation a greater chance to occur in an earlier or in a later stage of such a development? Or, as a further example, let us suppose it is noted that those hostilities are the bitterest that arise on the basis of a previous and somehow still felt communion or solidarity (hatred between blood relatives has been called the most burning hatred). As an occurrence, this can only be understood, or even described, psychologically. However, looking at this phenomenon as a sociological formation, we are not interested in the psychological processes that occur in each of the two individuals but in their subsumption under the categories of union and discord. We are interested in such problems as: Up to what point can the relation between two individuals or parties contain hostility and solidarity before depriving the relation of the character of solidarity or giving it that of hostility? What sort of solidarity—that which arises from remembered communion or that which is based on inextinguishable instinct—furnishes the means for more cruel, more profoundly wounding injury than is ever possible when the original relation was one of relatively great distance? In brief, how is our observation to be presented as the realization of forms of relation between people—what specific combination of social categories does it present? This is the point, and it is so in spite of the fact that the concrete description of the process, or the description of it as a typical process, can be nothing but psychological. Returning to an earlier illustration, we may (ignoring all differences) compare the procedure of sociology with the performance of a geometrical deduction using a figure drawn on a blackboard. All that is given and seen here is the physically produced chalk marks, but it is not in them that we are interested but in their significance from the viewpoint of geometry, which has nothing whatever to do with that physical figure as a deposit of chalk particles. (On the other hand, this figure, precisely as a physical structure, may be brought under scientific categories; its physiological genesis, its chemical composition, or its optical impression may become the object of special investigations.)

In this sense, then, the givens of sociology are psychological processes whose immediate reality presents itself first of all under psychological categories. But these psychological categories, although indispensable for the description of the facts, remains outside the purpose of sociological investigation. It is to this end that we direct our study to the objective reality of sociation, a reality which, to be sure, is embodied in psychic processes and can often be described only by means of them. Similarly, a drama, from beginning to end, contains only psychological processes and can be understood only psychologically; but its purpose is not to study psychological cognitions but to examine the syntheses which result when the contents of the psychic processes are considered from the viewpoints of tragedy and artistic form, or as symbolic of certain aspects of life.

4

THE CATEGORIES OF
HUMAN EXPERIENCE
1908

Mankind has created association as its general form of
life. This was not, so to speak, the only logical possibility. The human species could just as well have been unsocial; there are unsocial animal species as well as social ones. Because of the fact of
human sociality, however, we are easily misled into thinking that
categories which directly or indirectly are sociological ones are
the only, and universally applicable, categories in terms of which
we may contemplate the contents of human experience. This notion, however, is completely erroneous. That we are social beings
subjects these contents to a certain point of view, but it is by no
means the only possible one. To name a completely contrasting
point of view, one can observe, study, and systematize the contents which, to be sure, exist and are realized only within society
purely in terms of their objective content. The inner validity, coherence, and objective significance of all sciences, technologies,
and arts are completely independent of the fact that they are
realized within and find their preconditions in a social life, just
as independent as their objective sense is of the psychological
processes through which their discoverers found them. They can
naturally also be considered under the latter psychological or the
former social point of view. It is completely legitimate to inquire

From *Soziologie* (Munich and Leipzig: Duncker & Humblot, 1908), pp.
771–75. Translated by Donald N. Levine.

under what social circumstances the natural science we possess can come into being. But questions concerning the correctness of its propositions, their systematic coherence, and the adequacy or inadequacy of its methods have no sociological criterion whatsoever. Such matters are nowhere influenced by the fact of their social historical emergence, but are governed exclusively by immanent, timeless, that is, purely objective, norms.

All contents of life, therefore, are subject to this dual categorization. They can be considered as results of social development, as objects of human interactions, but they can with equal justification be considered with respect to their objective content—as elements of logical, technical, aesthetic, or metaphysical continua, possessing their meaning in themselves and not in the historical actualities which depend on social relationships.

In addition to these categories, now, we must consider two other essential ones. All those contents of life are directly borne by individuals. Some one person has conceived them. They fill the consciousness of someone; they bring someone pleasure or pain. Although they are social, they are at the same time individual, intelligible in terms of the psychic processes in this or that individual. From the teleological point of view, they issue in determinate meaning for this or that individual. It is of course true that they would not have come into being if this individual did not live in society, but just as little would they have become social if they had not been borne by individuals. If I ask what needs drive this individual to his religious activity, what personal destinies have moved him to found a sect, what value this action and experience has for the development of his psyche, this order of questioning does not in the slightest compete with one which subordinates the same facts to the point of view of society—what historical milieu has produced those inner needs; what forms of interactions among individuals and in their relationship to outsiders make them into a "sect"; what enrichments or cleavages the public mind experiences through that sort of religious movement.

Individual and society are, both for historical understanding and for normative judgment, *methodological concepts*. This is so either in that they divide given events and conditions among themselves or in that they deal with the unity of the given, which we cannot directly comprehend, by organizing it under two different points of view, comparable to the way a picture is considered now as a physiological and optical phenomenon, now as a cultural product, or now with respect to the technique of painting, now with respect to its content and aesthetic value. To express this with that radicalism of conception which in practice is naturally approached only fragmentarily, all human psychic events and ideal constructions are to be understood as contents and norms of individual life, and just as thoroughly as contents and norms of existence in social interaction, as for Spinoza the cosmic-absolute existence is to be conceived now under the attribute of extension, now (and just as completely) under that of thought—*una eademque res, sed duobus modis expressa* ["one and the same thing, but expressed in two modes."]

Beyond these last two standpoints, there is a third one[1] which is methodologically coordinate with them, even though our means to develop it with respect to the totality of individual problems are much more incomplete and its theoretical generality is restricted in actual cognition to very few considerations. I have already stressed that association was only the historical-social form which the human species gave to its life and which is by no means identical with the latter when it comes to scientific conceptual analysis. One can therefore examine the givens and contents of historical reality independent of their specific social genesis and significance according to the value and meaning which they possess as elements of the life of humanity, as stages of its development.

To say that this "humanity" possesses no concrete context, no unified consciousness, no continuous development is by no means a valid objection to using the concept. "Humanity" is, if you will, an "idea," just like "nature," perhaps also like "society." It is a category under which individual phenomena can be observed with-

---

[1]   Actually, at this point Simmel introduces a fourth category. All together, the fundamental categories in terms of which human experience may be viewed are: (1) society; (2) objective culture; (3) individual personality; and (4) humanity.—Ed.

out saying that what is designated thereby leads an isolated existence or is to be distilled as a special quality. We can, however, ask
of every human condition, quality, or action: What does this mean
as a stage of the development of humanity? What preconditions
must the entire species have attained for this to be possible? What
has humanity as a biological, ethical, and psychic type thereby
won or lost in value? If these questions can be answered in a
certain way, it is by no means excluded that they can be answered
in a completely opposite way from the standpoint of the society
to which the acting individual belongs. That may as a rule not
be true. It may be that what affects the entire history of humanity
for better or for worse usually has the same significance for the
narrower, socially bound circle; what is socially essential may
without further consideration even be something essential for the
development or for the system of humanity. Be all that as it may, it
does not affect the fact that the ordering and evaluation of any
given content of life according to the viewpoint of the whole of
humanity is in principle different from that which proceeds from
the viewpoint of society, and that both viewpoints are independent
of one another in their underlying motives, however much they
may consider one and the same fact, or human being, or cultural
content in terms of their respective hierarchies.

Although the category of the values and developments of the
human type is methodologically as distinct from the category of
the being and action of the individual as from that of the life of
social interaction, the first two of these categories nonetheless
stand in an inner relationship which places them as it were as *one*
party over against the social category as a second party. The material of the idea of humanity and the questions based on it are
individual. It is only a matter of secondary interest whether the
activities of these individuals contribute to the condition and development of humanity in the form of sociation or in that of a
purely personal activity in thought, sentiment, or artistic works,
in the biological improvement or deterioration of the race, or in
the religious relationship to gods and idols. The existence and
conduct of the individual must of course occur in some such
form, which provides the technique or the connecting link through

which individuality can become a practically effective element of humanity. But for all the indisputable indispensability of these individual forms, among which sociality stands uppermost, humanity and the individual remain the polar concepts for the observation of human life. Objectively and historically, this correlation may not be of very extensive importance when contrasted with the fact of society—although this chapter[2] has shown its efficaciousness in a series of historical epochs, and modern individualism has been traced back to it more than once. But at the very least it remains the ideal auxiliary construction by means of which "society" is shown its place in the series of concepts which methodically order the study of life. Just as within societal development the narrower, "more socialized" group attains its counterpart (internally or historically, on a cyclical or simultaneous basis) in that it expands to the larger group and is specialized to the individual element of society—so from this ultimate point of view society as a whole appears as a special form of aggregation beyond which, subordinating their contents to other forms of observation and evaluation, there stand the ideas of humanity and of the individual.

[2]   The earlier sections of the chapter to which Simmel alludes appear as chapter 16 of the present volume.—ED.

II. Forms of Social Interaction

5

EXCHANGE

1907

MOST RELATIONSHIPS among men can be considered under the category of exchange. Exchange is the purest and most concentrated form of all human interactions in which serious interests are at stake.

Many actions which at first glance appear to consist of mere unilateral process in fact involve reciprocal effects. The speaker before an audience, the teacher before a class, the journalist writing to his public—each appears to be the sole source of influence in such situations, whereas each of them is really acting in response to demands and directions that emanate from apparently passive, ineffectual groups. The saying "I am their leader, therefore I must follow them" holds good for politicians the world over. Even in hypnosis, which is manifestly the most clear-cut case where one person exercises influence and the other shows total passivity, reciprocity still obtains. As an outstanding hypnotist has recently stressed, the hypnotic effect would not be realized were it not for a certain ineffable reaction of the person hypnotized back on the hypnotist himself.

Interaction as Exchange

Now every interaction is properly viewed as a kind of exchange. This is true of every conversation, every love (even when

From *Philosophie des Geldes*, by Georg Simmel, 2d enlarged edition (Leipzig: Duncker & Humblot, 1907), pp. 33–61. Translated by Donald N. Levine.

requited unfavorably), every game, every act of looking one another over. It might seem that the two categories are dissimilar, in that in interaction one gives something one does not have, whereas in exchange one gives only what one does have, but this distinction does not really hold. What one expends in interaction can only be one's own energy, the transmission of one's own substance. Conversely, exchange takes place not for the sake of an object previously possessed by another person, but rather for the sake of one's own feeling about an object, a feeling which the other previously did not possess. The meaning of exchange, moreover, is that the sum of values is greater afterward than it was before, and this implies that each party gives the other more than he had himself possessed.

Interaction is, to be sure, the broader concept, exchange the narrower one. In human relations, however, interaction generally appears in forms which lend themselves to being viewed as exchange. The ordinary vicissitudes of daily life produce a continuous alternation of profit and loss, an ebbing and flowing of the contents of life. Exchange has the effect of rationalizing these vicissitudes, through the conscious act of setting the one *for* the other. The same synthetic process of mind that from the mere juxtaposition of things creates a with-another and for-another—the same ego which, permeated by sense data, informs them with its own unified character—has through the category of exchange seized that naturally given rhythm of our existence and organized its elements into a meaningful nexus.

The Nature of Economic Exchange

Of all kinds of exchange, the exchange of economic values is the least free of some tinge of sacrifice. When we exchange love for love, we release an inner energy we would otherwise not know what to do with. Insofar as we surrender it, we sacrifice no real utility (apart from what may be the external consequences of involvement). When we communicate intellectual matters in conversation, these are not thereby diminished. When we reveal a picture of our personality in the course of taking in that of others, this exchange in no way decreases our possession of ourselves. In all these exchanges the increase of value does not occur through the calculation of profit and loss. Either the contribution of each party stands beyond such a consideration, or else simply to be allowed to contribute is itself a gain—in which case we perceive the response of the other, despite our own offering, as an unearned gift. In contrast, economic exchange—whether it involves substances, labor, or labor power invested in substances—always entails the sacrifice of some good that has other potential uses, even though utilitarian gain may prevail in the final analysis.

The idea that all economic action is interaction, in the specific sense of exchange that involves sacrifice, may be met with the same objection which has been raised against the doctrine that equates all economic value with exchange value. The point has been made that the totally isolated economic man, who neither buys nor sells, would still have to evaluate his products and means of production —would therefore have to construct a concept of value independent of all exchange—if his expenditures and results were to stand in proper relation to one another. This fact, however, proves exactly what it is supposed to disprove, for all consideration whether a certain product is worth enough to justify a certain expenditure of labor or other goods is, for the economic agent, precisely the same as the appraisal which takes place in connection with exchange.

In dealing with the concept of exchange there is frequently a confusion of thought which leads one to speak of a relationship as though it were something external to the elements between which it occurs. Exchange means, however, only a condition of or a change within each of these elements, nothing that is *between* them in the sense of an object separated in space between the two other objects. When we subsume the two acts or changes of condition which occur in reality under the concept "exchange," it is tempting to think that with the exchange something has happened in addition to or beyond that which took place in each of the contracting parties.

This is just like being misled by the substantive concept of "the kiss" (which to be sure is also "exchanged") into thinking that a kiss is something that lies outside of the two pairs of lips, outside of their movements and sensations. Considered with reference to its immediate content, exchange is nothing more than the causally connected repetition of the fact that an actor now has something which he previously did not have, and for that has lost something which he previously did have.

That being the case, the isolated economic man, who surely must make certain sacrifices in order to gain certain fruits, behaves exactly like the one who makes exchanges. The only difference is that the party with whom he contracts is not a second free agent, but the natural order and regularity of things, which no more satisfy our desires without a sacrifice on our part than would another person. His calculations of value, in accordance with which he governs his actions, are generally the same as in exchange. For the economic actor as such it is surely quite immaterial whether the substances or labor capacities which he possesses are sunk into the ground or given to another man, if what he gains from the sacrifice is exactly the same in both cases.

This subjective process of sacrifice and gain within the individual psyche is by no means something secondary or imitative in relation to interindividual exchange. On the contrary, the give-and-take between sacrifice and attainment within the individual is the fundamental presupposition and, as it were, the essence of every two-sided exchange. The latter is only a subspecies of the former; that is, it is the sort in which the sacrifice is occasioned by the demand of another individual, whereas the sacrifice can be occasioned by things and their natural properties with the same sort of consequences for the actor.

It is extremely important to carry through this reduction of the economic process to that which takes place *in actuality*, that is, within the psyche of every economic actor. We should not let ourselves be misled because in exchange this process is reciprocal, conditioned by a similar process within another party. The natural and "solipsistic" economic transaction goes back to the same fundamental form as the two-sided exchange: to the process of balancing two subjective events within an individual. This is basically unaffected by the secondary question whether the process is instigated by the nature of things or the nature of man, whether it is a matter of purely natural economy or exchange economy. All feelings of value, in other words, which are set free by producible objects are in general to be gained only by foregoing other values. Such self-denial consists not only in that indirect labor for ourselves which appears as labor for others, but frequently enough in direct labor on behalf of our own personal ends.

Exchange as a Creative Process

This consideration makes it particularly clear that exchange is just as productive, as creative of values, as is so-called production. In both cases it is a matter of securing goods at the cost of others which one gives up, and in such a manner that the end result yields a surplus of satisfactions over what obtained before the action. We can create neither matter nor energy anew, but only so attack the given that as many quanta as possible ascend from the realm of reality to the realm of value as well. This formal displacement of given materials is effected by exchange between men just as by the exchange with nature which we name production. Both therefore belong to the same category of value: both involve filling the space vacated by some surrendered thing with an object of greater value. Only by virtue of this movement do objects become detached from the needing and enjoying ego with which they were fused, and thereby become values.

In one and the same area, value and exchange constitute the foundation of our practical life. This indicates the profound connection between them, such that value is determined by exchange just as the converse is true. Much as our life may appear to be determined by the mechanism and objectivity of things, we can in reality take no step nor think any thought without imparting values to things through our feelings and directing them in relation to our actions.

These actions themselves run their course according to the paradigm of exchange. From the satisfaction of our lowliest need to the acquisition of the highest intellectual and religious goods, value must always be offered up in order to obtain a value. What is starting point and what is consequence here is something that can perhaps not be determined. For either both are inseparable in the fundamental processes, constituting the unity of practical life which we must decompose into separate factors since we cannot directly grasp that unity as such, or else an unending process occurs between both, such that every exchange leads back to a value which in turn leads back to an exchange. The more fruitful and truly illuminating aspect of this, at least for our considerations, is the path from exchange to value, since the converse is better known and more self-evident.

The Significance of Sacrifice

The fact that value is the issue of a process of sacrifice discloses the infinity of riches for which our life is indebted to this basic form. Because we strive to minimize sacrifice and perceive it as painful, we tend to suppose that only with its complete disappearance would life attain its highest level of value. But this notion overlooks the fact that sacrifice is by no means always an external barrier to our goals. It is rather the *inner* condition of the goal and of the way to it. Because we dissect the problematic unity of our practical relations to things into the categories of sacrifice and profit, of obstacle and attainment, and because these categories are frequently separated into differentiated temporal stages, we forget that if a goal were granted to us without the interposition of obstacles it would no longer be the same goal.

The resistance which has to be eliminated is what gives our powers the possibility of proving themselves. Sin, after whose conquest the soul ascends to salvation, is what assures that special "joy in heaven" which those who were upright from the outset do not possess there. Every synthesis requires at the same time an effective analytic principle, which actually negates it (for without this it would be an absolute unity rather than a synthesis of several elements). By the same token every analysis requires a synthesis, in the dissolution of which it consists (for analysis demands always a certain coherence of elements if it is not to amount to a mere congeries without relations). The most bitter enmity is still more of a connection than simple indifference, indifference still more than not even knowing of one another. In short: the inhibiting countermovement, the diversion of which signifies sacrifice, is often—perhaps, seen from the point of view of elementary processes, even always—the positive presupposition of the goal itself. Sacrifice by no means belongs in the category of the undesirable, though superficiality and greed might portray it as such. It is not only the condition of individual values but, in what concerns us here, the economic realm, sacrifice is the condition of all value; not only the price to be paid for individual values that are already established, but that through which alone values can come into being.

Exchange occurs in two forms, which I shall discuss here in connection with the value of labor. All labor is indisputably a sacrifice if it is accompanied by a desire for leisure, for the mere self-satisfying play of skills, or for the avoidance of strenuous exertion. In addition to such desires, however, there exists a quantum of latent work energy which either we do not know what to do with or which presents itself as a drive to carry out voluntary labor, labor called forth neither by necessity nor by ethical motives. The expenditure of this energy is in itself no sacrifice, yet for this quantum of energy there compete a number of demands all of which it cannot satisfy. For every expenditure of the energy in question one or more possible and desirable alternative uses of it must be sacrificed. Could we not usefully spend the energy with which we accomplish task A also on task B, then the first would not entail any sacrifice; the same would hold for B in the event we chose it rather than A. In this utilitarian loss what is sacrificed is not labor, but *non-labor*. What we pay for A is not the sacrifice of labor—for our assumption here is that the latter in itself poses not the slightest hardship on us—but the giving up of task B.

The sacrifice which we make of labor in exchange is therefore of two sorts, of an absolute and a relative sort. The discomfort we accept is in the one case directly bound up with the labor itself, because the labor is annoying and troublesome. In the case where the labor itself is of eudaemonistic irrelevance or even of positive value, and when we can attain one object only at the cost of denying ourselves another, the frustration is indirect. The instances of happily done labor are thereby reduced to the form of exchange entailing renunciation, the form which characterizes all aspects of economic life.

The Relativity of Value

The idea that objects have established values before they enter into economic transactions, such that each of the two objects involved in a transaction represents a respective profit and loss for the two parties, is valid for describing a fully developed economic system, but not for the elementary processes which lead to its formation. To this view a logical objection can be readily put, for it would seem that two things can have the same value only if each of them already has its own value. The objection seems upheld by the analogous argument that two lines can be equally long only if each of them possesses a determinate length before the comparison. If we look at the matter closely, however, we see that a line possesses this length only at the moment of being compared with another line. A line is not "long" of and by itself. It cannot determine its length by itself, but only through another line by which it is measured, and which it measures as well, although the *result* of the measuring is not determined by the process of measuring, but depends on each of the two independent lines. This is reminiscent of the conception of objective value judgment which I have elsewhere termed metaphysical; namely, from the relation between us and things there emerges a demand to make a definite judgment, the content of which does not lie in the things themselves.

The same is true of judgments of length. The *demand* to make such a judgment emanates, as it were, from things, but the content of this judgment is not indicated by the things; it can only be realized through an act within ourselves. That length is not contained in the individual object but arises out of a process of comparison is easily hidden from us, because from the individual instances of relative length we have abstracted the universal concept of length

—from which the *determinacy* that is indispensable for any concrete length is excluded. We then project this concept back into things, and suppose that they must originally have had *length* even before this could be determined in the individual case through comparison. Out of numerous individual comparisons of length fixed measures are crystallized which are then used to determine the length of all spatial figures, such that these measures, the embodiment, as it were, of that abstract concept of length, seem removed from relativity, since everything is measured by them but they are not themselves measured. To think this is to commit an error no less egregious than to think that the falling apple is attracted by the earth, but not the earth by the apple.

We are further misled into thinking that a line possesses length intrinsically by the fact that its individual *parts* constitute the majority of elements in whose relation the totality consists. Yet were we to imagine that there was only one single line in the whole world, this line would not be "long," since it lacked any correlation with another line—just as one cannot express any determinate measure of the world as a whole, since it has nothing outside itself in relation to which it could have a size. This is the condition of every line insofar as it is regarded without comparison to another line, or without comparison of its parts among themselves: it is neither short nor long, but beyond the category altogether. The lineal analogy, therefore, instead of refuting the conception of the relativity of economic values, serves instead to render it more clear.

The Source of Value

If we regard economic activity as a special case of the universal life-form of exchange, as a sacrifice in return for a gain, we shall from the very beginning intuit something of what takes place within this form, namely, that the value of the gain is not, so to speak, brought with it, ready-made, but accrues to the desired object, in part or even entirely through the measure of the sacrifice demanded in acquiring it. These cases, which are as frequent as they are important for the theory of value, seem, to be sure, to harbor an inner contradiction: they have us making a sacrifice of a value for things which in themselves are worthless.

No one in his right mind would forego value without receiving for it at least an equal value; that, on the contrary, an end should receive its value only through the price that we must give for it could be the case only in an absurd world. Yet common sense can readily see why this is so.

The value which an actor surrenders for another value can never be greater, for the subject himself under the actual circumstances of the moment, than that for which it is given. All contrary appearances rest on the confusion of the value actually estimated by the actor with the value which the object of exchange in question usually has or has by virtue of some apparently objective assessment. Thus if someone at the point of death from hunger gives away a jewel for a piece of bread, he does so because the latter is worth more to him under the circumstances than the former. Some particular circumstances, however, are *always* involved when one attaches a feeling of value to an object. Every such feeling of value is lodged in a whole complex system of our feelings which is in constant flux, adaptation, and reconstruction. Whether these circumstances are exceptional or relatively constant is obviously in principle immaterial. Through the fact that the starving man gives away his jewel he shows unambiguously that the bread is worth more to him.

There can thus be no doubt that in the moment of the exchange, of the making of the sacrifice, the value of the exchanged object forms the limit which is the highest point to which the value of the object being given away can rise. Quite independent of this is the question whence that former object derives its exigent value, and whether it may not come from the sacrifices to be offered for it, such that the equivalence between gain and cost would be established a posteriori, so to speak, and by virtue of the latter. We will presently see how frequently value comes into being psychologically in this apparently illogical manner.

Given the existence of the value, however, it is psychologically necessary to regard it, no less than values constituted in every other way, as a positive good at least as great as the negative of what has been sacrificed for it. There is in fact a whole range of cases known to the untrained psychological observer in which sacrifice not only heightens the value of the goal, but even generates it by itself. What comes to expression in this process is the desire to prove one's strength, to overcome difficulties, indeed often to oppose for the sheer joy of opposition. The detour required to attain certain things is often the occasion, often the cause as well, of perceiving them as values. In human relationships, most frequently and clearly in erotic relations, we notice how reserve, indifference, or rejection inflames the most passionate desire to prevail over these obstacles, and spurs us to efforts and sacrifices which, without these obstacles, would surely seem to us excessive. For many people the aesthetic gain from climbing the high Alps would not be considered worth further notice if it did not demand the price of extraordinary exertion and dangers and thereby acquire character, appeal, and consecration.

The charm of antiques and curios is frequently of the same sort. Even if antiques possess no intrinsic aesthetic or historical interest, a substitute for this is furnished by the mere difficulty of acquiring them: they are worth as much as they cost. It then comes to appear that they cost what they are worth. Furthermore, all ethical merit signifies that for the sake of the morally desirable deed contrary drives and wishes must be combatted and given up. If the act occurs without any conquest, as the direct issue of uninhibited impulses, its content may be objectively desirable, but it is not accorded a subjective moral value in the same sense. Only through the sacrifice of the lower and yet so seductive goods does one reach the height of ethical merit; and the more tempting the seductions and the more profound their sacrifice, the loftier the height. If we observe which human achievements attain to the highest honors and evaluations, we find them always to be those which manifest, or at least appear to manifest, the most depth, the most exertion, the most persistent concentration of the whole being—which is to say the most self-denial, sacrifice of all that is subsidiary, and devotion of the subjective to the objective ideal.

And if, in contrast with all this, aesthetic production and everything sweet and light, flowing from the naturalness of impulse, unfolds an incomparable charm, this charm derives its special quality from feelings associated with the burdens and sacrifices which are ordinarily required to gain such things. The liability and inexhaustible richness of combination of the contents of our minds frequently transform the significance of a connection into its exact converse, somewhat as the association between two ideas follows equally whether they are asserted or denied of each other. We perceive the specific value of something obtained without difficulty as a gift of fortune only on the grounds of the significance which things have for us that are hard to come by and measured by sacrifice. It is the same value, but with the negative sign; and the latter is the primary from which the former may be derived—but not vice versa.

We may be speaking here of course of exaggerated or exceptional cases. To find their counterpart in the whole realm of the economy it seems necessary, first of all, to make an analytic distinction between the universal substance of value, and economic activity as a differentiated form thereof. If for the moment we take value as something given, then in accord with our foregoing discussion the following proposition is established beyond doubt: *Economic value as such does not inhere in an object in its isolated self-existence, but comes to an object only through the expenditure of another object which is given for it.* Wild fruit picked without effort, and not given in exchange, but immediately consumed, is no economic good. It can at most count as such only when its consumption saves some other economic expense. If, however, all of life's requirements were to be satisfied in this manner, so that at no point was sacrifice involved, men would simply not have *economic* activity, any more than do birds or fish or the denizens of fairyland. Whatever the way two objects, A and B, became values, A becomes an *economic* value only because I must give B for it, B only because I can obtain A for it. As mentioned above, it is in principle immaterial here whether the sacrifice takes place by transferring a value to another person, that is, through interindividual exchange, or within the circle of the individual's own interests, through a balancing of efforts and results. In articles of commerce there is simply nothing else to be found other than the meaning each one directly or indirectly has for our consumption needs and the exchange which takes place between them. Since, as we have seen, the former does not of itself suffice to make a given object an object of economic activity, it follows that the latter alone can supply to it the specific difference which we call economic.

This distinction between value and its economic form, is, however, an artificial one. If at first economy appears to be a mere form, in the sense that it presumes values as its contents, in order to be able to draw them into the process of balancing between sacrifice and profit, in reality the same process which forms the presumed values into an economy can be shown to be the creator of the economic *values themselves*. This will now be demonstrated.

The economic form of the value stands between two boundaries: on the one hand, *desire* for the object, connected with the anticipated feeling of satisfaction from its possession and enjoyment; on the other hand, this *enjoyment* itself which, strictly speaking, is not an economic act. That is, as soon as one concedes, as was shown above, that the immediate consumption of wild fruit is not an economic act and therefore the fruit itself is not an economic value (except insofar as it saves the production of economic values), then the consumption of real economic values is no longer economic, for the act of consumption in the latter case is not distinguishable from that in the former. Whether the fruit someone eats has been accidentally found, stolen, home-grown, or bought makes not the slightest difference in the act of eating and its direct consequences for the eater.

The Process of Value Formation: Creating Objects through Exchange

Now an object is not a value so long as it remains a mere emotional stimulus enmeshed in the subjective process—a natural part of our sensibility, as it were. It must first be separated from this subjective sensibility for it to attain the peculiar significance which we call value. For not only is it certain that desire in and of itself could not establish any value if it did not encounter obstacles

—trade in economic values could never have arisen if every desire was satisfied without struggle or exertion—but even desire itself would never have ascended to such a considerable height if it could be satisfied without further ado. It is only the postponement of satisfaction through impediment, the anxiety that the object may escape, the tension of struggle for it, that brings about the cumulation of desires to a point of intensified volition and continuous striving.

If, however, even the highest pitch of desire were generated wholly from within, we still would not confer value on the object which satisfies it if the object were available to us in unlimited abundance. The important thing in that case would be the total enjoyment, the existence of which guarantees to us the satisfaction of our wishes, but not that particular quantum which we actually take possession of, since this could be replaced quite as easily by another. Even that totality would acquire some sense of value only by virtue of the thought of its possible shortage. Our consciousness would in this case be filled simply with the rhythm of subjective desires and satisfactions, without attaching any attention to the mediating object. Neither need nor enjoyment contains in itself value or economic process. These are actualized simultaneously through exchange between two subjects, each of whom requires some self-denial by the other as a condition of feeling satisfied, or through the counterpart of this process in the solipsistic economy. Through exchange, economic process and economic values emerge simultaneously, because exchange is what sustains or produces the distance between subject and object which transmutes the subjective state of feeling into objective valuation.

Kant once summarized his theory of knowledge in the proposition: "The conditions of experience are at the same time the conditions of the objects of experience." By this he meant that the process we call experience and the concepts which constitute its contents or objects are subject to the same laws of reason. The objects can enter into our experience, that is, can be experienced by us, because they exist as concepts within us, and the same energy which forms and defines the experience manifests itself in the formation of those concepts. In the same spirit we may say here that the possibility of economy is at the same time the possibility of the objects of economy. The very transaction between two possessors of objects (substances, labor energies, rights) which brings them into the so-called economic relation, namely, reciprocal sacrifice, at the same time elevates each of these objects into the category of value. The logical difficulty raised by the argument that values must first exist, and exist as values, in order to enter into the form and process of economic action, is now removed. It is removed thanks to the significance we have perceived in that psychic relationship which we designated as the distance between us and things. This distance differentiates the original subjective state of feeling into (1) a desiring subject, anticipating feelings, and (2) counterposed to him, an object that is now imbued with value; while the distance, on its side, is produced in the economic realm by exchange, that is, by the two-sided operation of barriers, restraint, and self-denial. Economic *values* thus emerge through the same reciprocity and relativity in which the *economic condition* of values consists.

Exchange is not merely the addition of the two processes of giving and receiving. It is, rather, something new. Exchange constitutes a third process, something that emerges when each of those two processes is simultaneously the cause and the effect of the other. Through this process, the value which the necessity of self-denial for an object imparts to it becomes an economic value. If it is true that value arises in general in the interval which obstacles, renunciations, and sacrifices interpose between desire and its satisfaction, and if the process of exchange consists in that reciprocally conditioned taking and giving, there is no need to invoke a prior process of valuation which makes a value of an isolated object for an isolated subject. What is required for this valuation takes place in the very act of exchange itself. In empirical reality things are usually provided with the "value sign" the longest when they are involved in exchange. What we are speaking of here, be it understood, is the inner, systematic meaning of the concepts of value and exchange. In historical phenomena this meaning exists only in a rudimentary sense or else it constitutes their ideal meaning. It is not the form in which they actually exist, but the form which they take when projected on the plane of objective-logical understanding as contrasted with a historical-genetic approach. . . .[1]

Primitive Exchange

Still another observation teaches us just as well that exchange is in no way conditioned by a previously established conception of equal values. If one observes the trading behavior of children, of impulsive persons and, according to all appearance, of primitive peoples as well, one finds them giving any possession at all for an object for which they momentarily feel a violent desire, no matter whether the general opinion or their own unhurried reflection would find the price much too high. The reason this does not contradict the stipulation that every exchange must in the consciousness of the subject be an advantageous one is that subjectively this whole action stands *outside the question of the equality or inequality of the objects of exchange.* The notion that every exchange must be preceded by a weighing of losses and gains and at least eventuate in an equilibrating of the two is one of those rationalistic axioms that are so utterly unpsychological. This would require an objectivity regarding one's own desires which the kinds of psychic constitutions to which we have just alluded do not sustain. The undeveloped or prepossessed mind does not gain enough detachment from the momentary surging of his interest to make a comparison. At the moment he only wants the one thing; giving up something else therefore does not have the effect of being a detraction from the satisfaction he seeks. In other words, it does not count as a price.

In view of the mindlessness with which the childlike, inexperienced, impetuous creature appropriates what he immediately desires "at any price," it seems to me most likely that the judgment of equivalence is a later development, the issue of some number

[1] At this point Simmel digresses to refute alternative explanations of value, namely, those which derive value from considerations of utility or scarcity. The factors of utility and scarcity, he argues, do not in themselves generate value, but only when the objects they condition are desired in exchange.—ED.

of exchanges completed without any weighing. That wholly one-sided, obsessive desire must first have been pacified through actual possession of the object in order to permit other objects to be compared with it. That huge disparity of emphasis between immediate interests and all other concepts and valuations which prevails in the unschooled and ungoverned mind initiates exchange before a judgment about value, that is, about the relation of various quanta of desires to one another, has been formed. The fact that with well-developed concepts of value and tolerable self-control judgments about value equivalence precede the act of exchange must not delude us. The probability is that here, as so often is the case, the rational pattern has developed out of a process that is psychologically the reverse—even within the province of the soul *pros emas* is the last instance of which *physei* is the first—and that it is the experience of trading on the basis of purely subjective impulses which has then taught us about the relative value of things.

Value and Price

If value is, as it were, the offspring of price, then it seems logical to assert that their amounts must be the same. I refer now to what has been established above, that in each individual case no contrasting party pays a price which to him under the given circumstances is too high for the thing obtained. If, in the poem of Chamisso, the highwayman with pistol drawn compels the victim to sell his watch and ring for three coppers, the fact is that under the circumstances, since the victim could not otherwise save his life, the thing obtained in exchange is actually worth the price. No one would work for starvation wages if, in the situation in which he actually found himself, he did not prefer this wage to not working. The appearance of paradox in the assertion that value and price are equivalent in every individual case arises from the fact that certain conceptions of other kinds of equivalence of value and price are brought into our estimate.

Two kinds of considerations bring this about: (1) the relative stability of the relations which determine the majority of exchange transactions, and (2) the analogies which set still uncertain value-relations according to the norms of those that already exist. Together these produce the notion that if for a certain object this and that other object were exchange equivalents, then these two objects, or the circle of objects which they define, would have the same position in the scale of values. They also give rise to the related notion that if abnormal circumstances caused us to exchange this object for values that lie higher or lower in the scale, price and value would become discrepant—although in each individual case, considering *its* circumstances, we would find them actually to coincide. We should not forget that the objective and just equivalence of value and price, which we make the norm of the actual and individual case, holds good only under very specific historical and technical conditions; and that, with the change of these conditions, the equivalence vanishes at once. Between the norm itself and the cases which it defines as either exceptional or standard there is no difference of kind: there is, so to speak, only a quantitative difference. This is somewhat like when we say of an extraordinarily elevated or degraded individual, "He is really no longer a man." The fact is that this idea of man is only an average. It would lose its normative character at the moment a majority of men ascended or descended to that level of character, which would then pass for the generically "human."

To perceive this requires an energetic effort to disentangle two deeply rooted conceptions of value which have substantial practical justification. In relations that are somewhat evolved these conceptions are lodged in two superimposed levels. One kind of standard is formed from the traditions of society, from the majority of experiences, from demands that seem to be purely logical; the other, from individual constellations, from demands of the moment, from the constraints of a capricious environment. Looking at the rapid changes which take place within the latter sphere, we lose sight of the slow evolution of the former and its development out of the sublimation of the latter; and the former seems suitably justified as the expression of an objective proportion. In an exchange that takes place under such circumstances, when the feelings of loss and gain at least balance each other (for otherwise no actor who made any comparisons at all would consummate the exchange) yet when these same feelings of value are discrepant when measured by those general standards, one speaks of a divergence between value and price. This occurs most conspicuously under two conditions, which almost always go together: (1) when a single value-quality is counted as the economic value and two objects consequently are adjudged equal in value only insofar as the same quantum of that fundamental value is present in them, and (2) when a certain proportion between two values is expected not only in an objective sense but also as a moral imperative.

The conception, for example, that the real value-element in all values is the socially required labor time objectified in them has been applied in both of these ways, and provides a standard, directly or indirectly applicable, which makes value fluctuate positively and negatively with respect to price. The fact of that single *standard of value* in no way establishes how labor power comes to be a value in the first place. It could hardly have done so if the labor power had not, by acting on various materials and fashioning various products, created the possibility of exchange, or if the use of the labor power were not perceived as a sacrifice which one makes for the sake of its fruits. Labor energy also, then, is aligned with the category of value only through the possibility and reality of exchange, irrespective of the fact that subsequently *within* this category of value labor may itself provide a standard for the remaining contents. If the labor power therefore is also the content of every value, it receives its form as value in the first place only because it enters into the relations between sacrifice and gain, or profit and value (here in the narrower sense).

In the cases of discrepancy between price and value the one contracting party would, according to this theory, give a certain amount of immediately objectified labor power for a lesser amount of the same. Other factors, not involving labor power, would then lead the party to complete the exchange, factors such as the satisfaction of a terribly urgent need, amateurish fancy, fraud, monopoly, and so on. In the wider and subjective sense, therefore, the equivalence of value and countervalue holds fast in these cases, and the single norm, labor power, which makes the discrepancy possible, does not cease to derive the genesis of its character as a value from exchange.

The qualities of objects which account for their subjective desirability cannot, consequently, be credited with producing an absolute amount of value. It is always the relation of desires to one another, realized in exchange, which turns their objects into economic values. With respect to scarcity, the other element supposed to constitute value, this consideration is more directly apparent. Exchange is, indeed, nothing other than the interindividual attempt to improve an unfavorable situation arising out of a shortage of goods; that is, to reduce as much as possible the amount of subjective abstinence by the mode of distributing the available supply. Thereupon follows immediately a universal correlation between what is called scarcity-value (a term justly criticized) and what is called exchange-value.

For us, however, the connection is more important in the reverse direction. As I have already emphasized, the fact that goods are scarce would not lead us to value them unless we could not somehow modify that scarcity. It is modifiable in only two ways: by expending labor to increase the supply of goods, or by giving up objects already possessed in order to make whatever items an individual most desires less scarce for him. One can accordingly say that the scarcity of goods in relation to the desires directed to them objectively conditions exchange, but that it is exchange alone that makes scarcity a factor in value. It is a mistake of many theories of value to assume that, when utility and scarcity are given, economic value—that is, the exchange process—is something to be taken for granted, a conceptually necessary consequence of those premises. In this they are by no means correct. If, for instance, those conditions are accompanied by ascetic resignation, or if they instigated only combat or robbery—which, to be sure, is indeed true often enough—no economic value and no economic life would emerge.

Ethnology teaches us about the astonishing arbitrariness, vacillation, and incongruities which characterize concepts of value in primitive cultures the moment their people are concerned with anything more than the most pressing daily necessities. Now there is no doubt that this phenomenon is caused by—in any event, is connected with—another phenomenon, the primitive man's aversion to economic exchange. Several grounds for this aversion have been asserted. Since primitive man lacks an objective and generally accepted measure of value, he must constantly be afraid of being deceived when trading. Since any product of labor is brought forth by himself and for himself, he externalizes a part of his personality with it and may be giving the evil powers some control over him. Perhaps the aversion of nature people against work stems from the same source. Here, too, a reliable measure is wanting, for the balancing of travail and harvest; also from nature does he fear deception. The objective character of nature stands incalculable and terrifying before him before the time when he engages in tested and regulated exchange with her and thus places his own acts in the distance and category of objectivity. Because he is immersed in the subjectivity of his relations with objects, exchange—with nature as with individuals—which involves objectification of the thing and its value, appears to him as forbidding. It is actually as if the first flicker of consciousness of the object as an object brings with it a feeling of anxiety, as though with this awareness one felt a piece of ego being torn away. Thence the mythological and fetishistic interpretation which objects undergo—an interpretation which not only hypostatizes this anxiety and gives it the only possible intelligibility it can have for primitive man, but also alleviates it and by anthropomorphizing objects, brings them closer again to reconciliation with subjectivity.

Forms of Appropriation and Exchange

This state of affairs serves to explain numerous phenomena, including, first of all, the naturalness and honorableness of robbery, of the subjective and normatively unregulated seizure of what is immediately desired. Long after the Homeric era piracy remained a legitimate occupation in peripheral Greek territories. Indeed, among many primitive peoples armed robbery is held to be superior to honest payment. This latter point of view is thoroughly understandable: in exchange and payment one is subordinated to an objective norm, which the strong, autonomous personality must defer to, something it often is just not inclined to do. For this reason very aristocratic, self-willed natures disdain commerce. By the same token, however, trade favors peaceable relations among men, because they recognize the intersubjective, uniform objectivity and normative order which it places over them.

As one might suspect, there exists a continuum of intermediate phenomena between the purely subjective mode of changing ownership, exemplified by robbery and the giving of presents, and its purely objective form in trade, in which things are exchanged according to the equivalent quanta of value contained in them. Among these intermediate forms is the traditional pattern of reciprocal giving of gifts. Many peoples have the idea that one may accept a present only if one can requite it with a return present—a retroactive purchase, so to speak. This merges directly into regular exchange when it happens, as often occurs in the Orient, that the seller sends an object to the buyer as a "gift"—but woe to the buyer if he does not send a comparable "countergift." Another intermediate phenomenon of this sort is the universal form of "request work," whereby neighbors or friends assemble to lend assistance when urgently needed without being given any payment for their work. But it is the well-established custom in such instances to provide generous hospitality for those who come to work and if at all possible to give them a small feast; so that, for example, among the Serbs it is reported that only well-to-do individuals can afford to call together a voluntary work force of that sort.

Still today in the Orient and even in many parts of Italy one does not find the concept of the set price which establishes a fixed restraint on the subjective interests of both buyers and sellers. In those places everyone sells as dearly and buys as cheaply as he possibly can. Exchange there is exclusively a subjective transaction between two persons. Its outcome depends only on the cunning, greed, and tenacity of the parties, but not on the thing and its consensually grounded relation to price. Under these circumstances, as a Roman antique dealer explained to me, a business transaction consists of a process wherein the seller asks too much and the buyer offers too little and they only gradually approach one another to reach an acceptable point. This shows clearly how the objectively set price emerges out of the counterposition of subjects—the whole thing represents an intrusion of precommercial relations into a going exchange economy, but one that has not yet been consistently realized. The element of exchange is already there, it is already an objective event between values—but its implementation is thoroughly subjective, its mode and its quantities depend exclusively on the relation of person equalities.

The Cultural Foundations of Exchange

Herein probably lies the ultimate motive for the sacral forms, the legal guarantees, the various public and traditional assurances which lend support to commerce in all early cultures. They provide the transsubjective element which the nature of exchange demands but which men do not yet know how to establish through the objective relation to the object itself. So long as exchange and the idea that something like the equivalence of values could exist between things were not yet established, no two individuals would have come to an agreement by themselves. Therefore we find in all lands and far into the Middle Ages that commercial transactions take place in public, and above all that units of measure by which the customary wares are exchanged are exactly set and their use is not to be evaded by any pair of parties through private deals.

This sort of objectivity is, to be sure, mechanical and external, supported by motives and forces that lie beyond the realm of individual exchange transactions. Transaction-specific measurement does without such a priori arrangements and takes into account all the particularities which are suppressed by those conventional forms. But the intention and principle of both forms are the same: the trans-subjective fixing of values in exchange, an effort which only later finds a more germane, immanent way. The exchange carried out by free and self-sufficient individuals presumes a valuation based on standards that lie in the nature of the things. In the stages that precede this the contents of what is being exchanged must be fixed in a way that is socially guaranteed, for otherwise individuals would lack any stable point for evaluating objects. The same motive doubtless accounts for the social regulation of the direction and procedures of primitive labor, demonstrating once more the essential similarity between exchange and work, or more accurately, the subsumption of the latter under the former concept.

The manifold connections between what is objectively valid (valid practically as well as theoretically) and its social meaning and recognition often appear historically in the following way as well. Social interaction, expansion, and normative order provide the individual with that dignity and stability of life contents which they later attain as a matter of substantive right and demonstrable fact. Thus a child believes in something not because of intrinsic reasons but because he trusts the persons who communicate it to him: not something, but *someone* is believed. In matters of taste, similarly, we are dependent on fashion, that is, on the social dissemination of actions and judgments until, later on, we know enough to pass aesthetic judgment on the thing itself. Thus, too, the necessity for the individual to transcend himself and thereby to attain a solid, stable, supraindividual orientation in matters of law, knowledge, and morality is first manifest as the force of tradition. In place of this initially indispensable social regulation, which to be sure transcends the individual subject but not subjects in general, another type of standardization gradually develops from the knowledge of *things* and the apprehension of ideal norms. The external elements which we need for our orientation take the more readily accessible form of social generality before they come to us as the objective characteristics of realities and of ideas.

In this sense which holds true of all cultural development, then, exchange is originally a matter of social arrangements, until individuals become sufficiently acquainted with objects and their respective values to be able to set the terms of exchange from case to case. There may be doubt that these socially legislated rates which govern trade in all undeveloped cultures could only have resulted from numerous previous transactions which initially took place in irregular and unfixed form among individuals. This objection holds for exchange, however, no more than it does for lan-

guage, custom, law, religion—in short, for all the fundamental
forms of life which emerge from and regulate the group as a whole.
For a long time these forms, too, could only be explained as the
inventions of individuals, whereas they surely arose from the very
beginning as interindividual formations, as the product of interaction between individual and collectivity, so that no individual is
to be credited with their origin.

I hold it to be completely possible that the forerunner of socially fixed exchange was not individual exchange, but a form of
transfer of possessions that was not exchange at all—something
like robbery. Interindividual exchange would then have been nothing other than a peace treaty; exchange, and exchange under
fixed terms, would then have emerged as a single reality. An
analogy to this would be provided by cases where primitive steal-
ing of wives has preceded an exogamous peace treaty with neighbors, which legitimates and regulates the sale and exchange of
women. The radically new marriage form introduced thereby is
thus immediately set in a way that structures the choice of individuals. One does not need to assume the prior existence of a number
of separate arrangements of the same sort among individuals, but
rather a social regulation appears with the new marriage form at
one and the same time. It is a prejudice to think that every socially
regulated relationship must have developed historically out of relationships that are similar in content but appear only in individualistic, socially unregulated forms. The phenomenon can just as well
have been preceded by the same content in a social form *of a
wholly different kind*. The antecedents of exchange are the subjective forms of appropriation of alien possessions, robbery and
gift-giving—just as presents given to the chief and penalties imposed by the chief represent forestages of taxation. Social regulation appears as the first suprasubjective possibility which is
reached in the course of this development, and this in turn prepares
the way for objectivity in the factual sense. Only through this prior
stage of societal regulation does there develop in that free transfer
of possessions between individuals the condition of objectivity,
which is the essence of exchange.

From all the foregoing it appears that exchange is a sociologi-

cal structure sui generis, a primary form and function of interindividual life. By no means does it follow logically from those qualitative and quantitative properties of things which we call utility
and scarcity. On the contrary, both these properties derive their
significance as generators of value only under the presupposition
of exchange. Where exchange, offering a sacrifice for the sake of
a gain, is impossible for any reason, no degree of scarcity of a
desired object can convert it to an economic value until the possibility of that relation reappears.

The meaning that an object has for an individual always rests
solely in its desirability. For whatever an object is to accomplish
for us, its qualitative character is decisive. When we possess it, it
is a matter of indifference whether in addition there exist many,
few, or no other specimens of its kind. (I do not distinguish here
those cases in which scarcity itself is a kind of qualitative property
which makes the object desirable to us, such as old postage stamps,
curiosities, antiques without aesthetic or historical value, etc.)
The sense of difference, incidentally, important for enjoyment in
the narrower sense of the word, may be everywhere conditioned by
a scarcity of the object, that is, by the fact that it is not enjoyed
everywhere and at all times. This inner psychological condition of
enjoyment, however, is not a practical factor, because it would
have to lead not to the overcoming of scarcity but to its conservation, its increase even—which is patently not the case. The only
relevant question apart from the direct enjoyment of things for
their qualities is the question of the way to it. As soon as this way is
a long and difficult one, involving sacrifices in patience, disappointment, toil, inconvenience, feats of self-denial, and so on, we call the
object "scarce." One can express this directly: things are not difficult to obtain because they are scarce, but they are scarce because
they are difficult to obtain. The inflexible external fact that the
supply of certain goods is too small to satisfy all our desires for
them would be in itself insignificant. There are many objectively
scarce things which are not scarce in the economic sense of the
term. Whether they are scarce in this sense depends entirely upon
what measure of energy, patience, and devotion is necessary for

their acquisition—sacrifices which naturally presume the desirability of the object.

The difficulty of attainment, that is, the magnitude of the sacrifice involved in exchange, is thus the element that peculiarly constitutes value. Scarcity constitutes only the outer appearance of this element, only its objectification in the form of quantity. One often fails to observe that scarcity, purely as such, is only a negative property, an existence characterized by nonexistence. The nonexistent, however, cannot be operative. Every positive consequence must be the issue of a positive property and force, of which that negative property is only the shadow. These concrete forces are, however, manifestly the only ingredients of exchange. The aspect of concreteness is in no wise reduced because we are not dealing here with individuals as such. Relativity among things has a peculiar property: it involves reaching out beyond the individual, it subsists only within a plurality, and yet it does not constitute a mere conceptual generalization and abstraction.

Herewith is expressed the profound relation between relativity and society, which is the most immediate demonstration of relativity in regard to the material of humanity: society is the suprasingular structure which is nonetheless not abstract. Through this concept historical life is spared the alternatives of having to run either in mere individuals or in abstract generalities. Society is the generality that has, simultaneously, concrete vitality. From this can be seen the unique meaning which exchange, as the economic realization of the relativity of things, has for society. It lifts the individual thing and its significance for the individual man out of their singularity, not into the sphere of the abstract but into the liveliness of interaction, which is, so to speak, the body of economic value. We may examine an object ever so closely with respect to its self-sufficient properties, but we shall not find its economic value. For this consists exclusively in the *reciprocal relationship* which comes into being among several objects on the basis of these properties, each determining the other and each returning to the other the significance it has received therefrom.

6

CONFLICT

1908

THE SOCIOLOGICAL SIGNIFICANCE of conflict (*Kampf*) has in principle never been disputed. Conflict is admitted to cause or modify interest groups, unifications, organizations. On the other hand, it may sound paradoxical in the common view if one asks whether irrespective of any phenomena that result from conflict or that accompany it, it itself is a form of sociation. At first glance, this sounds like a rhetorical question. If every interaction among men is a sociation, conflict—after all one of the most vivid interactions, which, furthermore, cannot possibly be carried on by one individual alone—must certainly be considered as sociation. And in fact, dissociating factors—hate, envy, need, desire—are the *causes* of conflict; it breaks out because of them. Conflict is thus designed to resolve divergent dualisms; it is a way of achieving some kind of unity, even if it be through the annihilation of one of the conflicting parties. This is roughly parallel to the fact that it is the most violent symptoms of a disease which represent the effort of the organism to free itself of disturbances and damages caused by them.

But this phenomenon means much more than the trivial "si vis pacem para bellum" [if you want peace, prepare for war]; it is something quite general, of which this maxim only describes a spe-

Reprinted from *Conflict and the Web of Group-Affiliations* (Glencoe, Ill.: Free Press, 1955), pp. 13–28, 35–48. Translated by Kurt H. Wolff. Originally published as "Der Streit," in *Soziologie* (Munich and Leipzig: Duncker & Humblot, 1908).

cial case. Conflict itself resolves the tension between contrasts. The fact that it aims at peace is only one, an especially obvious, expression of its nature: the synthesis of elements that work both against and for one another. This nature appears more clearly when it is realized that both forms of relation—the antithetical and the convergent—are fundamentally distinguished from the mere indifference of two or more individuals or groups. Whether it implies the rejection or the termination of sociation, indifference is purely negative. In contrast to such pure negativity, conflict contains something positive. Its positive and negative aspects, however, are integrated; they can be separated conceptually, but not empirically.

The Sociological Relevance of Conflict

Social phenomena appear in a new light when seen from the angle of this sociologically positive character of conflict. It is at once evident then that if the relations among men (rather than what the individual is to himself and in his relations to objects) constitute the subject matter of a special science, sociology, then the traditional topics of that science cover only a subdivision of it: it is more comprehensive and is truly defined by a principle. At one time it appeared as if there were only two consistent subject matters of the science of man: the individual unit and the unit of individuals (society); any third seemed logically excluded. In this conception, conflict itself—irrespective of its contributions to these immediate social units—found no place for study. It was a phenomenon of its own, and its subsumption under the concept of unity would have been arbitrary as well as useless, since conflict meant the negation of unity.

A more comprehensive classification of the science of the relations of men should distinguish, it would appear, those relations which constitute a unit, that is, social relations in the strict sense, from those which counteract unity. It must be realized, however, that both relations can usually be found in every historically real situation. The individual does not attain the unity of his personality exclusively by an exhaustive harmonization, according to logical, objective, religious, or ethical norms, of the contents of his personality. On the contrary, contradiction and conflict not only precede this unity but are operative in it at every moment of its existence. Just so, there probably exists no social unit in which convergent and divergent currents among its members are not inseparably interwoven. An absolutely centripetal and harmonious group, a pure "unification" (*"Vereinigung"*), not only is empirically unreal, it could show no real life process. The society of saints which Dante sees in the Rose of Paradise may be like such a group, but it is without any change and development; whereas the holy assembly of Church Fathers in Raphael's *Disputa* shows if not actual conflict, at least a considerable differentiation of moods and directions of thought, whence flow all the vitality and the really organic structure of that group. Just as the universe needs "love and hate," that is, attractive and repulsive forces, in order to have any form at all, so society, too, in order to attain a determinate shape, needs some quantitative ratio of harmony and disharmony, of association and competition, of favorable and unfavorable tendencies. But these discords are by no means mere sociological liabilities or negative instances. Definite, actual society does not result only from other social forces which are positive, and only to the extent that the negative factors do not hinder them. This common conception is quite superficial. Society, as we know it, is the result of both categories of interaction, which thus both manifest themselves as wholly positive.[1]

[1]   This is the sociological instance of a contrast between two much more general conceptions of life. According to the common view, life always shows two parties in opposition. One of them represents the positive aspect of life, its content proper, if not its substance, while the very meaning of the other is non-being, which must be subtracted from the positive elements before they can constitute life. This is the common view of the relation between happiness and suffering, virtue and vice, strength and inadequacy, success and failure—between all possible contents and interruptions of the course of life. The highest conception indicated in respect to these contrasting pairs appears to me different: we must conceive of all these polar differentiations as of *one* life; we must sense the pulse of a central vitality even in that which, if seen from the standpoint of a particular ideal, ought not to be at all and is merely something negative; we must

Unity and Discord

There is a misunderstanding according to which one of these two kinds of interaction tears down what the other builds up, and what is eventually left standing is the result of the subtraction of the two (while in reality it must rather be designated as the result of their addition). The misunderstanding probably derives from the twofold meaning of the concept of unity. We designate as "unity" the consensus and concord of interacting individuals, as against their discords, separations, and disharmonies. But we also call "unity" the total group-synthesis of persons, energies, and forms, that is, the ultimate wholeness of that group, a wholeness which covers both strictly-speaking unitary relations and dualistic relations. We thus account for the group phenomenon

---

allow the total meaning of our existence to grow out of *both* parties. In the most comprehensive context of life, even that which as a single element is disturbing and destructive, is wholly positive; it is not a gap but the fulfillment of a role reserved for it alone. Perhaps it is not given to us to attain, much less always to maintain, the height from which all phenomena can be felt as making up the unity of life, even though from an objective or value standpoint, they appear to oppose one another as pluses and minuses, contradictions, and mutual eliminations. We are too inclined to think and feel that our essential being, our true, ultimate significance, is identical with one of these factions. According to our optimistic or pessimistic feeling of life, one of them appears to us as surface or accident, as something to be eliminated or subtracted, in order for the true and intrinsically consistent life to emerge. We are everywhere enmeshed in this dualism (which will presently be discussed in more detail in the text above)—in the most intimate as in the most comprehensive provinces of life, personal, objective, and social. We think we have, or are, a whole or unit which is composed of two logically and objectively opposed parties, and we identify this totality of ours with one of them, while we feel the other to be something alien which does not properly belong and which denies our central and comprehensive being. Life constantly moves between these two tendencies. The one has just been described. The other lets the whole really *be* the whole. It makes the unity, which after all comprises both contrasts, alive in each of these contrasts and in their juncture. It is all the more necessary to assert the right of this second tendency in respect to the sociological phenomenon of conflict, because conflict impresses us with its socially destructive force as with an apparently indisputable fact.

which we feel to be "unitary" in terms of functional components considered *specifically* unitary; and in so doing, we disregard the other, larger meaning of the term.

This imprecision is increased by the corresponding twofold meaning of "discord" or "opposition." Since discord unfolds its negative, destructive character between particular individuals, we naïvely conclude that it must have the same effect on the total group. In reality, however, something which is negative and damaging between individuals if it is considered in isolation and as aiming in a particular direction, does not necessarily have the same effect within the total relationship of these individuals. For a very different picture emerges when we view the conflict in conjunction with other interactions not affected by it. The negative and dualistic elements play an entirely positive role in this more comprehensive picture, despite the destruction they may work on particular relations. All this is very obvious in the competition of individuals within an economic unit.

Conflict as an Integrative Force in the Group

Here, among the more complex cases, there are two opposite types. First, we have small groups, such as the marital couple, which nevertheless involve an unlimited number of vital relations among their members. A certain amount of discord, inner divergence and outer controversy, is organically tied up with the very elements that ultimately hold the group together; it cannot be separated from the unity of the sociological structure. This is true not only in cases of evident marital failure but also in marriages characterized by a *modus vivendi* which is bearable or at least borne. Such marriages are not "less" marriages by the amount of conflict they contain; rather, out of so many elements, among which there is that inseparable quantity of conflict, they have developed into the definite and characteristic units which they are. Secondly, the positive and integrating role of antagonism is shown in structures which stand out by the sharpness and carefully preserved purity of their social divisions and gradations. Thus, the Hindu social system rests not only on the hierarchy, but also directly on the mutual repulsion, of the castes. Hostilities not only prevent boundaries within the group from gradually disappearing, so that these hostilities are often consciously cultivated to guarantee existing conditions. Beyond this, they also are of direct sociological fertility: often they provide classes and individuals with reciprocal positions which they would not find, or not find in the same way, if the causes of hostility were not accompanied by the *feeling* and the expression of hostility—even if the same objective causes of hostility were in operation.

The disappearance of repulsive (and, considered in isolation, destructive) energies does by no means always result in a richer and fuller social life (as the disappearance of liabilities results in larger property) but in as different and unrealizable a phenomenon as if the group were deprived of the forces of cooperation, affection, mutual aid, and harmony of interest. This is not only true for competition generally, which determines the form of the group, the reciprocal positions of its participants, and the distances between them, and which does so purely as a formal matrix of tensions, quite irrespective of its objective *results*. It is true also where the group is based on the attitudes of its members. For instance, the opposition of a member to an associate is no purely negative social factor, if only because such opposition is often the only means for making life with actually unbearable people at least possible. If we did not even have the power and the right to rebel against tyranny, arbitrariness, moodiness, tactlessness, we could not bear to have any relation to people from whose characters we thus suffer. We would feel pushed to take desperate steps—and these, indeed, would end the relation but do *not*, perhaps, constitute "conflict." Not only because of the fact (though it is not essential here) that oppression usually increases if it is suffered calmly and without protest, but also because opposition gives us inner satisfaction, distraction, relief, just as do humility and patience under different psychological conditions. Our opposition makes us feel that we are not completely victims of the circumstances. It allows us to prove our strength consciously and only thus gives vitality and reciprocity to conditions from which, without such corrective, we would withdraw at any cost.

Opposition achieves this aim even where it has no noticeable success, where it does not become manifest but remains purely covert. Yet while it has hardly any practical effect, it may yet achieve an inner balance (sometimes even on the part of *both* partners to the relation), may exert a quieting influence, produce a feeling of virtual power, and thus save relationships whose continuation often puzzles the observer. In such cases, opposition is an element in the relation itself; it is intrinsically interwoven with the other reasons for the relation's existence. It is not only a *means* for preserving the relation but one of the concrete functions which actually constitute it. Where relations are purely external and at the same time of little practical significance, this function can be satisfied by conflict in its *latent* form, that is, by aversion and feelings of mutual alienness and repulsion which upon more intimate contact, no matter how occasioned, immediately change into positive hatred and fight.

Without such aversion, we could not imagine what form modern urban life, which every day brings everybody in contact with innumerable others, might possibly take. The whole inner organization of urban interaction is based on an extremely complex hierarchy of sympathies, indifferences, and aversions of both the most short-lived and the most enduring kind. And in this complex, the sphere of indifference is relatively limited. Our psychological activity responds to almost every impression that comes from another person with a certain determinate feeling. The subconscious, fleeting, changeful nature of this feeling only *seems* to reduce it to indifference. Actually, such indifference would be as unnatural to us as the vague character of innumerable contradictory stimuli would be unbearable. We are protected against both of these typical dangers of the city by antipathy, which is the preparatory phase of concrete antagonism and which engenders the distances and aversions without which we could not lead the urban life at all. The extent and combination of antipathy, the rhythm of its appearance and disappearance, the forms in which it is satisfied, all these, along with the more literally unifying elements, produce the metropolitan form of life in its irresolvable totality; and what at first glance appears in it as dissociation, actually is one of its elementary forms of association.

Homogeneity and Heterogeneity in Social Relations

Relations of conflict do not by themselves produce a social structure, but only in cooperation with unifying forces. Only both together constitute the group as a concrete, living unit. In this respect, conflict thus is hardly different from any other form of relation which sociology abstracts out of the complexity of actual life. Neither love nor the division of labor, neither the common attitude of two toward a third nor friendship, neither party affiliation nor superordination or subordination is likely by itself alone to produce or permanently sustain an actual group. Where this seems so nevertheless, the process which is given one name actually contains several distinguishable forms of relation. Human nature does not allow the individual to be tied to another by one thread alone, even though scientific analysis is not satisfied until it has determined the specific cohesive power of elementary units.

Yet perhaps this whole analytic activity is purely subjective in a higher and seemingly inverse sense of the word: perhaps the ties between individuals are indeed often quite homogeneous, but our mind cannot grasp their homogeneity. The very relations that are rich and live on many different contents are apt to make us most aware of this mysterious homogeneity; and what we have to do is represent it as the co-efficiency of several cohesive forces which restrict and modify one another, resulting in the picture which objective reality attains by a much simpler and much more consistent route. Yet we cannot follow it with our mind even though we would.

Processes *within* the individual are, after all, of the same kind. At every moment they are so complex and contain such a multitude of variegated and contradictory oscillations that to designate them by any *one* of our psychological concepts is always imperfect and actually misleading. For the moments of the individual life, too, are never connected by only one thread—this is the picture analytic thought constructs of the unity of the soul, which is inaccessible to it. Probably much of what we are forced to represent to ourselves as mixed feelings, as composites of many drives, as the competition of opposite sensations, is entirely self-consistent.

But the calculating intellect often lacks a paradigm for this unity and thus must construe it as the result of several elements. When we are attracted and at the same time repelled by things; when nobler and baser character traits seem mixed in a given action; when our feeling for a particular person is composed of respect and friendship or of fatherly, motherly, and erotic impulses, or of ethical and aesthetic valuations—then certainly these phenomena in themselves, as real psychological processes, are often homogeneous. Only we cannot designate them directly. For this reason, by means of various analogies, antecedent motives, external consequences, we make them into a concert of several psychological elements.

If this is correct, then apparently complex relations between several individuals, too, must actually often be unitary. For instance, the distance which characterizes the relation between two associated individuals may appear to us as the result of an affection, which ought to bring about much greater closeness between them, and of a repulsion, which ought to drive them completely apart; and in as much as the two feelings restrict one another, the outcome is the distance we observe. But this may be entirely erroneous. The inner disposition of the relation itself may be those particular distances; basically the relation, so to speak, has a certain temperature which does not emerge as the balance of two temperatures, one higher, the other lower. We often interpret the quantity of superiority and suggestion which exists between two persons as produced by the strength of one of them, which is at the same time diminished by a certain weakness. While such strength and weakness may in fact exist, their separateness often does not become manifest in the actually existing relation. On the contrary, the relation may be determined by the total nature of its elements, and we analyze its immediate character into those two factors only by hindsight.

Erotic relations offer the most frequent illustrations. How often do they not strike us as woven together of love and respect, or disrespect; of love and the felt harmony of the individuals and, at the same time, their consciousness of supplementing each other through opposite traits; of love and an urge to dominate or the

need for dependence. But what the observer or the participant himself thus divides into two intermingling trends may in reality be
only one. In the relation as it actually exists, the total personality
of the one acts on that of the other. The reality of the relation does
not depend on the reflection that if it did not exist, its participants
would at least inspire each other with respect or sympathy (or
their contraries). Any number of times we designate such relations as mixed feelings or mixed relations, because we construe
the effects the qualities of one individual would have upon the
other *if* these qualities exerted their influence *in isolation*—which
is precisely what they do *not* do in the relation as it exists. Aside
from all this, the "mixture" of feelings and relations, even where
we are fully entitled to speak of it, always remains a problematic
expression. It uses a dubious symbolism to transfer a process which
is represented spatially into the very different realm of psychological conditions.

This, then, probably is often the situation in respect to the
so-called mixture of converging and diverging currents within a
group. That is, the structure may be *sui generis*, its motivation and
form being wholly self-consistent, and only in order to be able to
describe and understand it, do we put it together, *post factum*,
out of two tendencies, one monistic, the other antagonistic. Or else,
these two do in fact exist, but only, as it were, *before* the relation
itself originated. In the relation itself, they have fused into an
organic unity in which neither makes itself felt with his own, isolated power.

This fact should not lead us to overlook the numerous cases in
which contradictory tendencies really co-exist in separation and
can thus be recognized at any moment in the over-all situation. As
a special form of historical development, relations sometimes
show at an early stage undifferentiated unity of convergent and
divergent forces which separate only later with full distinctness.
At courts in Central Europe we find, up to the thirteenth century,
permanent bodies of noblemen who constitute a kind of council to
the prince and live as his guests; but at the same time, almost like
an estate, they represent nobility and must guard its interests even
against the prince. The interests in common with those of the king

(whose administration these nobles often serve) and the oppositional vigilance of their own rights as an estate exist in these coun-
cils not only separately side by side but in intimate fusion; and it
is most likely that the position was felt as self-consistent, no matter
how incompatible its elements appear to us now. In the England of
that period, the baronial parliament is hardly yet distinguished
from an enlarged royal council. Loyalty and critical or partisan
opposition are still contained in germ-like unity. In general, as
long as the problem is the crystallization of institutions whose task
it is to solve the increasingly complex and intricate problem of the
equilibrium within the group, it often is not clear whether the cooperation of forces for the benefit of the whole takes the form of
opposition, competition, and criticism, or of explicit unity and harmony. There thus exists an initial phase of undifferentiation which,
seen from a later, differentiated phase, appears as logically contradictory, but which is thoroughly in line with the undeveloped stage
of the organization.

Subjective or personal relations often develop in an inverse
manner. For it is usually in early cultural periods that the decisiveness of amity or enmity is relatively great. Halfway, unclear relations between persons—relations which have their roots in a twilight condition of feeling whose outcome might be hatred almost
as easily as love, or whose undifferentiated character is even sometimes betrayed by oscillation between the two—such relations are
more often found in ripe and overripe than in youthful periods.

Antagonism as an Element in Sociation

While antagonism by itself does not produce sociation, it
is a sociological element almost never absent in it. Its role can increase to infinity, that is, to the point of suppressing all convergent
elements. In considering sociological phenomena, we thus find a
hierarchy of relationships. This hierarchy can also be constructed
from the viewpoint of ethical categories, although ethical categories are generally not very suitable points of departure for the
convenient and complete isolation of sociological elements. The
value-feelings with which we accompany the actions of individual

wills fall into certain series. But the relation between these series, on the one hand, and constructs of forms of social relation according to objective-conceptual viewpoints, on the other, is completely fortuitous. Ethics conceived of as a kind of sociology is robbed of its deepest and finest content. This is the behavior of the individual soul in and to itself, which does not enter at all into its external relations: its religious movements, which exclusively serve its own salvation or damnation; its devotion to the objective values of knowledge, beauty, significance, which transcend all connections with other people. The intermingling of harmonious and hostile relations, however, presents a case where the sociological and the ethical series coincide. It begins with A's action for B's benefit, moves on to A's own benefit by means of B without benefiting B but also without damaging him, and finally becomes A's egoistic action at B's cost. In as much as all this is repeated by B, though hardly ever in the same way and in the same proportions, the innumerable mixtures of convergence and divergence in human relations emerge.

To be sure, there are conflicts which seem to exclude all other elements—for instance, between the robber or thug and his victim. If such a fight simply aims at annihilation, it does approach the marginal case of assassination in which the admixture of unifying elements is almost zero. If, however, there is any consideration, any limit to violence, there already exists a socializing factor, even though only as the qualification of violence. Kant said that every war in which the belligerents do not impose some restrictions in the use of possible means upon one another, necessarily, if only for psychological reasons, becomes a war of extermination. For where the parties do not abstain at least from assassination, breach of word, and instigation to treason, they destroy that confidence in the thought of the enemy which alone permits the materialization of a peace treaty following the end of the war. It is almost inevitable that an element of commonness injects itself into the enmity once the stage of open violence yields to any other relationship, even though this new relation may contain a completely undiminished sum of animosity between the two parties. After conquering Italy in the sixth century, the Lombards imposed on the conquered a tribute of one-third on the ground yield, and they did so in such a fashion that every single individual among the conquerors depended upon the tribute paid him by particular individuals among the conquered. In this situation, the conquered's hatred of their oppressors may be as strong as it is during the war itself, if not stronger, and it may be countered no less intensely by the conquerors—either because the hatred against those who hate us is an instinctive protective measure, or because, as is well known, we usually hate those whom we have caused to suffer. Nevertheless, the situation had an element of community. The very circumstance which had engendered the animosity—the enforced participation of the Lombards in the enterprises of the natives—at the same time made for an undeniable convergence of interests. Divergence and harmony became inextricably interwoven, and the content of the animosity actually developed into the germ of future commonness.

This formal type of relationship is most widely realized in the enslavement—instead of the extermination—of the imprisoned enemy. Even though slavery very often represents the extreme of absolute inner hostility, its occasion nevertheless produces a sociological condition and thus, quite frequently, its own attenuation. The sharpening of contrasts may be provoked directly for the sake of its own diminution, and by no means only as a violent measure, in the expectation that the antagonism, once it reaches a certain limit, will end because of exhaustion or the realization of its futility. It may also happen for the reason which sometimes makes monarchies give their own opposition princes as leaders—as did, for instance, Gustavus Vasa. To be sure, opposition is strengthened by this policy; elements which would otherwise stay away from it are brought to it by the new equilibrium; but at the same time, opposition is thus kept within certain limits. In apparently strengthening it on purpose, government actually blunts it by this conciliating measure.

Another borderline case appears to be the fight engendered exclusively by the lust to fight. If the conflict is caused by an object, by the will to have or control something, by rage or revenge, such a desired object or state of affairs makes for conditions which subject the fight to norms or restrictions applying to both warring parties. Moreover, since the fight is centered in a purpose outside itself, it is qualified by the fact that, in principle, every end can be attained by more than one means. The desire for possession or subjugation, even for the annihilation of the enemy, can be satisfied through combinations and events other than fight. Where conflict is merely a means determined by a superior purpose, there is no reason not to restrict or even avoid it, provided it can be replaced by other measures which have the same promise of success. Where, on the other hand, it is exclusively determined by subjective feelings, where there are inner energies which *can* be satisfied only through fight, its substitution by other means is impossible; it is its own purpose and content and hence wholly free from the admixture of other forms of relation. Such a fight for its own sake seems to be suggested by a certain formal hostility drive which sometimes urges itself upon psychological observation. . . .

Antagonistic Games

I really know only a single case in which the fascination of fight and victory itself—elsewhere only an *element* in the antagonisms over particular contents—is the exclusive motivation: this is the antagonistic game (*Kampfspiel*), more precisely, the game which is carried on without any prize for victory (since the prize would lie outside of it). The purely sociological attraction of becoming master over the adversary, of asserting oneself against him, is combined here, in the case of games of skill, with the purely individual enjoyment of the most appropriate and successful movement; and in the case of games of luck, with favor by fate which blesses us with a mystical, harmonious relation to powers beyond the realm of the individual and social. At any rate, in its *sociological motivation*, the antagonistic game contains absolutely nothing except fight itself. The worthless chip which is often contested as passionately as is a gold piece suggests the formal nature of this impulse, which even in the quarrel over gold often greatly exceeds any material interest.

But there is something else most remarkable: the realization of precisely this complete dualism presupposes sociological forms in the stricter sense of the word, namely, unification. One *unites* in order to fight, and one fights under the mutually recognized control of norms and rules. To repeat, these unifications do not enter into the *motivation* of the undertaking, even though it is through them that it takes shape. They rather are the technique without which such a conflict that excludes all heterogeneous or objective justifications could not materialize. What is more, the norms of the antagonistic game often are rigorous and impersonal and are observed on both sides with the severity of a code of honor —to an extent hardly shown by groups which are formed for co-operative purposes.

Legal Conflict

The principles of conflict and of unification, which holds the contrasts together in one whole, are shown in this example with the purity of almost an abstract concept. It thus reveals how each principle attains its full sociological meaning and effect only through the other. The same form which dominates the antagonistic game also governs legal conflict, even though not with the same neatness and separateness of the two factors involved. For legal conflict has an *object*, and the struggle can be satisfactorily terminated through the voluntary concession of that object. This does not occur in fights for the lust of fighting. In most cases, what is called the lust and passion of legal quarrels is probably something quite different, namely, a strong feeling of justice or the impossibility of bearing an actual or alleged interference with the sphere of law with which the ego feels identified. All the uncompromising stubbornness and obstinacy with which parties at a trial so often bleed themselves to death has, even on the defendant's part, hardly the character of an offensive but, in a deeper sense, that of a defensive, since the question is the self-preservation of the person. This self-preservation is so inseparable from the person's possessions and rights that any inroad on them destroys it. It is only consistent to fight with the power of one's whole existence. Hence it probably is this individualistic drive, rather than the sociological drive to fight, which determines such cases.

In respect to the *form* of conflict, however, legal quarrel is indeed absolute. That is, on both sides the claims are put through with pure objectivity and with all means that are permitted; the conflict is not deflected or attenuated by any personal or in any other sense extraneous circumstances. Legal conflict is pure conflict in as much as nothing enters its whole action which does not belong to the conflict *as such* and serves its purpose. Elsewhere, even in the wildest struggles, something subjective, or some mere turn of fate, or some interference by a third party is at least possible. In legal conflict, all this is excluded by the objectivity with which only the fight and absolutely nothing else proceeds.

This elimination of all that is not conflict can of course lead to a formalism which becomes independent of all contents. On the one hand, we here have legal pettifoggery. In legal pettifoggery, it is not objective points which are weighed against one another; instead, concepts lead an entirely abstract fight. On the other hand, the conflict is sometimes delegated to agents which have no relation to what their contest is to decide. The fact that in higher cultures legal quarrels are carried out by professional counsels certainly serves the clean separation of the controversy from all personal associations which have nothing to do with it. But if Otto the Great decrees that a legal question must be decided through ordeal by combat, only the mere form—the occurrence of fighting and winning itself—is salvaged from the whole conflict of interests; only the form is the element common to the fight to be decided and to the individuals who decide it.

This case expresses in exaggeration or caricature the reduction and restriction of legal conflict to the mere element of fight itself. It is the most merciless type of contestation because it lies wholly outside the subjective contrast between charity and cruelty. But precisely because of its pure objectivity, it is grounded entirely in the premise of the unity and commonness of the parties—and this to a degree of severity and thoroughness hardly required by any other situation. Legal conflict rests on a broad basis of unities and agreements between the enemies. The reason is that both parties are equally subordinated to the law; they mutually recognize that the decision is to be made only according to the objective weight of their claims; they observe the forms which are unbreakably valid for both; and they are conscious that they are surrounded in their whole enterprise by a social power which alone gives meaning and certainty to their undertaking. The parties to a negotiation or a commercial affair form a unity in the same manner, even though to a less extent, for they recognize norms binding and obligatory to both, irrespective of the opposition of their interests. The *common* premises which exclude everything personal from legal conflict have that character of pure objectivity to which (on the other hand) correspond the inexorability and the acute and unconditional character of the conflict itself. Legal conflict thus shows the interaction between the dualism and the unity of sociological relations no less than antagonistic games do. The extreme and unconditional nature of conflict comes to the fore in the very medium and on the very basis of the strict unity of common norms and conditions.

Conflicts over Causes

This same phenomenon is characteristic, finally, of all conflicts in which both parties have objective interests. In this case, the conflicting interests, and hence the conflict itself, are differentiated from the personalities involved. Here two things are possible. The conflict may focus on purely objective decisions and leave all personal elements outside itself and in a state of peace. Or on the contrary, it may involve precisely the persons in their subjective aspects without, however, thereby leading to any alteration or disharmony of the co-existing objective interests common to the two parties. The second type is characterized by Leibnitz's saying that he would run even after a deadly enemy if he could learn something from him. Such an attitude can obviously soften and attenuate the hostility itself; but its possible opposite result must also be noted. Hostility which goes along with solidarity and understanding in objective matters is indeed, so to speak, clean and certain in its justification. The consciousness of such a differentiation assures us that we do not harbor personal antipathy where it does not belong. But the good conscience bought with this discrimination may under certain circumstances lead to the very intensification of hostility. For where hostility is thus restricted to its real center, which at the same time is the most subjective layer of personality, we sometimes abandon ourselves to it more extensively, passionately, and with more concentration than when the hostile impulse carries with it a ballast of secondary animosities in areas which actually are merely infected by that center.

In the case in which the same differentiation inversely limits the conflict to impersonal interests, there too are two possibilities. On the one hand, there may be the elimination of useless embitterments and intensifications which are the price we pay for personalizing objective controversies. On the other hand, however, the parties' consciousness of being mere representatives of supra-individual claims, of fighting not for themselves but only for a cause, can give the conflict a radicalism and mercilessness which find their analogy in the general behavior of certain very selfless and very idealistically inclined persons. Because they have no consideration for themselves, they have none for others either; they are convinced that they are entitled to make anybody a victim of the idea for which they sacrifice themselves. Such a conflict which is fought out with the strength of the whole person while the victory benefits the cause alone has a noble character; for the noble individual is wholly personal but knows nevertheless how to hold his personality in reserve. This is why objectivity strikes us as noble. But once this differentiation has been achieved and the conflict thus objectified, it is, quite consistently, not subjected to a second restriction, which in fact would be a violation of the objective interest to which the fight has been limited. On the basis of this mutual agreement of the two parties, according to which each of them defends only his claims and his cause, renouncing all personal or egoistic considerations, the conflict is fought with unattenuated sharpness, following its own intrinsic logic, and being neither intensified nor moderated by subjective factors.

The contrast between unity and antagonism is perhaps most visible where both parties really pursue an identical aim—such as the exploration of a scientific truth. Here any yielding, any polite renunciation of the merciless exposure of the adversary, any peace prior to the wholly decisive victory would be treason against that objectivity for the sake of which the personal character has been eliminated from the fight. Ever since Marx, the social struggle has developed into this form, despite infinite differences in other respects. Since it has been recognized that the condition of labor is determined by the objective conditions and forms of production, irrespective of the desires and capacities of particular individuals, the personal bitterness of both general and local battles has greatly decreased. The entrepreneur is no longer a bloodsucker and damnable egoist, nor does the worker suffer from sinful greediness under all circumstances. Both parties have at least begun no longer to burden each other's consciences with their mutual demands and tactics as acts of personal meanness. In Germany, this objectification was started more nearly by means of theory, in as much as the personal and individualistic nature of antagonism was overcome by the more abstract and general character of the historical and class movement. In England, it was launched by the trade unions and was furthered by the rigorously supra-individual unity of their actions and those of the corresponding federations of entrepreneurs. The violence of the fight, however, has not decreased for that. On the contrary, it has become more pointed, concentrated, and at the same time more comprehensive, owing to the consciousness of the individual involved that he fights not only for himself, and often not for himself at all, but for a great superpersonal aim.

An interesting example of this correlation is the workers' boycott of the Berlin breweries in 1894. This was one of the most violent local fights in recent decades, carried out with the utmost force by both sides, but without any personal hatred of the brewers by the leaders of the boycott, or of the workers by the business leaders. In fact, in the middle of the fight, two leaders of the two parties published their opinions of the struggle in the same periodical, both being objective in their presentations of the facts and hence agreeing on them, but differing, in line with their respective parties, on the practical consequences that were to be drawn from the facts. It thus appears that conflict can exclude all subjective or personal factors, thus quantitatively reducing hostility, engendering mutual respect, and producing understanding on all personal matters, as well as the recognition of the fact that both parties are driven on by historical necessities. At the same time, we see that this common basis increases, rather than decreases, the intensity, irreconcilability, and stubborn consistency of the fight.

The objective common to the conflicting parties, on which alone their fight is based, can show itself in a much less noble manner than in the cases just discussed. This is true when the common feature is not an objective norm, an interest that lies above the egoism of the fighting parties, but their secret understanding in respect to an egoistic purpose which they both share. To a certain extent this was true of the two great English political parties in the eighteenth century. There was no basic opposition of political convictions between them, since the problem of both equally was the maintenance of the aristocratic regime. The strange fact was that two parties, which between themselves completely dominated the area of political struggle, nevertheless did not fight each other radically—because they had a silent mutual pact against something which was not a political party at all. Historians have connected the parliamentary corruptibility of that period with this strange limitation of the fight. Nobody thought too badly of a party's selling its conviction in favor of the opposing party because the conviction of that opposing party had a rather broad, even though hidden common basis, and the fight lay elsewhere. The ease of corruption showed that here the restriction of the antagonism through a common feature did not make the conflict more fundamental and objective. On the contrary, it blurred it and contaminated its meaning as necessarily determined by objective circumstances.

In other, purer cases, when unity is the point of departure and the basis of the relationship, and conflict arises over this unity, the synthesis between the monism and antagonism of the relation can have the opposite result. A conflict of this sort is usually more passionate and radical than when it does not meet with a prior or simultaneous mutual belongingness to the parties. While ancient Jewish law permitted bigamy, it forbade marriage with two sisters (even though after the death of one her husband could marry the other), for this would have been especially apt to arouse

jealousy. In other words, this law simply assumes as a fact of experience that antagonism on the basis of a common kinship tie is
stronger than among strangers. The mutual hatred of very small
neighboring states whose whole outlooks, local relations, and interests are inevitably very similar and frequently even coincide,
often is much more passionate and irreconcilable than between
great nations, which both spatially and objectively are complete
strangers to one another. This was the fate of Greece and of post-
Roman Italy, and a more intensive degree of it shook England
after the Norman Conquest before the two races fused. These two
lived scattered among one another in the same territory, were mutually bound by constantly operating vital interests, and were held
together by one national idea—and yet intimately, they were complete mutual strangers, were, in line with their whole character,
without reciprocal understanding, and were absolutely hostile to
one another in regard to their power interests. Their reciprocal
hatred, as has rightly been said, was more bitter than it can ever
be between externally and internally separate groups.

Some of the strongest examples of such hatred are church relations. Because of dogmatic fixation, the minutest divergence here
at once comes to have logical irreconcilability—if there is deviation at all, it is conceptually irrelevant whether it be large or small.
A case in point are the confessional controversies between Luth-
erans and Reformed, especially in the seventeenth century. Hardly
had the great separation from Catholicism occurred, when the
whole, over the most trivial matters, split into parties which frequently said about one another that one could more easily make
peace with the Popists than with the members of the other Protestant groups. And in 1875 in Berne, when there was some difficulty
over the place where Catholic services were to be held, the Pope did
not allow them to be performed in the church used by the Old-
Catholics, but in a Reformed church.

Common Qualities vs. Common Membership in a Larger Social Structure as Bases of Conflict

Two kinds of commonality may be the bases of particularly intense antagonisms: common qualities, and common mem-

bership in a larger social structure. The first case goes back simply to the fact that we are discriminating beings (*Unterschiedswesen*). A hostility must excite consciousness the more deeply and violently, the greater the parties' similarity against the background of which the hostility rises. Where attitudes are friendly or loving, this is an excellent protective measure of the group, comparable to the warning function of pain in the organism. For it is precisely the keen awareness of dissonance against the prevailing general harmony which at once warns the parties to remove the grounds of conflict lest conflict half-consciously creep on and endanger the basis of the relation itself. But where this fundamental intention to get along under all circumstances is lacking, the consciousness of antagonism, sensitized as this consciousness is by similarity in other respects, will sharpen the antagonism itself. People who have many common features often do one another worse or "wronger" wrong than complete strangers do. Sometimes they do this because the large area common to them has become a matter of course, and hence what is temporarily different, rather than what is common, determines their mutual position. Mainly, however, they do it because there is only little that is different between them; hence even the slightest antagonism has a relative significance quite other than that between strangers, who count with all kinds of mutual differences to begin with. Hence the family conflicts over which people profoundly in agreement sometimes break up. That they do so does by no means always prove that the harmonizing forces had weakened before. On the contrary, the break can result from so great a similarity of characteristics, leanings, and convictions that the divergence over a very insignificant point makes itself felt in its sharp contrast as something utterly unbearable.

We confront the stranger, with whom we share neither characteristics nor broader interests, objectively; we hold our personalities in reserve; and thus a particular difference does not involve us in our totalities. On the other hand, we meet the person who is very different from us only on certain points within a particular contact or within a coincidence of particular interests, and hence the spread of the conflict is limited to those points only. The more we have in common with another *as whole persons*, however, the more easily will our totality be involved in every single relation to him. Hence the wholly disproportionate violence to which normally well-controlled people can be moved within their relations to those closest to them. The whole happiness and depth of the relation to another person with whom, so to speak, we feel identical, lies in the fact that not a single contact, not a single word, not a single common activity or pain remains isolated but always clothes the whole soul which completely gives itself in it and is received in it. Therefore, if a quarrel arises between persons in such an intimate relationship, it is often so passionately expansive and suggests the schema of the fatal "Not you" (*"Du-überhaupt"*). Persons tied to one another in this fashion are too accustomed to investing every aspect of their relationship with the totality of their being and feeling not to endow conflict with accents and, as it were, a periph ery by virtue of which it far outgrows its occasion and the objective significance of that occasion, and drags the total personalities into it.

Conflict in Intimate Relations

At the highest level of spiritual cultivation it is possible to avoid this, for it is characteristic of this level to combine complete mutual devotion with complete mutual differentiation. Whereas undifferentiated passion involves the totality of the individual in the excitement of a part or an element of it, the cultivated person allows no such part or element to transcend its proper, clearly circumscribed domain. Cultivation thus gives relations between harmonious persons the advantage that they become aware, precisely on the occasion of conflict, of its trifling nature in compari son with the magnitude of the forces that unify them.

Furthermore, the refined discriminatory sense, especially of deeply sensitive persons, makes attractions and antipathies more passionate if these feelings contrast with those of the past. This is true in the case of unique, irrevocable decisions concerning a given relationship, and it must be sharply distinguished from the every day vacillations within a mutual belongingness which is felt, on the whole, to be unquestionable. Sometimes between men and women a fundamental aversion, even a feeling of hatred—not in regard to certain particulars, but the reciprocal repulsion of the total person —is the first stage of a relation whose second phase is passionate love. One might entertain the paradoxical suspicion that when individuals are destined to the closest mutual emotional relationship, the emergence of the intimate phase is guided by an instinctive pragmatism so that the eventual feeling attains its most passionate intensification and awareness of what it has achieved by means of an opposite prelude—a step back before running, as it were.

The inverse phenomenon shows the same form: the deepest hatred grows out of broken love. Here, however, not only the sense of discrimination is probably decisive but also the denial of one's own past—a denial involved in such change of feeling. To have to recognize that a deep love—and not only a sexual love—was an error, a failure of intuition (*Instinkt*), so compromises us before ourselves, so splits the security and unity of our self-conception, that we unavoidably make the object of this intolerable feeling pay for it. We cover our secret awareness of our own responsibility for it by hatred which makes it easy for us to pass all responsibility on to the other.

This particular bitterness which characterizes conflicts within relationships whose nature would seem to entail harmony is a sort of positive intensification of the platitude that relations show their closeness and strength in the absence of differences. But this platitude is by no means true without exception. That very intimate groups, such as marital couples, which dominate, or at least touch on, the whole content of life, should contain no occasions for conflict is quite out of the question. It is by no means the sign of the most genuine and deep affection never to yield to those occasions but instead to prevent them in far-ranging anticipation and to cut them short immediately by mutual yielding. On the contrary, this behavior often characterizes attitudes which though affectionate, moral, and loyal, nevertheless lack the ultimate, unconditional emotional devotion. Conscious of this lack, the individual is all the more anxious to keep the relation free from any shadow and to compensate his partner for that lack through the utmost friendliness, self-control, and consideration. But another function of this behavior is to soothe one's own consciousness in regard to its more or less evident untruthfulness which even the most sincere or even the most passionate will cannot change into truthfulness— because feelings are involved which are not accessible to the will but, like fate itself, exist or do not exist.

The felt insecurity concerning the basis of such relations often moves us, who desire to maintain the relation at all cost, to acts of exaggerated selflessness, to the almost mechanical insurance of the relationship through the avoidance, on principle, of every possibility of conflict. Where on the other hand we are certain of the irrevocability and unreservedness of our feeling, such peace at any price is not necessary. We know that no crisis can penetrate to the foundation of the relationship—we can always find the other again on this foundation. The strongest love can stand a blow most easily, and hence it does not even occur to it, as is characteristic of a weaker one, to fear that the consequences of such a blow cannot be faced, and it must therefore be avoided by all means. Thus, although conflict among intimates can have more tragic results than among less intimate persons, in the light of the circumstances discussed, precisely the most firmly grounded relation may take a chance at discord, whereas good and moral but less deeply rooted relationships apparently follow a much more harmonious and conflictless course.

This sociological sense of discrimination and the accentuation of conflict on the basis of similarity have a special nuance in cases where the separation of originally homogeneous elements occurs on purpose. Here separation does not follow from conflict but, on the contrary, conflict from separation. Typical of this is the way the renegade hates and is hated. The recall of earlier agreement has such a strong effect that the new contrast is infinitely sharper and bitterer than if no relation at all had existed in the past. Moreover often both parties realize the difference between the new phase and the similarity remembered (and the unambiguousness of this difference is of the greatest importance to them) only by allowing it to grow far beyond its original locus and to characterize every point which is at all comparable. This aim of securing the two respective positions transforms theoretical or religious defection into the reciprocal charge of heresy in respect to all moral, personal, internal and external matters—a charge not necessarily ensuing where the same difference occurs between strangers. In fact, the degeneration of a difference in *convictions* into hatred and fight ordinarily occurs only when there were essential, original similarities between the parties. The (sociologically very significant) "respect for the enemy" is usually absent where the hostility has arisen on the basis of previous solidarity. And where enough similarities continue to make confusions and blurred borderlines possible, points of difference need an emphasis not justified by the issue but only by that danger of confusion. This was involved, for instance, in the case of Catholicism in Berne, mentioned earlier. Roman Catholicism does not have to fear any threat to its identity from external contact with a church so different as the Reformed Church, but quite from something as closely akin as Old-Catholicism.

7

DOMINATION

1908

Domination, a Form of Interaction

NOBODY, IN GENERAL, wishes that his influence completely determine the other individual. He rather wants his influence, this determination of the other, to act back upon *him*. Even the abstract will-to-dominate, therefore, is a case of interaction. This will draws its satisfaction from the fact that the acting or suffering of the other, his positive or negative condition, offers itself to the dominator as the product of *his* will. The significance of this solipsistic exercise of domination (so to speak) consists, for the superordinate himself, exclusively in the consciousness of his efficacy. Sociologically speaking, it is only a rudimentary form. By virtue of it alone, sociation occurs as little as it does between a sculptor and his statue, although the statue, too, acts back on the artist through his consciousness of his own creative power. The practical function of this desire for domination, even in this sublimated form, is not so much the exploitation of the other as the mere consciousness of this possibility. For the rest, it does not represent the extreme case of egoistic inconsiderateness. Certainly, the desire for domination is designed to break the *internal* resistance of the subjugated (whereas egoism usually aims only at the victory over his *external* resistance). But still, even the desire for domination has some interest in the other person, who constitutes

Reprinted from "Superordination and Subordination," in *The Sociology of Georg Simmel* (Glencoe, Ill.: Free Press, 1950). Translated by Kurt H. Wolff. Originally published as "Uber- und Unterordnung," in *Soziologie* (Munich and Leipzig: Duncker & Humblot, 1908).

a value for it. Only when egoism does not even amount to a desire for domination; only when the other is absolutely indifferent and a mere means for purposes which lie beyond him, is the last shadow of any sociating process removed.

The definition of later Roman jurists shows, in a relative way, that the elimination of all independent significance of one of the two interacting parties annuls the very notion of society. This definition was to the effect that the *societas leonina*[1] must not be conceived of as a social contract. A comparable statement has been made regarding the lowest-paid workers in modern giant enterprises which preclude all effective competition among rivaling entrepreneurs for the services of these laborers. It has been said that the difference in the strategic positions of workers and employers is so overwhelming that the work contract ceases to be a "contract" in the ordinary sense of the word, because the former are unconditionally at the mercy of the latter. It thus appears that the moral maxim never to use a man as a mere means is actually the formula of every sociation. Where the significance of the one party sinks so low that its effect no longer enters the relationship with the other, there is as little ground for speaking of sociation as there is in the case of the carpenter and his bench.

Within a relationship of subordination, the exclusion of all spontaneity whatever is actually rarer than is suggested by such widely used popular expressions as "coercion," "having no choice," "absolute necessity," etc. Even in the most oppressive and cruel cases of subordination, there is still a considerable measure of personal freedom. We merely do not become aware of it, because its manifestation would entail sacrifices which we usually never think of taking upon ourselves. Actually, the "absolute" coercion which even the most cruel tyrant imposes upon us is always distinctly relative. Its condition is our desire to escape from the threatened punishment or from other consequences of our disobedience. More precise analysis shows that the super-subordination relationship destroys the subordinate's freedom only in the

[1]   "Sociation with a lion," that is, a partnership in which all the advantage is on one side.—TR.

case of direct physical violation. In every other case, this relationship only demands a price for the realization of freedom—a price, to be sure, which we are not willing to pay. It can narrow down more and more the sphere of external conditions under which freedom is clearly realized, but, except for physical force, never to the point of the complete disappearance of freedom. The moral side of this analysis does not concern us here, but only its sociological aspect. This aspect consists in the fact that interaction, that is, action which is mutually determined, action which stems exclusively from personal origins, prevails even where it often is not noted. It exists even in those cases of superordination and subordination—and therefore makes even those cases *societal* forms—where according to popular notions the "coercion" by one party deprives the other of every spontaneity, and thus of every real "effect," or contribution to the process of interaction.

Authority and Prestige

Relationships of superordination and subordination play an immense role in social life. It is therefore of the utmost importance for its analysis to clarify the spontaneity and co-efficiency of the subordinate subject and thus to correct their widespread minimization by superficial notions about them. For instance, what is called "authority" presupposes, in a much higher degree than is usually recognized, a freedom on the part of the person subjected to authority. Even where authority seems to "crush" him, it is based not *only* on coercion or compulsion to yield to it.

The peculiar structure of "authority" is significant for social life in the most varied ways; it shows itself in beginnings as well as in exaggerations, in acute as well as in lasting forms. It seems to come about in two different ways. A person of superior significance or strength may acquire, in his more immediate or remote milieu, an overwhelming weight of his opinions, a faith, or a confidence which have the character of objectivity. He thus enjoys a prerogative and an axiomatic trustworthiness in his decisions which excel, at least by a fraction, the value of mere subjective personality, which is always variable, relative, and subject to criticism. By acting "authoritatively," the quantity of his significance is transformed into a new quality; it assumes for his environment the physical state—metaphorically speaking—of objectivity.

But the same result, authority, may be attained in the opposite direction. A super-individual power—state, church, school, family or military organizations—clothes a person with a reputation, a dignity, a power of ultimate decision, which would never flow from his individuality. It is the nature of an authoritative person to make decisions with a certainty and automatic recognition which logically pertain only to impersonal, objective axioms and deductions. In the case under discussion, authority descends upon a person from above, as it were, whereas in the case treated before, it arises from the qualities of the person himself, through a *generatio aequivoca.*[2] But evidently, at this point of transition and change-over [from the personal to the authoritative situation], the more or less voluntary faith of the party subjected to authority comes into play. This transformation of the value of personality into a super-personal value gives the personality something which is beyond its demonstrable and rational share, however slight this addition may be. The believer in authority himself achieves the transformation. He (the subordinate element) participates in a sociological event which requires his spontaneous cooperation. As a matter of fact, the very feeling of the "oppressiveness" of authority suggests that the autonomy of the subordinate party is actually presupposed and never wholly eliminated.

Another nuance of superiority, which is designated as "prestige," must be distinguished from "authority." Prestige lacks the element of super-subjective significance; it lacks the identity of the personality with an objective power or norm. Leadership by means of prestige is determined entirely by the strength of the individual. This individual force always remains conscious of itself. Moreover, whereas the average type of leadership always shows a certain mixture of personal and superadded-objective factors, prestige leadership stems from pure personality, even as authority stems from the objectivity of norms and forces. Superiority through prestige con-

2   "Equivocal birth" or "spontaneous generation."—Tr.

sists in the ability to "push" individuals and masses and to make unconditional followers of them. Authority does not have this ability to the same extent. The higher, cooler, and normative character of authority is more apt to leave room for criticism, even on the part of its followers. In spite of this, however, prestige strikes us as the more voluntary homage to the superior person. Actually, perhaps, the recognition of authority implies a more profound freedom of the subject than does the enchantment that emanates from the prestige of a prince, a priest, a military or spiritual leader. But the matter is different in regard to the *feeling* on the part of those led. In the face of authority, we are often defenseless, whereas the *élan* with which we follow a given prestige always contains a consciousness of spontaneity. Here, precisely because devotion is only to the wholly personal, this devotion seems to flow only from the ground of personality with its inalienable freedom. Certainly, man is mistaken innumerable times regarding the measure of freedom which he must invest in a certain action. One reason for this is the vagueness and uncertainty of the explicit conception by means of which we account for this inner process. But in whatever way we interpret freedom, we can say that some measure of it, even though it may not be the measure we suppose, is present wherever there is the feeling and the conviction of freedom.[3] ...

Subordination under an Individual

The kinds of superordination may be divided according to a three-fold scheme. This is superficial, but convenient for our discussion. Superordination may be exerted by an individual, by a

[3] Here—and analogously in many other cases—the point is not to define the concept of prestige but only to ascertain the existence of a certain variety of human interactions, quite irrespective of their designation. The presentation, however, often begins appropriately with the concept which linguistic usage makes relatively most suitable for the discovery of the relationship, because it suggests it. This sounds like a merely definitory procedure. Actually, however, the attempt is never to find the content of a concept, but to describe, rather, an actual content, which only occasionally has the chance of being covered, more or less, by an already existing concept.

group, or by an objective force—social or ideal. I shall now discuss some of the sociological implications of these possibilities.

The subordination of a group under a single person results,
above all, in a very decisive unification of the group. This unification is almost equally evident in both of two characteristic forms
of this subordination. First, the group forms an actual, inner unit
together with its head; the ruler leads the group forces in their
own direction, promoting and fusing them; superordination, therefore, here really means only that the will of the group has found a
unitary expression or body. Secondly, the group feels itself in opposition to its head and forms a party against him.

In regard to the first form, every sociological consideration
immediately shows the immeasurable advantage which one-man
rule has for the fusion and energy-saving guidance of the group
forces. I will cite only two instances of common subordination to
one element. These cases are very heterogeneous as far as their
contents are concerned, but nevertheless show how irreplaceable
this subordination is for the unity of the whole. The sociology
of religion must make a basic distinction between two types of
religious organization. There may be the unification of group
members which lets the common god grow, as it were, out of this
togetherness itself, as the symbol and the sanctification of their
belonging together. This is true in many primitive religions. On
the other hand, only the conception of the god itself may bring the
members together into a unit—members who before had no, or
only slight, relations with one another. How well Christianity exemplifies this second type need not be described, nor is it necessary
to emphasize how particular Christian sects find their specific and
especially strong cohesion in the absolutely subjective and mystical
relation to the person of Jesus, a relation which each member
possesses as an individual, and thus quite independently of every
other member and of the total group. But even of the Jews it has
been asserted that they feel the contractual relation to Jehovah
which they hold in common, that is, which directly concerns every
one of them, as the real power and significance of membership in
the Jewish nation.

By contrast, in other religions which originated at the same time as Judaism, it was kinship that connected each member with every other, and only later, all of them with the divine principle. On the basis of its widely ramified personal dependencies and "services," medieval feudalism had frequent occasion to exemplify this same formal structure. It is perhaps most characteristically shown in the associations of the "ministers" (unfree court servants and house servants) who stood in a close, purely personal relation to the prince. Their association had no objective basis whatever, such as the village communities under bondage had by virtue of the nearby manor. The "ministers" were employed in highly varied services and had their residences in different localities, but nevertheless formed tightly closed associations which nobody could enter or leave without their authorization. They developed their own family and property laws; they had freedom of contract and of social intercourse among one another, and they imposed the expiation of breach of peace within their group. But they had no other basis for this close unit than the identity of the ruler whom they served, who represented them to the outside, and who was their legal agent in matters involving the law of the land. Here, as in the case of religion mentioned before, the subordination under an individual power is not the consequence or expression of an already existing organic or interest group (as it is in many, especially political, cases). On the contrary, the superordination of one ruler is the *cause* of a commonness which in the absence of it could not be attained and which is not predetermined by any other relation among its members.

It should be noted that not only the equal, but often precisely the unequal, relation of the subordinates to the dominating head gives solidity to the social form characterized by subordination under one individual. The varying distance or closeness to the leader creates a differentiation which is not less firm and articulate because the internal aspect of these relations to him often is jealousy, repulsion, or haughtiness. The social level of the individual Indian caste is determined by its relation to the Brahman. The decisive questions: Would the Brahman accept a gift from one of their members? Would he accept a glass of water from his hand without reluctance? Or with difficulty? Or would he reject it with abhorrence? That the peculiar firmness of caste stratification depends on such questions is characteristic of the form under discussion for the reason that the mere fact of a highest point determines, as a purely ideal factor, the structural position of every element, and thus the structure of the whole. That this highest layer should be occupied by a great many individuals is quite irrelevant, since the sociological form of the effect is here exactly like that of an individual: the relation to the "Brahman" is decisive. In other words, the formal characteristic of subordination under an individual *may* prevail even where there is a plurality of superordinate individuals. The *specific* sociological significance of such a plurality will be shown later, in connection with other phenomena.

UNIFICATION OF A GROUP IN OPPOSITION TO THE RULER   The unificatory consequence of subordination under one ruling power operates even when the group is in opposition to this power. The political group, the factory, the school class, the church congregation—all indicate how the culmination of an organization in a head helps to effect the unity of the whole in the case of either harmony or discord. Discord, in fact, perhaps even more stringently than harmony, forces the group to "pull itself together." In general, common enmity is one of the most powerful means for motivating a number of individuals or groups to cling together. This common enmity is intensified if the common adversary is at the same time the common ruler. In a latent, certainly not in an overt and effective, form, this combination probably occurs everywhere: in some measure, in some respect, the ruler is almost always an adversary. Man has an intimate dual relation to the principle of subordination. On the one hand, he wants to be dominated. The majority of men not only *cannot* exist without leadership; they also *feel* that they cannot: they *seek* the higher power which relieves them of responsibility; they seek a restrictive, regulatory rigor which protects them not only against the outside world but also against themselves. But no less do they need opposition to the leading power, which only through this opposition, through move and countermove, as it were, attains the right place in the life pattern of those who obey it.

One might even say that obedience and opposition are merely two sides or links of one human attitude which fundamentally is quite consistent. They are two sides that are oriented in different directions and only *seem* to be autonomous impulses. The simplest illustration here is from the field of politics. No matter of how many divergent and conflicting parties a nation may be composed, it nevertheless has a common interest in keeping the powers of the crown within limits or in restricting them—in spite of all the practical irreplaceability of the crown and even in spite of all sentimental attachment to it. For hundreds of years following the Magna Charta, there was a lively awareness in England that certain fundamental rights had to be preserved and increased for *all* classes; that nobility could not maintain its freedoms without the freedoms of the weaker classes being maintained at the same time; and that only the law which applied to nobility, burgher, and peasant alike represented a limitation of the personal reign. It has often been remarked that as long as this ultimate goal of the struggle—the restrictions upon monarchy—is endangered, nobility always has people and clergy on its side. And even where one-man rule does not engender this sort of unification, at least it creates a common arena for the fight of its subordinates—between those who are *for* the ruler and those who are *against* him. There is hardly a sociological structure, subject to a supreme head, in which this pro and con does not occasion a vitality of interactions and ramifications among the elements that in terms of an eventual unification is greatly superior to many peaceful but indifferent aggregates—in spite of all repulsions, frictions, and costs of the fight.

DISSOCIATING EFFECTS OF SUBORDINATION UNDER AN INDIVIDUAL   The present discussion is not concerned with constructing dogmatically one-sided series but with presenting basic processes whose infinitely varying extents and combinations often cause their superficial manifestations to contradict one another. It must therefore be emphasized that the common submission to a ruling power by no means always leads to unification but, if the submission occurs under certain conditions, to the very opposite of it. For instance, English legislation directed a number of measures and exclusions concerning military service, the right to vote, ownership, and government positions, against non-Conformists, that is, against Presbyterians, Catholics, and Jews alike. The member of the state church thus used his prerogative to give equal expression to his hatred of all these groups. But this did not fuse the oppressed into a community of any sort; on the contrary, the hatred of the Conformist was even surpassed by the Presbyterian's hatred of the Catholic, and of the Catholic's of the Presbyterian.

Here we seem to deal with a psychological "threshold phenomenon." There is a measure of enmity between social elements which becomes ineffectual if they experience a common pressure: it then yields to external, if not internal, unification. But if the original aversion surpasses a certain limit, a common oppression has the opposite effect. This has two reasons. The first is that once there is a dominating resentment in a certain direction, any irritation, no matter from what source it may come, only intensifies the *general* irritation and, contrary to all rational expectation, flows into the already existing river bed and thereby enlarges it. The second, even more important reason is that common suffering, though pressing the suffering elements closer together, reveals all the more strikingly their inner distance and irreconcilability, precisely by virtue of this enforced intimacy. Where unification, however it be created, cannot overcome a given antagonism, it does not preserve this antagonism at its former stage, but intensifies it. In all fields, contrast becomes sharper and more conscious in the measure in which the parties concerned come closer together.

Another, more obvious kind of repulsion among the subjects of a common ruler is created by means of jealousy. It constitutes the negative counterpart of the phenomenon mentioned before, namely, that common hatred is all the more powerful a bond if the object of the common hatred is at the same time the common ruler. We now add that a love shared by a number of elements makes them, by means of jealousy, all the more decisively into mutual enemies if the common loved one is also the common ruler. A student of Turkish conditions reports that the children of different mothers in a harem are always hostile to one another. The reason for this is the jealousy with which their mothers observe the father's manifestations of love for his children who are not their own. Jealousy takes on a particular nuance as soon as it refers to the power which is superordinate to both parties. Under this condition, the woman winning the love of the disputed person triumphs over the rival in a special sense, and has a special success of her power. The subtlety of the fascination consists in the fact that she becomes master over the rival inasmuch as she becomes master over the rival's master. By means of the reciprocity within which the commonness of the master allows this fascination to develop, it must lead to the highest intensification of jealousy.

THE "HIGHER TRIBUNAL" I leave these dissociating consequences of subordination under an individual power in order to return to its unifying functions. I will only note how much more easily discords between parties are removed if the parties stand under the same higher power than if each of them is entirely independent. How many conflicts which were the ruin of both the Greek and Italian city states would not have had this destructive consequence if a central power, if some ultimate tribunal, had ruled over them in common! Where there is no such power, the conflict among the elements has the fatal tendency to be fought out only in face-to-face battle between the power quanta. In the most general terms, we have to do here with the concept of "higher tribunal."[4] In varying forms, its operation extends through almost all of human collective life. The question whether or not a given society has a "higher tribunal" concerns a formal sociological characteristic of first-rank importance. The "higher tribunal" does not have to be a ruler in the ordinary or superficial sense of the word. For instance, above the obligations and controversies which are based on interests, instincts, and feelings, there is always

---

[4]   *"Höhere Instanz":* higher tribunal or court, but not necessarily in the technical, legal sense.—Tr.

a "higher tribunal," namely the realm of the *intellectual*, with its particular contents or representatives. This tribunal may make one-sided or inadequate decisions, and they may or may not be obeyed. But just as above the contradictory contents of our conceptions, logic remains the higher tribunal even where we think nonlogically, so in the same fashion, in a group that is composed of many elements, the most intelligent individual remains the higher tribunal in spite of the fact that in particular cases it is rather the person of strong will or warm feeling that may succeed in pacifying conflicts among the members. Nevertheless, the specific character of the "higher tribunal" to which one appeals for decisions or whose interference one accepts because it is felt to be legitimate, is typically on the side of intellectuality alone.

Another mode of unifying divergent parties, which is particularly favored if there exists a dominating "tribunal," is the following. Where it seems impossible to unify elements who are either in conflict or remain indifferent and alien toward one another—where they cannot be unified on the basis of the qualities they have—the unification can sometimes be brought about by so transforming the elements that they become adapted to a new situation which permits harmony, or by causing them to acquire new qualities which make their unification possible. The removal of ill-humor, the stimulation of mutual interest, the creation of thoroughly common features, can often be achieved (whether among children at play or among religious or political parties) by adding to the existing dissociative or indifferent intentions or delimitations of the elements some new trait which serves as a point of contact and, thus, reveals that even what was hitherto divergent can in fact be reconciled. Furthermore, features that cannot be directly unified often show the possibility of an indirect reconciliation if they can be developed further or can be augmented by a new element, and thus are placed upon a new and common basis. For instance, the homogeneity of the Gallic Provinces was decisively promoted when all of them in common became Latinized by Rome. Obviously, it is precisely this mode of unification which needs the "higher tribunal." Only a power which stands above the parties and in some manner dominates them can, more or less easily, give each of them interests and regulations which place them on a common basis. If left to themselves, they would perhaps never have found them; or their obstinacy, pride, and perseverance in the conflict would have prevented them from developing common interests. The Christian religion is praised for making its adherents "peaceful." The sociological reason for this is very probably the feeling that all beings alike are subordinate to the divine principle. The faithful Christian is convinced that above him and above each of his adversaries, whether Christian or not, there exists this "highest tribunal"—and this frees him from the temptation to measure his strength by violence. It is precisely because he stands immeasurably high above each individual Christian that the Christian God can be a bond among very large circles, all of which, by definition, are included in his "peace." At any given moment, each of them, along with every other, has a "higher tribunal" in God.

Subordination under a Plurality

Certain societal structures are characterized by the superordination of a plurality or social collectivity over individuals or other collectivities. In analyzing these structures, the first thing to be noted is that their significance for the subordinate is very uneven. The highest aim of the Spartan and Thessalian slaves was to become slaves of the state rather than of individuals. Prior to the emancipation of the feudal peasants in Prussia, the peasants on the state domains had a far better lot than private peasants had. In the large modern enterprises and warehouses, which are not characterized by very individual management but either are joint-stock companies or are administered as impersonally as if they were, employees are better situated than in small businesses, with their personal exploitation by the owner. This relationship is repeated where the question is not the differential impact of individuals as over collectivities, but of smaller *versus* larger collectivities. India's fate is considerably more favorable under British rule than under that of the East-India Company. In these cases, it is irrelevant, of course, whether the larger collectivity itself (for instance, England) is governed by a monarch—provided that the technique of the domination which it exercises has, in the largest sense, the character of super-individuality. Thus, the aristocratic regime of the Roman Republic oppressed the provinces by far more than did the Roman Empire, which was much more just and objective. Usually it is also more favorable for those who find themselves in a serving position to belong to a larger group. The great seigniories which developed in the seventh century in the Frankish realm often created a new, advantageous position for the subject population. The vast holdings permitted an organization and differentiation of the workers. They thus developed qualified, and therefore more highly esteemed, types of work which permitted the serf to rise socially within an individual seigniory. In the same sense, state criminal laws are often milder than those of smaller groups.

Yet, as has already been indicated, several phenomena run in exactly the opposite direction. The allies of Athens and Rome, as well as the territories which were once subject to particular Swiss cantons, were suppressed and exploited as cruelly as it would have hardly been possible under the tyranny of a single ruler. The same joint-stock company, which in consequence of the technique of its operation exploits its employees less than does the private entrepreneur, in many cases (for instance, in indemnifications and charities) *cannot* proceed as liberally as the private citizen, who owes nobody an account of his expenditures. And in regard to particular impulses: the cruelties committed for the pleasure of the Roman circus audiences—whose extreme intensification was often demanded by these audiences—would have hardly been committed by many, if the delinquent had faced them as an individual.

The basic reason for the difference in the results which the rule by a plurality has for its subordinates, lies, first of all, in its character of *objectivity*. This character excludes certain feelings, leanings, and impulses, which become effective only in the individual actions of the subjects, but not in their collective behavior. Within the given relationship and its particular contents, the situation of the subordinate may be influenced, favorably or unfavorably, by the objective or by the individually subjective character of this relationship; and, accordingly, differences result from this. Where the subordinate, in line with his situation, needs the tenderness, altruism, and favor of the superordinate, he will fare badly under the objective domination by a plurality. Inversely, under conditions where only legality, impartiality, and objectivity are favorable to his situation, the rule which has these features will be more desirable for him. It is characteristic of this phenomenon that the state, although it can legally condemn the criminal, cannot pardon him; and even in republics, the right to pardon is usually reserved for exercise by particular individuals. The principle is revealed most strikingly if we consider the material interests of communities. They are governed according to the profoundly objective axiom of greatest advantages and least sacrifices possible. This harshness and lack of consideration is by no means the same as the cruelty which individuals may commit for its own sake; but rather it is a wholly consistent objectivity. In a similar fashion, the brutality of a man purely motivated by monetary considerations and acting, to this extent, on the same axiom of greatest advantage and least sacrifice, often does not appear to him at all as a moral delinquency, since he is aware only of a rigorously logical behavior, which draws the objective consequences of the situation.

To be sure, this objectivity of collective behavior often merely implies something negative, namely, that certain norms to which the single individual ordinarily subjects himself, are suspended. Objectivity amounts to being a form that is designed to cover this suspension and to soothe the conscience. Every single individual who participates in a given decision can hide himself behind the fact, precisely, that it was a decision by the whole group. He can mask his own lust for gain and his brutality by maintaining that he only pursued the advantage of the totality. The idea that the possession of power—specifically, of rapidly acquired or long-lasting power—leads to its abuse, is true, for individuals, only with many and striking exceptions. By contrast, whenever it *cannot* be applied to social bodies and classes it is only because of especially fortunate circumstances.

It is very remarkable that the disappearance of the individual behind the totality serves, or even intensifies, the questionable character of this procedure, even in cases when also the subjugated

party is a collectivity. The psychological re-creation of suffering—
the essential vehicle of compassion and tenderness—fails easily if
the sufferer is not a namable or visible individual but only a totality, which has no subjective states of mind, so to speak. It has been
noted that English communal life has been characterized, throughout its history, by extraordinary justice toward persons and by
equally great injustice toward groups. In view of the strong feeling for individual rights, it is only this second psychological
peculiarity which accounts for the manner in which Dissenters,
Jews, Irishmen, Hindus, and, in earlier periods, Scotchmen, have
been treated. The immersion of the forms and norms of personality in the objectivity of collective life determines not only the
action, but also the suffering of the groups. Objectivity, to be sure,
operates in the form of law; but, where law is not compulsory and,
therefore, ought to be replaced by personal conscientiousness, it
frequently appears that the latter is no trait of collective psychology. This is shown even more decisively when, because of its collective character, the object of the procedure does not even stimulate the development of this personal trait. The misuses of power,
as, for instance, in American city administrations, would have
hardly attained their enormous dimensions if the rulers were not
corporations, and the ruled not collectivities. Characteristically, it
is sometimes believed that these misuses can be reduced by greatly
increasing the power of the mayor—so that there would be somebody who could personally be held responsible.

As a seeming exception to the objectivity of plurality action,
which in reality, however, only anchors the rule more solidly, there
is the behavior of the mass. It was already illustrated by the Roman
circus audience. Two phenomena must be fundamentally distinguished here. On the one hand, there is the effect resulting from
a plurality as a self-consistent and particular structure which, as it
were, embodies an abstraction. Such a plurality may be an economic association, a state, a church—any grouping which in reality or by analogy has to be designated as a legal person. On the
other hand, there is the plurality which is in fact physically present
as a mass. Both are characterized by the suspension of individual-
personal differences. But in the first case, this suspension causes

features to come to the fore which lie, as it were, above the individual character; whereas, in the second case, those are activated which lie below. For within a mass of people in sensory contact, innumerable suggestions and nervous influences play back and forth; they deprive the individual of the calmness and autonomy of reflection and action. In a crowd, therefore, the most ephemeral incitations often grow, like avalanches, into the most disproportionate impulses, and thus appear to eliminate the higher, differentiated and critical functions of the individual. It is for this reason that, in the theatre and at assemblies, we laugh about jokes which in a room would "leave us cold"; that spiritualistic manifestations succeed best in "circles"; that social games usually reach the highest degree of gaiety at the lowest intellectual level. Hence the quick, objectively quite understandable changes in the mood of a mass; hence the innumerable observations concerning the "stupidity" of collectivities.

As I have said, I ascribe the paralyzation of higher qualities and the lack of resistance to being swept away, to the incalculable number of influences and impressions which cross back and forth in a crowd between everybody and everybody else, mutually strengthening, crossing, deflecting, and reproducing themselves. On the one hand, because of this tangle of minimal excitations below the threshold of consciousness, there develops a great nervous excitement at the expense of clear and consistent intellectual activity; it arouses the darkest and most primitive instincts of the individual, which ordinarily are under control. On the other hand, there emerges a hypnotic paralysis which makes the crowd follow to its extreme every leading, suggestive impulse. In addition, there are the power intoxication and irresponsibility of the individual, whereby the moral inhibitions of the low and brutal impulses are eliminated. This satisfactorily explains the cruelty of crowds— whether they be composed of Roman circus goers, medieval Jew baiters, or American Negro lynchers—and the dire lot of those who become their victims.

But here, too, the typical, twofold result of this sociological relationship of subordination clearly appears. For, the impulsiveness and suggestibility of the crowd occasionally allows it to follow suggestions of magnanimity and enthusiasm which the individual could not attain without it any more than he could commit those acts of cruelty. The ultimate reason for the contradictions within this configuration can be formulated as follows: between the individual with his situations and needs, on the one hand, and all the super-individual or sub-individual phenomena and internal and external situations involved in collectivization, on the other, there is no fundamental and constant, but only a variable and contingent, relation. If, therefore, abstract social units proceed more objectively, coolly, and consistently than the individual; if, inversely, crowds in concrete physical proximity act more impulsively, senselessly, and extremely than each of its members alone; then, each of these two cases may be more favorable or more unfavorable for the person who is subject to such a plurality. There is, so to speak, nothing contingent about this contingency. It is the logical expression of the incommensurability between the specifically individual situations and claims at issue and the structures and moods that rule or serve the proximity and interaction of the many.

In the preceding analyses of subordination under a plurality, the single elements forming the plurality were coordinated, or, in all relevant regards, they behaved as if they were. New phenomena result, however, as soon as the superordinate plurality does not act as a unit of homogeneous elements. In this case, the superordinates may be either opposed to one another, or they may form a scale on which some of them are subordinate to higher superordinates....

Subordination under a Principle

SUBORDINATION UNDER A PRINCIPLE VS. A PERSON I now come, finally, to the third typical form of subordination, subordination neither to an individual nor to a plurality, but to an impersonal, objective principle. The fact that here a real interaction, at least an immediate interaction, is precluded, seems to deprive this form of the element of freedom. The individual who is subordinate to an objective law feels himself determined by it, while he, in turn, in no way determines the law, and has no possibility of reacting to it in a manner which could influence it—quite in contrast to even the most miserable slave, who, in some fashion at least, can still in this sense react to his master. For if one simply does not obey the law, one is, to this extent, not *really* subjected to it; and if one changes the law, one is not subordinate to the old law at all, but is again, in the same entirely unfree manner, subject to the new law. In spite of this, however, for modern, objective man, who is aware of the difference between the spheres of spontaneity and of obedience, subordination to a law which functions as the emanation of impersonal, uninfluenceable powers, is the more dignified situation. This was quite different at a time when the personality could preserve its self-esteem only in situations characterized by full spontaneity, which even in case of complete subordination were still associated with inter-personal effect and counter-effect. For this reason, as late as in the sixteenth century, princes in France, Germany, Scotland, and the Netherlands often met with considerable resistance, if they let their countries be ruled by administrative bodies or erudite substitutes—that is, more nearly by laws. The ruler's order was felt to be something personal; the individual wanted to lend him obedience only from personal devotion; and personal devotion, in spite of its unconditional character, is always in the form of free reciprocity.

This passionate personalism of the subordination relationship almost becomes its own caricature in the following circumstance, reported from Spain at the beginning of the modern period. An impoverished nobleman who became a cook or lackey did not thereby definitively lose his nobility: it only became latent and could be awakened again by a favorable turn of fate. But once he became a craftsman, his nobility was destroyed. This is entirely contrary to the modern conception, which separates the person from his achievement and, therefore, finds personal dignity to be preserved best if the content of subordination is as objective as possible. Thus, an American girl, who would work in a factory without the slightest feeling of humiliation, would feel wholly degraded as a family cook. Already in thirteenth-century Florence, the *lower* guilds comprised occupations in the immediate service of persons, such as cobblers, hosts, and school teachers; whereas the *higher* guilds were composed of occupations which, though still serving

the public, were yet more objective and less dependent on particular individuals—for instance, clothiers and grocers. On the other
hand, in Spain, where knightly traditions, with their engagement
of the whole person in all activity, were still alive, every relationship which (in any sense) took place between person and person,
was bound to be considered at least bearable; while every subordination to more objective claims, every integration into a system
of impersonal duties (impersonal, because serving many and anonymous persons), was bound to be regarded as wholly disgraceful.
An aversion to the objectivity of law can still be felt in the legal
theories of Althusius: the *summus magistratus* legislates, but he
does so, not because he represents the state, but because he is appointed by the people. The notion that the ruler could be designated
as the representative of the state by appointment through law, not
by personal appointment (actual or presumed) by the people—is
still alien to Althusius.

In antiquity, on the contrary, subordination to law appeared
thoroughly adequate, precisely because of the idea that law is free
from any personal characteristics. Aristotle praised law as *"tó
méson,"* that is, as that which is moderate, impartial, free from
passions. Plato, in the same sense, had already recognized government by impersonal law as the best means for counteracting selfish-
ness. His, however, was only a psychological motivation. It did
not touch the core of the question, namely, the fundamental transition of the relationship of obedience from personalism to objectiv-
ism, a transition which cannot be derived from the anticipation of
utilitarian consequence. Yet, in Plato, we also find this other theory: that, in the ideal state, the insight of the ruler stands above
the law; and as soon as the welfare of the whole seems to require
it of the ruler, he must be able to act even against the laws laid
down by him. There must be laws which may not be broken under
any circumstances, only if there are no true statesmen. The law,
therefore, appears here as the lesser evil—but not, as in the Germanic feeling, mentioned before, because subordination under a
person has an element of freedom and dignity in comparison with
which all obedience to laws has something mechanical and passive.
Rather, it is the rigidity of the law which is felt to be its weakness:

in its rigidity, it confronts the changing and unforeseeable claims of life in a clumsy and inadequate way; and this is an evil from which only the entirely unprejudiced insight of a personal ruler can escape; and only where there is no such insight, does law become relatively advantageous. Here, therefore, it is always the *content* of the law, its physical state, as it were, which determines its value or disvalue as compared with subordination under persons. The fact that the relationship of obedience is totally different in its inner principle and in terms of the whole feeling of life, on the part of the obeyer, according to whether it originates in a person or in a law—this fact does not enter these considerations. The most general or formal relation between government by law and government by person can (of course) be expressed in a preliminary, practical manner by saying that where the law is not forceful or broad enough a person is necessary, and where the person is inadequate, a law is required. But, far beyond this, whether rule by man is considered as something provisional in lieu of rule by perfect law, or, inversely, rule by law is considered a gap-filler or an inferior substitute for government by a personality which is absolutely qualified to rule—this choice depends upon decisions of ultimate, indiscussable feelings concerning sociological values.

SUBORDINATION UNDER OBJECTS   There is still another form in which an objective principle may become the turning point in the relationship between superordinates and subordinates, namely, when neither a law nor an ideal norm, but rather a concrete object governs the domination, as, for instance, in the principle of patrimony. Here—most radically under the system of Russian bondage—bonded subjects are only appurtenances of the land—"the air bonds the people." The terrible hardship of bondage at least excluded personal slavery which would have permitted the sale of the slave. Instead, it tied subordination to the land in such a way that the bondsman could be sold only along with the land. In spite of all contentual and quantitative differences, nevertheless, sometimes this same form occurs in the case of the modern factory worker, whose own interest, through certain arrangements, binds him to a given factory. For instance, the acquisition of his house was made possible for him, or he participated out of his own purse in certain welfare expenditures, and all these benefits are lost once he leaves the factory, etc. He is thus bound, merely by objects, in a way which in a very specific manner makes him powerless in respect to the entrepreneur. Finally, it was this same form of domination which, under the most primitive patriarchal conditions, was governed not by a merely spatial, but by a living object: children did not belong to the father because he was their progenitor, but because the mother belonged to him (as the fruits of the tree belong to the tree's owner); therefore, children begotten by other fathers were no less his property.

This type of domination usually involves a humiliatingly harsh and unconditional kind of subordination. For, inasmuch as a man is subordinate by virtue of belonging to a thing, he himself psychologically sinks to the category of mere thing. With the necessary reservations, one could say that where law regulates domination, the superordinate belongs in the sphere of objectivity; while, where a *thing* regulates it, the *subordinate* does. The condition of the subordinate, therefore, is usually more favorable in the first case, and more unfavorable in the second, than in many cases of purely personal subordination.

CONSCIENCE   Immediate sociological interest in subordination under an objective principle attaches to two chief cases of it. One case is when this ideal, superordinate principle can be interpreted as a psychological crystallization of an actual social power. The other is when, among those who are commonly subject to it, it produces particular and characteristic relationships. The first case must be taken into consideration, above all, when dealing with moral imperatives. In our moral consciousness, we feel subordinate to a command which does not seem to derive from any human, personal power. The voice of conscience we hear only in ourselves, although in comparison with all subjective egoism, we hear it with a force and decisiveness which apparently can stem only from a tribunal *outside* the individual. An attempt has been made, as is well known, to solve this contradiction by deriving the contents of morality from social norms. What is useful to the species and the group, the argument runs, and what the group, therefore, requests of its members for the sake of its own maintenance, is gradually bred into the individual as an instinct. He thus comes to contain it in himself, as his own, autonomous feeling, in addition to his personal feelings properly speaking, and thus often in contrast to them. This, it is alleged, explains the dual character of the moral command: that on the one hand, it confronts us as an impersonal order to which we simply have to submit, but that, on the other, no external power, but only our most private and internal impulses, imposes it upon us. At any rate, here is one of the cases where the individual, within his own consciousness, repeats the relationships which exist between him, as a total personality, and the group. It is an old observation that the conceptions of the single individual, with all their relations of association and dissociation, differentiation, and unification, behave in the same way in which individuals behave in regard to one another. It is merely a peculiar case of this correspondence that those intrapsychological relations are repeated, not only between individuals in general, but also between the individual and his group. All that society asks of its members—adaptation and loyalty, altruism and work, self-discipline and truthfulness—the individual also asks of himself.

In all of this, several very important motives cut across one another. Society confronts the individual with precepts. He becomes habituated to their compulsory character until the cruder and subtler means of compulsion are no longer necessary. His nature may thereby be so formed or reformed that he acts by these precepts as if on impulse, with a consistent and direct will which is not conscious of any law. Thus, the pre-Islamic Arabs were without any notion of an objectively legal compulsion; in all instances, purely personal decision was their highest authority, although this decision was thoroughly imbued with tribal consciousness and the requirements of tribal life, which gave it its norms. Or else, the law, in the form of a command which is carried by the authority of the society, does live in the individual consciousness, but irrespective of the question whether society actually backs it with its compulsory power or even itself supports it solely with its explicit will. Here then, the individual represents society to himself. The external confrontation, with its suppressions, liberations, changing accents, has become an interplay between his social impulses and the ego impulses in the stricter sense of the word; and both are included by the ego in the larger sense.

But this is not yet the really objective lawfulness, which was alluded to above, in whose consciousness no trace of any historical-social origin is left. At a certain higher stage of morality, the motivation of action lies no longer in a real-human, even though super-individual power; at this stage, the spring of moral necessities flows beyond the contrast between individual and totality. For, as little as these necessities derive from society, as little do they derive from the singular reality of individual life. In the free conscience of the actor, in individual reason, they only have their bearer, the locus of their efficacy. Their power of obligation stems from these necessities themselves, from their inner, super-personal validity, from an objective ideality which we must recognize, whether or not we want to, in a manner similar to that in which the validity of a truth is entirely independent of whether or not the truth becomes real in any consciousness. The *content*, however, which fills these forms is (not necessarily but often) the societal requirement. But this requirement no longer operates by means of its social impetus, as it were, but rather as if it had undergone a metempsychosis into a norm which must be satisfied for its own sake, not for my sake nor for yours.

We are dealing here with differences which not only are psychologically of the greatest delicacy, but whose boundaries are also constantly blurred in practice. Yet this mixture of motivations in which psychic reality moves, makes it all the more urgent that it be isolated analytically. Whether society and individual confront one another like two powers and the individual's subordination is effected by society through energy which seems to flow from an uninterrupted source and constantly seems to renew itself; or whether this energy changes into a psychological impulse in the very individual who considers himself a social being and, therefore, fights and suppresses those of his impulses that lean toward his "egoistic" part; or whether the Ought, which man finds above himself as an actuality as objective as Being, is merely filled with the content of

societal life conditions—these are constellations which only begin
to exhaust the kinds of individual subordination to the group. In
them, the three powers which fill historical life—society, individual, and objectivity—become norm-giving, in this order. But they
do so in such a way that each of them absorbs the social content,
the quantity of superordination of society over the individual; in
a specific manner, each of them forms and presents the power, the
will, and the necessities of society.

8

PROSTITUTION

1907

ONLY TRANSACTIONS for money have that character of a purely momentary relationship which leaves no traces, as is the case with prostitution. With the giving of money, one completely withdraws from the relationship; one has settled matters more completely than by giving an object, which, by its contents, its selection, and its use maintains a wisp of the personality of the giver. Only money is an appropriate equivalent to the momentary peaking and the equally momentary satisfaction of the desire served by prostitutes, for money establishes no ties, it is always at hand, and it is always welcomed.

Money is never an adequate means in a relationship between persons that depends on duration and integrity—like love, even when it is only of short duration. Money serves most matter-of-factly and completely for venal pleasure which rejects any continuation of the relationship beyond sensual satisfaction: money is completely detached from the person and puts an end to any further ramifications. When one pays money one is completely quits, just as one is through with the prostitute after satisfaction is attained.

In prostitution, the relation of the sexes is reduced to its generic content because it is perfectly unambiguous and limited to the sensual act. It consists of that which any member of the species can perform and experience. The most diverse personalities can engage

From *Philosophie des Geldes*, 2d enlarged edition (Leipzig: Duncker & Humblot, 1907), pp. 413–18. Translated by Roberta Ash.

121

in it and all individual differences appear to be of no importance. Therefore, the economic counterpart of this relation is money, for it, too, is beyond all individual differences; it is at the species level of economic value, the representation of what is common to all. Conversely, the nature of money resembles the nature of prostitution. The indifference with which it lends itself to any use, the infidelity with which it leaves everyone, its lack of ties to anyone, its complete objectification that excludes any attachment and makes it suitable as a pure means—all this suggests a portentous analogy between it and prostitution.

Kant stated as a moral law that man is never to be used as a mere means, but is always to be perceived and treated as an end in himself. Prostitution represents behavior that is the exact opposite of this, and indeed, *for both parties involved*. Of all human relationships, it is perhaps the most significant case of the mutual reduction of two persons to the status of mere means. This may be the most salient and profound factor underlying the very close historic tie between prostitution and the money economy—the economy of "means."

It is for this reason that the terrible humiliation inherent in prostitution finds sharpest expression in its equivalence to money. Certainly the nadir of human dignity is reached when what is most intimate and personal for a woman, that which should be given only on the basis of a genuine individual impulse and only when there is a comparable personal contribution from the man (even though it may have a different meaning for him), is offered for such thoroughly impersonal, externally objective remuneration. We perceive here the most total and painful imbalance between performance and recompense; or rather, the debasement of prostitution lies in the fact that the most personal possession of a woman, her area of greatest reserve, is considered equivalent to the most neutral value of all, one which is most remote from anything that is personal.

This characterization of prostitution in terms of monetary compensation leads, however, to certain contradictory considerations. These must now be discussed in order to let the meaning of money in this matter stand out quite clearly.

The completely personal, intimately individual character which the sexual contribution of the woman is supposed to have does not seem very consistent with the previously emphasized fact that merely sensual contact between the sexes is completely general in nature, and that in this contact which is common to all, even to animals, all personality and individual spirit is extinguished. If men are inclined to lump all women together and to judge them collectively, surely one reason for this is that the feature which men—particularly the coarser sort of men—find particularly attractive in women is shared by the seamstress and the princess.

So, it seems impossible to find individuated values in the sexual function. All other similar universals—eating and drinking, the habitual physiological and psychological activities, the self-preservation drive and the generic logical functions are never strongly entwined with the personality; one never feels that someone expresses his innermost, most essential and most comprehensive being in the behaviors that he indistinguishably shares with everyone else. Nevertheless, the woman's sexual contribution is indisputably anomalous. This completely general act, which is identical for all classes of humanity, is also really viewed—at least for women—as supremely personal, as involving the innermost self.

This can be understood if one assumes that women in general are more deeply embedded in the species type than are men, who emerge from the species type more differentiated and individualized. From this assumption it would follow first of all that, for women, species characteristics and personal characteristics coincide more. If women are indeed closer to the dark, primitive forces of nature, then their most essential and personal characteristics are more strongly rooted in the most natural, most universal, and most biologically important functions. And it further follows that this unity of womankind in which there is less distinction between universal and individual elements than among men must be reflected in the greater homogeneity of each woman's nature. Experience seems to confirm that the faculties, qualities, and impulses of a woman are more closely interwoven than those of a man, whose elements are more autonomous, so that the development and fate of each is relatively independent of that of the others.

According to general opinion on the matter, the nature of

woman is much more inclined to all-or-nothing. A woman's inclinations and activities are more closely linked to each other, and it is much easier to stimulate her entire being—with all its feelings, longings, and thoughts—from a single vantage point. If this is indeed so, then perhaps there is some truth in the assumption that for a woman, this single, vital function, with its contribution of one part of her self, involves more fully and unreservedly her entire person than is true for the more differentiated man in a sexual situation. This difference is already apparent in the less serious stage of the relationship between a man and a woman. Even primitive peoples set different fines for the bride and groom to pay in the event of unilateral abrogation of the engagement; thus, for instance, among the Bakaks the bride must pay five florins, but the groom must pay ten, and among the people of Bengkula, the contract-breaking bride must pay ten florins, but the groom must pay forty. The meaning and the consequences which society ascribes to the sexual contact of men and women are also based on the assumption that the woman contributes her entire self, with all of its worth, whereas the man contributes only part of his personality. Therefore a girl who has gone astray only once loses her reputation entirely, a woman's infidelity is more harshly judged than a man's (of whom it seems to be believed that an occasional purely sensual indulgence is compatible with loyalty to his wife in every spiritual and essential respect), and prostitutes become irredeemably déclassé; but the worst rake can still rise from the mire by virtue of other facets of his personality and no social status is closed to him.

Thus, in the purely sensual act, which is the point of prostitution, the man contributes only a minimal part of himself, but the woman her entire self—not, of course, in every case, but on the whole. Under these circumstances, the institution of the pimp and the alleged frequency of lesbianism among prostitutes become comprehensible, for in her contacts with men who are never involved as real and whole persons, the prostitute must feel a terrible loneliness and dissatisfaction which she seeks to diminish by relationships which involve at least some further aspects of the persons. Neither the thought that the sex act is general and impersonal nor the fact that objectively the man participates as fully as the woman can negate the claim; the contribution of the woman is infinitely more personal, more substantial, and more ego-involving than the man's, and thus money is the most inappropriate and inadequate remuneration, whose offer and acceptance is the greatest possible suppression of the woman's personality.

The humiliation of the prostitute does not lie in the polyandrous nature of prostitution, in her availability to many men; true polyandry often provides women with superior status, as among the high-caste Nayars of India. The key feature of prostitution is not polyandry, but polygyny; for everywhere polygyny incomparably diminishes uniqueness of a woman; she has lost the value of rarity. Objectively viewed, prostitution combines polygynous and polyandrous contacts. But the advantage of the buyer over the seller means that the polygynous features, which give the man a vast superiority, determine the character of prostitution. Even in affairs which do not have the remotest resemblance to prostitution, women find it embarrassing and humiliating to accept money from their lovers, although this feeling often does not extend to nonmonetary gifts. But they find enjoyment and satisfaction in giving money to their lovers. It was said of Marlborough that he was successful with women because he accepted money from them. The previously indicated superiority of the buyer over the seller, a superiority which in prostitution develops into a formidable social distance, in the reversed case gives the woman the satisfaction of making dependent on her the one whom she usually respects.

Now, however, we encounter the striking fact that in many primitive cultures, prostitution is not considered humiliating, nor does it lead to outcaste status. Similarly, in Asian antiquity, girls of all classes prostituted themselves to contribute to the temple treasury or to acquire a dowry, the latter also being the case among some African tribes. The girls, who often include the sovereign's daughter, do not lose their reputation, nor is their later married life in any way compromised. This opinion, so different from our own, indicates that the two factors—women's sexual honor and money—are related in a basically different way than they are among us. Among us prostitution is characterized by the unbridgeable gap between these two elements; where a totally different view of prostitution is held, these two elements must be closer together in value. This is a counterpart of the development of *wergeld*, the monetary penalty for the killing of a person. The increasing emphasis on the worth of the individual and the decreasing value of money have made the institution of *wergeld* impossible. The same process of differentiation which has led to a special emphasis on the individual and has made him unique and incomparable has made money the measure and equivalent of a completely opposite type of object; the growing indifference and objectivity of money which this entails has made it seem increasingly inappropriate to the balancing of human relations. This imbalance between the service and the payment, which in our culture is the most salient feature of prostitution, is not yet to be found in less differentiated cultures.

Explorers report that among a great many savage tribes, women are remarkably similar to men physically and frequently also mentally. This phenomenon is the result of these tribes' lack of the differentiation which provides the more cultivated woman and her sexual honor with a value that cannot be matched by money, even if she seems less differentiated and less phylogenetically specialized than the men of her milieu. Attitudes toward prostitution undergo the same development that can be observed in the case of ecclesiastical penance and blood money: human beings and their values are relatively unindividualistic in primitive periods, whereas owing to its rarity and infrequent use, money is relatively more individualized. As development causes the two to diverge, the counterbalancing of the two either becomes impossible or where it persists, as in prostitution, it leads to a terrible suppression of personal dignity.

9

SOCIABILITY

1910

THERE IS an old conflict over the nature of society. One side mystically exaggerates its significance, contending that only through society is human life endowed with reality. The other regards it as a mere abstract concept by means of which the observer draws the realities, which are individual human beings, into a whole, as one calls trees and brooks, houses and meadows, a "landscape." However one decides this conflict, he must allow society to be a reality in a double sense. On the one hand are the individuals in their directly perceptible existence, the bearers of the processes of association, who are united by these processes into the higher unity which one calls "society"; on the other hand, the interests which, living in the individuals, motivate such union: economic and ideal interests, warlike and erotic, religious and charitable. To satisfy such urges and to attain such purposes arise the innumerable forms of social life, all the with-one-another, for-one-another, in-one-another, against-one-another, and through-one-another, in state and commune, in church and economic associations, in family and clubs. The energy effects of atoms upon each other bring matter into the innumerable forms which we see as "things." Just so the impulses and interests which a man experiences in himself and which push him out toward other men bring

---

Reprinted from "The Sociology of Sociability," *American Journal of Sociology* 55, no. 3 (Nov. 1949). Translated by Everett C. Hughes. Originally published as "Soziologie der Geselligkeit," in *Verhandlungen des I. Deutschen Soziologentages (1910)* (1911).

about all the forms of association by which a mere sum of separate individuals are made into a "society."

Within this constellation called society, or out of it, there develops a special sociological structure corresponding to those of art and play, which draw their form from these realities but nevertheless leave their reality behind them. It may be an open question whether the concept of a play impulse or an artistic impulse possesses explanatory value; at least it directs attention to the fact that in every play or artistic activity there is contained a common element not affected by their differences of content. Some residue of satisfaction lies in gymnastics, as in card-playing, in music, and in plastic art, something which has nothing to do with the peculiarities of music or plastic art as such but only with the fact that both of the latter are art and both of the former are play. A common element, a likeness of psychological reaction and need, is found in all these various things—something easily distinguishable from the special interest which gives each its distinction. In the same sense one may speak of an impulse to sociability in man. To be sure, it is for the sake of special needs and interests that men unite in economic associations or blood fraternities, in cult societies or robber bands. But above and beyond their special content, all these associations are accompanied by a feeling for, by a satisfaction in, the very fact that one is associated with others and that the solitariness of the individual is resolved into togetherness, a union with others. Of course, this feeling can, in individual cases, be nullified by contrary psychological factors; association can be felt as a mere burden, endured for the sake of our objective aims. But typically there is involved in all effective motives for association a feeling of the worth of association as such, a drive which presses toward this form of existence and often only later calls forth that objective content which carries the particular association along. And as that which I have called artistic impulse draws its form from the complexes of perceivable things and builds this form into a special structure corresponding to the artistic impulse, so also the impulse to sociability distils, as it were, out of the realities of social life the pure essence of association, of the associative process as a value and a satisfaction. It thereby constitutes what we call sociability in the narrower sense. It is no mere accident of language that all sociability, even the purely spontaneous, if it is to have meaning and stability, lays such great value on form, on good form. For "good form" is mutual self-definition, interaction of the elements, through which a unity is made; and since in sociability the concrete motives bound up with life-goals fall away, so must the pure form, the free-playing, interacting interdependence of individuals stand out so much the more strongly and operate with so much the greater effect.

And what joins art with play now appears in the likeness of both to sociability. From the realities of life play draws its great, essential themes: the chase and cunning; the proving of physical and mental powers, the contest and reliance on chance and the favor of forces which one cannot influence. Freed of substance, through which these activities make up the seriousness of life, play gets its cheerfulness but also that symbolic significance which distinguishes it from pure pastime. And just this will show itself more and more as the essence of sociability; that it makes up its substance from numerous fundamental forms of serious relationships among men, a substance, however, spared the frictional relations of real life; but out of its formal relations to real life, sociability (and the more so as it approaches pure sociability) takes on a symbolically playing fulness of life and a significance which a superficial rationalism always seeks only in the content. Rationalism, finding no content there, seeks to do away with sociability as empty idleness, as did the savant who asked concerning a work of art, "What does that prove?" It is nevertheless not without significance that in many, perhaps in all, European languages, the word "society" [*Gesellschaft*] designates a sociable gathering. The political, the economic, the purposive society of any sort is, to be sure, always "society." But only the sociable gathering is "society" without qualifying adjectives, because it alone presents the pure, abstract play of form, all the specific contents of the one-sided and qualified societies being dissolved away.[1]

---

[1] The point is more striking in German, where the word *Gesellschaft* means both "society" and "party" (in the sense of a sociable gathering).— ED.

Sociability is, then, the *play-form of association*. It is related to the content-determined concreteness of association as art is related to reality. Now the great problem of association comes to a solution possible only in sociability. The problem is that of the measure of significance and accent which belongs to the individual as such in and as against the social milieu. Since sociability in its pure form has no ulterior end, no content, and no result outside itself, it is oriented completely about personalities. Since nothing but the satisfaction of the impulse to sociability—although with a resonance left over—is to be gained, the process remains, in its conditions as in its results, strictly limited to its personal bearers; the personal traits of amiability, breeding, cordiality, and attractiveness of all kinds determine the character of purely sociable association. But precisely because all is oriented about them, the personalities must not emphasize themselves too individually. Where real interests, co-operating or clashing, determine the social form, they provide of themselves that the individual shall not present his peculiarities and individuality with too much abandon and aggressiveness. But where this restraint is wanting, if association is to be possible at all, there must prevail another restriction of personal pushing, a restriction springing solely out of the form of the association. It is for this reason that the sense of tact is of such special significance in society, for it guides the self-regulation of the individual in his personal relations to others where no outer or directly egoistic interests provide regulation. And perhaps it is the specific function of tact to mark out for individual impulsiveness, for the ego and for outward demands, those limits which the rights of others require. A very remarkable sociological structure appears at this point. In sociability, whatever the personality has of objective importance, of features which have their orientation toward something outside the circle, must not interfere. Riches and social position, learning and fame, exceptional capacities and merits of the individual have no role in sociability or, at most, as a slight nuance of that immateriality with which alone reality dares penetrate into the artificial structure of sociability. As these objective qualities which gather about the personality, so also must the most purely and deeply personal qualities be excluded from sociability. The most personal things—character, mood, and fate—have thus no place in it. It is tactless to bring in personal humor, good or ill, excitement and depression, the light and shadow of one's inner life. Where a connection, begun on the sociable level—and not necessarily a superficial or conventional one—finally comes to center about personal values, it loses the essential quality of sociability and becomes an association determined by a content—not unlike a business or religious relation, for which contact, exchange, and speech are but instruments for ulterior ends, while for sociability they are the whole meaning and content of the social processess. This exclusion of the personal reaches into even the most external matters; a lady would not want to appear in such extreme *décolletage* in a really personal, intimately friendly situation with one or two men as she would in a large company without any embarrassment. In the latter she would not feel herself personally involved in the same measure and could therefore abandon herself to the impersonal freedom of the mask. For she is, in the larger company, herself, to be sure, but not quite completely herself, since she is only an element in a formally constituted gathering.

A man, taken as a whole, is, so to speak, a somewhat unformed complex of contents, powers, potentialities; only according to the motivations and relationships of a changing existence is he articulated into a differentiated, defined structure. As an economic and political agent, as a member of a family or of a profession, he is, so to speak, an *ad hoc* construction; his life-material is ever determined by a special idea, poured into a special mold, whose relatively independent life is, to be sure, nourished from the common but somewhat undefinable source of energy, the ego. In this sense, the man, as a social creature, is also a unique structure, occurring in no other connection. On the one hand, he has removed all the objective qualities of the personality and entered into the structure of sociability with nothing but the capacities, attractions, and interests of his pure humanity. On the other hand, this structure stops short of the purely subjective and inward parts of his personality. That discretion which is one's first demand upon others in sociability is also required of one's own ego, because a breach of it in either direction causes the sociological artifact of sociability to break down into a sociological naturalism. One can therefore speak of an upper and a lower sociability threshold for the individual. At the moment when people direct their association toward objective content and purpose, as well as at the moment when the absolutely personal and subjective matters of the individual enter freely into the phenomenon, sociability is no longer the central and controlling principle but at most a formalistic and outwardly instrumental principle.

From this negative definition of the nature of sociability through boundaries and thresholds, however, one can perhaps find the positive motif. Kant set it up as the principle of law that everyone should have that measure of freedom which could exist along with the freedom of every other person. If one stands by the sociability impulse as the source or also as the substance of sociability, the following is the principle according to which it is constituted: everyone should have as much satisfaction of this impulse as is consonant with the satisfaction of the impulse for all others. If one expresses this not in terms of the impulse but rather in terms of success, the principle of sociability may be formulated thus: everyone should guarantee to the other that maximum of sociable values (joy, relief, vivacity) which is consonant with the maximum of values he himself receives. As justice upon the Kantian basis is thoroughly democratic, so likewise this principle shows the democratic structure of all sociability, which to be sure every social stratum can realize only within itself, and which so often makes sociability between members of different social classes burdensome and painful. But even among social equals the democracy of their sociability is a play. Sociability creates, if one will, an ideal sociological world, for in it—so say the enunciated principles—the pleasure of the individual is always contingent upon the joy of others; here, by definition, no one can have his satisfaction at the cost of contrary experiences on the part of others. In other forms of association such lack of reciprocity is excluded only by the ethical imperative which govern them but not by their own immanent nature.

This world of sociability, the only one in which a democracy of equals is possible without friction, is an *artificial* world, made up of beings who have renounced both the objective and the purely personal features of the intensity and extensiveness of life in order to bring about among themselves a pure interaction, free of any disturbing material accent. If we now have the conception that we enter into sociability purely as "human beings," as that which we really are, lacking all the burdens, the agitations, the inequalities with which real life disturbs the purity of our picture, it is because modern life is overburdened with objective content and material demands. Ridding ourselves of this burden in sociable circles, we believe we return to our natural-personal being and overlook the fact that this personal aspect also does not consist in its full uniqueness and natural completeness, but only in a certain reserve and stylizing of the sociable man. In earlier epochs, when a man did not depend so much upon the purposive, objective content of his associations, his "formal personality" stood out more clearly against his personal existence: hence personal bearing in the society of earlier times was much more ceremonially, rigidly, and impersonally regulated than now. This reduction of the personal periphery, of the measure of significance which homogeneous interaction with others allowed the individual, has been followed by a swing to the opposite extreme; today one may even find in society that courtesy by which the strong, outstanding person not only places himself on a level with the weaker but goes so far as to assume the attitude that the weaker is the more worthy and superior. If association itself is interaction, it appears in its purest and most stylized form when it goes on among equals, just as symmetry and balance are the most outstanding forms of artistic stylizing of visible elements. Inasmuch as sociability is the abstraction of association—an abstraction of the character of art or of play—it demands the purest, most transparent, most engaging kind of interaction—that among *equals*. It must, because of its very nature, posit beings who give up so much of their objective content, who are so modified in both their outward and their inner significance, that they are sociably equal, and every one of them can win sociability values for himself only under the condition that the others, interacting with him, can also win them. It is a game in which one "acts" as though all were equal, as though he especially esteemed everyone. This is just as far from being a lie as is play or art in all their departures from reality. But the instant the intentions and events of practical reality enter into the speech and behavior of sociability, it does become a lie—just as a painting does when it attempts, panorama fashion, to be taken for reality. That which is right and proper within the self-contained life of sociability, concerned only with the immediate play of its forms, becomes a lie when this is mere pretense, which in reality is guided by purposes of quite another sort than the sociable or is used to conceal such purposes—and indeed sociability may easily get entangled with real life.

It is an obvious corollary that everything may be subsumed under sociability which one can call sociological play-form; above all, play itself, which assumes a large place in the sociability of all epochs. The expression "social game" is significant in the deeper sense which I have indicated. The entire interactional or associational complex among men: the desire to gain advantage, trade, formation of parties and the desire to win from another, the movement between opposition and co-operation, outwitting and revenge —all this, fraught with purposive content in the serious affairs of reality, in play leads a life carried along only and completely by the stimulus of these functions. For even when play turns about a money prize, it is not the prize, which indeed could be won in many other ways, which is the specific point of the play; but the attraction for the true sportsman lies in the dynamics and in the chances of that sociologically significant form of activity itself. The social game has a deeper double meaning—that it is played not only *in* a society as its outward bearer but that with its help people actually "play" "society."

Further, in the sociology of the sexes, eroticism has elaborated a form of play: *coquetry*, which finds in sociability its lightest, most playful, and yet its widest realization. If the erotic question between the sexes turns about consent or denial (whose objects are naturally of endless variety and degree and by no means only of strictly physiological nature), so is it the essence of feminine coquetry to play hinted consent and hinted denial against each other to draw the man on without letting matters come to a decision, to rebuff him without making him lose all hope. The coquette brings her attractiveness to its climax by letting the man hang on the verge of getting what he wants without letting it become too serious for herself; her conduct swings between yes and no, without stopping at one or the other. She thus playfully shows the simple and pure form of erotic decision and can bring its polar opposites together in a quite integrated behavior, since the decisive and fateful content, which would bring it to one of the two decisions, by definition does not enter into coquetry. And this freedom from all the weight of firm content and residual reality gives coquetry that character of vacillation, of distance, of the ideal, which allows one to speak with some right of the "art"—not of the "arts"—of coquetry. In order, however, for coquetry to spread as so natural a growth on the soil of sociability, as experience shows it to be, it must be countered by a special attitude on the part of men. So long as the man denies himself the stimulation of coquetry, or so long as he is—on the contrary—merely a victim who is involuntarily carried along by her vacillations from a half-yes to a half-no—so long does coquetry lack the adequate structure of sociability. It lacks that free interaction and equivalence of the elements which is the fundamental condition of sociability. The latter appears only when the man desires nothing more than this free moving play, in which something definitively erotic lurks only as a remote symbol, and when he does not get his pleasure in these gestures and preliminaries from erotic desire or fear of it. Coquetry, as it unfolds its grace on the heights of sociable cultivation, has left behind the reality of erotic desire, of consent or denial, and becomes a play of shadow pictures of these serious matters. Where the latter enter or lurk, the whole process becomes a private affair of the two persons, played out on the level of reality; under the sociological sign of sociability, however, in which the essential orientation of the person to the fulness of life does not enter, coquetry is the teasing or even ironic play with which eroticism has distilled the pure essence of its interaction out from its substantive or individual content. As sociability plays at the forms of society, so coquetry plays out the forms of eroticism.

In what measure sociability realizes to the full the abstraction of the forms of sociological interaction otherwise significant because of their content and gives them—now turning about themselves, so to speak—a shadow body is revealed finally in that most extensive instrument of all human common life, *conversation*. The decisive point is expressed in the quite banal experience that in the serious affairs of life men talk for the sake of the content which they wish to impart or about which they want to come to an understanding—in sociability talking is an end in itself; in purely sociable conversation the content is merely the indispensable carrier of the stimulation, which the lively exchange of talk as such unfolds. All the forms with which this exchange develops: argument and the appeals to the norms recognized by both parties; the conclusion of peace through compromise and the discovery of common convictions; the thankful acceptance of the new and the parrying-off of that on which no understanding is to be hoped for—all these forms of conversational interaction, otherwise in the service of innumerable contents and purposes of human intercourse, here have their meaning in themselves; that is to say, in the excitement of the play of relations which they establish between individuals, binding and loosening, conquering and being vanquished, giving and taking. In order that this play may retain its self-sufficiency at the level of pure form, the content must receive no weight on its own account; as soon as the discussion gets businesslike, it is no longer sociable; it turns its compass point around as soon as the verification of a truth becomes its purpose. Its character as sociable converse is disturbed just as when it turns into a serious argument. The form of the common search of the truth, the form of the argument, may occur; but it must not permit the seriousness of the momentary content to become its substance any more than one may put a piece of three-dimensional reality into the perspective of a painting. Not that the content of sociable conversation is a matter of indifference; it must be interesting, gripping, even significant—only it is not the purpose of the conversation that these qualities should square with objective results, which stand by definition outside the conversation. Outwardly, therefore, two conversations may run a similar course, but only that one of them is sociable in which the subject matter, with all its value and stimulation, finds its justification, its place, and its purpose only in the functional play of conversation as such, in the form of repartee with its special unique significance. It therefore inheres in the nature of sociable conversation that its object matter can change lightly and quickly; for, since the matter is only the means, it has an entirely interchangeable and accidental character which inheres in means as against fixed purposes. Thus sociability offers, as was said, perhaps the only case in which talk is a legitimate end in itself. For by the fact that it is two-sided—indeed with the possible exception of looking-each-other-over the purest and most sublimated form of mutuality among all sociological phenomena—it becomes the most adequate fulfilment of a relation, which is, so to speak, nothing but relationship, in which even that which is otherwise pure form of interaction is its own self-sufficient content. It results from this whole complex that also the telling of tales, witticisms, anecdotes, although often a stopgap and evidence of conversational poverty, still can show a fine tact in which all the motives of sociability are apparent. For, in the first place, the conversation is by this means kept above all individual intimacy, beyond everything purely personal which would not fit into the categories of sociability. This objective element is brought in not for the sake of its content but in the interest of sociability; that something is said and accepted is not an end in itself but a mere means to maintain the liveliness, the mutual understanding, the common consciousness of the group. Not only thereby is it given a content which all can share but it is a gift of the individual to the whole, behind which the giver can remain invisible; the finest sociably told story is that in which the narrator allows his own person to remain completely in the background; the most effective story holds itself in the happy balance of the sociable ethic, in which the subjectively individual as well as the objectively substantive have dissolved themselves completely in the service of pure sociability.

It is hereby indicated that sociability is the play-form also for the ethical forces of concrete society. The great problems placed before these forces are that the individual has to fit himself into a whole system and live for it: that, however, out of this system values and enhancement must flow back to him, that the life of the individual is but a means for the ends of the whole, the life of the whole but an instrument for the purposes of the individual. Sociability carries the seriousness, indeed the frequent tragedy of these requirements, over into its shadow world, in which there is no friction, because shadows cannot impinge upon one another. If it is, further, the ethical task of association to make the coming-together and the separation of its elements an exact and just expression of their inner relations, determined by the wholeness of their lives, so within sociability this freedom and adequacy are freed of their concrete and substantively deeper limitations; the manner in which groups form and break up at parties, and conversation spins itself out, deepens, loosens, cuts itself off purely according to impulse and opportunity—that is a miniature picture of the social ideal that one might call the freedom of bondage.

If all association and separation shall be the strictly appropriate representation of inner realities, so are the latter here fallen by the way, and only the former phenomenon is left, whose play, obedient to its own laws, whose closed charm, represents *aesthetically* that moderation which the seriousness of realities otherwise demands of its ethical decisions.

This total interpretation of sociability is evidently realized by certain historical developments. In the earlier German Middle Ages we find knightly fraternities which were founded by friendly patrician families. The religious and practical ends of these unions seem to have been lost rather early, and in the fourteenth century the chivalrous interests and conduct remain their only specific content. Soon after, this also disappears, and there remain only purely sociable unions of aristocratic strata. Here the sociability apparently develops as the residuum of a society determined by a content—as the residuum which, because the content has been lost, can exist only in form and in the forms of with-one-another and for-one-another. That the essential existence of these forms can have only the inner nature of play or, reaching deeper, of art appears even more clearly in the court society of the *ancien régime*. Here by the falling-off of the concrete life-content, which was sucked away from the French aristocracy in some measure by the monarchy, there developed free-moving forms, toward which the consciousness of this class was crystallized—forms whose force, definitions, and relations were purely sociable and in no way symbols or functions of the real meanings and intensities of persons and institutions. The etiquette of court society became an end in itself; it "etiquetted" no content any longer but had elaborated immanent laws, comparable to those of art, which have validity only from the viewpoint of art and do not at all have the purpose of imitating faithfully and strikingly the reality of the model, that is, of things outside art.

With this phenomenon, sociability attains its most sovereign expression but at the same time verges on caricature. To be sure, it is its nature to shut out realities from the interactive relations of men and to build its castle in air according to the formal laws of these relations which move within themselves and recognize no purpose outside themselves. But the deep-running source, from which this empire takes its energies, is nonetheless to be sought not in these self-regulating forms but only in the vitality of real individuals, in their sensitivities and attractions, in the fulness of their impulses and convictions. All sociability is but a symbol of life, as it shows itself in the flow of a lightly amusing play; but, even so, a symbol of *life*, whose likeness it only so far alters as is required by the distance from it gained in the play, exactly as also the freest and most fantastic art, the furthest from all reality, nourishes itself from a deep and true relation to reality, if it is not to be empty and lying. If sociability cuts off completely the threads which bind it to real life and out of which it spins its admittedly stylized web, it turns from play to empty farce, to a lifeless schematization proud of its woodenness.

From this context it becomes apparent that men can complain both justly and unjustly of the superficiality of social intercourse. It is one of the most pregnant facts of mental life that, if we weld certain elements taken from the whole of being into a realm of their own, which is governed by its own laws and not by those of the whole, this realm, if completely cut off from the life of the whole, can display in its inner realization an empty nature suspended in the air; but then, often altered only by imponderables, precisely in this state of removal from all immediate reality, its deeper nature can appear more completely, more integrated and meaningful, than any attempt to comprehend it realistically and without taking distance. According as the former or the latter experience predominates, will one's own life, running its own course according to its own norms, be a formal, meaningless dead thing —or a symbolic play, in whose aesthetic charm all the finest and most highly sublimated dynamics of social existence and its riches are gathered. In all art, in all the symbolism of the religious life, in great measure even in the complex formulations of science, we are thrown back upon this belief, upon this feeling, that autonomies of mere parts of observed reality, that the combinations of certain superficial elements possess a relation to the depth and wholeness of life, which, although often not easy to formulate, makes such a part the bearer and the representative of the fundamental reality. From this we may understand the saving grace and blessing effect of these realms built out of the pure forms of existence, for in them we are released from life but have it still. The sight of the sea frees us inwardly, not in spite of but because of the fact that in its rushing up only to recede, its receding only to rise again, in the play and counterplay of its waves, the whole of life is stylized to the simplest expression of its dynamic, quite free from all reality which one may experience and from all the baggage of individual fate, whose final meaning seems nevertheless to flow into this stark picture. Just so art perhaps reveals the secret of life; that we save ourselves not by simply looking away from it but precisely in that in the apparently self-governing play of its forms we construct and experience the meaning and the forces of its deepest reality but without the reality itself. Sociability would not hold for so many thoughtful men who feel in every moment the pressure of life, this emancipating and saving exhilaration if it were only a flight from life, the mere momentary lifting of its seriousness. It can often enough be only this negative thing, a conventionalism and inwardly lifeless exchange of formulas; so perhaps in the *ancien régime*, where gloomy anxiety over a threatening reality drove men into pure escape, into severance from the powers of actual life. The freeing and lightening, however, that precisely the more thoughtful man finds in sociability is this; that association and exchange of stimulus, in which all the tasks and the whole weight of life are realized, here is consumed in an artistic play, in that simultaneous sublimation and dilution, in which the heavily freighted forces of reality are felt only as from a distance, their weight fleeting in a charm.

III. Social Types

10

THE STRANGER

1908

IF WANDERING, considered as a state of detachment from every given point in space, is the conceptual opposite of attachment to any point, then the sociological form of "the stranger" presents the synthesis, as it were, of both of these properties. (This is another indication that spatial relations not only are determining conditions of relationships among men, but are also symbolic of those relationships.) The stranger will thus not be considered here in the usual sense of the term, as the wanderer who comes today and goes tomorrow, but rather as the man who comes today and stays tomorrow—the potential wanderer, so to speak, who, although he has gone no further, has not quite got over the freedom of coming and going. He is fixed within a certain spatial circle —or within a group whose boundaries are analogous to spatial boundaries—but his position within it is fundamentally affected by the fact that he does not belong in it initially and that he brings qualities into it that are not, and cannot be, indigenous to it.

In the case of the stranger, the union of closeness and remoteness involved in every human relationship is patterned in a way that may be succinctly formulated as follows: the distance within this relation indicates that one who is close by is remote, but his strangeness indicates that one who is remote is near. The state of being a stranger is of course a completely positive relation; it is a specific form of interaction. The inhabitants of Sirius are not

From "Der Fremde," in *Soziologie* (Munich and Leipzig: Duncker & Humblot, 1908), pp. 685–91. Translated by Donald N. Levine.

exactly strangers to us, at least not in the sociological sense of the word as we are considering it. In that sense they do not exist for us at all; they are beyond being far and near. The stranger is an element of the group itself, not unlike the poor and sundry "inner enemies"—an element whose membership within the group involves both being outside it and confronting it.

The following statements about the stranger are intended to suggest how factors of repulsion and distance work to create a form of being together, a form of union based on interaction.

In the whole history of economic activity the stranger makes his appearance everywhere as a trader, and the trader makes his as a stranger. As long as production for one's own needs is the general rule, or products are exchanged within a relatively small circle, there is no need for a middleman within the group. A trader is required only for goods produced outside the group. Unless there are people who wander out into foreign lands to buy these necessities, in which case they are themselves "strange" merchants in this other region, the trader *must* be a stranger; there is no opportunity for anyone else to make a living at it.

This position of the stranger stands out more sharply if, instead of leaving the place of his activity, he settles down there. In innumerable cases even this is possible only if he can live by trade as a middleman. Any closed economic group where land and handicrafts have been apportioned in a way that satisfies local demands will still support a livelihood for the trader. For trade alone makes possible unlimited combinations, and through it intelligence is constantly extended and applied in new areas, something that is much harder for the primary producer with his more limited mobility and his dependence on a circle of customers that can be expanded only very slowly. Trade can always absorb more men than can primary production. It is therefore the most suitable activity for the stranger, who intrudes as a supernumerary, so to speak, into a group in which all the economic positions are already occupied. The classic example of this is the history of European Jews. The stranger is by his very nature no owner of land—land not only in the physical sense but also metaphorically as a vital substance which is fixed, if not in space, then at least in an ideal position within the social environment.

Although in the sphere of intimate personal relations the stranger may be attractive and meaningful in many ways, so long as he is regarded as a stranger he is no "landowner" in the eyes of the other. Restriction to intermediary trade and often (as though sublimated from it) to pure finance gives the stranger the specific character of *mobility*. The appearance of this mobility within a bounded group occasions that synthesis of nearness and remoteness which constitutes the formal position of the stranger. The purely mobile person comes incidentally into contact with *every* single element but is not bound up organically, through established ties of kinship, locality, or occupation, with any single one.

Another expression of this constellation is to be found in the objectivity of the stranger. Because he is not bound by roots to the particular constituents and partisan dispositions of the group, he confronts all of these with a distinctly "objective" attitude, an attitude that does not signify mere detachment and nonparticipation, but is a distinct structure composed of remoteness and nearness, indifference and involvement. I refer to my analysis of the dominating positions gained by aliens, in the discussion of superordination and subordination,[1] typified by the practice in certain Italian cities of recruiting their judges from outside, because no native was free from entanglement in family interests and factionalism.

Connected with the characteristic of objectivity is a phenomenon that is found chiefly, though not exclusively, in the stranger who moves on. This is that he often receives the most surprising revelations and confidences, at times reminiscent of a confessional, about matters which are kept carefully hidden from everybody with whom one is close. Objectivity is by no means nonparticipation, a condition that is altogether outside the distinction between subjective and objective orientations. It is rather a positive and definite kind of participation, in the same way that the objectivity of a theoretical observation clearly does not mean that the mind is a passive tabula rasa on which things inscribe their qualities, but rather signifies the full activity of a mind working according to its own laws, under conditions that exclude accidental distortions and

[1]   Simmel refers here to a passage which may be found in *The Sociology of Georg Simmel*, pp. 216–21.—Ed.

emphases whose individual and subjective differences would produce quite different pictures of the same object.

Objectivity can also be defined as freedom. The objective man is not bound by ties which could prejudice his perception, his understanding, and his assessment of data. This freedom, which permits the stranger to experience and treat even his close relationships as though from a bird's-eye view, contains many dangerous possibilities. From earliest times, in uprisings of all sorts the attacked party has claimed that there has been incitement from the outside, by foreign emissaries and agitators. Insofar as this has happened, it represents an exaggeration of the specific role of the stranger: he is the freer man, practically and theoretically; he examines conditions with less prejudice; he assesses them against standards that are more general and more objective; and his actions are not confined by custom, piety, or precedent.[2]

Finally, the proportion of nearness and remoteness which gives the stranger the character of objectivity also finds practical expression in the more *abstract* nature of the relation to him. That is, with the stranger one has only certain *more general* qualities in common, whereas the relation with organically connected persons is based on the similarity of just those specific traits which differentiate them from the merely universal. In fact, all personal relations whatsoever can be analyzed in terms of this scheme. They are not determined only by the existence of certain common characteristics which the individuals share in addition to their individual differences, which either influence the relationship or remain outside of it. Rather, the kind of effect which that commonality has on the relation essentially depends on whether it exists only among the participants themselves, and thus, although general within the relation, is specific and incomparable with respect to all those on the outside, or whether the participants feel that what they have

[2] Where the attacked parties make such an assertion falsely, they do so because those in higher positions tend to exculpate inferiors who previously have been in a close, solidary relationship with them. By introducing the fiction that the rebels were not really guilty, but only instigated, so they did not actually start the rebellion, they exonerate themselves by denying that there were any real grounds for the uprising.

in common is so only because it is common to a group, a type, or mankind in general. In the latter case, the effect of the common features becomes attenuated in proportion to the size of the group bearing the same characteristics. The commonality provides a basis for unifying the members, to be sure; but it does not specifically direct *these* particular persons to one another. A similarity so widely shared could just as easily unite each person with every possible other. This, too, is evidently a way in which a relationship includes both nearness and remoteness simultaneously. To the extent to which the similarities assume a universal nature, the warmth of the connection based on them will acquire an element of coolness, a sense of the contingent nature of precisely *this* relation—the connecting forces have lost their specific, centripetal character.

In relation to the stranger, it seems to me, this constellation assumes an extraordinary preponderance in principle over the individual elements peculiar to the relation in question. The stranger is close to us insofar as we feel between him and ourselves similarities of nationality or social position, of occupation or of general human nature. He is far from us insofar as these similarities extend beyond him and us, and connect us only because they connect a great many people.

A trace of strangeness in this sense easily enters even the most intimate relationships. In the stage of first passion, erotic relations strongly reject any thought of generalization. A love such as this has never existed before; there is nothing to compare either with the person one loves or with our feelings for that person. An estrangement is wont to set in (whether as cause or effect is hard to decide) at the moment when this feeling of uniqueness disappears from the relationship. A skepticism regarding the intrinsic value of the relationship and its value for us adheres to the very thought that in this relation, after all, one is only fulfilling a general human destiny, that one has had an experience that has occurred a thousand times before, and that, if one had not accidentally met this precise person, someone else would have acquired the same meaning for us.

Something of this feeling is probably not absent in any relation, be it ever so close, because that which is common to two is perhaps never common *only* to them but belongs to a general conception which includes much else besides, many *possibilities* of similarities. No matter how few of these possibilities are realized and how often we may forget about them, here and there, nevertheless, they crowd in like shadows between men, like a mist eluding every designation, which must congeal into solid corporeality for it to be called jealousy. Perhaps this is in many cases a more general, at least more insurmountable, strangeness than that due to differences and obscurities. It is strangeness caused by the fact that similarity, harmony, and closeness are accompanied by the feeling that they are actually not the exclusive property of this particular relation, but stem from a more general one—a relation that potentially includes us and an indeterminate number of others, and therefore prevents that relation which alone was experienced from having an inner and exclusive necessity.

On the other hand, there is a sort of "strangeness" in which this very connection on the basis of a general quality embracing the parties is precluded. The relation of the Greeks to the barbarians is a typical example; so are all the cases in which the general characteristics one takes as peculiarly and merely human are disallowed to the other. But here the expression "the stranger" no longer has any positive meaning. The relation with him is a nonrelation; he is not what we have been discussing here: the stranger as a member of the group itself.

As such, the stranger is near and far *at the same time*, as in any relationship based on merely universal human similarities. Between these two factors of nearness and distance, however, a peculiar tension arises, since the consciousness of having only the absolutely general in common has exactly the effect of putting a special emphasis on that which is not common. For a stranger to the country, the city, the race, and so on, what is stressed is again nothing individual, but alien origin, a quality which he has, or could have, in common with many other strangers. For this reason strangers are not really perceived as individuals, but as strangers of a certain type. Their remoteness is no less general than their nearness.

This form appears, for example, in so special a case as the tax levied on Jews in Frankfurt and elsewhere during the Middle Ages. Whereas the tax paid by Christian citizens varied according to their wealth at any given time, for every single Jew the tax was fixed once and for all. This amount was fixed because the Jew had his social position as a *Jew*, not as the bearer of certain objective contents. With respect to taxes every other citizen was regarded as possessor of a certain amount of wealth, and his tax could follow the fluctuations of his fortune. But the Jew as taxpayer was first of all a Jew, and thus his fiscal position contained an invariable element. This appears most forcefully, of course, once the differing circumstances of individual Jews are no longer considered, limited though this consideration is by fixed assessments, and all strangers pay exactly the same head tax.

Despite his being inorganically appended to it, the stranger is still an organic member of the group. Its unified life includes the specific conditioning of this element. Only we do not know how to designate the characteristic unity of this position otherwise than by saying that it is put together of certain amounts of nearness and of remoteness. Although both these qualities are found to some extent in all relationships, a special proportion and reciprocal tension between them produce the specific form of the relation to the "stranger."

11

THE POOR

1908

I

INSOFAR AS MAN is a social being, to each of his obligations
there corresponds a right on the part of others. Perhaps even the
more profound conception would be to think that originally only
rights existed; that each individual has demands which are of a
general human character and the result of his particular condition,
and which afterward become the obligation of others. But since
every person with obligations in one way or another also possesses
rights, a network of rights and obligations is thus formed, where
right is always the primary element that sets the tone, and obligation is nothing more than its correlate in the same act and, indeed,
an inevitable correlate. . . .

A fundamental opposition between the sociological and ethical
categories manifests itself here. Inasmuch as all relations of presta-
tion are derived from a *right*—in the widest sense of this concept
which includes, among other elements, legal right—the relationship between man and man has totally imbued the moral values of
the individual and determined his course. However, in contrast to
the undoubted idealism of this point of view, there is the no less
deeply based rejection of any interindividual genesis of duty. Our
duties (from this standpoint)—it is said—are duties only toward
ourselves and there are no others. Their content may be the conduct

Reprinted from "The Poor," *Social Problems* 13, no. 2 (Fall 1965). Translated by Claire Jacobson. Originally published as "Der Arme," in *Soziologie*
(Munich and Leipzig: Duncker & Humblot, 1908).

toward other men, but their form and motivation as duty do not derive from others, but are generated with full autonomy by the self and its own purely internal demands, being independent of anything that lies outside of it. It is only in the case of right that the other is the *terminus a quo* of motivation in our moral actions, but for morality itself he is no more than the *terminus ad quem*. In the final analysis, we ourselves are the only ones responsible for the morality of our acts; we are responsible for them only to our better selves, to our self-esteem, or whatever we wish to call this enigmatic focus which the soul finds in itself as the final judge that decides freely up to what point the rights of others are obligations.

This fundamental dualism in the basic sentiments which govern the course of moral action is exemplified or empirically symbolized by various conceptions that exist in relation to assistance to the poor. The obligations we have toward the poor may appear as a simple correlate of the rights of the poor. Especially in countries where begging is a normal occupation, the beggar believes more or less naively that he has a right to alms and frequently considers that their denial means the withholding of a tribute to which he is entitled. Another and completely different characteristic—in the same category—implies the idea that the right to assistance is based on the group affiliation of the needy. One point of view according to which the individual is merely the product of his social milieu confers upon that individual the right to solicit from the group compensation for every situation of need and every loss. But even if such an extreme dissolution of individual responsibility is not accepted, one may stress, from a social viewpoint, that the rights of the needy are the basis of all assistance to the poor. For only if we assume such rights, at least as a socio-legal fiction, does it appear possible to protect public assistance from arbitrariness and dependence upon a chance financial situation or other uncertain factors. Everywhere the predictability of functions is improved whenever in the correlation between the rights and obligations that underlie them right constitutes the methodological point of departure; for man, in general, is more easily disposed to demand a right than to fulfill an obligation.

To this may be added the humanitarian motive of making it

easier for the poor person to request and accept assistance, when by doing so he only exercises his due right; for the humiliation, shame, and *déclassement* that charity implies are overcome for him to the extent that it is not conceded out of compassion or sense of duty or utility, but because he can lay claim to it. Since this right naturally has limits, which must be determined in each individual case, the right to assistance will not modify these motivations in the material quantitative aspect with respect to other motivations. By making it a right, its inner meaning is determined and is raised to a fundamental opinion about the relationship between the individual and other individuals and between the individual and the totality. The right to assistance belongs in the same category as the right to work and the right to life. It is true in this case that the ambiguity of the quantitative limits, which characterizes this as well as other "human rights," reaches its maximum, especially if assistance is in cash; for the purely quantitative and relative character of money makes it much more difficult objectively to delimit requests than assistance in kind—except in complex or highly individualized cases in which the poor person may make a more useful and fruitful application of money than of assistance in kind, with its providential character.

It is also unclear to whom the rights of the poor ought to be addressed, and the solution of this question reveals very deep sociological differences. The poor person who perceives his condition as an injustice of the cosmic order and who asks for redress, so to speak, from the entire creation will easily consider any individual who is in better circumstances than he jointly liable for his claims against society. This leads to a scale which goes from the delinquent proletarian who sees in any well-dressed person an enemy, a representative of the "exploiting" class who can be robbed in good conscience, to the humble beggar who asks for charity "for the love of God," as though each individual had the obligation of filling the holes of the order which God desired but has not fully implemented. The poor man addresses his demands in this case to the individual; however, not to a specific individual, but to the individual on the basis of the solidarity of mankind. Beyond this correlation which allows any particular individual to appear as a representative of the totality of existence with respect to the demands directed to that totality, there are multiple particular collectivities to which the claims of the poor are addressed. The State, municipality, parish, professional association, circle of friends, family, may, as total entities, maintain a variety of relationships with their members; but each of these relationships appears to include an element which is manifested as the right to assistance in the event of impoverishment of the individual. This characteristic is the common element of such sociological relationships, although in other respects they are of highly heterogeneous character. The rights of the poor which are generated by such ties are curiously mixed under primitive conditions, where the individual is dominated by the tribal customs and religious obligations that constitute an undifferentiated unity. Among the ancient Semites, the right of the poor to participate in a meal is not associated with personal generosity, but rather with social affiliation and with religious custom. Where assistance to the poor has its *raison d'être* in an organic link between elements, the *rights of the poor are* more highly emphasized, whether their religious premise derives from a metaphysical unity or their kinship or tribal basis from a biological unity. We will see, in contrast, that when assistance to the poor derives teleologically from a goal one hopes to pursue in this way, rather than from the causal basis of a real and effective unity among all the members of the group, the rights of the poor dwindle to nothingness.

In the cases examined so far, a right and an obligation seemed to be two aspects of an absolute relationship. Completely new forms appear, however, when the point of departure is the obligation of the giver rather than the right of the recipient. In the extreme case, the poor disappear completely as legitimate subjects and central foci of the interests involved. The motive for alms then resides exclusively in the significance of giving for the giver. When Jesus told the wealthy young man, "Give your riches to the poor," what apparently mattered to him were not the poor, but rather the soul of the wealthy man for whose salvation this sacrifice was merely a means or symbol. Later on, Christian alms retained the same character; they represent no more than a form of asceticism, of "good works," which improve the chances of salvation of the giver. The rise of begging in the Middle Ages, the senseless distribution of alms, the demoralization of the proletariat through arbitrary donations which tend to undermine all creative work, all these phenomena constitute the revenge, so to speak, that alms take for the purely subjectivistic motive of their concession—a motive which concerns only the giver but not the recipient.

II

As soon as the welfare of society requires assistance to the poor, the motivation turns away from this focus on the giver without, thereby, turning to the recipient. This assistance then takes place voluntarily or is imposed by law, so that the poor will not become active and dangerous enemies of society, so as to make their reduced energies more productive, and so as to prevent the degeneration of their progeny. The poor man as a person, and the perception of his position in his own mind, are in this case as indifferent as they are to the giver who gives alms for the salvation of his own soul. In this case, the subjective egoism of the latter is overcome not for the sake of the poor, but for the sake of society. The fact that the poor receive alms is not an end-in-itself but merely a means to an end, the same as in the case of the man who gives alms for the sake of his salvation. The predominance of the social point of view with reference to alms is shown in the fact that the giving can be refused from that same social point of view, and this

frequently happens when personal compassion or the unpleasantness of refusing would move us strongly to give.

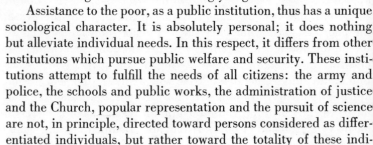

Assistance to the poor, as a public institution, thus has a unique sociological character. It is absolutely personal; it does nothing but alleviate individual needs. In this respect, it differs from other institutions which pursue public welfare and security. These institutions attempt to fulfill the needs of all citizens: the army and police, the schools and public works, the administration of justice and the Church, popular representation and the pursuit of science are not, in principle, directed toward persons considered as differentiated individuals, but rather toward the totality of these individuals; the unity of many or all is the purpose of these institutions. Assistance to the poor, on the other hand, is focused in its concrete activity on the individual and his situation. And indeed this individual, in the abstract modern type of welfare, is the *final* action but in no way the *final purpose*, which consists solely in the protection and furtherance of the community. The poor cannot even be considered as a *means* to this end—which would improve their position—for social action does not make use of them, but only of certain objective material and administrative means aimed at suppressing the dangers and losses which the poor imply for the common good. This formal situation is not only valid for the total collectivity, but also for smaller circles. Even within the family there are many acts of assistance, not for the sake of the recipient himself, but so that the family need not be ashamed and lose its reputation owing to the poverty of one of its members. The aid which English trade unions grant to their unemployed members does not purport so much to alleviate the personal situation of the recipient as to prevent that the unemployed, prompted by necessity, should work more cheaply and that this should result in lower wages for the entire trade.

If we take into consideration this meaning of assistance to the poor, it becomes clear that the fact of taking away from the rich to give to the poor does not aim at equalizing their individual positions and is not, even in its orientation, directed at suppressing the social difference between the rich and the poor. On the contrary, assistance is based on the structure of society, whatever it may be; it is in open contradiction to all socialist and communist aspirations which would abolish this social structure. The goal of assistance is precisely to mitigate certain extreme manifestations of social differentiation, so that the social structure may continue to be based on this differentiation. If assistance were to be based on the interests of the poor person, there would, in principle, be no limit whatsoever on the transmission of property in favor of the poor, a transmission that would lead to the equality of all. But since the focus is the social whole—the political, family, or other sociologically determined circles—there is no reason to aid the person more than is required by the maintenance of the social *status quo*.

When this purely social and centralist teleology prevails, assistance to the poor offers perhaps the greatest sociological tension between the direct and the indirect goals of an action. The alleviation of personal need is emotionally so categorical an end-in-itself, that to deprive it of this ultimate purpose and to convert it into a mere technique for the transsubjective ends of a social unit constitutes a significant triumph for the latter. This distantiation between the individual and the social unit—despite its lack of visibility—is more fundamental and radical in its abstractness and coldness than sacrifices of the individual for the collectivity in which the means and the ends tend to be bound together by a chain of sentiments.

This basic sociological relationship explains the peculiar complications of rights and duties which we find in modern assistance to the poor by the State. Frequently we find the principle according to which the State has the obligation to assist the poor, but to this obligation there is no corresponding right to assistance on the part of the poor. As has been expressly declared in England for example, the poor person has no recourse to action for unjust refusal of assistance, nor can he solicit compensation for illegally refused assistance. All the relations between obligations and rights are located, so to speak, above and beyond the poor. The right which corresponds to the obligation of the State to provide assistance is not the right of the poor, but rather the right of every citizen that the taxes he pays for the poor be of such a size and applied in such a manner that the public goals of assistance to the poor be truly attained. Consequently, in the case of negligence in assistance to the poor, it would not be the poor who are entitled to take action against the State, but rather the other elements indirectly harmed by such negligence. In case it should be possible, for instance, to prove that a thief might not have carried out a robbery if the legal assistance requested by him had been granted, it would in principle be the robbed one who would be entitled to claim compensation from the welfare administration. Assistance to the poor holds, in legal teleology, the same position as the protection of animals. No one is punished in Germany for torturing an animal, except if he does it "publicly or in a manner that results in scandal."

It is not, therefore, consideration for the mistreated animal but rather for the witnesses that determines punishment.

This exclusion of the poor, which consists in denying them the status of a final end in the teleological chain and, as we have seen, does not even permit them to stand there as a means, is also manifested in the fact that within the modern relatively democratic State public assistance is perhaps the *only* branch of the administration in which the interested parties have no participation whatsoever. In the conception to which we are referring, assistance to the poor is, in effect, an application of public means to public ends; and, since the poor find themselves excluded from its teleology— something that is not the case for the interested parties in other branches of administration—it is logical that the principle of self-government, which is recognized to a varying degree in other matters, should not be applied to the poor and to their assistance. When the State is obligated by a law to channel a stream to provide irrigation for certain districts, the stream is approximately in the situation of the poor supported by the State: it is the object of obligation but is not entitled to the corresponding right, which is rather that of the adjacent property holders. And every time that this centralist interest prevails, the relationship between right and obligation may be altered for the sake of utilitarian considerations. The draft of the Prussian Poor Law of 1842 asserts that the State must organize assistance to the poor in the interest of public prosperity. With this objective, it creates legal public bodies which are obligated to the State to assist needy individuals; but they are not so obligated to the latter since these have no legal claim. . . .

III

The image of a channeled stream which we used previously was, however, inaccurate. For the poor are not only poor, they are also citizens. *As such,* they participate in the rights which the law grants to the totality of citizens, in accordance with the obligation of the State to assist the poor. To use the same image, let us say that the poor are at the same time the stream and the adjacent landowner, in the same sense as the wealthiest citizens could be. Undoubtedly, the functions of the State, which formally stand at the same ideal distance from all citizens, have, insofar as content is concerned, very different connotations, in accordance with the different positions of citizens; and though the poor participate in assistance, not as subjects with their own ends but merely as members of the teleological organization of the State which transcends them, their role in that function of the State, however, is distinct from that of well-to-do citizens.

What matters sociologically is to understand that the special position which the assisted poor occupy does not impede their incorporation into the State as members of the total political unit. This is so despite the fact that their overall situation makes their individual condition the external endpoint of a helping act and, on the other hand, an inert object without rights in the total goals of the State. In spite of, or better yet, because of these two characteristics which appear to place the poor outside the State, the poor are ordered organically within the whole, belong as poor to the historical reality of society which lives in them and above them, and constitute a formal sociological element, like the civil servant or the taxpayer, the teacher or the intermediary in any interaction. The poor are approximately in the situation of the stranger to the group who finds himself, so to speak, materially outside the group in which he resides. But precisely in this case a large total structure emerges which comprises the autochthonous parts of the group as well as the stranger; and the peculiar interactions between them create the group in a wider sense and characterize the true historical circle. Thus the poor are located in a way outside the group; but this is no more than a peculiar mode of interaction which binds them into a unity with the whole in its widest sense.

It is only with this conception that we resolve the sociological antinomy of the poor, which reflects the ethical-social difficulties of assistance. The solipsist tendency of the medieval type of almsgiving of which I spoke bypassed internally, so to say, the poor to whom the action was directed externally; in so doing, it neglected the principle according to which man must never be treated exclusively as a means but always as an end. In principle, the one who receives alms also gives something; there is a diffusion of effects from him to the giver and this is precisely what converts the donation into an interaction, into a sociological event. But if—as in the case previously cited—the recipient of alms remains completely excluded from the teleological process of the giver, if the poor fulfill no role other than being an almsbox into which alms for Masses are tossed, the interaction is cut short; the donation is no social fact, but a purely individual fact.

As we were saying, neither does the modern conception of assistance to the poor consider the poor as ends-to-themselves; but nevertheless, according to it, the poor, although they are located in a teleological series which bypasses them, are an element which belongs organically to the whole and are—on the basis given— closely related to the goals of the collectivity. Certainly neither now nor in the medieval form is their reaction to the donation directed to any specific individual; but by rehabilitating their economic activity, by preserving their bodily energy, by preventing their impulses from leading them to the use of violent means to enrich themselves, the social collectivity gets back from the poor a reaction to what it has done to them.

A purely individual relationship is sufficient from the ethical point of view and perfect from the sociological point of view only when each individual is an end for the other—although naturally not merely an end. But this cannot be applied to the actions of a transpersonal collective entity. The teleology of the collectivity may quietly pass by the individual and return to itself without resting on him. From the moment the individual belongs to this whole he is placed thereby, from the beginning, at the final point of action and not, as in the other case, outside of it. Although he is denied as individual the character of an end-in-itself, he participates as member of the whole in the character of an end-in-itself which the whole always possesses.

A long time before this centralist conception of the essence of assistance to the poor became clear, its organic role in the life of the collectivity was revealed through visible symbols. In old England, assistance to the poor was exercised by monasteries and ecclesiastical corporations, and the reason for this, as has been duly noted, is that only the property of mortmain possesses the

indispensable permanence on which assistance to the poor necessarily depends. The numerous secular donations derived from
booties and penances did not suffice to attain this end, because
they were not yet sufficiently integrated into the administrative
system of the State and they were consumed without lasting results.
Assistance to the poor then became based on the only substantial
and fixed point in the midst of social chaos and turmoil; and this
connection is shown negatively by the indignation aroused by the
clergy sent from Rome to England, because they neglected to help
the poor. The foreign priest does not feel intimately related to the
life of the community; and the fact that he does not care for the
poor appears as the clearest sign of this lack of connection.

This same link of assistance with the firm substratum of social
existence appears clear in the later tie established in England between the poor tax and landed property; and this was cause as
much as effect of the fact that the poor counted as an organic element of the land, belonging to the land. The same tendency is
manifested in 1861, when part of the welfare charges were legally
transferred from the parish to the welfare association. The costs
of assistance to the poor were no longer to be carried in isolation
by parishes, but rather by a fund to which the parishes contributed
in relation to the value of their landed property. The proposition
that in order to make a distribution the number of inhabitants
should also be taken into consideration was repeatedly and expressly rejected; with it, the individualistic element was completely excluded. A suprapersonal entity, with its substratum in the
objectivity of landed property, and not a sum of persons, appeared
as the carrier of the obligation to assist the poor. Assistance in this
case is so basic to the social group that the local administration
only gradually added to this main activity, first the administration
of schools and roads, and then public health and the system of
registration. Elsewhere, also, the welfare administration has become a basis of political unity because of its success. The North
German Confederation decided that in all of the territory of the
Confederation no needy person should remain without assistance
and that none of the poor in the Confederation should receive a
different treatment in one region than in another. If in England

external and technical reasons contributed to establish a link between assistance to the poor and landed property, this connection
does not lose its profound sociological meaning when the addition
of other branches of administration to public assistance institutions led to the crossing of county boundaries by the welfare associations despite the technical disadvantages involved. It is precisely this contradiction in the technical conditions which makes
the unity of sociological meaning even more conspicuous.

Consequently, the conception that defines assistance to the poor
as an "organization of the propertied classes in order to fulfill the
sentiment of moral duty which is associated with property" is completely one-sided. Assistance is rather a part of the organization of
the *whole*, to which the poor belong as well as the propertied
classes. It is certain that the technical and material characteristics
of their social position make them a mere object or point of intersection within a transcending collective life. But, in the final analysis, this is the role that each concrete individual member of society
performs; about which one can say, in accordance with the viewpoint temporarily accepted here, what Spinoza says of God and
the individual; that we may love God, but that it would be contradictory that He, the whole which contains us, should love us, and
that the love which we dedicate to Him is a part of the infinite love
with which God loves Himself. The singular exclusion to which the
poor are subjected on the part of the community which assists them
is characteristic of the role which they fulfill *within* society, as
members of it in a special situation. If technically they are mere
objects, in turn in a wider sociological sense they are subjects who,
on the one hand, like all the others, constitute social reality and,
on the other hand, like all the others, are located beyond the abstract and suprapersonal unity of society.

IV

Owing to this also it is the general structure of the group
that decides the question: Where do the poor belong? To the extent
that a poor person carries out some economic activity, he belongs
to the segment of the general economy which includes that activity.

If a church member, he belongs in its sphere as marked off from that of any other [religious organization]. As member of a family, he belongs in the personally and spatially defined circle of his relatives. But where does he belong insofar as he is poor?

A society maintained or organized on the basis of tribal consciousness includes the poor within the circle of their tribe. Other societies, whose ethical connections are fulfilled essentially through the Church, will turn the poor over to one or another type of pious associations, which are the answer of the society to the fact of poverty. The explanatory reasons of the German law of 1871 on place of residence for assistance answers this question in the following manner: the poor belong to that community—that is, that community is obligated to assist them—which utilized their economic strength before their impoverishment. The principle just mentioned is a manifestation of the social structure which existed prior to the complete triumph of the idea of the modern State, since the municipality is the place which enjoyed the economic fruits of those who are now impoverished. But the modern mobility, the interlocal exchange of all forces, have eliminated this limitation; so that the whole State must be considered the *terminus a quo* and *ad quem* of all prestations. If the laws actually permit everybody to establish his residence in whatever community he wishes, then the community no longer has an integrated relationship with its inhabitants. If there is no right to oppose establishment of residence on the part of undesirable elements, one can no longer demand of the community a solidary give-and-take relationship with the individual. Only for practical reasons, and then only as organs of the State—thus read the explanatory reasons of the legislation—do the municipalities have the obligation to take over the care of the poor.

This is, then, the extreme condition which the formal position of the poor has attained, a condition in which their dependence on the general level of social evolution is revealed. The poor belong to the largest effective circle. No part of the totality but the totality itself, to the extent that it constitutes a unit, is the place or power to which the poor as poor are linked. It is only for this circle, which, being the largest, has no other outside it to which to transfer an obligation, that a problem pointed out by the practitioners of welfare in the small corporative entities ceases to exist: the fact that they frequently avoid giving assistance to the poor, for fear that once they have taken care of them they will always have them on their hands. We see manifested here a very important character-istic for human sociation, a trait which might be called moral in-duction: when an act of assistance has been performed, of whatever type, although it be spontaneous and individual and not demanded by any obligation, there is a duty to continue it, a duty which is not only a claim on the part of the one who receives the assistance but also a sentiment on the part of the one who gives. It is a very common experience that the beggars to whom alms are given with regularity consider these very rapidly as their right and as the duty of the giver, and if the latter fails in this supposed obligation they interpret it as a denial of their due contribution and feel a bitter-ness which they would not feel against someone who always denied them alms. There is also the person in better circumstances who has supported for some time a needy person, fixing in advance the pe-riod for which he will do so, and who, however, when he stops his gifts, is left with a painful feeling, as if he were guilty. With full consciousness, this fact is recognized by a Talmudic law of the ritual code "Jore Deah": he who has assisted three times a poor person with the same amount, although he had in no way the in-tention of continuing the assistance, tacitly acquires the obligation of continuing it; his act assumes the character of a vow, from which only weighty reasons can dispense him, such as, for example, his own impoverishment.

The case just mentioned is much more complicated than the related principle, homologous to *odisse quem laeseris*, which says that one loves the one to whom he has done good. It is understand-able that one projects the satisfaction of his own good action on the one who has given him the opportunity for it: in the love for the one for whom he has made sacrifices he loves in essence him-self, just as in the hate against the one to whom he has done an injustice he hates himself. The sense of obligation that the good action leaves in the doer of good, that particular form of *noblesse oblige*, cannot be explained with so simple a psychology. I believe that, in effect, an *a priori* condition is involved here: that each ac-

tion of this type—despite its apparent free will, despite its apparent
character of *opus supererogationis*—derives from an obligation;
that in such behavior a profound obligation is implicit which, in a
certain way, is manifested and made visible through action. What
happens here is the same as in scientific induction: if the similarity is accepted between a past process and a future one, it is not
simply because the first one has this or that structure, but because
a *law* can be derived from the first process that determines it in
the same way as it determines any other future process. There must
be, therefore, a moral instinct which tells us that the first act of
charity already corresponded to an obligation which also demands
the second no less than the first action. This is clearly related to the
motives which we touched on at the beginning of this study. If, in
the final analysis, any altruism, any good action, any self-sacrifice,
is nothing but a duty and an obligation, this principle may, in the
individual case, be manifested in such a form that any act of assistance is, in its profound sense—if one wishes, from the viewpoint of a metaphysics of ethics—the mere fulfillment of a duty
which, naturally, is not exhausted with the first action but rather
continues to exist as long as the determining occasion obtains. According to this, assistance given to someone would be the *ratio
cognoscendi*, the sign which makes us see that one of the ideal lines
of obligation between man and man runs here and reveals its timeless aspect in the continuing effects of the bond established.

V

We have seen so far two forms of the relation between right
and obligation: the poor have a *right* to assistance; and there exists
an *obligation* to assist them, an obligation which is not oriented
toward the poor as having a right, but toward society to whose
preservation this obligation contributes and which the society demands from its organs or from certain groups. But along with
these two forms there exists a third, which probably dominates the
moral consciousness: the collectivity and well-to-do persons have
the obligation to assist the poor, and this obligation has its sufficient goal in the alleviation of the situation of the poor; to this

there corresponds a right of the poor, as the correlative end of the purely moral relation between the needy and the well-to-do. If I am not mistaken, the emphasis has shifted within this relation since the 18th century. The ideal of humanitarianism and of the rights of man, mostly in England, displaced the centralist spirit of the Elizabethan Poor Law, according to which work had to be provided for the poor for the benefit of the community. The ideal of humanitarianism substituted for this principle another one: every poor person has a right to minimal subsistence, whether he wants and is able to work or not. On the other hand, modern assistance, in the correlation between moral duty (of the giver) and moral right (of the recipient) prefers to emphasize the former. Evidently, this form is realized above all by private assistance, in contrast to public assistance. We are attempting now to determine its sociological significance in this sense.

First, we should point out here the already noted tendency to consider assistance to the poor as a matter pertaining to the widest political circle (the State), while initially it was based everywhere in the local community. This ascription of assistance to the smallest circle was, first of all, a consequence of the corporative ties that bound the community. As long as the supraindividual organism around and above the individual had not changed from the municipality to the State and freedom of mobility had not completed this process factually and psychologically, it was the most natural thing in the world for neighbors to assist needy persons. To this may be added an extremely important circumstance for the sociology of the poor: that of all the social claims of a non-individualistic character based on a general quality, it is that of the poor which most impresses us. Laying aside acute stimuli, such as accidents or sexual provocations, there is nothing such as misery that acts with such impersonality, such indifference, with regard to the other qualities of the object and, at the same time, with such an immediate and effective force. This has given at all times to the obligation of assisting the poor a specific *local* character. Rather, to centralize it in the largest circle and thereby to bring it about not by immediate visibility but only through the general concept of poverty—this is one of the longest roads which sociological forms have had to travel to pass from the immediate sensate form to the abstract.

When this change occurred, whereby assistance to the poor became an abstract obligation of the State—in England in 1834, in Germany since the middle of the 19th century—its character was modified with respect to this centralizing form. Above all, the State maintains in the municipality the obligation to participate in assistance, but considers the municipality as its delegate; local organization has been made into a mere technique in order to attain the best result possible; the municipality is no longer the point of departure, but rather a point of transmission in the process of assistance. For this reason welfare associations are organized everywhere according to principles of utility—for example, in England, they are organized in such a fashion that each of them may support a workhouse—and they have the deliberate tendency to avoid the partiality of local influences. The growing employment of salaried welfare officials works in the same way. These officials stand vis-à-vis the poor much more clearly as representatives of the collectivity from which they receive a salary than do the unpaid officials who work, so to speak, more as human beings and attend not so much to the merely objective point of view as to the human, man-to-man point of view. Finally, a sociologically very important division of functions takes place. The fact that assistance to the poor is still essentially delegated to the municipalities is especially useful for two reasons; first, because every case must be handled individually, something that can only be done by someone close at hand and with intimate knowledge of the milieu, and second because if the municipality has to grant assistance it also has to provide the money, since it might otherwise hand out the funds of the State too freely. On the other hand, there are cases of need in which bureaucratic handling is not a threat, since action can be determined on the basis of objective criteria: sickness, blindness, deaf-mutism, insanity, chronic illness. In these cases, assistance has a more technical character and consequently the State, or the larger institution, is much more efficient. Its greater abundance of means and its centralized administration show their advantages in those cases where personal and local circumstances have little importance. And aside from the qualitative determination of the direct prestations of the State, there is the quantitative determination that particularly differentiates public from private assistance: the State and, in general, public organizations attend only to the most urgent and immediate needs. Everywhere, and particularly in England, assistance is guided by the firm principle that only the minimum necessary for the life of the poor should leave the purse of taxpayers. . . .

If the objective point of view goes hand in hand with the tendency to turn over all assistance to the State—a tendency which certainly until now has nowhere been fully realized—the normative measure, whose logical application implies objectivity, is derived not only from the poor but also from the interest of the State. We see manifested here an essential sociological form of the relationship between the individual and the totality. Wherever prestations or interventions are transferred from individuals to society, regulation by the latter tends to be concerned either with an excess or with a deficiency in individual action. In compulsory education the State requires that the individual should not learn too little, but leaves it up to him whether to learn more or even "too much." With the legal workday, the State provides that the employer should not require too much from his workers, but leaves it up to him whether to ask for less. Thus this regulation always refers only to one side of the action, while the other side is left to the freedom of the individual. This is the scheme within which our socially controlled actions appear; they are limited only in one of their dimensions; society, on the one side, sets limits to their excess or deficiency, while on the other side their deficiency or excess is left to the indefiniteness of subjective choice. But this scheme sometimes deceives us; there are cases in which social regulation includes in fact *both* sides, although practical interest only focuses attention on one side and overlooks the other. Wherever, for example, the private punishment of a crime has been transferred to society and objective criminal law, one only takes into account, as a rule, that thereby one acquires greater certainty in retribution, that is, a sufficient degree and certitude in its application. But, in reality, the goal pursued is not only to punish enough, but also not to punish too much. Society not only protects the person who has suffered damage, but also the criminal against the excess of subjective reaction; that is to say, society establishes as an objective measure of punishment that which corresponds to its social interest and not to the desires or interests of the victim. And this occurs not only in relations which are legally established. Any social class which is not too low sees to it that its members spend a minimum on their clothing; establishes a standard of "decent" dress; and the one who does not attain this standard will no longer belong to that class. But it also establishes a limit at the other extreme, although not with the same determination nor in such a conscious manner; a certain measure of luxury and elegance and even at times modernity is not proper, indeed, for this or that group, and he who overreaches this upper limit is treated on occasion as not belonging fully to the group. Thus the group does not allow the freedom of the individual to expand completely in this second direction, but rather it sets an objective limit to his subjective choice, that is to say, a limit required by supraindividual life conditions.

VI

This fundamental form is repeated whenever the community takes over assistance to the poor. While apparently it seems to have an interest only in setting a lower limit to assistance, that is, in seeing to it that the poor should receive the part to which they are entitled—in other words, that they should not receive too little—there is also the other consideration: that the poor should not receive too much. This latter consideration is in practice less significant. The disadvantage of private assistance lies not only in the "too little," but also in the "too much," which leads to laziness, uses the available means in an economically unproductive way, and arbitrarily favors some at the expense of others. The subjective impulse to do good sins in both directions and, although the danger of excess is not as great as that of deficiency, an objective norm —which determines a standard that is not derived from the subject but from the interest of the collectivity—is directed against that danger of excess.

The transcendence of the subjective point of view is as valid for the recipient as for the giver. English public assistance, by intervening only when there is an objectively determined absolute lack of means, renounces the investigation as to whether a person deserves assistance. This is so because the workhouse is such an unpleasant experience that no one, except in extreme need, would choose it, and consequently the lack of means is objectively determined. For this reason its complement is private assistance, which is directed to a specific worthy individual and which can select individually, since the State already cares for the most urgent needs. The task of private assistance consists in rehabilitating the poor, who are already protected from starvation, and in curing need, for which the State offers only a temporary alleviation. It is not need as such, the *terminus a quo*, that determines the task of private assistance, but rather the ideal of creating independent and economically productive individuals. The State operates in a causal sense, private assistance in a teleological sense. To put it in other words: the State assists poverty; private assistance assists the poor. . . .

This distinction may be elaborated further. It is necessary to start from poverty as an objectively determined phenomenon and to attempt to eliminate it as such. Whoever the poor may be and whatever the individual causes that produce it and the individual consequences it produces, poverty requires assistance, compensation for this social deficiency. But, on the other hand, interest may be directed to the poor person, who is assisted unquestionably because he is poor, not for the purpose of eliminating poverty in general *pro rata*, but rather to help this particular poor person. His poverty operates here as an individal and specific characteristic; it serves as the immediate occasion for being concerned with him; but the individual as a whole should be put into such a situation that poverty would disappear by itself. For this reason assistance derived from the first attitude is directed more to the fact of poverty; and assistance derived from the second attitude, on the other hand, to its cause. Incidentally, it is of sociological importance to observe that the natural distribution of the two types of assistance between the State and private individuals is modified as soon as one follows up the causal chain one step further. The State—in

England more clearly than elsewhere—meets externally visible need; private assistance attends to its individual causes. But the fundamental economic and cultural circumstances which create those personal conditions can only be changed by the collectivity. The task of changing those circumstances in such a way that they should offer the least chance for impoverishment due to individual weakness, unfavorable propensities, misfortune, or mistakes belongs to the collectivity. Here, as in many other respects, the collectivity, its circumstances, interests, and actions, surrounds and affects the individual in his specificity. The collectivity represents a kind of immediate reality to which the elements contribute their own existence, the results of their own life. But, on the other hand, it is also the ground in which individual life grows, a ground in which it grows in such a way that the diversity of individual proclivities and situations contributes an endless variety of unique and colorful manifestations to that overall reality. . . .

VII

We said above that the relationship between the collectivity and its poor contributes to the formation of society in a formal sense as much as the relationship between the collectivity and the civil servant or the taxpayer. We are going to develop this assertion from the point of view which we have just reached in our discussion. We compared above the poor person with the stranger, who also finds himself *confronted* by the group. But this "being confronted" implies a specific *relationship* which draws the stranger into group life as an element of it. Thus the poor person stands undoubtedly *outside* the group, inasmuch as he is a mere object of the actions of the collectivity; but being outside, in this case, is only, to put it briefly, a particular form of being inside. All this occurs in society in the same way as, in the Kantian analysis, spatial separateness occurs in consciousness: even though in space everything is separate and the subject, too, as perceiver, is outside of the other things, the space itself is "in me," in the subject, in the wider sense.

If we consider things more closely, this twofold position of the poor—as well as that of the stranger—can be found in all elements of the group with mere variations of degree. However much an individual may contribute positively to group life, however much his personal life may be tied with social life and submerged in it, he also stands *vis-à-vis* that totality: giving or receiving, treated well or poorly by it, feeling inwardly or only outwardly committed to it; in short, as part or as object in relation to the social group as subject, to which he nevertheless belongs as a member, as a part-subject, through the very relationships based on his actions and circumstances. This twofold position, which appears logically difficult to explain, is a completely elementary sociological fact.

We have already seen this in such simple structures as marriage. Each of the spouses, in certain situations, sees the marriage as an independent structure distinct from himself, confronting him with duties and expectations, good things and bad, which proceed not from the other spouse as a person, but from the whole, that makes each of its parts an object, in spite of the fact that the whole consists only of these parts. This relationship, this fact of finding onself simultaneously within and without, becomes more and more complicated and more and more visible as the number of members of the group increases. And this is true not only because the whole then acquires an independence that dominates the individual, but because the most marked differentiations among individuals lead to a whole scale of nuances in this twofold relationship. The group has a special and different relationship with respect to the prince and the banker, the society woman and the priest, the artist and the civil servant. On the one hand, it makes the person into an object, it "handles" him differently, it subjects him or recognizes him as a power standing against power. On the other hand, the group incorporates him as an element of its life, as a part of the whole, which in turn stands in contrast to other elements. This is perhaps a completely unitary attitude of social reality, which manifests itself separately in these two directions or which appears different from these two distinct viewpoints: comparably, a particular representation stands with respect to the soul, so distinct from it that it can be influenced by the total mood—colored, heightened or toned down, formed or dissolved—while at the same time it is still an integral part of that whole, an element of the soul, of that soul which consists only of the coexistence and interlocking of such represen-tations.

In that scale of relationships with the collectivity the poor oc-cupy a well-defined position. Assistance, to which the community is committed in its own interest, but which the poor person in the large majority of cases has no right to claim, makes the poor person into an object of the activity of the group and places him at a dis-tance from the whole, which at times makes him live as a *corpus vile* by the mercy of the whole and at times, because of this, makes him into its bitter enemy. The State expresses this by depriving those who receive public alms of certain civic rights. This separa-tion, however, is not absolute exclusion, but a very specific relation-ship with the whole, which would be different without this element. The collectivity, of which the poor person is a part, enters into a relationship with him, confronting him, treating him as an object.

These norms, however, do not appear to be applicable to the poor in general but only to some of them, those who receive assist-ance, while there are poor who do not receive assistance. This leads us to consider the relative character of the concept of poverty. He is poor whose means are not sufficient to attain his ends. This con-cept, which is purely individualistic, is narrowed down in its prac-tical application in the sense that certain ends may be considered as independent of any arbitrary and purely personal decision. First, the ends which nature imposes: food, clothing, shelter. But one can-not determine with certainty the level of these needs, a level that would be valid in all circumstances and everywhere and below which, consequently, poverty exists in an absolute sense. Rather, each milieu, each social class has typical needs; the impossiblity of satisfying them means poverty. From this derives the banal fact that in all advanced civilizations there are persons who are poor within their class and would not be poor within a lower class, be-cause the means they have would be sufficient to satisfy the typical ends of that class. Undoubtedly, it may happen that a man who is really poor does not suffer from the discrepancy between his means and the needs of his class, so that poverty in the psychological sense does not exist for him; just as it may also happen that a wealthy man sets himself goals higher than the desires proper to his class and his means, so that he feels psychologically poor. It may be, therefore, that individual poverty—insufficiency of means for the ends of a person—does not exist for someone, while social poverty exists; and it may be, on the other hand, that a man is individually poor while socially wealthy.

The relativity of poverty does not refer to the relation between individual means and actual individual ends, but to the status-related ends of the individual, to a social *a priori* which varies from status to status. The relationship between individual means and actual ends, on the other hand, is something absolute, independent in its basic meaning from anything outside of the individual. It is a very significant socio-historical difference *which* level of needs each group considers as a zero point above which or below which wealth or poverty begins. In a somewhat complex civilization there is always a margin, often a considerable one, to determine this level. In relation to this problem there are many important sociological differences; for example: the relationship of this zero point to the *real average*; whether it is necessary to belong to the favored minority in order not to be considered poor or whether a class, out of an instinctive utilitarian criterion to prevent the growth of feelings of poverty, sets the boundary below which poverty begins very low; or whether an individual case can modify the boundary, as for example the moving into a small town or into a closed social circle of a wealthy person; or whether the group holds on rigidly to the boundary set between rich and poor.

VIII

A result of poverty's being found within all social strata, which have created a typical level of needs for each individual, is that often poverty is not susceptible to assistance. However, the principle of assistance is more extensive than what its official manifestations would indicate. When, for example, within a large family the poorer and richer members give one another presents, the latter take advantage of a good opportunity to give the former a value which exceeds the value of what they have received; and not only that, but also the quality of presents reveals this character of assistance: *useful* objects are given to the poorer relatives, that is, objects which help them to maintain themselves within the level of their class.

For this reason, presents from a sociological point of view turn out to be completely different in the various social classes. The sociology of the gift coincides in part with that of poverty. In the gift it is possible to discover a very extensive scale of reciprocal relationships between men, differences in the content, motivation, and manner of giving as well as in that of accepting the gift. Gift, theft, and exchange are the external forms of interaction which are directly linked with the question of ownership and from which an endless wealth of psychological phenomena that determine the sociological process are derived. They correspond to the three motives of action: altruism, egoism, and objective norms; the essence of exchange is in the substitution of some values by others which are objectively equal, while subjective motives of goodness or greed are eliminated since in the pure concept of exchange the value of the object is not measured by the desire of the individual but by the value of the other object. Of these three forms, gift is that which offers the greatest wealth of sociological situations, because here the intention and position of the giver and of the recipient are combined in the most varied ways with all their individual nuances.

Of the many categories which make possible, so to speak, a systematic ordering of these phenomena, the most important for the problem of poverty seem to be the following basic alternatives. On the one hand, does the meaning and purpose of the gift consist in the final condition achieved by it, in the fact that the recipient will have a valuable specific object, or, on the other hand, does it consist in the action itself, in the gift as the expression of the giver's intention, of a love desirous of sacrifice, or of a reaching out of the self which is manifested more or less arbitrarily by the gift? In the latter case, the process of giving is, so to say, its own ultimate end and the question of wealth or poverty evidently plays no role whatever, except in terms of the practical problem of what people can afford. But when the one to whom one gives is a *poor man*, the emphasis is not on the process but on its results: the main thing is that the poor person receive something.

Between these two extremes of the concept of gift there are innumerable mixed forms. The more the latter type predominates in its purest form, the more impossible it often is to give the poor person what he lacks in the form of a gift, because the other sociological relationships between individuals are incongruent with that of giving. The gift is almost always possible when a great social distance intervenes or when a great personal intimacy prevails; but it becomes difficult to the extent that social distance decreases or personal distance increases. In the upper classes, the tragic situation frequently occurs in which the needy person would willingly accept assistance and he who is in a well-to-do position would also willingly grant it; but neither can the former ask for it nor the latter offer it. In the higher classes the economic *a priori*, below which poverty begins, is set in such a way that this poverty very rarely occurs and is even excluded in principle. The acceptance of assistance thus excludes the assisted person from the premises of his status and provides visible proof that the poor person is formally *déclassé*. Until this happens, class prejudice is strong enough to make poverty, so to say, invisible; and until then poverty is individual suffering, without social consequences. All the assumptions on which the life of the upper classes is based determine that a person may be poor in an individual sense, that is, that his resources may be insufficient for the needs of his class, without his having to recur to assistance. For this reason, no one is socially poor until he has been assisted. And this has a general validity: sociologically speaking, poverty does not come first and then assistance—this is rather fate in its personal form—but a person is called poor who receives assistance or should receive it given his sociological situation, although perchance he may not receive it.

The social-democratic assertion that the modern proletarian is definitely poor but not a *poor man* fits this interpretation. The poor, as a sociological category, are not those who suffer specific deficiencies and deprivations, but those who receive assistance or should receive it according to social norms. Consequently, in this sense, poverty cannot be defined in itself as a quantitative state, but only in terms of the social reaction resulting from a specific situation; it is analogous to the way crime, the substantive definition of which offers such difficulties, is defined as "an action punished by public sanctions." Thus today some do not determine the essence of morality on the basis of the inner state of the subject but from the result of his action; his subjective intention is considered valuable only insofar as it normally produces a certain socially useful effect. Thus too, frequently, the concept of personality is not defined by an inner characteristic that qualifies the individual for a specific social role, but, on the contrary, those elements of society that perform a specific role are called personalities. The individual state, in itself, no longer determines the concept, but social teleology does so; the individual is determined by the way in which the totality that surrounds him acts toward him. Where this occurs, we find a certain continuation of modern idealism, which does not attempt to define things by an essence inherent to them, but by the reactions that occur in the subject with respect to them. The binding function which the poor person performs within an existing society is not generated by the sole fact of being poor; only when society—the totality or particular individuals—reacts toward him with assistance, only then does he play his specific social role.

This social meaning of the "poor man," in contrast to the individual meaning, makes the poor into a kind of estate or unitary stratum within society. The fact that someone is poor does not mean that he belongs to the specific social category of the "poor." He may be a poor shopkeeper, artist, or employee but he remains in this category, which is defined by a specific activity or position. In this category he may occupy, as a consequence of his poverty, a gradually modified position; but the individuals who, in different statuses and occupations, are in this state are not grouped in any way into a particular sociological whole different from the social stratum to which they belong. It is only from the moment they are assisted—perhaps already when their total situation would normally require assistance, even though it has not yet been given—that they become part of a group characterized by poverty. This group does not remain united by interaction among its members, but by the collective attitude which society as a whole adopts toward it. However, an explicit tendency toward sociation has not always been lacking. Thus in the 14th century, for example, there was in Norwich a *Poorman's Gild*, and in Germany the so-called "guilds of the miserable." Some time later, we find in the Italian cities a party of the wealthy, of the *Optimates* as they called themselves, whose members were united only by the fact of their wealth. Similar unions of the poor soon became impossible because, with the growing differentiation of society, the individual differences in education and ideas, in interests and background, among those who might have belonged to the unions were too great to lend to such groups the necessary strength for true sociation.

It is only when poverty implies a positive *content*, common to many poor, that an association of the poor, as such, arises. Thus, the result of the extreme phenomenon of poverty, the lack of shelter, is that those who find themselves in such a situation in the large cities congregate in specific places of refuge. When the first stacks of hay arise in the vicinity of Berlin, those who lack shelter, the *Penner*, go there to take advantage of the opportunity to spend a comfortable night. One finds among them a type of incipient organization, whereby the *Penner* of each district have a kind of headman who assigns to the members of the district their places in the night shelter and arbitrates their quarrels. The *Penner* scrupulously see to it that no criminal infiltrates them, and, when this happens, they denounce him to the police to whom they often render good services. The headmen of the *Penner* are well-known persons whom the authorities always know how to find when they need information about some obscure character. Such a specification of poverty, as the lack of shelter implies, is necessary today to contribute an element of association. Moreover, one may note that the increase of general prosperity, the greater police vigilance and, above all, social conscience which, with a strange mixture of good and bad motives, "cannot tolerate" the sight of poverty, all contribute to impose on poverty increasingly the tendency to hide. And this tendency to hide logically isolates the poor increasingly from one another and prevents them from developing any feeling of belonging to a stratum, as was possible in the Middle Ages.

The class of the poor, especially in modern society, is a unique sociological synthesis. It possesses a great homogeneity insofar as its meaning and location in the social body is concerned; but it lacks it completely insofar as the individual qualification of its elements is concerned. It is the common end of the most diverse destinies, an ocean into which lives derived from the most diverse social strata flow together. No change, development, polarization, or breakdown of social life occurs without leaving its residuum in the stratum of poverty. What is most terrible in poverty is the fact that there are human beings who, in their social position, are just poor and nothing but poor. This is different from the simple fact of being poor which each one has to face for himself and which is merely a shade of another individually qualified position. The fact of being just poor and nothing but poor is particularly apparent where expanding and indiscriminate almsgiving prevails, such as during the Christian Middle Ages and in Islamic lands. However, so long as one accepted it as an official and unchangeable fact, it did not have the bitter and contradictory character which the progressive and activistic tendency of modern times imposes on a whole class: a class which bases its unity on a purely passive characteristic, specifically the fact that the society acts toward it and deals with it in a particular way. To deprive those who receive alms of their political rights adequately expresses the fact that they are nothing but poor. As a result of this lack of positive qualification, as has already been noted, the stratum of the poor, notwithstanding their common situation, does not give rise to sociologically unifying forces. In this way, poverty is a unique sociological phenomenon: a number of individuals who, out of a purely individual fate, occupy a specific organic position within the whole; but this position is not determined by this fate and condition, but rather by the fact that others—individuals, associations, communities—attempt to correct this condition. Thus, what makes one poor is not the lack of means. The poor person, sociologically speaking, is the individual who receives assistance because of this lack of means.

12

THE MISER AND
THE SPENDTHRIFT

1907

THE MISER [is one who] finds bliss in the sheer possession of money, without proceeding to the acquisition and enjoyment of particular objects. His sense of power is therefore more profound and more precious to him than dominion over specific objects could ever be. As we have seen, the possession of concrete objects is inherently circumscribed; the greedy soul who ceaselessly seeks satisfaction and penetration to the ultimate, innermost absolute nature of objects is painfully rebuffed by them. They are and remain separate, resisting incorporation into the self and thus terminating even the most passionate possession in frustration. The possession of money is free of this contradiction latent in all other kinds of possession. At the cost of not obtaining things and of renouncing all the specific satisfactions that are tied to particulars, money can provide a sense of power far enough removed from actual empirical objects that it is not subject to the limitations imposed by possession of them. Money alone do we own completely and without limitations. It alone can be completely incorporated into the use which we plan for it.

The pleasures of the miser are almost aesthetic. For aesthetic pleasures likewise lie beyond the impermeable reality of the world and depend on its appearance and luster, which are fully accessible to the mind and can be penetrated by it without resistance. The phenomena associated with money are only the clearest and

---

From *Philosophie des Geldes*, 2d enlarged edition (Leipzig: Duncker & Humblot, 1907), pp. 351–54; 254–57. Translated by Roberta Ash.

most transparent instances of a series of phenomena in which the same principle is realized in other contexts. I once met a man who, though no longer young and a well-to-do family man, spent all his time learning every skill he could—languages, which he never employed, superb dancing, which he never pursued; accomplishments of every sort, which he never made use of and did not even want to use. This characteristic is precisely that of the miser: satisfaction in the complete possession of a potentiality with no thought whatsoever about its realization. At the same time, it exemplifies an attraction akin to the aesthetic, the mastery of both the pure form and the ideal of objects or of behavior, in respect to which every step toward reality—with its unavoidable obstacles, setbacks, and frustrations—could only be a deterioration, and would necessarily constrain the feeling that objects are potentially absolutely to be mastered.

Aesthetic contemplation, which is possible for any object and only especially easy for the beautiful, most thoroughly closes the gap between the self and the object. It allows as easy, effortless, and harmonious formation of the image of the object as if this image were determined only by the nature of the self. Hence the sense of liberation which accompanies an aesthetic mood; it is characterized by emancipation from the stuffy dull pressure of life, and the expansion of the self with joy and freedom into the objects whose reality would otherwise violate it. Such is the psychological tone of joy in the mere possession of money. The strange coalescing, abstraction, and anticipation of ownership of property which constitutes the meaning of money is like aesthetic pleasure in permitting consciousness a free play, a portentous extension into an unresisting medium, and the incorporation of all possibilities without violation or deterioration by reality. If one defines beauty as *une promesse de bonheur* ["a promise of happiness"], this definition is yet another indicator of the similarity between aesthetic attraction and the attraction of money, because the latter lies in the promise of the joys money makes possible.

There have been attempts to combine the attraction of as yet formless value with the attraction of forming; this is one of the meanings of jewelry and trinkets. Their owner appears as the representative and master of a possibly very great sum which symbolizes his coalesced power; but also in jewelry the absolute liquidity and sheer potentiality of money has been shaped into some measure of definiteness of form and of specific qualities. Especially striking is the following instance of such an attempt at combination (of liquidity and definite form): In India it was long the custom to keep and especially to save money in the form of jewelry. That is, one had the rupees melted and made into jewelry (with only a very small loss of value), and stored it to be given out as silver should the need arise. Apparently value in the form of jewelry is both more condensed and richer in quality. This combination permits value to appear more closely linked to the person in that it becomes more individualistic and temporarily loses its atomized nature. So convincing is this appearance that since Solomon's day royal treasuring of precious metals in the form of utensils has been based on the treacherous belief (or delusion) that the treasure is closest to the family and safest from the grasp of enemies in this form. The direct use of coins as jewelry often is done to keep the fortune about one's person, under constant supervision. Jewelry, which is an ornament for the person, is also a symbol of its bearer, and it is hence essential that it be valuable; both this ideal purpose of jewelry and the previously mentioned practical purpose depend on the close association of jewelry with the self. In the Orient the most important requirement of all wealth is that one can flee with it, that is, that it be absolutely obedient to the owner and his fate.

It should also be noted that joy in the possession of money also doubtlessly contains an idealistic moment whose importance only appears paradoxical because on the one hand, the means to obtain it are necessarily diminished in the process of obtaining it and on the other hand because this feeling of joy is usually expressed by the individual in a nonidealistic form. This should not obscure the fact that joy in the sheer possession of money is one of the abstract joys, one of the furthest removed from sensuous immediacy, and one of those mediated most exclusively by the process of thinking and fantasy. In this respect it is similar to the joy of victory, which is so strong in some individuals that they simply do not ask what they really gain by winning. . . .

The spendthrift is far more similar to the miser than their apparent polarization would seem to indicate. Let us note that in primitive economies the miserly conservation of valuables is not consistent with the nature of these valuables, that is, with the very limited storage time of agricultural products. Therefore, when their conversion into indefinitely storable money is not practical or is at any rate not a matter of course, one only rarely finds miserly hoarding. Where agricultural products are produced and consumed immediately there usually exists a certain liberality, especially toward guests and the needy. Money is much more inviting to collect and therefore makes such liberality much less likely. Thus Petrus Martyr praises the cocoa-bags which served the ancient Mexicans as money, because they cannot be long hoarded or cached and therefore cannot engender miserliness. Similarly, natural conditions limit the feasibility and attractiveness of prodigality. Prodigal consumption and foolish squandering (except for senseless destruction) are limited by the capacity of household members and outsiders to consume.

But the most important fact is that the waste of money has a different meaning and a new nuance that completely distinguish it from the waste of concrete objects. The latter means that value for any reasonable purposes of the individual is simply destroyed, whereas in the former case it has been purposelessly converted into other values. The wastrel in the money economy (who alone is significant for a philosophy of money) is not someone who senselessly gives his money to the world but one who uses it for senseless purchases, that is, for purchases that are not appropriate to his circumstances. The pleasure of waste must be distinguished from pleasure in the fleeting enjoyment of objects, from ostentation, and from the excitement of the alteration of acquisition and consumption. The pleasure of waste depends simply on the instant of the expenditure of money for no-matter-what objects. For the spendthrift, the attraction of the instant overshadows the rational evaluation either of money or of commodities.

At this point the position of the spendthrift in the instrumental nexus becomes clear. The goal of enjoying the possession of an object is preceded by two steps—first, the possession of money and, second, the expenditure of money for the desired object. For the miser, the first of these grows to be a pleasurable end in itself; for the spendthrift, the second. Money is almost as important to the spendthrift as to the miser, only not in the form of possessing it, but in its expenditure. His appreciation of its worth swells at the instant that money is transformed into other values; the intensity of this feeling is so great that he purchases the enjoyment of this moment at the cost of dissipating all more concrete values.

It is therefore clear to the observer that the indifference about the value of money which constitutes the essence and the charm of prodigality is possible only because money is actually treasured and assumed to be special. For the indifferent man's throwing away of his money would itself be done with indifference. The following case is typical of the enormous waste of the ancien régime: when a lady returned the 4,000–5,000 franc diamond that Prince Conti had sent her, he had it shattered and used the fragments as blotting sand for the note in which he informed her of the incident. Taine adds the following remark about the attitudes of that age: one is the more a man of the world the less one is concerned about money. But precisely herein lies the self-delusion. For as in a dialectic, the conscious and strongly negative stance toward money has the opposite sentiment as its basis, which alone provides it with meaning and attraction.

The same is true of those shops that may be found in the metropolis which, in direct contrast to stores that advertise bargains, smugly boast that they have the *highest* prices. Thus they imply that their customers are the Best People—those who do not ask about prices. But the noteworthy fact is that they do not emphasize what really matters—the quality of their merchandise. Thus they unconsciously do place money above all else, albeit with a reversal of value. Because of its close association with money, a spendthrift's lust easily grows to a monstrous extent and robs its victim of all reasonable sense of proportion. For money lacks the regulation that human capacity imposes on concrete objects. This is exactly the same immoderation that characterizes miserly avarice. The pure potentiality which it seeks instead of the enjoyment of real objects tends toward the infinite. Unlike the latter, it has no inherent or external reasons for restraint. When avarice lacks positive external constraints and limitations, it tends to become completely amorphous and increasingly passionate. This is the reason for the peculiar immoderation and bitterness of inheritance disputes. Since neither effort nor objective apportionment determines one's own claim, no one is inclined a priori to recognize the claims of others. One's own claims, therefore, lack all restraint and any encroachment upon them is perceived as a particularly unreasonable injustice. This inherent lack of a relationship between the wish and any assessment of its object, which in inheritance disputes stems from the personal relations involved in the inheritance situation, in the case of avarice arises from the nature of the object. A coinage rebellion in Braunschweig in 1499 is an excellent illustration of the lack of principle which is encouraged by the nature of money and which prevents the limitation of demands. The government wanted only the good coinage to be valid, whereas previously bad coinage had also existed. And thereupon the same persons who had taken only good coinage for their goods and labor revolted violently because their payments in bad coinage were no longer accepted! The frequent coexistence of good and bad coinage provides the fullest opportunities for the immoderation of avarice, compared to which the most intense other passions seem to have only a partial hold over the emotions. Even in China there have been revolutions because the government paid in bad coinage but collected taxes in good coinage.

This tendency to immoderation inherent in the pure interest in money as such is also, I should like to hypothesize, the hidden source of a peculiar phenomenon found in stock exchanges. The small grain speculators, known in English as the *Outsiders*, almost without exception assume a bull market. I believe that the logically undeniable, if practically irrelevant, fact that the gain of bear market speculation is potentially limited whereas that of a bull market speculation is not provides the emotional attraction for this behavior. The large-scale grain speculators whose goal is the actual delivery of merchandise calculate the probabilities for both market trends, but for the pure money speculation such as is found in gambling in futures, any trend is adequate as long as the trend is potentially infinite.

Such a trend, which constitutes the inner motivational structure of an interest in money, is still more evident as the basis of the following events.

The German agricultural economy in the period from 1830 to 1880 provided constantly rising returns. This led to the illusion that the boom would continue forever. Consequently, farms were no longer bought at their current value, but at that which they were expected to acquire at current rates of increase. This is the cause of the present plight of the agricultural economy. It is the monetary nature of the returns that produces the wrong conception of value: When [returns] are based only on "utility value," on an immediate concrete amount, the idea of increase is cautiously limited; but the potentiality and anticipation of monetary value is unbounded.

This is the basis of the nature of miserliness and prodigality. Both reject on principle that calculation of value which alone can stop and limit the instrumental nexus: a calculation based on the consummatory enjoyment of the object. The spendthrift—who is not to be confused with the epicure and the merely frivolous, although all these elements can be blended in a given case—becomes indifferent to the object once he possesses it. For this reason his enjoyment of it is marred by the curse of restlessness and transience. The moment of its beginning is also that of its undoing. The life of the spendthrift is marked by the same demonic formula as that of the miser: every pleasure attained arouses the desire for further pleasure, which can never be satisfied. Satisfaction can never be gained because it is being sought in a form that from the beginning foregoes its ends and is confined to means and to the moment before fulfillment. The miser is the more abstract of the two; *his* goal is reached even earlier than the usual goal. The spendthrift gets somewhat closer to real objects. He abandons the movement toward a rational goal at a later point [than the miser], at which he stops as though it were the real goal. This formal identity of the two types despite the diametrical opposition of their visible behaviors—and the lack of a regulating substantive aim which suggests a capricious interplay between the two equally senseless tendencies—explain why miserliness and prodigality are often found in the same person, sometimes in different areas of interest and sometimes in connection with different moods. Constricting or expansive moods are expressed in miserliness or prodigality, as though the impulse were the same and merely the valence differed.

13

THE ADVENTURER

1911

EACH SEGMENT of our conduct and experience bears a twofold meaning: it revolves about its own center, contains as much breadth and depth, joy and suffering, as the immediate experiencing gives it, and at the same time is a segment of a course of life—not only a circumscribed entity, but also a component of an organism. Both aspects, in various configurations, characterize everything that occurs in a life. Events which may be widely divergent in their bearing on life as a whole may nonetheless be quite similar to one another; or they may be incommensurate in their intrinsic meanings but so similar in respect to the roles they play in our total existence as to be interchangeable.

One of two experiences which are not particularly different in substance, as far as we can indicate it, may nevertheless be perceived as an "adventure" and the other not. The one receives the designation denied the other because of this difference in the relation to the whole of our life. More precisely, the most general form of adventure is its dropping out of the continuity of life. "Wholeness of life," after all, refers to the fact that a consistent process runs through the individual components of life, however crassly and irreconcilably distinct they may be. What we call an

Reprinted from *Georg Simmel, 1858–1918: A Collection of Essays, with Translations and a Bibliography*, edited by Kurt H. Wolff. Copyright 1959 by the Ohio State University Press. All rights reserved. Translated by David Kettler. Originally published in German as "Das Abenteuer," in Georg Simmel, *Philosophische Kultur: Gesammelte Essays* (Leipzig: W. Klinkhardt, 1911).

adventure stands in contrast to that interlocking of life-links, to
that feeling that those countercurrents, turnings, and knots still,
after all, spin forth a continuous thread. An adventure is certainly
a part of our existence, directly contiguous with other parts which
precede and follow it; at the same time, however, in its deeper
meaning, it occurs outside the usual continuity of this life. Nevertheless, it is distinct from all that is accidental and alien, merely
touching life's outer shell. While it falls outside the context of life,
it falls, with this same movement, as it were, back into that context
again, as will become clear later; it is a foreign body in our existence which is yet somehow connected with the center; the outside,
if only by a long and unfamiliar detour, is formally an aspect of
the inside.

Because of its place in our psychic life, a remembered adventure tends to take on the quality of a dream. Everyone knows how
quickly we forget dreams because they, too, are placed outside the
meaningful context of life-as-a-whole. What we designate as
"dreamlike" is nothing but a memory which is bound to the unified,
consistent life-process by fewer threads than are ordinary experiences. We might say that we localize our inability to assimilate to
this process something experienced by imagining a dream in which
it took place. The more "adventurous" an adventure, that is, the
more fully it realizes its idea, the more "dreamlike" it becomes in
our memory. It often moves so far away from the center of the ego
and the course of life which the ego guides and organizes that we
may think of it as something experienced by another person. How
far outside that course it lies, how alien it has become to that
course, is expressed precisely by the fact that we might well feel
that we could appropriately assign to the adventure a subject other
than the ego.

We ascribe to an adventure a beginning and an end much
sharper than those to be discovered in the other forms of our experiences. The adventure is freed of the entanglements and con-
catenations which are characteristic of those forms and is given a
meaning in and of itself. Of our ordinary experiences, we declare
that one of them is over when, or because, another starts; they
reciprocally determine each other's limits, and so become a means

whereby the contextual unity of life is structured or expressed. The adventure, however, according to its intrinsic meaning, is independent of the "before" and "after"; its boundaries are defined regardless of them. We speak of adventure precisely when continuity with life is thus disregarded on principle—or rather when there is not even any need to disregard it, because we know from the beginning that we have to do with something alien, untouchable, out of the ordinary. The adventure lacks that reciprocal interpenetration with adjacent parts of life which constitutes life-as-a-whole. It is like an island in life which determines its beginning and end according to its own formative powers and not—like the part of a continent—also according to those of adjacent territories. This factor of decisive boundedness, which lifts an adventure out of the regular course of a human destiny, is not mechanical but organic: just as the organism determines its spatial shape not simply by adjusting to obstacles confining it from right and left but by the propelling force of a life forming from inside out, so does an adventure not end because something else begins; instead, its temporal form, its radical being-ended, is the precise expression of its inner sense.

Here, above all, is the basis of the profound affinity between the adventurer and the artist, and also, perhaps, of the artist's attraction by adventure. For the essence of a work of art is, after all, that it cuts out a piece of the endlessly continuous sequences of perceived experience, detaching it from all connections with one side or the other, giving it a self-sufficient form as though defined and held together by an inner core. A part of existence, interwoven with the uninterruptedness of that existence, yet nevertheless felt as a whole, as an integrated unit—this is the form common to both the work of art and the adventure. Indeed, it is an attribute of this form to make us feel that in both the work of art and the adventure the whole of life is somehow comprehended and consummated—and this irrespective of the particular theme either of them may have. Moreover, we feel this, not although, but because, the work of art exists entirely beyond life as a reality; the adventure, entirely beyond life as an uninterrupted course which intelligibly connects every element with its neighbors. It is because the work of art and the adventure stand over against life (even though in very different senses of the phrase) that both are analogous to the totality of life itself, even as this totality presents itself in the brief summary and crowdedness of a dream experience.

For this reason, the adventurer is also the extreme example of the ahistorical individual, of the man who lives in the present. On the one hand, he is not determined by any past (and this marks the contrast between him and the aged, of which more later); nor on the other hand, does the future exist for him. An extraordinarily characteristic proof of this is that Casanova (as may be seen from his memoirs), in the course of his erotic-adventurous life, ever so often seriously intended to marry a woman with whom he was in love at the time. In the light of his temperament and conduct of life, we can imagine nothing more obviously impossible, internally and externally. Casanova not only had excellent knowledge of men but also rare knowledge of himself. Although he must have said to himself that he could not stand marriage even two weeks and that the most miserable consequences of such a step would be quite unavoidable, his perspective on the future was wholly obliterated in the rapture of the moment. (Saying this, I mean to put the emphasis on the moment rather than on the rapture.) Because he was entirely dominated by the feeling of the present, he wanted to enter into a future relationship which was impossible precisely because his temperament was oriented to the present.

In contrast to those aspects of life which are related only peripherally—by mere fate—the adventure is defined by its capacity in spite of its being isolated and accidental, to have necessity and meaning. Something becomes an adventure only by virtue of two conditions: that it itself is a specific organization of some significant meaning with a beginning and an end; and that, despite its accidental nature, its extraterritoriality with respect to the continuity of life, it nevertheless connects with the character and identity of the bearer of that life—that it does so in the widest sense transcending, by a mysterious necessity, life's more narrowly rational aspects.

At this point there emerges the relation between the adventurer and the gambler. The gambler, clearly, has abandoned himself to the meaninglessness of chance. In so far, however, as he counts on its favor and believes possible and realizes a life dependent on it, chance for him has become part of a context of meaning. The typical superstition of the gambler is nothing other than the tangible and isolated, and thus, of course, childish, form of this profound and all-encompassing scheme of his life, according to which chance makes sense and contains some necessary meaning (even though not by the criterion of rational logic). In his superstition, he wants to draw chance into his teleological system by omens and magical aids, thus removing it from its inaccessible isolation and searching in it for a lawful order, no matter how fantastic the laws of such an order may be.

The adventurer similarly lets the accident somehow be encompassed by the meaning which controls the consistent continuity of life, even though the accident lies outside that continuity. He achieves a central feeling of life which runs through the eccentricity of the adventure and produces a new, significant necessity of his life in the very width of the distance between its accidental, externally given content and the unifying core of existence from which meaning flows. There is in us an eternal process playing back and forth between chance and necessity, between the fragmentary materials given us from the outside and the consistent meaning of the life developed from within.

The great forms in which we shape the substance of life are the syntheses, antagonisms, or compromises between chance and necessity. Adventure is such a form. When the professional adventurer makes a system of life out of his life's lack of system, when out of his inner necessity he seeks the naked, external accidents and builds them into that necessity, he only, so to speak, makes macroscopically visible that which is the essential form of every "adventure," even that of the non-adventurous person. For by adventure we always mean a third something, neither the sheer, abrupt event whose meaning—a mere given—simply remains outside us nor the consistent sequence of life in which every element supplements every other toward an inclusively integrated meaning. The adventure is no mere hodgepodge of these two, but rather that incomparable experience which can be interpreted only as a particular encompassing of the accidentally external by the internally necessary.

Occasionally, however, this whole relationship is comprehended in a still more profound inner configuration. No matter how much the adventure seems to rest on a differentiation within life, life as a whole may be perceived as an adventure. For this, one need neither be an adventurer nor undergo many adventures. To have such a remarkable attitude toward life, one must sense above its totality a higher unity, a super-life, as it were, whose relation to life parallels the relation of the immediate life totality itself to those particular experiences which we call adventures.

Perhaps we belong to a metaphysical order, perhaps our soul lives a transcendent existence, such that our earthly, conscious life is only an isolated fragment as compared to the unnamable context of an existence running its course in it. The myth of the transmigration of souls may be a halting attempt to express such a segmental character of every individual life. Whoever senses through all actual life a secret, timeless existence of the soul, which is connected with the realities of life only as from a distance, will perceive life in its given and limited wholeness as an adventure when compared to that transcendent and self-consistent fate. Certain religious moods seem to bring about such a perception. When our earthly career strikes us as a mere preliminary phase in the fulfillment of eternal destinies, when we have no home but merely a temporary asylum on earth, this obviously is only a particular variant of the general feeling that life as a whole is an adventure. It merely expresses the running together, in life, of the symptoms of adventure. It stands outside that proper meaning and steady course of existence to which it is yet tied by a fate and a secret symbolism. A fragmentary incident, it is yet, like a work of art, enclosed by a beginning and an end. Like a dream, it gathers all passions into itself and yet, like a dream, is destined to be forgotten; like gaming, it contrasts with seriousness, yet, like the *va banque* of the gambler, it involves the alternative between the highest gain and destruction.

Thus the adventure is a particular form in which fundamental categories of life are synthesized. Another such synthesis it achieves is that between the categories of activity and passivity, between what we conquer and what is given to us. To be sure, their synthesis in the form of adventure makes their contrast perceptible to an extreme degree. In the adventure, on the one hand, we forcibly pull the world into ourselves. This becomes clear when we compare the adventure with the manner in which we wrest the gifts of the world through work. Work, so to speak, has an organic relation to the world. In a conscious fashion, it develops the world's forces and materials toward their culmination in the human purpose, whereas in adventure we have a nonorganic relation to the world. Adventure has the gesture of the conqueror, the quick seizure of opportunity, regardless of whether the portion we carve out is harmonious or disharmonious with us, with the world, or with the relation between us and the world. On the other hand, however, in the adventure we abandon ourselves to the world with fewer defenses and reserves than in any other relation, for other relations are connected with the general run of our worldly life by more bridges, and thus defend us better against shocks and dangers through previously prepared avoidances and adjustments. In the adventure, the interweaving of activity and passivity which characterizes our life tightens these elements into a coexistence of conquest, which owes everything only to its own strength and presence of mind, and complete self-abandonment to the powers and accidents of the world, which can delight us, but in the same breath can also destroy us. Surely, it is among adventure's most wonderful and enticing charms that the unity toward which at every moment, by the very process of living, we bring together our activity and our passivity—the unity which even in a certain sense *is* life itself— accentuates its disparate elements most sharply, and precisely in *this* way makes itself the more deeply felt, as if they were only the two aspects of one and the same, mysteriously seamless life.

If the adventure, furthermore, strikes us as combining the elements of certainty and uncertainty in life, this is more than the view of the same fundamental relationship from a different angle. The certainty with which—justifiably or in error—we know the outcome, gives our activity one of its distinct qualities. If, on the contrary, we are uncertain whether we shall arrive at the point for which we have set out, if we know our ignorance of the outcome, then this means not only a quantitatively reduced certainty but an inwardly and outwardly unique practical conduct. The adventurer, in a word, treats the incalculable element in life in the way we ordinarily treat only what we think is by definition calculable. (For this reason, the philosopher is the adventurer of the spirit. He makes the hopeless, but not therefore meaningless, attempt to form into conceptual knowledge an attitude of the soul, its mood toward itself, the world, God. He treats this insoluble problem as if it were soluble.) When the outcome of our activity is made doubtful by the intermingling of unrecognizable elements of fate, we usually limit our commitment of force, hold open lines of retreat, and take each step only as if testing the ground.

In the adventure, we proceed in the directly opposite fashion: it is just on the hovering chance, on fate, on the more-or-less that we risk all, burn our bridges, and step into the mist, as if the road will lead us on, no matter what. This is the typical fatalism of the adventurer. The obscurities of fate are certainly no more transparent to him than to others; but he proceeds as if they were. The characteristic daring with which he continually leaves the solidities of life underpins itself, as it were, for its own justification with a feeling of security and "it-must-succeed," which normally only belongs to the transparency of calculable events. This is only a subjective aspect of the fatalist conviction that we certainly cannot escape a fate which we do not know: the adventurer nevertheless believes that, as far as he himself is concerned, he is certain of this unknown and unknowable element in his life. For this reason, to the sober person adventurous conduct often seems insanity; for, in order to make sense, it appears to presuppose that the unknowable is known. The prince of Ligne said of Casanova, "He believes in nothing except in what is least believable." Evidently, such belief is based on that perverse or at least "adventurous" relation between the certain and the uncertain, whose correlate, obviously, is the skepticism of the adventurer—that he "believes in nothing": for him to whom the unlikely is likely, the likely easily becomes unlikely. The adventurer relies to some extent on his own strength, but above all on his own luck; more properly, on a peculiarly undifferentiated unity of the two. Strength, of which he is certain, and luck, of which he is uncertain, subjectively combine into a sense of certainty.

If it is the nature of genius to possess an immediate relation to these secret unities which in experience and rational analysis fall apart into completely separate phenomena, the adventurer of genius lives, as if by mystic instinct, at the point where the course of the world and the individual fate have, so to speak, not yet been differentiated from one another. For this reason, he is said to have a "touch of genius." The "sleepwalking certainty" with which the adventurer leads his life becomes comprehensible in terms of that peculiar constellation whereby he considers that which is uncertain and incalculable to be the premises of his conduct, while others consider only the calculable. Unshakable even when it is shown to be denied by the facts of the case, this certainty proves how deeply that constellation is rooted in the life conditions of adventurous natures.

The adventure is a form of life which can be taken on by an undetermined number of experiences. Nevertheless, our definitions make it understandable that one of them, more than all others, tends to appear in this form: the erotic—so that our linguistic custom hardly lets us understand by "adventure" anything but an erotic one. The love affair, even if short-lived, is by no means always an adventure. The peculiar psychic qualities at whose meeting point the adventure is found must be added to this quantitative matter. The tendency of these qualities to enter such a conjuncture will become apparent step by step.

A love affair contains in clear association the two elements which the form of the adventure characteristically conjoins: conquering force and unextortable concession, winning by one's own abilities and dependence on the luck which something incalculable outside ourselves bestows on us. A degree of balance between these forces, gained by virtue of his sense of their sharp differentiation, can, perhaps, be found only in the man. Perhaps for this reason, it is of compelling significance that, as a rule, a love affair is an "adventure" only for men; for women it usually falls into other categories. In novels of love, the activity of woman is typically permeated by the passivity which either nature or history has imparted to her character; on the other hand, her acceptance of happiness is at the same time a concession and a gift.

The two poles of conquest and grace (which manifest themselves in many variations) stand closer together in woman than in man. In man, they are, as a matter of fact, much more decisively separated. For this reason, in man their coincidence in the erotic experience stamps this experience quite ambiguously as an adventure. Man plays the courting, attacking, often violently grasping role: this fact makes one easily overlook the element of fate, the dependence on something which cannot be predetermined or compelled, that is contained in every erotic experience. This refers not only to dependence on the concession on the part of the other, but to something deeper. To be sure, every "love returned," too, is a gift which cannot be "earned," not even by any measure of love—because to love, demand and compensation are irrelevant; it belongs, in principle, in a category altogether different from a squaring of accounts—a point which suggests one of its analogies to the more profound religious relation. But over and above that which we receive from another as a free gift, there still lies in every happiness of love—like a profound, impersonal bearer of those personal elements—a favor of fate. We receive happiness not only from the other: the fact that we do receive it from him is a blessing of destiny, which is incalculable. In the proudest, most self-assured event in this sphere lies something which we must accept with humility. When the force which owes its success to itself and gives all conquest of love some note of victory and triumph is then combined with the other note of favor by fate, the constellation of the adventure is, as it were, preformed.

The relation which connects the erotic content with the more general form of life as adventure is rooted in deeper ground. The adventure is the exclave of life, the "torn-off" whose beginning and end have no connection with the somehow unified stream of existence. And yet, as if hurdling this stream, it connects with the most recondite instincts and some ultimate intention of life as a whole—and this distinguishes it from the merely accidental episode, from that which only externally "happens" to us. Now, when a love affair is of short duration, it lives in precisely such a mixture of a merely tangential and yet central character. It may give our life only a momentary splendor, like the ray shed in an inside room by a light flitting by outside. Still, it satisfies a need, or is, in fact, only possible by virtue of a need which—whether it be considered as physical, psychic, or metaphysical—exists, as it were, timelessly in the foundation or center of our being. This need is related to the fleeting experience as our general longing for light is to that accidental and immediately disappearing brightness.

The fact that love harbors the possibility of this double relation is reflected by the twofold temporal aspect of the erotic. It displays two standards of time: the momentarily climactic, abruptly subsiding passion; and the idea of something which cannot pass, an idea in which the mystical destination of two souls for one another and for a higher unity finds a temporal expression. This duality might be compared with the double existence of intellectual contents: while they emerge only in the fleetingness of the psychic process, in the forever moving focus of consciousness, their logical meaning possesses timeless validity, an ideal significance which is completely independent of the instant of consciousness in which it becomes real for us. The phenomenon of adventure is such that its abrupt climax places its end into the perspective of its beginning. However, its connection with the center of life is such that it is to be distinguished from all merely accidental happenings. Thus "mortal danger," so to speak, lies in its very style. This phenomenon, therefore, is a form which by its time symbolism seems to be predetermined to receive the erotic content.

These analogies between love and adventure alone suggest that the adventure does not belong to the life-style of old age. The decisive point about this fact is that the adventure, in its specific nature and charm, is a *form of experiencing*. The *content* of the experience does not make the adventure. That one has faced mortal danger or conquered a woman for a short span of happiness; that unknown factors with which one has waged a gamble have brought surprising gain or loss; that physically or psychologically disguised, one has ventured into spheres of life from which one returns home as if from a strange world—none of these are necessarily adventure. They become adventure only by virtue of a certain experiential tension whereby their substance is realized. Only when a stream flowing between the minutest externalities of life and the central source of strength drags them into itself; when the

peculiar color, ardor, and rhythm of the life-process become decisive and, as it were, transform its substance—only then does an
event change from mere experience to adventure. Such a principle
of accentuation, however, is alien to old age. In general, only youth
knows this predominance of the process of life over its substance;
whereas in old age, when the process begins to slow up and coagulate, substance becomes crucial; it then proceeds or perseveres in
a certain timeless manner, indifferent to the tempo and passion of
its being experienced. The old person usually lives either in a
wholly *centralized* fashion, peripheral interests having fallen off
and being unconnected with his essential life and its inner necessity; or his center atrophies, and existence runs its course only in
isolated petty details, accenting mere externals and accidentals.
Neither case makes possible the relation between the outer fate
and the inner springs of life in which the adventure consists;
clearly, neither permits the perception of contrast characteristic of
adventure, viz., that an action is completely torn out of the inclusive context of life and that simultaneously the whole strength and
intensity of life stream into it. . . .

14

THE NOBILITY

1908

I

LIKE THE MIDDLE CLASS, the nobility is an "intermediate structure," located between the highly stationed and the lower elements of the wider group; yet its position is formally distinct from that of the middle class. The sociological characteristic of the middle class is its openness at either boundary, whereas it is typical of the nobility, albeit with modifications, to be closed at both. Upward and downward, the middle class expands; the nobility repulses. Although the nobility tends for obvious reasons to shift its upper boundary more readily than its lower, there are numerous historical instances in which the nobility has confronted even the ruler himself as an entirely self-sufficient, closed stratum, centered on its own interests.

Through this doubly independent position the nobility has exerted two kinds of influence. It has inserted itself as a wedge between the ruler and large segments of the people, paralyzing the actions of the former in the interest of the latter. This happened quite often during the period of peasant serfdom and frequently under feudal regimes. On the other hand, the nobility has exercised a unifying influence, mediating the representation of each side to the other (especially in England).

Whenever in monarchical countries these two boundaries are

From *Soziologie* (Munich and Leipzig: Duncker & Humblot, 1908), pp. 732–46. Translated by Richard P. Albares.

not sharply drawn, the formation of nobility remains at a rudimentary level. This is the case in Turkey, where a true nobility has
never arisen. On the one hand, this results from the Mohammedan
view that lets the whole people feel itself to be an aristocracy, to be
something [divinely] elected in contrast to the infidels. On the
other hand, it results from the absolute grandeur of the sultan,
which cannot be mediated by anything at all and which lets no
level develop that in principle and by its own right would stand
closer to the sultan than any other. Similarly in Russia, because of
the absolutistic position of the czar, there is no aristocracy as a cohesive status group—only individual aristocrats who occasionally
establish circles (details below). But then, too, this is because
the lower mass of the people do not constitute such a practically
unified status group that they provoke the unification of those stationed above them.

Conversely, the twofold boundary of the nobility—which is
also a twofold relationship—will become more variegated in countries with a developed status-group system and with rich interstrata
relations variously mixed in syntheses and antitheses. This diversification must displace the nobility from its true position, although
new significance may accrue to it in the process. The motives that
Napoleon I imputed to his newly created nobility show this to the
point of caricature. Of this *caste intermédiaire*, he is reported to
have said to the democrats: it is thoroughly democratic, for it is
accessible to anyone at any time without hereditary prejudice; to
the great lords: it will support the throne; to the limited monar-
chists: it will inhibit all absolute rule, for it will itself become a
power in the state; to the Jacobins: only this will truly destroy the
old nobility; to the nobility: in that you are thus adorned with new
dignity, your old dignity will revive again in them. Here, therefore, the dual position of the nobility has become hypertrophied
into a multiple ambiguity which reveals that this particular dualism is the only appropriate and essential one for it.

The position of the nobility with its two fronts rests directly
upon its self-assurance and autonomy, attributes that will be specific in greater detail below. That position is further reflected in a
distinctive duality that is more inwardly directed. The nobility

emerges from among those personalities that are better off than others for whatever reason; but once it has emerged, personalities are then better off—retroactively, as it were—because they belong to it. There is no need here for examples of the "privileges" of nobility, but rather for examples of the other side of the noble position, of its restrictions and limitations.

In Florence around the year 1300, a far-reaching democratic movement arose during whose course the nobles were subjected to such exceptionally severe limitations and burdens that one could be ennobled then for punishment. The original distinction of nobility continued, but with a minus sign, as it were. It was as though the exceptional situation of nobility had endured, only that instead of the special advantages the situation would otherwise have bestowed, it entailed peculiar sacrifices and restrictions.

Something similar is found in a regulation from the eighteenth century in the very democratic canton of Thurgau in Switzerland. Since all status privileges were being eliminated at the time, it was stipulated in the constitution that anyone wishing to occupy public office would first have to renounce his nobility. Thus the nobility was encumbered to some extent by the penalty of exclusion from holding public office. This was the restriction imposed on the nobility to counterbalance their social prerogatives.

These detriments to the nobility appear most characteristically when they involve reversals of its penal exemptions. Although there are countless times when the nobleman's crime is punished more leniently than the commoner's, such phenomena as the following also occur. In medieval Dortmund, there was an extraordinarily elegant corporation, the Reinold Guild, which is always called Major Gilda. If one of its members committed any crime against the life and limb of another, then in addition to the generally applicable amends fine for such crimes, he had to pay the council a special fine as well.

A twelfth-century stipulation in the municipal code of Valenciennes reaches even more deeply. This code sets a particular penalty for thievery committed by an apprentice or a burgher. But if a knight steals, it is another matter. A noble simply does not steal: he robs. Theft lies entirely outside his competence, so to speak. If he acquires something illegitimately, it is assumed that he took it by force, by an act of robbery; and robbery is far more severely punished in the code than theft! The knight's noble position thus prevents him from suffering the milder penalty. From the very outset, he is at a level where one can only sin more fundamentally— where one absolutely cannot commit a sin like theft, which, because of its pettiness, can be atoned for more easily.

More subtle, but perhaps marked by more radical tension, is the contrast of the rights and burdens of the priestly aristocracy of Brahmans. Perhaps there was never any other hierarchy that ruled so unconditionally and that possessed such fantastic prerogatives as this one. But consider the life of the Brahman, this man who was endowed with unsurpassed power, against whose word there was absolutely no appeal, who seemed to be the only man with rights in the entire people such that even the king was no more than a subordinate of the priest. One sees there a life of unbearable harshness, of such constriction by forms and rules and mortifications and limitations that there would probably have been extraordinarily few Europeans who would have wanted even the unsurpassed rights of the Brahman priest at such a price. He was the most powerful, but also the most unfree man in India.

But perhaps freedom would have been despicable to him just as for Giordano Bruno, necessity was of inferior worth to God, but freedom was of inferior worth to man, for freedom would have meant to the Brahman that some vital impulse of his was a matter of indifference. It may be immaterial whether the rabble do this or that; the man of highest nobility must have every moment fixed by a law, since each one is unconditional and equally important. Phenomena of this type are summarized in the principle of noblesse oblige.

These impediments to, and detractions from, the advantages of the noble situation really define the full measure of the situation's elegance and exclusiveness. In the allowance to the lower masses of much that is forbidden to nobility lies the most profound disdain and devaluation: they are not thought worthy of the more stringent standard. If the non-noble wishes, he may make the same renunciations, but that bears no relation to this social position; it is an irrelevant private affair. But for the nobility, it is social duty to be forbidden many things; or more correctly it is the nobility's privilege. Perhaps the prototype of this is the prohibition on trading that runs through the whole history of the nobility since ancient Egypt.

Although the nobility has always emphasized the principle, *quod licet Jovi non licet bovi*, the converse is implicit: *quod licet bovi non licet Jovi*. If it is the case that the sociological form of the nobility is built above all upon its sharp group insularity, which bears on the whole being of the personalities in it in such a way that all individual differences are merely symbols of an absolutely self-sufficient and whole mode of being, then the distinction from everything non-noble is encompassed by *two* rules: the nobility is permitted what others are not, and the nobility is forbidden what others are allowed.

II

Apparently the social life of a group produces the particular structure of a nobility simply out of its own internal dynamics. The formal character of this structure is revealed by an identity of essential features under the endlessly diverse circumstances of these groups with respect to other formal and material attributes. The noble strata of ancient Rome, the Norman Empire, the American Indians, or the ancien régime all have corresponding sociological features despite the incomparability of their life contents. These features also emerge in a more rudimentary, labile, and transitory way in any other kind of smaller grouping within which some segment coalesces and separates off as "the aristocracy," be it in large family circles, among associations of labor, or within priesthoods.

For the nobility in the narrower sense, this similarity has been illustrated in the observation that "nobles often get to know one another better in the course of an evening than bourgeois do in a month." This is apparently because the common conditions of their existence penetrate very far into the personal sphere and are brought along into the relationship as self-evident assumptions. In

interests, *Weltanschauung,* consciousness of personality, feel for
the point at which they stand in the social order—in all these,
aristocrats apparently coincide to such an extent, and the coincidence is so clear and self-evident to them that they are able to
come to personal matters among themselves much sooner than
others who must first ascertain what basis they have in common. In
order to "get to know one another," that is, to reveal their individualities, nobles do not need as many preliminaries as those who
first must search for the a priori from which to present particulars
of thoughts, interests, and modes of being.

This homogeneity of formal-sociological setting appears very
significantly in the following historical phenomena. Attention has
been called to the peculiar fact that many families of high noble
status in European countries have foreign origins. In England, the
Fitzgeralds and the Dukes of Leicester come from Florence, the
Dukes of Portland from Holland. In France, the Broglies come
from Piedmont, the Dukes des Cars from Perugia, the Luynes
from Arezzo. In Austria, the Clarys come from Florence. In Prussia, the Lynars come from Faenza. In Poland, the Poniatowskis
come from Bologna. In Italy, the Roccas come from Croatia, the
Ruspolis from Scotland, the Torlonias from France, and so on. One
would expect members of the nobility to be little disposed to such
transplantation by virtue of their attachment to landed property
and their traditional nationalism, which is usually tied to a conservative *Weltanschauung.* All the more potent, then, must be the
assimilating forces that are involved in such a changing about
within what has been called the republic of nobility.

This pattern continues in particular unifications of national nobility. Until sometime around the beginning of the nineteenth century, the attachment of German nobles to one another was very
slight. Most looked after their interests within the narrower circles
of their estates or of their immediate homelands. But when German nobles from the various locales met during the Napoleonic
Wars, a contact developed among them that led to some quite notable structures, for example, the so-called Chain of Nobility. The
Chain of Nobility was a semisecret society that probably arose
at the time of the Congress of Vienna. The nobles felt that their

role had diminished even in Germany since the French Revolution, especially because of the emancipation of the serfs. By drawing on the solidarity that exists among all nobles, they tried to create a collective structure in order to regain somehow their lost importance.

The Chain of Nobility explicitly emphasized in its charter that everything political was foreign to it. Although this may have involved a certain deception or self-delusion, it nevertheless expresses the essential point, namely, the inconsequentiality of political and geographic boundaries compared to that which is common to all nobles simply because they are nobles. The identity of purely material interests would not have been sufficiently great to have brought into being this inter-Germanic society of nobles had not the deeper bond of the form of the nobility itself—a concept whose explication remains—been effective.

Finally, a last example. The great importance of nobility in Austria and the considerable prerogatives invariably conceded to it there might be traced to the fact that among the extraordinarily heterogeneous and fractious components of the Austrian monarchy, the nobility is still a thoroughly uniform, qualitatively coherent element, thereby aiding considerably in the maintenance of the whole. The identical formal setting of the nobility in the various parts of this hodgepodge country makes it possible for there to be a unitary Austrian nobility even though there is no unitary Austrian nationality. The unity inherent in the nobility by virtue of its invariant sociological position makes it tend to serve the unity of the whole like cement.

III

But everything presented so far has been external appearance, more or less, grounded in the inner sociological structure of the nobility, but not yet making it discernible. The sociological analysis of the nobility must focus now on the quite singular relation that the socially shared life content of this special group has to the individual being of its members. Here the decisive consideration is not merely that the individual is taken up into a group of individuals who exist before, alongside, and after him and who are bound together by means of a uniquely effective formula. It is, rather, that what is best and most valuable in that whole alignment accrues to every one of its members.

It has been stressed frequently in these investigations that the collective level of a group, the value of what is really common to all members, lies very close to the lowliest among them because, as a rule, the top can sink to the bottom, but the bottom cannot rise to the top. Thus, on the whole, whatever it may be that is common to all members will be the possession of the bottom part, much as when a hundred men are to march in step, the tempo will be set by whoever has the least marching ability.

With the nobility, however, the presumption is the opposite. In a noble group (the noble family, in the narrower sense, or the nobility of a country or an epoch, in the broader one), each constituent personality has in its value a share in the glory attained by the most outstanding members of it. The personality assumes the legacy of the status group *sub beneficio inventarii*, as it were; and it is precisely the positive values accumulated there in merits, distinctions, and honors that shine upon the individual more unrefractedly than in any other kind of group. This is the prejudice with which other status groups favor the nobility; which nobles cherish among themselves; and last, which forms the precondition, as it were, for every member's self-awareness, constituting an individual support that is just as strong as the social support it makes for the totality of the status group.

The nobility has within its sociological structure a singular tenacity in the conservation of its "objective spirit," the achievement of individuals that is crystallized in tradition, rigid form, the products of labor, and so on. That which exists in single families as their distinction, renown, value, coalesces to some degree in the general position of "nobility"; and to that degree, the position of nobility is to be distinguished from their merely external power and property holdings.

This even appears in a configuration whose actual orientation is the reverse. It has been observed with regard to ancient clan organizations that a nobility would very frequently emerge when the head of the gens was always elected from the same lineage. That lineage was thus not preferred from the outset, but rather only came to be preferred once the expectation existed that it would always supply someone qualified for the leadership position. In that the entire family thereupon became a nobility, it discounted the merit and honor which any of its members would probably acquire someday and which, radiating back from the future, as it were, provided the ennobling substance for the whole lineage.

It is an instructive simile when one speaks of noble metals, of the "nobility" of gold and silver. This nobility of metal exists chiefly, it seems to me, in its relative indestructibility. Because of its value, it is constantly conserved; in its continuous recastings, it changes only its form, while the value substance is relatively imperishable. A similar conception lies at the foundation of the feeling of and for the nobility: it is as though its individual members were, so to speak, nothing but different recastings, nothing but different forms of a constant-value substance that endures throughout the whole succession of inheritances. This gives a quite special accent to the relation of the individual to the group that historically leads down to him. An imperishability of value, so to speak, is what the nobility claims for itself and what its sociological patterns seek to realize.

The reason no aristocracy arose in Russia as a compact status group, at least before Czar Fedor,[1] predecessor to Peter the Great, is as follows. Everyone's prestige and honor were dependent exclusively on his "services," his performance in office, from which a classification of families was made. That is, the extraordinary principle held sway that no one might serve under a statutory superior who in his time had served under the candidate's father. To determine the possible right and positions of everyone in accord with this principle special records were kept. The consequence of this was incessant disputes among families under consideration concerning facts and rights—a plethora of overt and covert competi-

[1]   Theodore II.—TRANS.

tions and rivalries. Thus the creation of a centripetal status group, the coalescence of separate powers and qualities into a common unitary and persisting substance, was frustrated from the outset.

IV

This structure, even as far as it has been described already, makes clear at once why the nobility must hold to equality of birth. Already in the constitution of ancient clans, it has been argued, nobles from different clans belonged to a single status group; and although as a rule the clan as such was exogamous (permitting no marriage among its members), that noble stratum always tended to become endogamous, that is, to marry only within itself. If it is the case that nobility presumes solid substance, as it were, with which everyone belonging to it is endowed, and which must be transmitted undiminished to succeeding generations, then every member must have originated in the one circle. No circle in which the superior qualities which created that substance are not hereditary may mix in with it. Only in this way can one be sure, generally speaking, that each member truly participates in the force, sentiment, and significance of the totality—that that peculiar relationship will be realized in which the value of the whole grows through every single individual.

This recruiting from within conveys the unique insularity and self-sufficiency of this status group which, so to speak, can and may need nothing that lies outside itself. The nobility is, thereby, like an island in the world. It is comparable to a work of art, within which each part also takes its meaning from the whole, and which shows through its frame that the world cannot enter, that it is absolutely sufficient unto itself.

This form surely gives the nobility a large part of the aesthetic attraction that it has exerted in every period. For it is not just the individual that is attractive, in which event the attraction would derive only from good stock and from the superior care and cultivation that nobles have devoted to the body and to social forms over long generations. Rather, there hovers in the *collective image* of the nobility a certain charm, dependent surely on the aesthetically satisfying form of autonomy and insularity, of the solidarity of parts—all of which are analogues to the work of art.

This fulfillment of individual being with psychologically and historically transmitted substance can lead, to be sure, to a decadent emptiness. It seems as though socially transmitted contents and meanings only attain true value in life if they are balanced to a certain extent by a creative power flowing out of the individual. In the more excellent manifestations of nobility, therefore, it is especially a self-assured personal existence that emerges, a feeling of the equally strong qualities of *independence* and *responsibility* of the individual. This is due to the sociologically unique intimacy with which a perduring substance, extending in the three dimensions of past, present, and future, has grown together with the individual's existence, transposing itself into an awareness of the higher values of that existence. Whenever the individual factor is too weak to impart form to that superpersonal substance, then, as stated, signs of decay appear: unavoidably, the substance itself becomes form, and the meaning of life is no more than the preservation of specific status honors and of "good demeanor"—as finally occurred in the nobility of the ancien régime.

V

For the relation of the family—and furthermore, of the noble group generally—to the individual, the significance of the "family tree" is profoundly symbolic: the substance that makes up the individual must have passed through the trunk of the whole, just as the substance of fruit and branch in a tree is the same as that composing the trunk. Perhaps this sociological constitution explains the aversion to "labor" that the nobility has shown throughout social history, until the most recent period, with the democratization of economic activity, has tended to effect a change. In every instance of true "labor," subject is devoted to object; and regardless whether the *product* of labor reverts back to the subject, the action itself remains oriented toward an impersonal structure and finds its culmination in the forming of that structure, be it the shaping or reshaping of concepts in intellectual labor, the pedagogic forming of a pupil, or the working of physical substances. But this directly contradicts aristocracy's basic ethos [*Lebensgefühl*], which is absolutely personal. Its center is in the being of the subject, whose value, like the value of everything that arises directly from him, is determined by the *terminus a quo*. However, labor is action that is eminently a means, that is oriented toward something external, that is determined by the *terminus ad quem*. It is on this point that Schiller distinguishes between low natures, who pay with what they do, and noble natures, who pay with what they are.

The nobleman is occupied, but he does not labor (all these specifications naturally appear in particular empirical cases with thousandfold modifications). War and the hunt, the historically typical occupations of nobility, are not, despite all the toil involved, "labor" in the true sense. The subjective factor has decisive dominance over the objective factor in them; and unlike the case in labor, the product is not an object severed from the personality from which it has absorbed energy; rather, the emphasis lies in the preservation of the powers of the subject himself.

A certain analogy to the aristocracy's type of achievement can be found, if at all, in artistic labor. This is not actually labor on an object, but much more a forming of the object by outflows of subjective stirrings whose determination is purely internal. Yet the action of the artist and its value flow from the mysterious point of uniqueness of his individuality, behind which there is no detectable factor conveying it or transposing itself therein. The particular action and consciousness of the aristocrat, however, are based on that substance transmitted by family and stratum which has only taken individual form in him, one that is quite self-assured and internally grounded nevertheless.

VI

There is a peculiar exception to this characterization of nobility in terms of the amassing or ideal crystallization of dignities and deserts, wealth and honors, duties and rights that are acquired within family and status group and that each member takes part in—not pro rata as through division, but rather as an indivisible property that is the a priori, as it were, of each person's being and action. This exception is the condition in China, wherein inheritable nobility gradually decreases. Nobility is never simply bestowed that would remain continually in the family, thus making possible the accumulation of importance just described; rather, there exists an infinitely fine gradation of honor for whose degrees we have no appropriate expressions. The son always stands one level below the father in this continuum so that after a particular sequence of generations, all nobility is extinguished. If I am rightly informed, highest nobility, princely status, is conferred every twenty-six generations; so after their passage—and this also applies to princes of the royal household who have not risen to power—the family reverts back to commoner status. This anomaly, which can only occur in a bureaucratic or paper-work nobility, denotes normal development with a minus sign, so to speak. For the sense of that normal development is the gradual accumulation of transmitted values, although this may begin with an original conferral; in China, however, that substance is given all at once, as it were, and then it is gradually used up.

In contrast, the current order in Tahiti demonstrates the normal form in a very instructive, pointed way. When a son is born to a nobleman there, the father abdicates social dignity to him, "for the son has one more ancestor than the father." In a satirical poem by Glassbrenner from the middle of the nineteenth century, the hollow dignity and puffed-up nullity of a noble are depicted with the conclusion that there is *one* thing in which he could rightfully take pride: "Once blessedly deceased, He too will be an ancestor." This is fundamentally the same feeling as in the Tahitian case. Given the sociological base to which the nobility have clung with the greatest historical success, this feeling is hardly as senseless as it is made to seem by certain decadent examples and by macrosocial structures within which that base cannot persist.

VII

The specification of that base in terms of the broadest categories of life can now be completed somewhat as follows. Every human being emerges as a certain combination of predetermination and accident; of received material for, and unique formation of, his life; of social inheritance and the individual administration of it. In each person, we see the stereotypings of his race, his stratum, his traditions, his family, in brief, of everything that makes him a bearer of preexisting contents and norms; we see these combined with the incalculable and the personal, with free autonomy. The earlier factors are the a priori, as it were, and the latter are the singular givenness, which combine to produce the empirical phenomenon. Both are diversely mixed in the great social construction of types; and in the nobility, indeed, they are mixed in a highly unique manner. The scientific specification of that mixture in abstract concepts is naturally independent of the fact that the complications of reality cause these pure patterns to be constantly affected by obscuring, diverting, and particularizing forces.

Stereotypings have coalesced here as into the bed of a river. Since collective life contents, child rearing and marriage, occupation and political standpoint, aesthetic inclination and economic means, are all "status specific," all standardizations, which give the individual the material of his life half-finished, as it were, are channeled through a single canal. Certainly there were universally binding stereotypings of equal or greater power in guild and priesthood, in hereditary callings and in the compulsions of caste and class. Yet the distinguishing characteristic of the nobility is that that other element—personality, freedom, the internally grounded —became of greater value and of greater significance here than in other structures. This is because the substance transmitted in the nobility did not take on an objective, individual-transcending configuration; rather, only the particular form and power of the individual makes the whole transmitted material come alive. Although the individual will not infrequently experience compulsion, the sense of the whole constellation is nevertheless that this substance of values accumulated by status group and family should benefit the self-exalting, individually justified being of each member. The substance thereby experiences not a diminution, but an increase. The existence that rests upon itself, that takes responsibility for and joy in itself, is not, as in many other highly socialized structures, a detraction from the common welfare and from common possessions; rather, that existence is their elaboration, preservation, increase.

Nobility's special synthesis is one between the extremes in which the individual is either swallowed up by his group or comes to regard it with oppositional self-centeredness. The rigor of the status-specific form of life produces a maximally broad contact surface among the members. The insistence on equality of birth effects a physiological guarantee of qualitative and historical continuity. Through the technique of the noble tradition, the values and achievements of family and status group coalesce as though into a reservoir. By these sociological means, the nobility has smelted individuals into the common grouping to a degree not otherwise attained. But the superpersonal structure thus created has its goal and meaning, here more than anywhere else, in the existence of individuals, in their might and significance, in the freedom and self-sufficiency of their lives.

In its purest historical manifestations, the nobility pulls the worth of individual lives into its collective structure with unique power. Its development aims with unconditional unanimity at the formation, growth, and self-sufficiency of the individual. To the equation between the totality and the individual, between the predetermined givenness and the personal elaboration of life, the nobility has thus arrived at an historically unique solution.

IV. Forms of Individuality

15

FREEDOM AND THE INDIVIDUAL

Posthumous

THE GENERAL European consensus is that the era of the Italian Renaissance created what we call individuality. By this is meant a state of inner and external liberation of the individual from the communal forms of the Middle Ages, forms which had constricted the pattern of his life, his activities, and his fundamental impulses through homogenizing groups. These had, as it were, allowed the boundaries of the individual to become blurred, suppressing the development of personal freedom, of intrinsic uniqueness, and of the sense of responsibility for one's self. I will set aside the question whether the Middle Ages lacked all traces of individuality. The conscious emphasis on individuality as a matter of principle certainly does seem to have been the original accomplishment of the Renaissance. This took place in such a way that the will to power, to distinction, and to becoming honored and famous was diffused among men to a degree never before known. If for a time in Florence at the beginning of this period, as has been reported, there was no pervasive fashion in masculine attire, since each man wished to deport himself in a manner peculiar to himself, it was not a matter of simple distinctiveness, of being different. The individual wanted to be *conspicuous;* he wanted to present himself more propitiously and more remarkably than was possible by means of the established forms. This is the

---

From "Das Individuum und die Freiheit," in *Brücke und Tür*, ed. Michael Landmann and Margarete Susman (Stuttgart: Koehler, 1957), pp. 260–69. Translated by Richard P. Albares.

behavioral reality of the individualism of distinction, which is associated with the ambition of Renaissance man, with his ruthless self-aggrandizement, with his value emphasis on being unique.

It is self-evident that such yearning and realization as this cannot remain a constant condition of men and society, but must pass away like an intoxication. Appearing here as a striving for aggrandizement, individualism still left behind in the lowlands and commonplaces of existence so many restrictions, so many impossibilities for the individual to develop his powers, to live out his life freely, to sense the self-sufficiency of his person—so many of these that the accumulation of this pressure led once again to an explosion in the eighteenth century. But this occurred from a different direction; it was led by a different ideal of individuality, one whose innermost impulse was not to distinction, but to freedom.

Freedom becomes for the eighteenth century the universal demand which the individual uses to cover his manifold grievances and self-assertions against society. This is readily observable in a variety of contexts. One sees it under the garb of political economy among the physiocrats, who extol the free competition of individual interests as the natural order of things; in its sentimental elaboration by Rousseau, for whom the ravaging of man by historical society is the source of all atrophy and all evil; in its political manifestation in the French Revolution, which elevated the idea of individual freedom to the point of forbidding workers to form unions even for the protection of their own interests; and in its philosophical sublimation by Kant and Fichte, who conceived the ego as the bearer of the knowable world and made its absolute autonomy *the* moral value.

The inadequacy of the socially sanctioned forms of life in the eighteenth century, compared with the material and intellectual productivity of the period, struck the consciousness of individuals as an unbearable restriction of their energies. Those restrictive forms included the privileges of the higher estates as well as the despotic control of commerce; the still powerful survivals of the guild system as well as to the intolerant pressure of the church; the corvée expected from the peasant population as well as paternalism in the life of the state and the restrictions imposed on municipal constitutions. The oppressiveness of such institutions, which had lost their intrinsic justification, gave rise to the ideal of pure freedom for the individual. If only these restraints would collapse and cease forcing the powers of the personality into their own unnatural channels, then all the internal and external values that were already in full vigor, but which were politically, religiously, and economically crippled, would unfold, leading society out of the era of historical unreason and into the era of natural rationality.[1]

The individualism that sought its realization in this way was based on the notion of the *natural equality* of individuals, on the conception that all the restrictions just mentioned were artifically produced inequalities and that once these had been banished along with their historical fortuitousness, their injustice, and their burdensomeness, perfected man would emerge. And since he was perfect, perfect in morality, in beauty, and in happiness, he could show no differences. The deep cultural-historical movement that generated this conception flows out of the eighteenth century's concept of nature, which is entirely mechanistic and scientific in orientation. In that concept, nothing exists except the general law, and every phenomenon, be it a human being or a nebula in the Milky Way, is merely a single instance of some law or laws. Even if the form of an individual phenomenon is absolutely unrepeatable, it is still a mere crosspoint and a resolvable constellation of purely universal laws. This is why it is man in general, universal man, who occupies the center of interest for this period instead of historically given, particular, and differentiated man. The latter is in principle reduced to the former; in each individual person, man in general lives as his essence, just as every piece of matter, peculiar as its configuration may be, exhibits in its essence the pervasive laws of matter in general.

It is at this point that freedom and equality can be seen to belong together by right from the very outset. For if universal humanity—natural-law man, as it were—exists as the essential core of every man, who is individualized by empirical traits, social

[1]   Some of these formulations are drawn from my two books, *Kant, 16 Vorlesungen* and *Goethe.*

position, and accidental configuration, all one need do is *free* him from all these historical influences and diversions that ravage his deepest essence, and then what is common to all, man as such, can emerge in him as this essence.

Here lies the pivotal point of this concept of individuality, which is one of the great conceptions of intellectual history: when man is freed from everything that is not wholly himself, what remains as the actual substance of his being is man in general, mankind, which lives in him and in everyone else, the ever identical fundamental essence that is merely empiricohistorically disguised, diminished, and distorted. It is this significance of the universal which makes the literature of the Revolutionary period continually speak about the "people," the "tyrant," and "freedom" in such general terms. It is for this reason that "natural religion" has a providence in general, a justness in general, a divine education in general, but does not recognize the right of any particular manifestations of this generality. It is for this reason that "natural law" is based on the fiction of isolated and identical individuals. And this is why Frederick the Great can call the prince "the first judge, the first man of finance, the first minister of society," but then in the same breath, call him "a *man* like the least of his subjects."

The basic metaphysical motif that finds expression during the eighteenth century in the practical demand for "freedom and equality" is this: the worth of each individual's configuration is based, to be sure, on him alone, on his personal responsibility, but along with that it is based on what the individual has in common with all others. Perhaps it was also part of this motif that the individual felt it to be an extraordinary demand that he should bear the sum total of his existence with his own solitary powers, which center upon the point of his uniqueness, and that he lightened or threw off this burden through having the human species, man in general, living within him and actually accomplishing the task. The deepest point of individuality is the point of universal equality, regardless whether this lies in "nature," whose universal lawfulness we are all the more merged into as we increasingly rely on our free ego aside from all historical diversities and restrictions or whether it is the universality of "reason," which is where our ego has its roots for Kant and Fichte, or whether it is "mankind." Whether it is nature, reason, or man, it is always something shared with others in which the individual discovers himself when he has discovered his own freedom, his own selfhood.

By freeing individuality from every restriction and special determination, and hence by making perpetually identical individuality—man in the abstract—the ultimate substance of personality, this era simultaneously elevated that abstraction to the ultimate *value* of personality. A man, says Kant, is certainly profane, but the mankind in him is sacred. For Rousseau, who certainly had a strong sense for individual diversities, this is still at a superficial level: the more a man returns to his own heart, holding to his inner absoluteness rather than to external relations, the more strongly does the fountainhead of goodness and happiness flow into him, that is, into everyone equally. Once a man is truly himself in this way, he possesses an accumulated power that is sufficient for more than his own self-preservation, a power that he can let overflow, so to speak, onto others, through which he can take them into himself and identify himself with them. We are morally more worthy, more compassionate and authentic, the more each person is merely himself, that is, the more each person allows this inner core to become sovereign within himself, the core in which all men are identical beyond the muddle of their social bonds and accidental guises.

In the practical dimension, this concept of individuality obviously flows into laissez faire, laissez aller. If in all men, ever identical "man in general" exists as what is essential to them, and if the full, unhampered development of this core is assumed, there is naturally no need for special regulating intervention into human relations. The play of forces must take place there in the same natural-law harmony as in the events in the heavens which, if a supernatural power were suddenly to change their intrinsic movements, could only collapse into chaos.

To be sure, the shadow that lay across the freedom of individuals could not be banished entirely. Their equality, by which their freedom was justified, never did exist in reality as accomplished fact, and at the instant individuals received unlimited freedom, unmistakable inequality would generate a new repression, a repression of dullards by the smart, of the weak by the strong, of the shy by the aggressive. And it seems to me that it was an instinctive sense for this that resulted in the extension of the demand for *liberté* and *égalité* to include *fraternité*. For it was only through the voluntary act of renunciation as expressed in this concept that it would be possible to prevent *liberté* from being accompanied by the total opposite of *égalité*. Nevertheless, this contradiction between the equality and the freedom of individuality remained latent in the general eighteenth-century conception of the essence of individuality, and it was the nineteenth century that first [brought it out into the open. . . .[2]]

I shall now sketch the peculiar form of individualism that dissolved the eighteenth-century synthesis which based equality on freedom, and freedom on equality. In place of that idea of equality which expresses the deepest being of man and yet is still to be realized, this other form of individualism substitutes inequality. As was true for equality under the other form of individualism, so now inequality requires nothing but freedom in order for it to shape human existence as it emerges from its mere latency and potentiality. Freedom remains the common denominator, despite this opposition between its two correlates. As soon as the ego had become sufficiently strengthened by the feeling of equality and universality, it sought once again inequality—but this time an inequality determined only from within. After the individual had been liberated in principle from the rusty chains of guild, hereditary status, and church, the quest for independence continued to the point where individuals who had been rendered independent in this way wanted also to distinguish themselves *from one another*. What mattered now was no longer that one was a free individual as such, but that one was a particular and irreplaceable individual.

With this development, the modern striving for differentiation is heightened to the point of repudiating the form it has just won.

[2]   There is a gap in the manuscript at this point, probably because Simmel took some pages from this essay when reworking the general topic for a later publication. The latter has been translated as "Individual and Society in Eighteenth- and Nineteenth-Century Views of Life," in *The Sociology of Georg Simmel*, pp. 58–84.—ED.

At the same time, the drive underlying this development remains one and the same: throughout the modern era, the quest of the individual is for his self, for a fixed and unambiguous point of reference. He needs such a fixed point more and more urgently in view of the unprecedented expansion of theoretical and practical perspectives and the complication of life, and the related fact that he can no longer find it anywhere outside himself.

All relations with others are thus ultimately mere stations along the road by which the ego arrives at its self. This is true whether the ego feels itself to be basically identical to these others because it still needs this supporting conviction as it stands alone upon itself and its own powers, or whether it is strong enough to bear the loneliness of its own quality, the multitude being there only so that each individual can use the others as a measure of his incomparability and the individuality of his world.

In the eighteenth century, to be sure, the latter ideal is adumbrated in the works of Lessing, Herder, and Lavater; and it achieves its first full artistic expression in *Wilhelm Meister's Apprenticeship*. Here, for the first time, a world is depicted that is based entirely on the personal peculiarities of its individuals and that is organized and developed on this basis alone—quite irrespective of the fact that these figures were intended as types. No matter how often these character types may be repeated in reality, it remains the intrinsic meaning of each of them that he is fundamentally different from the others with whom fate has brought him into contact, that the *accent* of his life and development does not fall on what is similar to others, but on the absolutely idiosyncratic. Here we have the absolute opposite of the ideal of free and equal personalities that is speaking—which Fichte, condensing the intellectual movement of the eighteenth century in a single sentence, formulated thus: "A rational being must necessarily be an individual, but *not* this or that particular one." In pointed antithesis to that ideal, Friedrich Schlegel captured the *new* individualism with the formula: "It is precisely individuality that is primordial and eternal in man; in personality, not so much is involved."

This form of individualism found its philosopher in Schleiermacher. For him, the moral task is that each person should represent mankind in a *particular* manner. Certainly, each individual is a synthesis of the forces that constitute the universe. Yet out of this material that is common to all, each one creates an entirely unique configuration. It is the realization of this incomparability, the filling of a space held in reserve for him alone, that is the moral duty of the individual. Each person is called to realize his own, his very own prototype. Through Schleiermacher, the great world-historical idea that not only the equality of men but also their differentiation is a moral imperative becomes the pivotal point for a world view.

This individualism could be called qualitative, in contrast to the numerical individualism of the eighteenth century, or it could be named the individualism of uniqueness [*Einzigkeit*] in contrast to that of singleness [*Einzelheit*]. Romanticism was perhaps the broadest channel through which the new individualism penetrated the consciousness of the nineteenth century. Goethe created its artistic, Schleiermacher its metaphysical basis; Romanticism created for it a basis in feeling, in experience. Following Herder, the Romantics first immersed themselves again in the particularity and uniqueness of historical realities. It is in this sense that Novalis wants to allow his "one spirit" to transform itself into infinitely many alien spirits. But above all, the Romantic experiences in his internal rhythm the incomparability, the special claims, and the sharp contrast of elements and motives—the same contrast that this form of individualism sees between the components of *society*. The Romantic psyche feels its way through an endless succession of contrasts. At the instant it is being experienced, each one of them seems absolute, complete, self-contained; at the next instant, it is overcome by another, and in the difference between the two, the self of each is first fully appreciated. "He who holds fast to only one point," says Friedrich Schlegel, "is nothing but a rational oyster." The life of the Romantic translates the synchronic opposition of a social scene in which each individual finds the meaning of his life in his difference from all others, in the personal uniqueness of his nature and his activities, into a protean succession of contrasting moods and tasks, beliefs and feelings.

Incessantly, these great forces of modern culture strain toward accommodation in countless external and internal domains and in countless permutations. One force is the yearning for the autonomous personality that bears the cosmos within itself, whose isolation has the great compensation of being identical to all others at its deepest, natural core. The other is the yearning for the incomparability of being unique and different, which is compensated for its isolation by the fact that each person can exchange with another some good that he alone possesses and whose exchange weaves both of them into the interaction of organic parts of the whole. By and large, one can say that the individualism of simply free personalities that are thought of as equal in principle has determined the rationalistic liberalism of France and England, whereas the individualism that is based on qualitative uniqueness and immutability is more a concern of the Germanic mind.

In their elaboration into economic principles, to be sure, the nineteenth century let the two forms coalesce. For clearly the doctrine of freedom and equality is the basis for free competition; and the doctrine of differentiated personality is the basis for the division of labor. The liberalism of the eighteenth century set the individual on his own two feet, and he could go quite as far as they would carry him. The theory left it up to the natural order of things to see to it that unlimited competition among individuals would yield a harmony of all interests, that the whole would fare best in the setting of ruthless individual strivings for advantage. That is the metaphysic with which eighteenth-century optimism about nature socially justified free competition.

In the individualism of otherness, of the deepening of individuality to the point of incomparability in essence as in the performances of one's calling, the metaphysic of the division of labor was found. The two great principles which operate, inseparably, in nineteenth-century economic theory and practice—competition and the division of labor—thus appear to be the economic projections of metaphysical aspects of social individualism. To be sure, unlimited competition and individual specialization in the division of labor have affected the subjective culture of individuals in ways that show that they are not exactly the most suitable processes for promoting that culture.

But perhaps, over and above the economic form in which these two ideals are mutually operative—the only one thus far realized —there is a higher form that constitutes the hidden ideal of our culture. I would prefer to believe that the idea of free personality as such and the idea of unique personality as such are not the last words of individualism—that, rather, the unforeseeable work of mankind will produce ever more numerous and varied forms with which the human personality will affirm itself and prove the worth of its existence. And if, in fortunate periods, these varied forms may order themselves harmoniously, even their possible contradiction and struggle will not merely disrupt that work, but rather will stimulate it to new demonstrations of strength and lead to new creations.

16

SUBJECTIVE CULTURE

1908

ALL SEQUENCES of events based on human activity can be viewed as natural—that is, as causally determined developments in which every stage must be understood with reference to the combinations and tensions of the preceding stage. In this sense one does not need to distinguish between nature and history, since what we call "history," if seen purely as a course of events, takes its place as part of the natural interrelationships of world happenings and their causal order. But as soon as some of the contents of these sequences move under the concept of culture, the concept of nature acquires a narrower and, so to speak, local meaning. For in that case, the "natural" development extends only to a certain point, beyond which cultural development replaces it.

The wild pear tree bears woody, sour fruit. Such is the end point of its development in the wild. At this point, human will and intellect have intervened and have led the tree by means of a variety of influences to the production of edible pears, that is, have "cultivated" it. Similarly, we believe that the development of the human species through its physical and psychological struc- ture, by heredity and adaptation, arrives at certain forms and con- tents of existence. At this point, teleological processes set in that raise existing energies to a level that was in principle unattainable

From "Vom Wesen der Kultur," in *Brücke und Tür*, ed. Michael Landmann and Margarete Susman (Stuttgart: Koehler, 1957), pp. 86–94. Translated by Roberta Ash. Originally published in a slightly expanded version in *Österreichische Rundschau XV*, 1908.

with their previous developmental possibilities. The point at which this unleashing of developmental forces occurs marks the boundary between the state of nature and the state of culture.

Since, however, the state of culture can also be shown to be caused by its "natural" originating conditions, we see that nature and culture are only two different ways of looking at the same phenomenon; and that the concept of nature appears here in two different meanings. In one sense of the term, nature signifies the all-inclusive complex of phenomena connected in causal chains. In the other sense, it signifies a particular phase in the development of a subject—namely, the phase in which it enfolds its own potential, and which ends as soon as a more intelligent and purposive will takes over these forces and thereby brings the subject to a condition which it could not reach by itself.

Inasmuch as the concept of culture thus seems to be coterminous with the concept of human purposive action, there is need for a more circumscribed definition that will bring out its distinctive nature. When a schoolboy trips his fellow to make him fall and to get the other boys to laugh, he has certainly engaged in an eminently teleological act, an exploitation of natural occurrences by intellect and will; but one can hardly categorize it under the concept of culture! So the use of the term depends on a further series of perhaps unconsciously effective conditions which become apparent only after a not entirely self-evident analysis has been carried out.

Cultivation implies that some being existed before the appearance of cultivation in an uncultivated, that is, "natural," state, and it further implies that the ensuing transformation of this subject is somehow latent in *its natural structural potential*, even though it could not be realized by itself, but only through culture. For cultivation brings its object to a fulfillment determined by the essential and fundamental tendencies of the object's nature.

The pear tree, therefore, seems to us cultivated because the work of the gardener really only develops potentialities inherent in it but unawakened in its natural state—brings it to the most complete unfolding of its own nature. By contrast, when the trunk of a tree is made into a mast, this, too, is a work of culture, but not a "cultivation" of the trunk; because the form which the labor of the shipbuilder gives it is not inherent in its nature. This form is given to it purely from the outside, under the impact of a purposive system foreign to its own tendencies.

To use the word appropriately, then, all cultivation is not merely the development of a being beyond the morphological stage attainable through its nature alone, but development in the direction of an original inner core, a fulfillment of this being according to the law of its own meaning, its deepest dispositions. This perfection cannot be attained in the "natural" stage that emerges from the purely causal development of qualities native to the being. It emerges, rather, through the interaction of the natural forces with a new, teleological intervention, an intervention which follows the inherent proclivities of the being and as such may be called *its* culture.

From this it follows that, to use the term precisely, man alone is a proper object for culture; for he is the only being known to us in which the challenge of perfectibility exists from the outset. His "potentialities" are not merely the simple condition of quiescent tensions, nor are they the reflections and idealized contributions of a bystander—as with the garden pear whose potential is dormant in the wild pear—but they already have a language of their own, as it were. The state to which the soul can in fact develop is already present in its initial condition as a striving, as though etched into it with invisible lines. Even if it is vague and fragmented in its contents, it already has a definite direction. The *should* and *can* of man's full development are inseparably bound to the *being* of man's soul. Only the human soul contains the developmental potentialities whose goals are determined purely in the teleology of its own nature. It does not attain these goals by mere inherent growth processes, which we call natural, but through the application, at a certain point of a technique, of a deliberate intervention.

Therefore when we talk of the "cultivation" of lower organisms, of plants and animals (this word cannot even be applied to inorganic things), we are obviously only using an analogy between mankind and other organisms. For even if the state to which culture leads the latter is inherent in their organization and is indeed produced by means of their own forces, still it is not rooted in the meaning of their existence. In their natural state, perfection is never predetermined as an attainable goal, as it is in the human soul.

But at this point a further delimitation of the concept is necessary. Culture is a perfection of man, but not every perfection of man is culture. On the contrary, there are developments which perfect the soul purely internally, or which appear as a relationship with transcendental powers or which involve it in an immediate ethical, erotic, suggestive relation to other persons, and which cannot be included in the concept of culture. Religious enthusiasm, moral sacrifices, the stern insistence of the personality on *its* own mode of existence and duty—all these are values which the soul derives from the instincts of its own inspiration or by acting upon itself. They may very well satisfy a first approximation to the concept of culture, for they develop qualities of the person beyond the "natural" stage to a high level, which admittedly coincides with the most essential orientation of the person and his Idea, and which can be attained only through the application of the most elevated spiritual energies. But all that still does not exhaust the meaning of the concept of culture.

For culture exists only if man draws into his development *something that is external to him.* Cultivation is certainly a state of the soul, but one that is reached only by means of the use of purposely created *objects.* This externality and objectivity is not to be understood only in a spatial sense. The forms of comportment, the refinement of taste expressed in judgments, the education of moral tact which make an individual a delightful member of society—they are all cultural formations in which the perfection of the individual is routed through real and ideal spheres outside of the self. The perfection does not remain a purely immanent process, but is consummated in a unique adjustment and teleological interweaving of subject and object. Where there is no inclusion of an objective construct in the developmental process of the subjective soul, where the soul does not return to itself via the inclusion of an object as a means and stage of its path to perfection—it may realize values of the highest order within itself or outside of itself, but it does not thereby attain culture in the specific sense. Thus we comprehend why very inner-oriented persons, who shun every detour of the soul into the surrounding world in the course of seeking their own perfection, can feel hatred for culture.

This necessary duality of the elements of culture is also evident if we examine the object. We are accustomed simply to designate as cultural values great works of artistic, moral, scientific, and economic production. It is possible that they all are; but in no way are they cultural by virtue of their purely objective, independent meaning, and in no way does the cultural importance of the individual product exactly correspond to its importance within its own objective category. A work of art is subjected to quite different rankings and norms when it is considered in terms of the categories of art history or aesthetics than when its cultural value is in question. Each of the former categories can be considered an end in itself, so that each single product in it represents a value measured by immediate enjoyment and worthwhileness. On the other hand, it can all be placed in a cultural perspective, that is, considered from the point of view of its importance for the total development of the single individual and the sum total of individuals. On their own ground, the former values strain against being subsumed under the category of culture. The work of art seeks only perfection in terms of the yardstick of purely aesthetic criteria, scientific inquiry in terms of the truth of its findings, and the economic product only in terms of its efficient manufacture and its profit-making capacity. Mental and physical constructs can be stretched beyond their "natural" development to a teleological one and thus could function as cultural values. Viewed with regard to their autonomous substantive character, however, they *are* not as yet such, but are subordinated to ideals and norms which are drawn only from the objective contents and not from the demands of that unified central point of the personality.

What these constructs accomplish for the development of cultural values is another question. The height they attain in connection with cultural development is by no means the same as that demanded by the specific interests which relate to the objective, specialized aspects of our nature. Even if they serve our single interests well, their contribution to our whole existence, to the growth-hungry core of our ego, may be slight. Conversely, they may be incomplete and unimportant with respect to objective, technical, specialized spheres of life, but contribute perfectly to what our being needs for the harmony of its elements, to that mysterious unity that transcends all specific needs and forces.

Since "unity" appears to us only as interaction and dynamic interweaving, as an interrelating, a balance within a multiplicity, that core of unity within us, whose inner meaning and strength are perfected in the cultural process through the integration of more elevated and perfect objects, can be articulated as follows. The several aspects of our being stand in close interaction, each supporting the others and supported by them, harmoniously balancing and reciprocating their vital energies. Therefore we are not yet cultivated just because we possess certain facts or skills; specialization is not equivalent to culture, no matter how excellent the objective contents it produces. Culture is created only when these one-sided perfections are ordered within the total structure of the soul, when the disharmonies of the soul's elements are resolved by elevation to a higher plane; in short, when each contributes to the perfection of the whole. So we should not confuse the measure applied to each of our accomplishments or abilities in order to rank it in a specialized substantive category with that other measure, the one which is applied to the same contents under the category of culture, that is, to judge the development of our inner *totality*.

In light of this distinction the paradoxical fact becomes clear that what are precisely the highest accomplishments in several fields, namely, those of a personal sort in art, religion, and speculation, are of relatively little value from the point of view of *culture*.

The most impressive works and thoughts bind us so strongly to what they are in themselves, within their own spheres and measured by their own internal criteria, that their cultural significance is thereby diminished. They resist, so to speak, entering into that cooperation with other elements that is necessary for the development of our general nature. They are too much the master of their own province to accept the role of servant which would be necessary if they were to be factors of culture, means for the creation of a spiritual wholeness.

This will clearly be most emphatically true of those cultural products in which a personal life is speaking. The more separated a product is from the subjective spirituality of its creator, the more it is integrated into an objective order—the more distinct is its *cultural* significance and the more suited it is to become a general means for the cultivation of many individual souls.

A similar observation may be made about the "style" of a work of art. The great masterpiece in which a sovereign soul has expressed only himself is hardly ever considered from the point of view of style. For style refers to a *general* mode of expression, one that is common to many creations, a form ideationally separable from its various contents. In the very greatest masterpieces, the general foundation and the particular configuration are a unified manifestation in which what is shared with others contributes very little to the impression the work makes. It asks to be taken purely by itself, not as an example of a general principle of style.

And thus, generally, the very great and the very personal, even if they are culturally impressive, are not primarily important for their cultural meaning. For cultural importance by its inner nature is most marked in more general, less personal accomplishments, which are objectified at a greater distance from the subject of their creator and thus serve the stages of the psychic development of others more "selflessly."

Since culture places life-contents in an incomparably tangled knot of subject and object, two meanings of the concept are justifiable. The term "objective culture" can be used to designate things in that state of elaboration, development, and perfection which leads the psyche to its own fulfillment or indicates the path to be traversed by individuals or collectivities on the way to a heightened existence. By subjective culture I mean the measure of development of persons thus attained. Thus subjective and objective culture are only in a figurative sense the concepts we discussed above, when we credited things with an independent drive to perfection, with the thrust toward development beyond their merely natural condition, and conceived of the human force which brings about this development as the means for this process. When one speaks of the cultivation of things, of the objective contents of life, one reverses the order of the actual cultural process that takes place in man. One is only creating a metaphor when one separates the development of things into a natural and a cultivated stage, as though the development were an intrinsically teleological event and the cultivated stage were self-sufficient and definitive—as though the thing merely passes through the stage of man's intervention as an episode in its ascent.[1]

In a more precise sense, the two uses of the culture concept are in no way analogous, for subjective culture is the overarching goal. Its measure is the extent to which the psychic life-process makes use of those objective goods and accomplishments. Obviously there can be no subjective culture without objective culture, because the development or condition of a subject is culture only through its incorporation of the cultivated objects which it encounters. In contrast, objective culture can be partially independent from subjective culture, insofar as "cultivated"—that is, cultivating—objects have been created whose availability for cultural purposes is not fully utilized by subjects. Particularly in periods of social complexity and an extensive division of labor, the accomplishments of culture come to constitute an autonomous realm, so to speak. Things become more perfected, more intellectual, and to some degree more controlled by an internal, objective logic tied to their instrumentality; but the supreme cultivation, that of subjects, does not increase proportionately. Indeed, in view of the enormous increase of objective culture, in which the world of things is parcelled out to countless workers, subjective culture *could* not increase. Thus far at least, historical development has moved toward a steadily increasing separation between objective cultural production and the cultural level of the individual. The dissonance of modern life—in particular that manifested in the improvement of technique in every area and the simultaneous deep dissatisfaction with technical progress—is caused in large part by the fact that things are becoming more and more cultivated, while men are less able to gain from the perfection of objects a perfection of the subjective life.

---

[1]   In this passage Simmel appears to be saying that it is not so much things that are cultivated by man (the common conception) but rather man who is cultivated by virtue of his interaction with objects.—TRANS.

17

EROS, PLATONIC AND MODERN

1921

THE HISTORY of philosophy reveals the peculiar and not particularly praiseworthy fact that its claim to provide a deeper estimation of life has been left unfulfilled with respect to a number of the most important and problematic elements of life. Apart from occasional observations, philosophy has nothing to tell us about the concept of fate; nothing on the enigmatic structure of what we call "experience"; nothing, before Schopenhauer, about the deep meaning which happiness and suffering have for life insofar as this meaning is morally significant. Perhaps the most neglected of all the great vital issues has been love—as though this were an incidental matter, a mere adventure of the subjective soul, unworthy of the seriousness and rigorous objectivity of philosophical endeavor.

In reality, the preference for the problem of knowledge, which has frequently been treated in depth, over the problem of Eros betrays a certain subjectivity on the part of philosophers. For since they personally are men of a passionate drive for knowledge, but seldom of a passionate drive for love, their *subjective* nature is reflected in the fact that they continually make cognition the object of their thought, but most infrequently do the same for love. Were they actually to do their job properly—something for which there

---

From "Der platonische und der moderne Eros," in *Fragmente und Aufsätze* (Munich: Drei Masken Verlag, 1923), pp. 125–45. Translated by Donald N. Levine. Originally published as a section of a posthumous essay "Über die Liebe," in *Logos* 10 (1921–22).

is still no better description than the somewhat old-fashioned expression, wisdom about life—and thus rank their labors according to the potency of life's elements, the preponderance of these labors would most surprisingly have to shift to the question of the meaning which love has for the soul, for fate, and for being.

The only one of the great philosophers who confronted this question and answered it in a profound way is Plato. For Schopenhauer, the only philosopher one could name beside him, did not actually inquire into the nature of love, but of sexuality. Plato, however, saw that love was an absolute vital power and that the way of understanding would therefore have to lead through love to the ultimate ideals and metaphysical potencies, to all the places where life as experienced is connected to these potencies. To be sure the curves and the terminal points of this way are different from those traversed by modern men, even if its point of departure, the immediate subjective fact of the feeling of love, has not undergone a comparable change. The different philosophical interpretations of this show all the more clearly the difference between the ultimate intentions of the Greek spirit, culminating in Plato, and those which the law of the modern spirit prescribes.

The world view of the Greek was based on the idea of *being*, of a unified real cosmos, the self-contained plastic representation of which he revered as divine. Even where his thinking led to the universal principles of movement, of relativity, of dualism, still the ultimate form and the ultimate yearning of his intellectual world view was determined by the immutable, all-encompassing, self-sufficient, and intelligible Being. Ever since Christianity raised this significance of the human soul to infinity and located all the values of existence in a personal God who stands over against the world, the firm unity of the cosmos, which in every part existed as simply valuable and divine, has been sundered. Existence has been stretched out between the two poles of soul and God, or has actually been absorbed by them, and a concept of God needed only to lose its original power in the course of the centuries for the soul to remain alone, so to speak—a development which then attains its purest expression in modern idealism, for which the world only exists as an idea within a consciousness that takes notice of it. That the soul should thus possess a primordial productivity is a notion that is very far from the theoretical consciousness of the *Greeks*— so immeasurably productive was their reality. Thought was too closely tied to the living being of the *cosmos*, in whose unity the soul grew, for that; they lived too unconditionally in the intelligible stability of the object to entrust the subject with an independent creativity. Inasmuch as the contrast between subject and object, self and world, is thereby spared the decisiveness it later attains, the practical application of this opposition—egoism and altruism —is also less harsh, be it that a naive egoism is not even conscious of it, or be it that the self feels itself borne by the universal life, by cosmic and ideal necessities. This is the bottommost layer of the features out of which the characteristics of Platonic love develop in contrast with the modern conception.

In apparent contradiction to the unbroken unity of the Greek world view, which fuses reality and its divine sense—a contradiction whose resolution is not in question here—Plato transposed all value and all actual reality of things into the realm of ideas, that is, of metaphysical substances which are the metaphysical counterpart of our concepts of things, the bearers of truth transcending them. An earthly thing acquires meaning and value only insofar as a ray from that realm lights on it and every element thereby takes part, however incompletely, in its other, absolute nature. In a myth whose mixture of serious belief and poetic fantasy we shall probably never clearly disentangle, Plato has the soul inhabit that realm in its preearthly existence—giving an old dream of humanity its classic form. The fact that after its fall to earth the soul can recognize earthly beings and can love them is then due to the dark, yet remarkable, recollection of those original images in heaven, a dim reflection of which sometimes appears in the earthly particulars. If now, as is self-evident for Plato, the *beauty* of a person causes us to love him—at first the beauty of his body, then, following somewhat diffidently, also of his soul—this is because he awakes in us the memory of that formerly viewed idea of beauty, of that original image of the beautiful in general, for which we carry within us an eternal yearning here below from our former existence. Beauty, of all ideas the only visible one, leads the idea down to the earthly realm; love leads the earthly phenomenon by the same path up to the Idea. All the features which seem to constitute what is distinctive of the Platonic mind are brought together here as in a focal point.

First of all, the direction of attention to the firm, sculptured substance. For us being beautiful is a *property* of a human being, a relationship among the parts of his appearance, perhaps a symbolic expression of his inner life, perhaps even only the reaction which he evokes in the consciousness of the beholder. For Plato this property must itself be an object. It must be able to be viewed as a substance in order to have reality and meaning in the world. And since it does not exist thus in the empirical human being, the soul must therefore have seen it *before* in such a condition that it could be viewed and grasped. The beautiful person is only the empirical medium needed to call forth the memory of it. For in him beauty is something that comes and goes, and in any case is never present in absolute perfection. Even when it arouses the highest degree of passion, it still does not really concern the person himself: but the love of the higher human being has need of lasting, visible, and self-contained objects. Because the earthly world does not offer this, the beautiful person evokes love, whereby he yet remains attached to the *panta rei*, not because he is beautiful, but because a ray of that substantial beauty which has been seen in its purity and substantiality has fallen on him and stayed there.

The *dynamic* vital character of the modern life-feeling, and the fact that it is manifest to us as a form of vital *movement*, consumed in a continuous flux in spite of all persistence and faithfulness, and adhering to a rhythm that is always new—this runs counter to the Greek's sense of substance and its eternal outline. The great task of modern man—to comprehend the eternal as something which immediately dwells within the transient, without its having to forfeit anything for being transplanted from the transcendental to the earthly plane—is alien to him through and through. This is clearly related to the previously mentioned difference between Greek and modern thought; that the former involves a much slighter theoretical awareness of the creativity of the soul. For as we conceive the term, soul means to exercise a continuous creativity. For all his actual intellectual power and independence, the Greek must, so to speak, hold fast to something. The fact that his life-feeling is determined by being immersed in the cosmos is expressed by the following: the Greek in thought and feeling inevitably confronts the given existence somehow, but he always grasps, imitates, or reshapes only what is given. The contents of the soul are presented to the Greek as brought from something existing, not as produced from within the creative soul itself. Looked at from this point of view, Plato's theories of truth and of love develop in an exactly parallel manner. Truth is a product of our capacity to know, even if this product stands in a determinate relation to reality; the general concepts, however, which carry the truths are not freely created constructs out of the stuff of experience. They are only the reawakened memories which the soul maintained unconsciously ever since it *viewed* in its pre-existence their metaphysical counterimages, the ideas, the truths in substance as it were. And similarly love is for him no free act of the soul, aroused to be sure from outside, but arising unpredictably and freely out of its innermost mood and powers; it is a kind of logical necessity imposed by that looking at pure beauty, the moment its former presence again appears in the apprehension of an earthly phenomenon in which, so to speak, a part or a reflection of that absolute beauty dwells. Therefore it is always only the perception of beauty which produces love. He misses the significant converse case which finds the secret of love in a much more profound layer; that we find someone beautiful whom we love—a construction which is thinkable only by attributing spontaneity and a creative life of its own to the affect of love.

Coming back now to Plato himself, the active force which permitted his depiction of the experience of love to be fundamentally off base nevertheless breaks through, as it were, at the other end. The object of Platonic love was not woman, but male youth. This was not inconsistent with Greek sensibilities, but is scarcely imaginable for latter-day modern men. Of course, we should not understand by this a form which is covered by our penal law. Rather, the relationship which Plato conceived in its perfected form not only stops before that boundary, but also, where it is overstepped, the sensual element is absorbed, permeated, and uplifted by the intellectual element in such a way that the whole tendency of the relationship is one of intellectual idealism, albeit one that remains most alien to our way of thinking. As things stood in Greece at the time, precisely that metaphysical grounding of love, making it equivalent with the yearning for a purely suprasensual, only-intellectual—precisely this conception must have caused the man to appear as the appropriate object in love. (Aristophanes says explicitly of male lovers: "They act thus not out of shamelessness; no, their courage, their masculinity loves its own kind.") For higher intellectual development was considered peculiar to the male. In this connection one thinks of how the continuous gymnastic care and training of the male body also must have served to intellectualize it, to make it an expression of conative energy, of sensibility, of a total inner character, whereas today's thorough veiling of the body, which concentrates all expression in the face, and the virtual restriction of body care to cleanliness have the effect of making the body a merely material, intrinsically indifferent earthly residue. The capacity for abstract thought, which for Plato paves the way to the highest realms of value, he found only in males; only they could be his traveling companions. And it is one of the most fundamental characteristics of the Greek nature in contrast to the modern that it bases the bonds among men above all on their equality of being, their commonality of goals instead of on the complementary integration of differences, as has been increasingly true in the modern world. The feeling of *friendship* among the Greeks, similar in certain respects to our idea of love (since it is based on mutuality and individuality), presumes the *equality* of friends. The thought that friendship could encompass both masculine and feminine structures is remote from them. Insofar as a Hellenic national consciousness existed, moreover, it appears to have been based on an equality of tribes rather than on a unity produced out of heterogeneity.

Herein lies a decisive motive of psychic structure which at least helped to facilitate the love of men among the Greeks as much as it makes this more remote for later men. That the Eternal Feminine attracts the constantly striving and toiling man, that, as Goethe confessed for himself, women were the only vessel into which he could pour his idealism—is about the opposite of what was felt by the Platonic man, perhaps by the typical Greek generally. But one understands that the practical side of this love, so to speak— always conceived only in terms of the love of an older man for a younger—went over to education in a way that would lift up the beloved to the highest intellectual and personal level, would draw him along as a comrade in the striving toward the Idea. All activity and productivity, apart from the grounding of feeling in the soul itself, was transplanted into this pedagogical striving. This and probably the self-sufficiency of the feeling as such fulfilled the meaning of this love, which, therefore, was protected from sentimentality in a totally different way than is the modern.

All the vehemence of the passion of love is directed, in Plato's portrayal of it, to the suprapersonal: to the Idea of absolute goodness and beauty which has been incarnated, accidentally as it were and always fragmentarily, in the person of the beloved. It is as though this orientation to something of the highest rationality, to the idea which is the counterpart of our rational concepts and accessible through them, should justify the irrationality of the passion. What decisively separates this from the modern attitude is that the rays of Eros only pass through the beloved individual, but their focal point lies over and above him. Plato characterizes love as a "daemon," that is, a being that makes contact by mediating between the human and the divine. Whereas for us love only mediates between persons, Plato moves the mediating effect out of interpersonal relations and assigns it to the relationship with the *supraindividual.* The ultimate goal is the visionary beholding of Beauty itself, and love is only an aid to the *synergos* for that. And thus Plato can go on to teach that the perfect erotic disposition does not stop at any individual beauty, but recognizes in one the same beauty which he finds in another and in everyone else, and that it is therefore slavish and foolish to bind one's feelings exclusively to a single beautiful person; he will pour his love into the "great sea of beauty" in general. What to us appears as the definitive high point of the love experience is distant from his conception: that love concerns precisely this unique, irreplaceable being:

that even where the love is turned on by external beauty only this particular individual manifestation of it is involved: and that once this has happened, an objectively equivalent amount does not affect us erotically at the same time. For us the *beauty* of individuality and the *individuality* of beauty comprise an indivisible unity. What separates us most profoundly from Plato is that for him individuality and beauty are divisible, and it is precisely love which draws the dividing line between them: it encompasses beauty and leaves individuality out.

The development of Platonism in the Renaissance seeks to connect its metaphysical nature with the individualism in whose name the Renaissance has conquered. Here, too, an existence of creatures before the earthly one is assumed—be it that the beloved there shines with a perfection, meaning, and purity of which the mere empirical manifestation presents no adequate expression, or be it that in an encounter in that world his earthly fate is blueprinted. Thus speaks Petrarch of the portrait of Laura of Simone Memmi; thus Michelangelo of his beloved wife. Now it is no longer the general idea of Beauty that is beheld in that "supercelestial realm," but the individual person himself: no longer is the elevation of personality to an unindividual universal borrowed from Plato, but rather indeed that of an earthly form to a transcendental one. This is doubtless an intermediate conception, as it were, leading over to our concept of love rooted in concrete individuality. What has been inherited from Plato, by us as well, is the feeling that in love there lives something mysterious, beyond the contingent individual existence and meeting, beyond the momentary sensual desire, and beyond the mere relations between personalities. In the sacrament of marriage, this metaphysicalizing has just grasped a historical-social form.

Because in Plato's rational thought individuality appeared as something unsubstantial, all-too-fleeting, all inner events connected with it as free-floating willfulness, he believed that one could do justice to that feeling only by completely removing it from its own sphere, what to us seems like a dissipation of love into a universal. Nevertheless, in the last reaches of our instinctual structure even we have not abandoned this conviction. We, too, perceive in love something of a metaphysical, timeless significance—except that we cannot dispose of it in the simple manner of the Greeks with their disposition to think in terms of visual substances and locate it in a realm beyond that of immediate experience. Rather, the great problem of the modern spirit comes forward here as well: to find a place for everything which transcends the givenness of vital phenomena within those phenomena themselves, instead of transposing it to a spatial beyond. *Ding an sich*—Michelangelo—Nietzsche —*life* contains that which is more than life. No *synthesis* of the finite and the infinite, but a grown unity of life.

In that supraindividual there lay—this we do not fail to appreciate—a value, a deliverance, a support which we in no way renounce. The effort to preserve this without metaphysical hypostatization is directed first of all to the species life. The latter leads the individual out of himself, makes him participant in an unending process of development in which the impulses of love join one link of its chain with the other. (A frequent motif of recent times: species, society as a third or intermediate element between the abstract-universal and the concrete-individual.)[1]

However, although the erotic sphere is thereby removed from the narrowness of individual existence, this is still not sufficient. For precisely in the depths within and out of this individual existence as such there lies an accent, something definitive which cannot be replaced by organically incorporating it in an ongoing stream of collective development. As in the moral sphere the "Individual Law" hovers over us—the strict normative regulation of individual conduct which nonetheless we can no longer apprehend within an abstract universal imperative[2]—so must there also be something like an Individual Law of erotic life. In the incomparable relationship of incomparable individuals there lies a meaning which is wholly limited to that relationship and yet extends beyond its surface manifestation, not dominated or justified by a universal idea of Beauty, of Value, or of Amiability, but just by the idea of these

[1]   This motif is discussed more fully at the end of chapter 4 above.— Ed.

[2]   This conception of the "Individual Law" is articulated in "Das individuelle Gesetz," published as chapter 4 of *Lebensanschauung.*—Ed.

individual existences and their perfection. And if we say that this would be somewhere beyond their fleeting individual existence, the Beyond is but an inadequate designation of the form of its presence within the individual exclusiveness of this love.

I stressed above the fundamental difference: that beauty, which for us is an attribute of a person, affected by the changes and dissolution of his life, acquires in the Platonic way of thinking an existence of its own; it becomes a tangible substance in the metaphysical sense. If one turns back from this height and looks at the role which beauty plays below, one may express the above distinction as follows. In the Platonic interpretation love gets attached to a nameable property of its object, to beauty, which is conceived as strictly universal, equivalent in all of its manifestations. For us, however, the ultimate mystery of love resides in the fact that there is no single attribute which is responsible for it—as Meister Eckhardt said with respect to God, we should not love him because he possesses these and those attributes, but simply because he just is. However valuable the qualities of a person may be, feelings are attached to the unity and totality which lies behind them. Its superiority over all particular attributes which stimulate love (which only serve to form bridges to that totality) is evident from the fact that love survives the disappearance of these several attributes—a possibility which Plato, to be sure, mentions in a fragmentary way, thereby departing from a fully consistent interpretation of love. Much has been said about mysticism in Plato's vision of Eros. The deepest mystery of *our* world view, however, Individuality—this unanalyzable unity, which is not to be derived from anything else, not subsumable under any higher concept, set within a world otherwise infinitely analyzable, calculable, and governed by general laws —this individuality stands for us as the actual focal point of love, which for this very reason becomes entwined in the darkest problematic aspects of our concept of the world in contrast with the rational clarity of the Platonic attitude. Precisely this is, so to speak, passed over by Plato, and in its place is put the clear, intelligible relation of the soul to the universal, to the qualitative characteristics of the perceptible—if only *wholly* perceptible by a transcendent vision—Idea.

This negative significance of individuality is the definitive point which distinguishes the Platonic and modern views of Eros. All the great motifs which undergird Plato's theory of love leads up to it; all the traits which give this theory its special hue branch out from it. Heading the list of these is something which is most astonishing for us: that mutuality is no decisive, internally essential element for this love. What this brings out is that the Greeks have no pure relational concept. It escapes them that love is the side of a *relationship* existing in the subject. As a reciprocal relationship one categorizes it under friendship (*philia*). Plato further indicates that also in the beloved a certain degree of counterlove arises as through contagion or gratitude, but this is only accidental and without significance for the erotic of the lover himself. The force and style of the latter is independent of response, and the loneliness of its self-sufficiency is modified only through being attached to the realm of the universal Ideas. But the Idea to which this love is directed does not love in return, and so neither does its earthly representative, in whom the first stage of love takes place. The unique value-relation which is based on love and counterlove is not taken into account by Plato. That the Platonic Socrates discusses the statement that the beautiful youth would do better to form a relationship with one who does not love him but only desires him, though not in the purely sensual sense of the term, than with one who passionately loves him—the very fact that he considers this statement at length, if only to refute it angrily, is something still scarcely imaginable for us.

The Greek Eros is a wish to possess, in the nobler sense of the term as well, of course; to have in the beloved a vessel for ideal instruction and morally elevating cultivation. Therefore for him love can be an intermediate state between not-having and having. As a logical consequence of this, therefore, love would have to be extinguished once this state of possession is reached. It would seem to me wrong to give to the fact that he locates love on this side of possession the more subtle interpretation that "having" appeared to him as an unattainable goal, one lying in the infinite. Inasmuch as the real goal of modern love is reciprocal love, in relation to which everything else only follows as something secondary and accidental, modern love is the first to recognize that there is something unattainable in the other: that the absoluteness of the individual self erects a wall between two human beings which even the most passionate willing of both cannot remove and that renders illusory any actual "possession" that would be anything more than the fact and consciousness of being loved back. This is the consequence of that ultimate deepening and individualization of the self-feeling. What this leads to is a becoming rooted in oneself and an isolation within oneself which turns the wish to "possess" into a contradiction and a grasping into the void.

Now to perceive the Greek's autonomous majesty of love, needing no reciprocal response, as a kind of egoism—while the *"Wenn ich dich liebe, was geht's dich an?"* is taken to signify only conscious resignation, and therefore the very opposite of egoism—this is but a foolishness of modern thought. The Platonic lover feels himself so attached to the realm of the "Idea" that the sharp boundaries of his ego dissolve in it, so that his ego-related desire still stands beyond the exclusiveness associated with the concept of egoism that corresponds to the later ego concept. And as the beloved is here loved not as an individual but as the messenger of a supraindividual beauty, so is the lover himself also deindividualized, because his love, as I indicated, comes not from the creative personality but from his former beholding of the Idea of the beautiful. Both object and subject are only vessels of the Idea. Obviously, love must first be removed from this sphere outside of both of them, every ego must first have found a definite, secure boundary for *itself*, for love to move on the shortest line between them, as it were, and for love therefore to be able to quiet their yearning only through reciprocal love.

That peculiar indifference between the ego and that which reaches beyond the ego is unmistakably revealed, finally, in Plato's great interpretation of love as the desire for immortality. The mature human being has a longing to procreate—a divine act by which the mortal attains immortality. A love for our children is nothing other than this passion to survive beyond death. We are so constituted, however, that only the beautiful person arouses our wish to procreate with him; our nature resists doing this with one who is ugly. For this reason our love concerns the beautiful, that is, not really him but now one's own continued life—either through the procreation of offspring, or through informing the beautiful soul of a youth with our best thoughts and impulses. That "education" of the beloved is nothing other than elevating him to a higher nature which then in the deepest sense is an offspring which we have produced with him—our own continued life, our own maturity reproducing itself. With respect to this Platonic doctrine, the Greek's boundless desire for fame provided the point at which strivings related to one's own ego and those aimed at the pure ideal meet. He wishes to be immortal in the memory of men, but he wishes this by virtue of the inner *value* of his thought and action which are carried on by his offspring. If his loving adoration of the beautiful person was previously justified on the grounds that the latter makes possible a reaching out, as it were, toward one dimension of eternity, toward the timeless idea of beauty—so now toward the other dimension, toward the eternal living on in the memory and higher development of men. The more objective, somewhat abstract character of the earlier justification is suddenly permeated here by a stream of life that is very personal. Now we do not abandon ourselves when the love for the beautiful carries us off, but we take ourselves along beyond the threshold of our temporally bounded life. But the love of individual to individual as a primordial phenomenon is acknowledged here no more than there. This emotion, too, does not stop at the individual whose beauty aroused it. Whereas there the individual only pointed the direction to be taken by our ultimate striving, here it is the vessel in which our best powers are collected, to be preserved and brought to fruition so that we may follow the path of immortality in the memory of men.

Even so, this more simple, so to speak, more human motivation of love also overlooks the irrational dimension which we feel in individuality as the ultimate element of Eros. Insofar as it makes the emotional relationship between lover and beloved into a mere *transitional* stage of a movement either toward the metaphysical realm or toward immortality, love takes on the rational tone of every instrumental relationship. If the visionary passion and the soaring forth from the ultimate depths of the soul with which Plato proclaims all of this tend to deceive us on this matter and to bring the thrust of his erotic philosophy close to ours, it is just at this point that the separation between his whole intellectual approach and ours becomes clear. For whether he is interpreting love or knowledge, it is always the impersonal energy of the soul, the conceptualizing reason, which elevates their existence and through which they are connected with the world of true reality and of values. But because he did not see the true boundaries of logical reason, whose miraculous powers he had discovered, boundaries which it would take millenia to determine with certainty, he was led by this discovery to an intoxication unparalleled in the history of philosophy. Around the Apollonian clarity of cool thought danced the Dionysian joy of this unprecedented victory of the soul in becoming conscious of attaining the *essence* of things with its conceptual thinking. The birth of scientific thought, which was destined to suppress so much of religion, was greeted with religious consecration. The rational interpretation of love released a suprarational enthusiasm which to *us* seems to radiate only from love itself—just because we honor it as a primordial phenomenon. That the most subjective and individual of all passions is led in the direction of rational-metaphysical meaning and that this meaning could be fully enthroned only by overcoming such a huge tension— therein lies the meaning of Eros for Plato's world view.

The great themes of Plato's thought have been infinitely fruitful in the course of intellectual history. But what mankind grown old, differentiated, and sophisticated can no longer support is this: to transform the world in its reality, its love, its meaning, and its spiritual values into a logical structure of abstract concepts and analogous metaphysical essences and to perceive this as the deepest happiness of the spirit; to derive from logical thought those tremors and awesome relations to the ground of things which later times can attain precisely only by a rejection of pure thought, through a cleavage between logical structure and that living, feeling existence whose immediacy is caught neither in the Platonic concepts nor in ours, but can only be experienced in its own depths.

V. Individuality and Social Structure

18

GROUP EXPANSION
AND THE DEVELOPMENT
OF INDIVIDUALITY[1]

1908

EACH OF THE THEMES around which the inquiries in this
book have thus far been organized into chapters is a single concept
from the general domain of sociology. They have made room for
considerable diversity and often contrariety in the historical configurations and types of configurations that present these concepts.
The assemblages of material required by the practical need for
organization have had no other internal justification than the fact
that the phenomena and reflection on them have involved the particular concept in question. The content in each of these chapters
could not have been expressed as a central argument whose proof
is gradually adduced, but only as a collection of arguments that
find themselves under the title of a concept.

The following inquiry is of a different sort. It is devoted to the
demonstration of a relational pattern, of a *single* pattern, even
though it emerges in conjunction with many modifications, wrappings, and admixtures. What is common to the sections of the present chapter is not a concept, but a proposition. Rather than pursuing a single abstracted form in the phenomena where it happens
to appear, phenomena whose contents are not constrained in any
particular direction by the form, this chapter presents a particular

From "Die Erweiterung der Gruppe und die Ausbildung der Individualität,"
in *Soziologie*, 5th ed. (Berlin: Duncker & Humblot, 1968 [1908]), pp.
527–45, 552–65, 568–70. Translated by Richard P. Albares.
    Part of this chapter is taken from my *Soziale Differenzierung*, chap-
ter 3.

correlation, an interactionally determined pattern of development among forms of association.

Group Expansion and the Transformation of Social Bonds

Individuation of personality, on the one hand, and the influences, interests, and relationships that attach the personality to its social circle, on the other hand, show a pattern of interdependent development that appears in the most diverse historical and institutional setting as a typical form. *Individuality in being and action generally increases to the degree that the social circle encompassing the individual expands.*

Of the diverse modalities in which group expansion occurs and gives rise to the correlation just underscored, I will first mention the one that occurs when circles that are isolated from one another become approximately alike. Imagine that there are two social groups, M and N, that are sharply distinguished from one another both in characteristic attributes and in opposing systems of shared belief; and imagine further that each of these groups is composed of homogeneous and tightly cohesive elements. This being so, quantitative expansion will produce an increase in social differentiation. What were once minimal differences in inner predilection, external resources, and actualizations of these will be accentuated by the necessity of competing for a livelihood with more and more people using more and more specialized means. Competition will develop the speciality of the individual in direct ratio to the number of participants.

Different as its points of origin in M and N may have been, this process will inevitably produce a gradually increasing likeness between the two groups. After all, the number of fundamental human formations upon which a group can build is relatively limited, and it can only slowly be increased. The more of these formations that are present in a group—that is, the greater the dissimilarity of constituent elements in M and N respectively—the greater is the likelihood that an ever increasing number of structures will develop in one group that have equivalents in the other. Deviation in all directions from what had thus far been the prevailing norm in each group complex must necessarily result in a likening—at first a qualitative or ideal equivalence—between parts of the two complexes.

This likening will come about if for no other reason than because even within very diverse groups, the forms of social differentiation are identical or approximately the same. What I have in mind here are such forms as the relational pattern of simple competition, the alliance of many who are weak against one who is strong, the pleonexy of lone individuals, the progression in which relationships among individuals, once initiated, become stabilized, the attraction or repulsion that arises between individuals by virtue of their qualitative differentiation, and so on.

This process, quite apart from all bonds based on shared substantive interests, will often lead to actual relations between the elements of any two—or of many—groups that have been made alike in this way. One observes this, for example, in the international sympathy that aristocrats hold for one another. To an astonishing degree, these feelings of solidarity are independent of the specific character of the individuals concerned, a matter that is otherwise decisive in determining personal attraction and repulsion. In the same way, by specialization within groups that were originally independent of one another, solidarities also develop at the other end of the social scale, as in the internationalism of social democrats and in the sentiments underlying the earlier journeymen's unions.

After the process of social differentiation has led to a separation between high and low, the mere formal fact of occupying a particular social position creates among the similarly characterized members of the most diverse groups a sense of solidarity and, frequently, actual relationships. Accompanying such a differentiation of social groups, there arise a need and an inclination to reach out beyond the original spatial, economic, and mental boundaries of the group and, in connection with the increase in individualization and concomitant mutual repulsion of group elements, to supplement the original centripetal forces of the lone group with a centrifugal tendency that forms bridges with other groups.

For example, the guilds were once ruled by the spirit of strict equality. On the one hand, the individual's production was limited to the level of quality and quantity that all other guild members attained; on the other hand, the guild's norms of sale and exchange sought to protect the individual from being outdone by other members. In the long run, it was impossible to maintain this condition of undifferentiation. The master who became rich under whatever circumstances was not inclined to submit further to regulations stipulating that he might sell only his own products, might maintain no more than one salesplace, might have no more than a very limited number of apprentices, and so forth.

Once the affluent masters had won the right—partly after intense struggle—to ignore these restrictions, a certain duality began to appear. The once homogeneous mass of guild members became differentiated with increasing decisiveness into rich and poor, capitalists and laborers. Once the principle of equality had been broken through to the extent that one member could have another labor for him and that he could select his sales market on the basis of his own personal capacity and energy, his knowledge of the market, and his assessment of its prospects, it was inevitable that just these personal attributes, once given the opportunity to unfold, would continue to develop, leading to an ever increasing specialization and individualization within the fellowship of the guild and, finally, to the dissolution of that fellowship. On the other hand, however, structural change made possible an extension far beyond the confines of previous sales regions. Formerly, producer and merchant had been united in *one* person; once they had been differentiated from one another, the merchant won an incomparable freedom of movement, and previously unattainable commercial relations were established.

Individual freedom and the expansion of commercial enterprise are interdependent. Thus, in the case of the coexistence of guild restrictions and large, factory-style workshops around the beginning of the nineteenth century in Germany, it always proved necessary to let the factories have freedoms of production and trade that could or would have been collectivistically restricted in the circles of smaller and more modest enterprises. In this manner, the development away from narrow, homogeneous guild circles prepared their dissolution along two lines: one led to individualizing differentiation, the other to expansion involving ties across great distances. For this reason, the differentiation of English guild members into merchants and actual workers was exhibited most strikingly by those, such as tanners and textile manufacturers, who produced articles of foreign demand.

A fissioning is inherent in this correlation with group expansion that involves not only the content of labor but also its sociological dimension. Even given a certain technical division of labor, as long as the small, primitive group is self-sufficient, a pervasive equality exists in that each member of the group works for the group itself; every achievement is sociologically centripetal. However, as soon as the boundaries of the group are ruptured and it enters into trade in special products with another group, internal differentiation develops between those who produce for export and those who produce for domestic consumption—two wholly opposed inner modes of being.

The history of the emancipation of the serfs, as for example in Prussia, demonstrates a process that is similar in this regard. As he existed in Prussia until about 1810, the enserfed peasant found himself in a peculiar intermediate position regarding both his lord and his land. The land belonged to the lord, to be sure, but not in such a way that the peasant himself could have no right at all to it. Likewise, the peasant was of course bound to work the lord's fields for him, but close by he also worked the land that had been allotted to him for his own benefit. With the abolition of serfdom, a certain part of the land that the peasant had formerly owned in a limited sense was converted into true, free property. The lord was left to seek wage laborers, whom he recruited for the most part from among the owners of smaller parcels that he had purchased. Thus, whereas the peasant had had within himself the partial attributes of owner and of laborer for another's benefit, a sharp differentiation of these attributes followed the abolition of serfdom: one part became pure owner, the other part pure laborer.

It is obvious how free movement of the person and his involvement in spatially more distant relations emerged from this situation. Not only the eradication of the external bond to the soil was involved, but also the very condition of the laborer as one who receives work first in one place, then in another. On the other hand, alienable property was involved, since it made possible sale and hence commercial relations, resettlement, and so on.

So it is that the observation made at the beginning of this section has its justification: differentiation and individualization loosen the bond of the individual with those who are most near in order to weave in its place a new one—both real and ideal—with those who are more distant. . . .[2]

An Englishman who had lived for many years in India once told me that it was impossible for a European to get at all close to the natives where castes existed; but that where caste divisions did not prevail this was very easy. The insularity of the caste—maintained by an internal uniformity no less strict than its exclusion of outsiders—seems to inhibit the development of what one has to call a more universal humanity, which is what makes relationships between racial aliens possible.

Consistent with the above, the broad uneducated masses of one civilized people are more homogeneous internally, and they are separated from the masses of a second people by more distinct characteristics, than is the case either within or between the educated strata of these populations. This same pattern of synthesis and antithesis repeats itself intraculturally. The older German corporate system set out to unite guild *members* tightly in order to keep guild *memberships* strictly separated. The modern voluntary association, on the other hand, restricts its members and imposes uniformity upon them only so far as the strictly circumscribed organizational goal requires. In all other matters, it allows members complete freedom and tolerates every individuality and heterogeneity of their full personalities. But for all that, the modern association gravitates toward an all-embracing union of organizations by virtue of interpenetrating division of labor, leveling that results from equal justice and the cash economy, and solidarity of interests in the national economy.

These examples hint at a relation that will be found everywhere in the course of this inquiry. The nonindividuation of ele-

[2]   Simmel digresses here briefly to speculate on analogies with the plant and animal kingdoms.—ED.

ments in the narrower circle and their differentiation in the wider one are phenomena that are found, synchronically, among coexistent groups and group elements, just as they appear, diachronically, in the sequence of stages through which a single group develops.

The Relation between Personal and Collective Individuality

This basic idea can be generalized to the proposition that in each person, other things being equal, there is, as it were, an unalterable ratio between individual and social factors that changes only its form. The narrower the circle to which we commit ourselves, the less freedom of individuality we possess; however, this narrower circle is itself something individual, and it cuts itself off sharply from all other circles precisely because it is small. Correspondingly, if the circle in which we are active and in which our interests hold sway enlarges, there is more room in it for the development of our individuality; but *as parts of this whole*, we have less uniqueness: the larger whole is less individual as a social group. Thus, the leveling of individual differences corresponds not only to the relative smallness and narrowness of the collectivity, but also—or above all—to its own individualistic coloring.

Expressed in a very terse schema, the elements of a distinctive social circle are undifferentiated, and the elements of a circle that is not distinctive are differentiated. Of course this is not a sociological "natural law," but rather what might be called a phenomenological formula that seeks to conceptualize the regular outcome of regularly coexisting sequences of events. It designates no cause of phenomena; instead, it designates a single phenomenon whose underlying, general structure is represented in each individual case as the effect of very diverse causes, but causes whose combined effect is always to release identical formative energies.

Illustrations of the Formula in Religious and Political Settings

The first aspect of this relationship—lack of differentiation among the members of a differentiated group—is exhibited by the social order of the Quakers, in a form that is based on the deepest motives of its members. As a whole, as a religious principle of the most extreme individualism and subjectivism, Quakerism binds members of the congregation to a style of life and a mode of being that are highly uniform and democratic, seeking to exclude, as far as possible, all individual differences. And in turn, Quakerism lacks all understanding for the higher political union and its goals so that the individuality of the smaller group not only precludes the individuality of the person, but also his commitment to the large group. The specific manifestation of this is as follows: in the affairs of the congregation, in the assemblies of worship, each person may act as preacher and may say whatever he likes whenever he likes. On the other hand, the congregation watches over personal affairs such as marriage, and these cannot occur without the permission of a committee that is appointed to investigate each case. Thus, the Quakers are individual only in collective matters, and in individual matters, they are socially regulated.

Both aspects of the formula are exemplified in the differences between the political structures in the Northern and Southern states in the United States, most clearly so during the period before the Civil War. The New England states in North America had a pronounced local orientation from the very beginning. They developed townships in which the individual was tightly bound by his obligations to the whole, and although this whole was relatively small, it was also self-sufficient. The Southern states, by contrast, were populated to a greater extent by lone adventurers who were not particularly predisposed to local self-government. The South very early developed extensive counties as units of administration. Indeed, for the Southerner, the state as a whole is the site of true political significance, whereas in New England, the state is more a combination of towns. The more abstract, less colorful general political structure corresponds to the more independent—to the point of anarchistic inclinations—Southern personalities that were included in it, whereas the more strictly regulated Northern personalities were inclined toward narrower municipal structures that each, as wholes, possessed strongly individual coloring and autonomous characters.

The Basic Relation as a Dualistic Drive

With all the above qualifications in mind, one could speak of a particular quantum of the tendency toward individualization and of the tendency toward nondifferentiation. This quantum is determined by personal, historical, and social circumstances; and it remains constant, whether it applies to purely psychological configurations or to the social community to which the personality belongs.

We lead, as it were, a doubled, or if one will, a halved existence. We live as an individual within a social circle, with tangible separation from its other members, but also as a member of this circle, with separation from everything that does not belong to it. If now there is a need within us both for individuation and for its opposite, then this need can be realized on either side of our existence. The differentiation drive receives satisfaction from the contrast of one's particular personality with one's fellow members, but this plus corresponds to a minus in the satisfaction that the same person, as a purely social being, derives from oneness with his fellows. That is to say: intensified individualization within the group is accompanied by decreased individualization of the group itself, and vice versa, whenever a certain portion of the drive is satiated.

A Frenchman has made the following observation about the mania for clubs in Germany: "It is this that accustoms the German, on the one hand, not to count solely on the state; on the other hand, not to count solely on himself. It keeps him from locking himself up in his particular interests, and from relying on the state in all matters of general interest." Thus, in this negative mode of expression it is argued that a tendency to the most individual and one to the most general are present, but that they cannot both be satisfied in radically separated special structures; rather, the club is said to constitute an intermediate structure that satiates the dualistic drive quantum in a certain fusion.

The Differentiation Drive as a Heuristic Principle

If one uses this notion as a heuristic principle (i.e., not as designating the actual causality of phenomena, but merely as maintaining that phenomena occur *as if* they were governed by such a dual drive whose manifestations on the two sides of our existence balance one another), then what we have here is a most universal norm that is particularly salient when differences in group size are involved, but one that also applies to other arrangements. For example, in certain circles, and perhaps even in certain peoples, where extravagance, nervous enthusiasm, and moody impulsiveness predominate, we notice nonetheless a decidedly slavish preoccupation with fashion. One person perpetrates some madness, and it is aped by all the others as though they were automatons. In contrast, there are other circles whose life style is of a more sober and soldierly cut, hardly as colorful as the former, but whose members have a far stronger individuality drive, and distinguish themselves much more sharply and concisely within their uniform and simple life style than do those others in their bright and transitory way. So in one case, the totality has a very individual character, but its parts are very much alike; in the other, the totality is less colorful and less modeled on an extreme, but its parts are strikingly differentiated from one another.

Fashion, in and of itself, as a form of social life, is a preeminent case of this correlation. The adornment and accentuation that it lends to the personality is accorded to it only as the member of a class that is collectively distinguishing itself from other classes by adopting the new fashion. (As soon as a fashion has diffused into the other classes, it is abandoned and replaced with another.) The adoption of a fashion represents an internal leveling of the class and its self-exaltation above all other classes.

For the moment, however, our principal concern is with the correlation that involves the *extent* of social circles, the one that generally relates the freedom of the group to the restriction of the individual. A good example of this is the coexistence of communal restrictions and political freedom as found in the Russian governmental system during the preczarist period. Especially in the period of the Mongol wars, Russia had a large number of territorial units, principalities, cities, and village communes that were not held together by any kind of unifying political bond; and thus on the whole they enjoyed great political freedom. For all that, however, the restriction of the individual in commune society was the narrowest imaginable, so much so that there was absolutely no private ownership of land, which only the commune possessed. This narrow confinement in the circle of the commune, which deprived the individual of personal property and often of freedom of movement as well, is the counterpart of the lack of all binding relations with a wider political circle.

Bismarck once said that there was a much more narrow-minded small-town provincialism in a French city of 200,000 than in a German city of 10,000, and he explained this by the fact that Germany was composed of a large number of smaller states. Apparently the very large state allows the local community to have a certain mental self-sufficiency and insularity; and if even a relatively small community views itself as a whole, it will exhibit that cherishing of minutiae which constitutes small-town provincialism. In a smaller state, the community can view itself more as a part of the whole; it is not so much thrown back upon itself. Because the community does not have so much individuality, it can dispense with that internal, coercive leveling of individuals which, because of our psychological sensitivity to differences, must produce a heightened awareness of the smallest and most petty events and interests.

In a narrow circle, one can preserve one's individuality, as a rule, in only two ways. Either one leads the circle (it is for this reason that strong personalities sometimes like to be "number one in the village"), or one exists in it only externally, being independent of it in all essential matters. The latter alternative is possible only through great stability of character or through eccentricity—both traits that are conspicuous most often in small towns.

Stages of Social Commitment

We are surrounded by concentric circles of special interests. The more narrowly they enclose us, the smaller they must be. However, a person is never merely a collective being, just as he is never merely an individual being. For that reason we are naturally speaking here only in terms of more or less, of single aspects and determinants of human existence in which we can see the development away from an excess of one and into an excess of the other.

This development can go through stages in which memberships in both the small and the larger social circle coincide in characteristic sequences. Thus, although commitment to a narrower circle is generally less conducive to the strength of individuality as such than it is in the most general realm possible, it is still psychologically significant that in a very large cultural community, belonging to a family promotes individuation. The lone individual cannot save himself from the totality: only by surrendering a part of his absolute ego to a few others, joining himself in with them, can he preserve his sense of individuality and still avoid excessive isolation, bitterness, and idiosyncrasy. And by extending his personality and his interests around those of a set of other persons, the individual opposes himself in the broader mass, as it were, to the remaining whole. To be sure, individuality in the sense of eccentricity and every kind of abnormality is given broader scope by life without a family in a wider social circle; but for the differentiation that also benefits the greatest whole, for the sort that derives from strength, not from succumbing to one-sided drives—for this, belonging to a narrower circle within the widest is often useful, frequently, to be sure, only as preparation or transition.

The family's significance is at first political and real; then with the growth of culture, it is more and more psychological and ideal. The family as a collective individual offers its members a preliminary differentiation that at least prepares them for differentiation in the sense of absolute individuality; on the other hand, the family offers members a shelter behind which that absolute individuality can develop until it has the strength to stand up against the greatest universality. Belonging to a family in a more advanced culture, where the rights of individuality and of the widest circle developed simultaneously, represents a mixture of the characteristic significance of the narrow and of the expanded circle.

The same observation has been made with respect to the animal kingdom. The tendencies to the creation of families and to the creation of large groups are inversely related. Monogamous and even polygamous relations have something so exclusive about them, and concern for the progeny demands so much from the par-

ents, that a more extensive socialization suffers among such animals. Hence, organized groups are relatively rare among birds,
whereas among wild dogs, to name an example in which complete
sexual promiscuity and mutual indifference after the act are the
rule, the animals live mostly in tightly cohesive packs.

Among the mammals that have both familial and social drives,
we invariably notice that during those periods in which the former
predominate, that is, during the period of pairing off and mating,
the latter decline significantly. The union of parents and offspring
is also tighter if the number of young is smaller. I will cite only
one distinctive example: within the class of fishes, those whose offspring are left entirely on their own lay countless millions of eggs,
whereas among the brooding and nesting fish, where the beginnings of a familial cohesion are found, few eggs are produced.

It is in this sense that it has been argued that social relations
among the animals originated not in conjugal or filial ties, but
rather in sibling ties alone, since the latter allow much greater freedom to the individual than do the former; hence, they make the
individual more inclined to attach itself closely to the larger circle,
which certainly first proffers itself in the individual's siblings. Being confined in an animal family has thus been viewed as the
greatest hindrance to becoming involved in a larger animal society.

The Sociological Duality of the Family

The family has a peculiar sociological double role. On the
one hand, it is an extension of one's own personality; it is a unit
through which one feels one's own blood coursing, one which
arises in being closed to all other social units and in enclosing us
as a part of itself. On the other hand, the family also constitutes
a complex within which the individual distinguishes himself from
all others and in which, in opposition to other members, he develops a selfhood and an antithesis. This double role unavoidably
results in the sociological ambiguity of the family: it appears sometimes as a unitary structure that acts as an individual, thereby assuming a characteristic position in larger and in the largest circles;
and sometimes it appears as an intermediate circle that intervenes

between the individual and the larger circle that encloses both family and individual.

The developmental history of the family, at least as it still seems to be recognizable from a series of points, recapitulates this schema. The family appears first as the embracing circle that entirely encloses the life horizons of the individual, while it is itself largely independent and exclusive. Then it contracts into a narrower structure and thereby becomes adapted to playing the role of an individual in a social circle that has expanded considerably beyond the boundaries of the previous one. After the matriarchal family had been displaced by the rise of masculine force, at first it was much less the fact of procreation by the father that established a family as *one* than it was the domination that he exercised over a particular number of people. Under his unitary authority, he held together not only his offspring, but also his followers, those whom he had bought, those whom he had married and their entire families, and so on. From this primal patriarchal family, the more recent family of mere blood relationship differentiated itself, a family in which parents and their children constitute an autonomous household. This one was naturally far smaller and more individual in character than the embracing patriarchal family had been. That older group had been self-sufficient in all matters, in gaining a livelihood as in carrying out warlike activity; but once it had individualized itself into small families, it became possible and necessary for these to be amalgamated into a newly expanded group, the superfamilial community of the state. The Platonic Ideal State merely extended this line of development by dissolving the family altogether, setting in place of this intermediate structure only individuals, on the one hand, and the state, on the other.

Methodological Implications

Incidentally, there is a typical epistemological difficulty in sociology that finds its clearest example in the double role of the family: when instead of having simply a larger and a smaller group standing opposed to one another so that the position of the individual in them can readily be compared, one has several continuously expanding, superimposed circles, this relation can seem to shift, since a circle can be the narrower one in relation to a second, but it can be the wider one in relation to a third. Short of the largest circle around us that is still effective, all circles included therein have a double meaning: on the one hand, they function as entities with an individual character, often directly as sociological individualities; while on the other hand, depending on their makeup, they function as higher-order complexes that may also include complexes of lower order in addition to their individual members.

It is always precisely the *intermediate* structure that exhibits the pattern in question—internal cohesion, external repulsion—when contrasted with a more general higher structure and a more individual lower structure. The latter is a *relative individual* in relation to the former, regardless of whether in relation to still others it is a collective structure. Thus, wherever one seeks, as we do here, the normal correlation between three levels that are distinguished by their magnitudes—between the primarily individual element, and the narrower and the wider circle—there one will find that under different circumstances one and the same complex can play all three roles, depending on the relationships into which it enters. This hardly diminishes the theoretical value of the statement of this correlation; on the contrary, it proves that the correlation has a formal character that is open to every determinate content.

The Individuation of Collectivities

There are naturally more than enough sociological constellations in which the value of individuality and the need for it focus exclusively on the individual person, where in comparison to him, every complex of several persons emerges under all circumstances as the essentially other level. But on the other hand, it has already been demonstrated that the meaning and the motive power of individuality do not always stop at the boundaries of individual personality, that this is something more general and more formal that can affect the group as a whole and the individual as its element as soon as something is present that is more inclusive, antithetical; over against this something, the (now relatively individual) collective structure can gain its conscious particularity, its character of uniqueness or indivisibility.

Given this formulation, we can explain phenomena that would seem to disconfirm the correlation at issue here, one of which is the following from the history of the United States. The Anti-Federalist party, which first called itself the Republicans, then the Whigs, then the Democrats, defended the autonomy and the sovereignty of the states at the expense of centralization and of national authority—but always with an appeal to the principle of individual freedom, of noninterference by the totality in the affairs of the individual. On no account does this contradict the relationship of individual freedom to just the relatively *large* circle, for here the sense of individuality has permeated the *narrower* circle enclosing many individual persons, and thus the narrower circle serves here the same sociological function as the discrete individual would otherwise.

The Indeterminacy of Collective Individuality

The boundary between those spheres that the individuality drive infuses and those that it requires as its antithesis is indeterminate in principle because the drive can spread from the locus of personality over an indefinite number of concentric structures around the personality. The power of the drive manifests itself, on the one hand, in the fact that any sphere infused by it immediately defines all neighboring spheres as antithetical and anti-individualistic, and on the other hand, by the fact that the need for diversity does not arise so quickly there, so that these neighboring spheres also become individualistically colored.

The political disposition of the Italians, for example, is regionalistic on the whole: every province, and often as not every city, is extraordinarily jealous of its idiosyncrasies and its rights, frequently in complete opposition to all others and with complete indifference toward the values and rights of the whole. One would seemingly have to conclude, in keeping with our general formula, that the elements in these single individuated divisions had a collectivistic, egalitarian disposition. But this is not at all true; rather, among families, and then again among individuals, there is a most extreme craving for autonomy and distinction. Just as in the American case, all three levels of our correlation—single individuals, smaller circles composed of them, and a large group embracing everyone—are clearly present here. But there is no impetus for the characteristic relation between the first and third strata as they orient themselves in common opposition to the second, since in practical awareness, the second is subsumed under the aspect of the first. The sense of individuality has overstepped the boundary of the individual, as it were, and has absorbed the social aspect of the person that normally constitutes the antithesis to his individual aspect.

Attachments between the First and Third Levels

Now, in general, the first and third parts of this three-part structure are oriented toward one another and create a common antithesis—in all the different meanings of that word—against the middle part; and this is manifested, no less than in objective relational patterns, by the subjective relations of the person with these levels. A personal, passionate commitment by the individual human being usually involves the narrowest and the widest circles, but not the intermediate ones. Whoever will sacrifice himself for his family will perhaps do the same for his homeland, perhaps also for an abstract idea such as "mankind" and the demands implicit in the concept, perhaps also for his city and its honor in those eras when "the city" constitutes the widest practical circle of life. For intermediate structures, however, he will scarcely do it, neither for his province nor for a voluntary association. One might sacrifice oneself for a *single* human being or for the very few who make up a family circle; and then again, for an incomprehensible multitude; but for a hundred people, hardly anyone brings himself to martyrdom.

The psychological significance of purely spatial "near and far" thoroughly corresponds to the figurative meaning in which it subsumes the quite "near" and the quite "far" under what is practically speaking a single category. The deepest sentimental interest attaches itself, on the one hand, to the person whom we constantly have before our eyes, with whom we are involved in our daily lives, and, on the other hand, to the person from whom we are separated by vast, unbridgeable distance with as much agitation as unappeased yearning. But a relative coolness, a lesser stimulation of consciousness, befits the person who is neither quite near to us nor unreachably far from us.

This same form squares exactly with a fact that has been noted by a prominent expert on North America. He observes that the county has very little significance there: "It is too large for the personal interest of the citizens: that goes to the township. It is too small to have traditions which command the respect or touch the affections of its inhabitants: these belong to the state."

This "touching of extremes" holds just as good when its sign is reversed to the negative. The Indian caste is endogamous, but in it there is another very narrow circle within which marriage is forbidden. Marriage prospects are thus confined to the narrower circle, a state of affairs that is also found elsewhere; and indeed, in a certain sense, it may be universal, at least for the behavioral reality of marital arrangements. In the Indian case, both the widest and the ultimately narrowest circles are proscribed. This mode of the correlation is exhibited yet again in historically sequential stages: the strength and extent of control with which the guild formerly grasped the individual is no longer exercised by this type of circle at all, but rather by the family, on the one hand, and by the state, on the other.

Freedom and Individuality

THE MEANINGS OF FREEDOM   The relatively most individual and the relatively most extensive configurations relate to one another over the head of the intermediate one, as it were. And at this point we have arrived at the basis of a fact that figures prominently in the foregoing discussion as well as in what now follows: the larger circle encourages individual freedom, the smaller one restricts it.

As it is used here, the concept of individual freedom covers various meanings that are differentiated according to the diversity of our provinces of interest. They range, say, from freedom in choosing a spouse to freedom in economic initiative. I will cite one example each for just these two.

During periods of strict group separation by clans, families, occupational and hereditary estates, castes, and so on, the circle within which a man or woman can marry tends to be a relatively narrow one—narrow, that is, relative to advanced or liberal conditions. But so far as we can survey this state of affairs, and so far as we can judge by certain contemporary analogies, selecting a partner from among the available individuals was not at all difficult. The lesser differentiation of persons and of marital relations had its counterpart in the fact that the individual male could take almost any girl from the appropriate circle, choosing on the basis of external attractiveness, since there were no highly specific internal impulses or aloof reservations to be considered by either side.

Culture as it has matured has now displaced this earlier condition in two directions. The circle of possible marriage partners has been vastly expanded by the mixing of status groups, the elimination of religious barriers, the decline of parental authority, free mobility in both the geographic and the social sense, and so forth. But for all that, individual selection is far more stern, a fact and a right of wholly personal inclination. The conviction that out of all mankind, two and only two people are "meant" for each other has now reached a stage of development that was still unheard of by the bourgeoisie of the eighteenth century.

A more profound meaning of freedom emerges here: individual freedom is freedom that is limited by individuality. Out of the uniqueness of the individual's being, there arises a corresponding uniqueness of that which can complement and free him, a specificity of needs whose correlate is the availability of the largest possible circle of possible selections, since as one's wishes and inner drives become more individual, it becomes that much less likely that they will find satisfaction in a narrowly bounded domain. In the earlier condition, conversely, there was far less restriction by the rigidity of personalities: *from the standpoint of his own concerns*, the individual was much more free in making a choice, since instead of a compelling differentiation of choice objects, there was an approximate equivalence of all those that might come under consideration. For this reason, there was no need for the circle of choice objects to be significantly more extensive. So the relatively undeveloped condition certainly imposed a social constraint on the individual; however, this was linked to the negative freedom of nondifferentiation, to the *liberum arbitrium* that was provided by the mere identical worth of objects. In the more advanced state, on the other hand, social possibilities are much enlarged, but now they are restricted by the positive meaning of freedom in which every choice is—or at least ideally should be— the unambiguously determined expression of an unalterable kind of personality.

Now in the general, societal meaning of freedom, I would say that feudalism generated nothing but narrow circles that bound individual to individual and restricted each by his obligation to the other. For this reason, within the feudal system there was room neither for national enthusiasm or public spirit, nor for the spirit of individual enterprise and private energy. The same restrictions that prevented the emergence of conceptions of a higher social union also prevented, at the lower level, the actualization of individual freedom. For just this reason, it is especially pertinent and profound that during the feudal period, the "freeman" is defined as a man who is subject to the law of the realm; bound and unfree is the man who is party to a feudal tie, that is, whose law derives from this narrower circle to the exclusion of the wider one.

If freedom swings to extremes; if the largest group, as I indicated above, affords greater play to extreme formations and malformations of individualism, to misanthropic detachment, to baroque and moody life styles, to crass egoism—then all this is merely the consequence of the wider group's requiring less of us, of its being less concerned with us, and thus of its lesser hindering of the full development even of perverse impulses. The size of the circle has a negative influence here, and it is more a matter, so to speak, of developments outside rather than inside the group, developments in which the larger circle gives its members more opportunity to get involved than does the smaller one.

THE MEANINGS OF INDIVIDUALITY   The meaning of individuality in general can be separated into two more specific meanings. One has been emphasized in the above, namely, individuality in the sense of the freedom and the responsibility for oneself that comes from a broad and fluid social environment, whereas the smaller group is "narrower" in a dual sense: not only with regard to its extent, but also with regard to the restraints it imposes upon the individual, the control it exercises over him, the trifling radius of the prospects and the kinds of impetus it allows him. The other meaning of individuality is qualitative: it means that the single human being distinguishes himself from all others; that his being and conduct—in form, content, or both—suit him alone; and that being different has a positive meaning and value for his life.

The elaborations that the principle or ideal of individualism has undergone in the modern era differ according to the accentuation given to the first or the second of these meanings. On the whole, the eighteenth century sought individuality in the form of freedom, the lack of every kind of restraint on personal powers, regardless whether this restraint came from the estates or from the church, whether it was political or economic. But at the same time, the assumption prevailed that once men had been freed from all sociohistorical fetters, they would show themselves to be essentially equal; that "man in general," along with all the goodness and perfection of his nature, was inherent in every personality, needing only to be emancipated from those distorting and diverting bonds. That once men had freedom, they would use it to differentiate themselves; to rule or to become enslaved; to be better or worse than others; in short, to unfold the full diversity of their individual powers—this fact escaped the kind of individualism for which "freedom and equality" were two peacefully coexisting—indeed, two mutually necessary—values.

It should be obvious how this kind of individualism was involved in blowing apart every narrow and narrowing accommodation; partly, this was its historical, real effect, and at least partly, it was involved as a yearning and a demand. In the French Revolution, even the workers were forbidden to join into unions for better working conditions: such a federation would limit the freedom of individual members! So it is that the correlate of this kind of individualism is a wholly "cosmopolitan" disposition; even national integration recedes behind the idea of "mankind." The particularistic rights of status groups and of circles are replaced in principle by the rights of the individual, and these, quite significantly, are called "human rights"; that is, they are the rights that derive from belonging to the widest conceivable circle.

It was the other meaning of individuality that was developed by the nineteenth century, and its contradiction of the meaning just described was not seen on the whole by the eighteenth. This other meaning found its preeminent theoretical expression in Romanticism and its practical expression in the ascendancy of the division of labor. Here individualism means that the person assumes and should assume a position that he and no one else can fill; that this position awaits him, as it were, in the organization of the whole, and that he should search until he finds it; that the personal and social, the psychological and metaphysical meaning of human existence is realized in this immutability of being, this intensified differentiation of performance. This ideal image of individualism seems to have nothing at all to do with the earlier notion of "the generally human," with the idea of a uniform human nature that is present in everyone and that only requires freedom for its emergence. Indeed, the second meaning fundamentally contradicts the first. In the first, the value emphasis is on what men have in common; in the second, it is on what separates them. But with regard to the correlation I am seeking to verify, they coincide.

The enlargement of the circle that is associated with the first conception of individuality also promotes the emergence of the

second. Although the second conception does not look to the totality of mankind; although it makes individuals mutually complementary and dependent instead of atomizing society into uniform
and absolutely "free" individuals; although historically it promotes nationalism and a certain illiberalism instead of free cosmopolitanism—nevertheless, it too requires a group of relatively
considerable size for its origination and survival. One need only
refer to the manner in which the mere expansion of the economic
circle, the increase in population, or the geographic boundlessness
of competition has directly compelled a specialization of performance.

It is no different for mental differentiation, especially since
this usually originates in the meeting of latent mental abilities
with objectively preexisting mental products. The unmediated interaction of subjectivities or the purely inner energy of a human
being rarely elicits all the mental distinctiveness that one possesses; rather, this seems to be associated with the extent of what
has been called "objective mind," that is, the traditions and the
experiences of one's group, set down in thousands of forms; the art
and learning that are present in tangible structures; all the cultural
materials that the historical group possesses as something super-
subjective and yet available to everyone. The peculiarity of this
generally accessible Mind that crystallizes itself in objective structures is that it provides both the material and the impetus for the
development of a distinct personal mental type. It is the essence of
"being cultured" that our purely personal dispositions are sometimes realized as the *form* of what is given as a content of objective
culture [*Geist*], sometimes as the *content* of what is given as a
form in objective culture. Only in this synthesis does our mental
life attain its full idiom and personality; only thereby do its unique
and wholly individual attributes become tangibly incarnated.

This, then, is the connection that links mental differentiation
to the size of the circle in which objective mind originates. The
circle may be a social, real one, or it may be of a more abstract,
literary, historical sort: as that circle enlarges, so too do the possibilities of developing our inner lives; as its cultural offerings increase, regardless of how objective or abstract they may be, so too

do the chances of developing the distinctiveness, the uniqueness, the sufficiency of existence of our inner lives and their intellectual, aesthetic, and practical productivity.

The individualism of equality is not, from the very beginning, a *contradictio in adjecto* only if one takes it to mean the freedom and self-sufficiency that are not limited by narrower social bonds. The individualism of inequality is a consequence of that freedom, given the infinite variability of human capacities, and therefore it is incompatible with equality. In the fundamental antithesis of these two forms of individualism, there is one point at which they coincide: each of them has a potential for development to the degree that quantitative expansion of the circle that encloses the individual provides the necessary room, impetus, and material.

INDIVIDUALISM AND COSMOPOLITANISM I now return to the relation that was mentioned above, the one between the strong development and high prestige of individuality, on the one hand, and a cosmopolitan disposition that leaps, as it were, over the individual's *nearest* social milieu. I would remind you first of the teachings of the Stoics.

Whereas for Aristotle the sociopolitical milieu of the individual was still the source of ethical valuation, the Stoical interest in the practical actually involved only the individual, and the elevation of the individual to the system's prescribed ideal became so exclusively the arbiter of Stoical practice that the interrelations of individuals became no more than a means to that ideal, individualistic end. This goal, of course, was defined in content by the idea of a universal Reason that infused all individual beings. Every person was thought to partake in this Reason, and its realization in the individual constituted the Stoical ideal. Transcending all barriers of nationality and social exclusiveness, Reason wove a bond of equality and brotherhood around all human creatures. Thus, the individualism of the Stoics had its complement in cosmopolitanism; the rending of narrower social bonds, which during this period was promoted no less by the political situation than by theoretical contemplation, shifted the center of gravity toward the individual, on the one hand; and on the other, toward that widest circle to which every human belongs simply by virtue of his humanity.

In countless variations, historical reality has conformed to the same pattern. The medieval knight combined his ethos of purely individual authenticity and worth with a firm, cosmopolitan bent. His self-reliance made room for the forms that produced a European knighthood transcending all national boundaries. And with this formula, one also describes the forms that came to life throughout the Holy Roman Empire and that eventually dissolved it. The empire collapsed, on the one hand, because of the particularism of its constituent parts, and on the other hand, because of binding relations with the remaining components of pan-European politics; that is, because of the contraction and expansion that shattered intermediate national structures.

That particularism was evoked essentially by an identical constellation, although one that extended in another dimension. When elements that are already differentiated or that press toward differentiation are forced into an embracing union, the outcome, more often than not, is an increased incompatibility, a more intense mutual repulsion. The large, embracing framework, which naturally requires differentiation, on the one hand, in order to exist at all, causes a friction of elements against one another, on the other hand, an actualization of antitheses that would not have come to pass except for this crowding. Unification into a great amalgam is the means—even if a transient one—to individualization and to its emergence in consciousness. Thus, the politics of world domination pursued by the medieval empire only served to release the particularisms of peoples, tribes, and princes; indeed, that policy brought them to life in the first place. The intended, partially successful fusion into a great whole contained the instrument of its own destruction, namely, the individuation of its components, which it created, intensified, and brought to awareness.

In a more intuitively obvious configuration, the culture of the Italian Renaissance has conformed to this norm. On the one hand, it developed perfect individuality; on the other hand, it developed a disposition and a morality that transcended by far the boundaries of the narrower social milieu. This is explicit, for example, in the words of Dante where he says that—with all his passionate love for Florence—the world is as much home to him and his kind as the sea to fish. Indirectly and a posteriori, as it were, this is shown in the adoption of the life styles created by the Italian Renaissance by the entire cultured world, an adoption that came to pass precisely because these styles gave free play to individuality, whatever kind it might be, to a degree that had never before been imagined.

As a symptom of this development, I will mention only the low prestige of the nobility in this epoch. Nobility is of real significance only so long as it defines a social circle that is highly cohesive and that hence sets itself off all the more energetically from the mass of all other circles; from those below *and* from those above. To deny the worth of the nobility signifies a breakdown of both these criteria: on the one hand it signifies a recognition of the value of the personality, whatever circle of birth it belongs to; on the other hand, it signifies a leveling with regard to those above whom one would otherwise raise oneself. Both of these find unequivocal expression in the literature of the Renaissance.[3]

Individuation in the Economic Sphere

The preeminent historical instance of the correlation between social expansion and the individuation of life contents and forms is provided by the emergence of the cash economy. The primitive economy engenders small, relatively insular economic circles; the difficulty of transportation alone restricts their perimeters, and it accordingly prevents the technology of the primitive economy from arriving at a significant degree of the differentiation and individualization of activities.

The cash economy changes this condition along two lines. The general acceptance of money, its ease of transport, its eventual sublimation into cashless transactions in bank drafts and bills of exchange—all these allow the effects of money to extend into unboundable distances, and ultimately to engender from the whole civilized world a single economic circle with interpenetrating interests, complementary sectors of productivity, and similar prac-

[3]   In the original text, the lengthy "Note on the Nobility" appears between this section and the next. In this volume it appears separately as chapter 14.—ED.

tices. In the other line of development, money causes an enormous individualization of the participant in the economy. The form of cash wages makes the worker infinitely more independent than does any kind of payment in the primitive economy. The possession of money gives a man previously unheard of freedom of movement. The liberal norms that are regularly associated with the cash economy set each individual in a free competitive struggle with every other. And finally, no less than the dilation of the economic circle, this competition compels a specialization of function that would not otherwise come into question, one whose extremes of compartmentalization are made possible only by accommodations in the framework of a very large circle.

Within the economy, money is the connection that relates maximal expansion of the economic group to maximal differentiation of its members, both in the dimension of freedom and a sense of responsibility for oneself, and in the dimension of a qualitative differentiation of labor. A more precise formulation is that money develops the smaller, more insular, internally more uniform group of the primitive economy into another whose unitary character bifurcates into the two aspects of expansion and individualization.

The Political Sphere

Political developments actualize this constellation in a great number of domains, although of course with multiple variations on the basic relationship. From the smaller, constrictingly socialized circle to the large group and the differentiation of personalities, there is no necessary pari passu progression; rather, there are processes of selection and alternation. The emphasis in the more evolved condition falls *either* on the creation of an embracing public realm and the enhancement of the significance of its central organs, *or* on the autonomy of individual elements. Then too, the expansion of the group may not be related to the development of personality for the members of the group themselves, but instead to the idea of an ultimate personality to whom individual will is surrendered, as it were. I will cite a few examples from the various domains of politics.

In the agrarian domain, the dissolution of the peasantry's communal property since the end of the Middle Ages has taken place in just these forms. The evolving centralist states struck down community holdings, the common pasture land. Part of this, as a public commodity, was absorbed into the property of the state and was attached to the administrative organism of the polity. The rest, to the degree that this did not occur, was distributed among enfranchised persons as private property. In this latter fact alone, the simultaneous tendencies toward both individual and general outcomes are evident once again: on the one hand, the distribution was guided by concepts of Roman law with their enthronement of individual interests; on the other hand, it was guided by the notion that the partitioning of common holdings would bring about a betterment in the state of national culture, that is, precisely in the broadest public realm.

Under very different material and overall conditions, a particular phase of the history of the common pasture, the case of the collective property of Swiss communities, exhibited the same form, and that as recently as the nineteenth century. To the degree that common pasture was annexed to the holdings of partial communities, of local and village corporations, it was dealt with in a few cantons (Zurich, Saint Gallen, and others) by legislation that tended either to distribute the pasture land among individual community members or else to let it be incorporated into larger national communities, the idea being that the smallest communities lacked the personal and territorial resources to make their holdings adequately productive for the commonwealth.

In the course of postmedieval developments in Germany, the form of agrarian policy measure that is stressed above was diffused throughout domestic politics generally. The higher authorities manipulated separate, self-segregating circles in a manner that tended to differentiate them: some into creatures of private law that would be merely the personal affairs of their members, and others into institutions of the state. The corporations that had dominated medieval society had become so hardened and constricted that public life threatened to collapse into an incoherent mass of egotistic factions. Counterposed to these, and dissolving them as the modern era began, was the idea of an all-embracing public realm, an idea that first took the form of princely absolutism. In accordance with its inner principle, absolutism generated "equal justice for all," that is, it detached the individual, on the one hand, from the restraint placed on his practical life by the privileges of the corporations; and on the other hand, it canceled the privileges that he himself enjoyed as a member of the corporations, but which often forced him into unnatural alliance with his fellow members. Thus, it was fundamentally a matter of destroying the narrow, internally homogeneous, "intermediate" association whose hegemony had characterized the earlier condition in order to conduct development upward toward the state and downward toward the unprejudiced freedom of the individual. That the state, in turn, found its practical effectiveness in the form of an ultimate personality, the absolute ruler, is hardly a counterinstance to the fundamental pattern; indeed, the pattern is actualized in just this manner, both diachronically and synchronically, in an extraordinarily large number of cases.

This is the often-stressed relationship that history demonstrates between republicanism and tyranny, between despotism and leveling. Every system of government that derives its character from the aristocracy or the bourgeoisie—in short, all those that offer social and political consciousness to a plurality of contiguously bounded narrower circles—as soon as it attempts to go beyond itself at all, surges, on the one hand, toward consolidation in a personal, guiding power, and on the other hand, toward an anarchistically tinged socialism that seeks to establish, with the obliteration of all differences, the absolute right of the free personality. The shattering of group constraints within a whole that somehow belongs together is so intimately related to the accentuation of individuality that both the cohesion of the ruling personality and the individual freedom of all group members center upon it like two variations on a single theme.

It is noteworthy that political aristocracies, which are always constructed after the type of closed and rigorously bounded circles, are often militarily unsuccessful under conditions of social expansion. This may result from their aversion to those two forces that, alone or in combination, appoint their disintegration: on the one hand, the aristocracies shrink from summoning the whole populace to united action; on the other, they distrust individual generals who have broad power of authority and striking success.

The correlation between the *volonté générale* and autocracy is one in which the latter has not infrequently been used as the official cloak for designs leading ultimately to the suppression of the former. When the Earl of Leicester had been called to the governor-generalship of the Netherlands (1586), he sought to establish an unlimited dominion over the heads of the narrower bodies that had ruled previously, the states general and provincial status groups. He proceeded under cover of unqualifiedly democratic principles: the will of the people, so it was said, was the absolute ruler; and it had called upon Leicester. Yet it was explicitly stressed along with this that tradesmen and lawyers, peasants and craftsmen had nothing to say in that rule and could do no more than simply obey. Thus, the—purportedly—democratic leveling was carried so far that the higher as well as the lower status groups were disfranchised, and only the ideal entity of "the people as a whole" remained. Opponents soon declared that this newly discovered concept of "the people" served only to transfer "the people's" unlimited sovereignty to a single man.

Further elaborations of our basic relationship are found in the domain of municipal politics. As early as the Middle Ages, English cities exhibited a pattern in which the larger municipalities were ruled by single corporations or magnates, whereas in the smaller cities, the people as a whole held dominion. Corresponding to the smaller circle, there is a homogeneity of elements that underlies the unvarying rate of their political participation; but in the larger circles, this homogeneity is fragmented, allowing only for the mass of private individuals on one side, and for the single ruling personality on the other.

In a certain rudimentary form, the administrative arrangements of North American cities exhibit the same pattern. As long as cities are small, administration of each office by a majority of persons presents itself as the most suitable mode; but if they grow into metropoles, it would seem more practical to entrust each office to a single person. Largeness of scale requires representation and guidance by an individual, fully responsible personality; the smaller circle could administer itself in a less differentiated fashion, since a greater number of its elements was always directly at the helm.

This sociological distinction fully corresponds to a line of development in which the general political tendency of the individual states of the Union conforms to the basic type at issue here: that development is said to have loosed, in recent decades, a thorough weakening of parliamentarianism, which it is replacing along two other dimensions—on the one hand, with direct plebiscite; and on the other hand, with monarchistic institutions, with the surrender of power to individual persons.

The Religious Sphere

Finally, ecclesiastical politics provides us with examples, and these have analogies even in purely religious developments. The polytheism of antiquity had many of the essential characteristics that I have subsumed here under the concept of "the narrower circle." For the most part, the cults set themselves off from one another by sharp internal and local boundaries. The circles of believers were centripetal; often they were mutually indifferent to one another, often hostile. The gods themselves were often aristocratically ranked, with complicated relationships of superordination and subordination, and with segregated spheres of potency. At the outset of the Christian era in the domain of classical culture, this condition led to monotheism, to the enthronement of a single and personal God who united in himself all the powers of those discrete and segregated deities.

A religious individual originated who had an unconditional sense of responsibility for himself. A "religiosity of the closet" developed. And there came to pass an independence from all bonds to world and man except for the one inherent in the undiverted and unmediated relation of the individual's soul to his God, to a God who was no less "his" because he was the God of all, but rather who was "his" precisely because of that universality. Individuality within the large, leveled collectivity, as it originated in the dissolution and fusion of all previous discrete gods, was the reflected image of the absolute and unitary personality of a God who had grown out of the same processes of analysis and synthesis of all earlier gods.

The developmental form exhibited by Christianity in its original purity was recapitulated in the politics of the Catholic church. Within the church, the tendency toward the generation of particularized circles rose anew, leading to sharp demarcations of rank and interest, to the rise of an aristocracy of the clergy over the status group of the laity. Yet Gregory VII early united his quest for absolute power with a decided demagoguery that pulled together the most powerful antitheses and reached over the heads of the exclusive aristocratic bishops. After celibacy had most effectively supported this endeavor—since a married priest would have had attachment to a narrower circle and thus would have engendered a closed opposition within the church, whereas as a celibate, a priest's only recourse in his individual isolation would be to the unqualified totality—the Jesuits took it up with the greatest success. They fought the status aspirations of the clergy on all fronts, and they laid stress on the universal character of the priest that permitted him to feel at one with all believers, whatever their status. In opposition to all aristocratic systems of church rule, their goals were a thorough leveling of all believers, on the one hand, and papal absolutism, on the other.

General Modes of Actualization of the Correlation

The entire relational pattern under discussion here takes shape in the most diverse modes of simultaneity, sequentiality, and alternation. Perhaps one could symbolically express this complex of relations by saying that the narrower circle constitutes in some measure an intermediate proportionality between individuality and the expanded group. Thus the narrower circle, closed upon itself and requiring no other factor, can be seen to result in the same outcome of life chances as results from the conjunction of individuality and the large circle.

I will now select a few examples from the realm of law, examples from domains that are absolutely different, historically and materially. The idea of total power that was contained in the Roman concept of the state had its correlate in the notion that next to the *jus publicum*, there was a *jus privatum*. The norm of behavior that the all-inclusive whole defined for itself required that there be a corresponding norm for the individuals whom it enveloped. On the one side, there was only the community in the broadest sense; on the other side, there were only single persons. The oldest Roman law recognized no corporations, and this spirit generally remained with it.

Conversely, German law did not have different legal principles for the community and for individuals; however, these collectivities were hardly as all-embracing as those of the Roman state; rather they were smaller ones that were called into being by the many shifting needs of individuals. In smaller commonwealths, there is no need for anything like the Roman divorce of public from private law, since in them, the individual is more intimately bound up in the whole.

As a unitary development, the correlation is demonstrated in the right of blood vengeance, for example, in Arabia. The essence of this right resided entirely in the solidarity and the autonomy of sharply bounded tribal groups: it applied to the whole tribe or family of the murderer, and it was executed by the whole tribe or family of the victim. Mohammed's intention clearly ran counter to this in the direction of the bifurcation I have emphasized. Over these particularized groups, leveling them with the common religion, a national or political collectivity was to have arisen, and from it the legal judgment would be promulgated that the law of particularistic interest would be replaced by an ultimate, universally recognized authority. Correspondingly, judgment would henceforth be passed on the guilty individual alone, and the collective responsibility of particularized groups would be abolished. The largest collectivity and the individually circumscribed personality, as products of the differentiation of those intermediate structures, were to face one another alone.

With the same clarity, although in the setting of completely different contents, this type of form appears as the final stage in an unbroken sequence when, in ancient Rome, developments shattered the patriarchal family grouping. When civil rights in war and peace accrued to both father and sons, and when the sons were able to acquire personal significance, influence, booty, and so on, a fissure had been opened in the *patria protestas* that inevitably split the patriarchal relation more and more widely apart to the benefit of the expanded needs of the state and of the law of the great whole over each of its members, but also to the benefit of the personality. Out of its relation to this whole, the personality could gain an importance that the patriarchal relation had incomparably restricted.

Finally, a formally identical process runs its course in an oddly mixed phenomenon where it can be recognized only by holding rigorously to our basic idea. Until the Norman period, each English sheriff, each royal judge, seems to have been assigned a single community, so that adjudication had a certain local coloring or constraint in which the interest of the community and that of the state were fused. These two interests began to separate after the middle of the twelfth century; royal jurisdiction then came to be executed by judicial commissions that rode large circuits, and their administration was obviously of a more general, locally unconstrained sort, while the interests of the community were protected by the growing significance of the local jury. Here the community, in its purely internal interests, played the role of the individual in our correlation; it was a social individual whose judicial life had once run its course along with that of the political state collectivity, but which later gained a purer autonomy of being with which it then stood along side of, or in opposition to, the equally more purely elaborated law of the large collectivity.

The Ideals of the Equality and Unity of Mankind

It is no more than a corollary of the idea of such a relation between individuality and sociality if we state the following: as man as individual, and so his attributes as man qua man, come to replace man as social element in the foreground of interest, the bond must tighten that pulls him—over the head of his social group, as it were—toward all that is human, suggesting to him the notion of an ideal unity of mankind. There need be no mistake about this developmental tendency, even though in generating this notion of ideal unity—which is really logically required—it has been restricted by all manner of historical limitations.

So in Plato, we find, on the one hand, an interest in pure individuality and the perfection of personality, an interest that broadened to include the ideal of friendship, and on the other hand, an interest in pure statehood that was completely indifferent to intermediate confederations and their respective interests. The manner of his emphasis on the cultivation and practical exemplification of the individual human being, on the value of his psyche as a self-sufficient and discrete entity, should logically have led to the rejection of the final barrier, the barrier of the form of the Greek state, which other philosophers of his epoch did reject. It was only the accident of his political inclination and his Greek nationalist disposition that prevented Plato from drawing out of his ideal construction the real conclusion for the individual: beyond the individual conceived of by Plato, only all mankind could stand as a collective value.

Similarly, Christianity lays stress on the absolute concentration of all values in the soul and its salvation, and yet fails to recognize the link which this position establishes between Christianity and all human beings. The process of unification and equalization (gradated as that equality may be), rather than extending into all mankind, tends far more to stop at the barrier of affiliation with the church. It is roughly this spirit that one finds in Zwingli's declaration that all orders, sects, special confederations, and so forth must be abolished because all Christians are brothers—but all Christians, not all men.

Altogether consistently, in contrast to the above cases, extreme individuality has frequently been associated with the doctrine of the equality of all men. It is, psychologically speaking, quite obvious that the frightful inequality into which the individual was born during certain epochs of social history would elicit a reaction along two lines, one leading in the direction of the right to individuality, and the other toward the right to universal equality, since either of these alone tends to be inadequate in the same degree for the broader masses. Only in this dualistic connection can a phenomenon such as Rousseau be understood.

The increasing development of education exhibits the same tendency. It seeks to eliminate glaring differences in mental level and, precisely via the creation of a certain equality, to secure for each person the previously denied chance of making good his individual capacities.

I have already spoken of the form assumed by our correlation in the idea of "human rights." Eighteenth-century individualism wanted only freedom, only the removal of the "intermediate" circles and middle levels that separated men from mankind, that is, those that inhibited the development of the pure humanity that supposedly constituted the value and core of each individual's existence, but which was hidden and truncated by particularistic historical groupings and bonds. So as soon as the individual is made reliant upon *himself*, upon the ultimate and essential within himself, he is on the same footing as everyone else, and freedom has revealed equality. Individuality that truly is such, that is not diverted by social coercion, represents the absolute unity of human kind and is fused with it. There is no need to discuss how this theoretical, ethical conviction of the eighteenth century was perfected in thoroughly practical, real situations, and how it came to have an immense effect on them.

The later meaning of individualism—according to which the factual reality of human nature is comprised of the uniqueness of individuals' qualities and values, a uniqueness whose development and intensification are moral imperatives—this meaning of individualism is the denial of every kind of equality. For it seems inadmissible to me to construe equality from the fact that each individual is as special and incomparable as every other. That an individual is incomparable is hardly his own positive quality; rather, this arises only out of comparison with others, who are different only in the judgment of an observer who does not find in one person what he found in another. This point is perfectly obvious when one compares only two objects: a black object and a white object certainly do not have the common quality of one's being not white, and the other not black.

But even if to speak of the *equality* of mankind in the presence of the qualitative singularity of individuals is no more than a misuse of words, the ideal of the *unity* of mankind is not at all incompatible with this supposition. For one can conceive of the diversity of individuals, even if it implies neither economic production nor more generally a direct cooperation of everyone, as a kind of division of labor. To be sure, this takes us into the speculations of sociological metaphysics.

As the individual becomes more incomparable, as he comes more and more to occupy—in his being, his conduct, and his destiny—a position that can be filled only by him and that is reserved for him alone in the organization of the whole, all the more must this whole be grasped as a unity, as a metaphysical organism in which each psyche is a vital element, exchangeable with no other, but presupposing all others and their interaction for its own life. Wherever the need exists to perceive the totality of psychic existence in the world as a unity, it will sooner be satisfied by an individuation in which single beings necessarily complement and need one another, each taking the place left for it by all the others; this need for unity and hence apprehension of the totality of being will sooner be satisfied by that than by an equality of beings in which any one could essentially replace any other, in which each member seems actually to be superfluous and without proper relation to the whole.

Nevertheless, the ideal of equality, which unifies, in quite another sense, the most extreme individualization with the most extreme expansion of the circle of associated beings, has never been more encouraged than by the Christian doctrine of the immortal and eternal soul. The soul that faces its God with reliance only upon itself in its metaphysical individuality, the only absolute value of all being, is identical to all others in what ultimately matters. For in the eternal and the absolute, there are no distinctions: men's empirical differences, confronting the eternal and transcendental, are of no consequence. These individuals are not just the sums of their attributes, in which event they would be as diverse as those; rather, beyond those attributes, each of them is an absolute entity by virtue of personality, freedom, and immortality.

Thus, the sociology of Christianity offers the greatest historical as well as metaphysical example of the asserted correlation: the psyche that is free from all bonds and from all relations, whatever the ends for whose sake they were instituted, the psyche that is oriented only toward the powers beyond that are the same for everyone—such a psyche, in conjunction with all others, constitutes a homogeneous being that encompasses all sentience. Unconditionality of personality and unconditional expansion of the circle of its kind are but two expressions for the unity of this religious conviction. And insofar as this has become the metaphysics or the given meaning for life in general, it is unmistakable in the extent to which it influences, as a priori disposition and mood, the historical patterns of relation among men and the attitude with which they approach one another.

Group Expansion and the Determinants of Will

OBJECTIVITY AND SUBJECTIVITY   Indeed, the sociological significance of a universal world view, both as cause and as effect within our correlation, is manifest even when inquiry into the narrowness or breadth of environmental image does not halt at the borders of the human world. Its significance still holds when inquiry apprehends objectivity in general, whose forms we frequently construe by way of analogy with socially habituated forms.

One may well say that antiquity lacked both the broadest and purest conception of objectivity and the deepest and most precise conception of subjectivity. The concept of natural law as an absolutely substantive, universal rule, indifferent to all "values," was as foreign to antiquity as the real concept of the ego, with its productivity and its freedom, its problematics, and its value that outweighs the world. The psyche neither went so far beyond itself nor so deeply into itself as it later did via the synthesis—or also the antithesis—of the Christian ethos with modern natural and historical sciences. This cannot have been without internal and at least indirect connection with the sociopolitical structure of the Greek world. The enormous internal prerogatives of the narrower state circles bound the individual by and large to a certain intermediate image of life and the world that fell between universality and ultimate personality; and the whole form of existence inherent in these restrictions had to be abolished in order to make room for development toward those two extremes.

ETHICS AND INTERESTS   More directly than in its significance for metaphysical images of the cosmos, our correlation becomes intuitively clear in the domain of ethics. Very early, the Cynics had already rejected the otherwise typically Greek link with narrower social structures by embracing a cosmopolitan disposition, on the one hand; and on the other hand, by eliminating the intermediate element of patriotism. The expansion of the circle that fills the view and interest of individuals may frequently give rise to a particular form of egoism that engenders a real and ideal restriction of social spheres. It may promote a greatheartedness and an enthusiastically outreaching vault of the psyche, both of which are inhibited by the amalgamation of personal life with a narrow interest circle of solidary comrades. But whenever circumstances or character retard this outcome, then, quite significantly, its exact opposite easily results. To the greatest extent, as I have already discussed, the cash economy and its associated liberalistic tendencies have loosened or dissolved narrower confederations—from guild to nation—and have inaugurated a world economy; and on the other hand, they have encouraged economic egoism to every degree of remorselessness. The less, as a result of enlargement of the economic circle, the producer knows his consumers, the more exclusively is his interest focused on the level of the price that he can extract from them. The more impersonal and qualitatively empty is the public that confronts him, the more his own orientation comes to rest exclusively on the qualitatively empty result of labor, that is, on money. Apart from those lofty domains where the energy of labor stems from abstract idealism, the worker will impart his person and his ethical interest to his labor to the degree that his circle of consumers is personally known to him, and this occurs only under conditions of smaller scale. Along with the growing size of the group for which he works, and along with the growing indifference with which he is able only to confront it, many factors are lost that once restricted economic egoism.

Along many dimensions, human nature and human situations

are so positioned that when the individual's relations begin to exceed a certain extensiveness, he becomes all the more thrown back upon himself. This is not only a matter of the quantitative extension of the circle, which must inevitably reduce the personal interestedness in it of each of its points down to a minimum; it is also a matter of qualitative diversification within the circle that impeded the focusing of interest upon any one point, and which thus leaves egoism as the logical outcome of the general paralysis of irreconcilable demands. In keeping with this formal motif, for example, one of the factors giving rise to the colorfulness and internal heterogeneity of the Habsburg possessions has been held to be the fact that in all their political activity, the Habsburgs had nothing in view except the interests of their house.

Finally, spatial extension of the interest circle into greater distances—not necessarily coinciding with its actual enlargement—is what enables the individual to confront at least his narrower circle in an egoistic way. Until the time of Henry III and Edward I, English status groups were deeply divided because their interests extended variously beyond their homeland. An English nobleman had a much more intense interest in a foreign war conducted by other nobles than in domestic struggles over the law. An urbanite was much more interested in the orderliness of the commercial situation in the Netherlands than in that of English cities, unless some matter directly touched his own concerns. The great officers of the church felt themselves to be members of an international ecclesiastical entity, rather than showing any specifically English sympathies. Only after Henry and Edward did these classes begin to merge into a unified nation, and with that the segregation ceased whose egoistic character had been associated in every respect with the earlier cosmopolitan extensions of interest.

Group Expansion and Consciousness of the Ego

Beyond the significance that expansion of the circle has for the differentiation of the determinants of will, one sees its significance for the emergence of the *sensation* of a personal ego. Surely no one can fail to recognize that the style of modern life—

precisely because of its mass character, its rushing diversity, its unboundable equalization of countless previously conserved idio-syncrasies—has led to unprecedented levelings of the personality form of life. But neither should one fail to recognize the counter-tendencies, much as these may be diverted and paralyzed in the joint effect that ultimately appears.

Life in a wider circle and interaction with it develop, in and of themselves, more consciousness of personality than arises in a narrower circle; this is so above all because it is precisely through the *alternation* of sensations, thoughts, and activities that personal-ity documents itself. The more uniformly and unwaveringly life progresses, and the less the extremes of sensate experience depart from an average level, the less strongly does the sensation of per-sonality arise; but the farther apart they stretch, and the more energetically they erupt, the more intensely does a human being sense himself as a personality. Just as duration can be determined only in the presence of alternation, and just as it is only the alter-nation of nonessential properties that throws constancy of sub-stance into bold relief, so too the ego is apparently perceived as the one constant in all the alternation of psychological con-tents, especially when these contents provide a particularly rich opportunity.

Personality is *not* a single immediate state, not a single quality or a single destiny, unique as this last may be; rather it is some-thing that we sense beyond these singularities, something grown into consciousness out of their experienced reality. This is so even if this retroactively generated personality, as it were, is only the sign, the *ratio cognoscendi* of a more deeply unitary individuality that lies at the determinative root of the diverse singularities, an individuality that we cannot become aware of directly, but only as the gradual experience of these multiple contents and variations.

As long as psychic stimulations, especially the stimulations of sensation, occur only in small number, the ego is fused with them and stays latently embedded in them; it rises above them only to the degree that, precisely via a fullness of dissimilarity, it becomes clear to our awareness that the ego itself is common to all this varia-tion. This is just the same as when a general concept cannot be abstracted out of single phenomena if we are familiar with only one or a few of their elaborations, but only if we know very many of them; and its abstractness and purity are all the greater as dissimilarity contrasts more distinctly with the generality. Now this alternation of the contents of the ego, which is what actually first poses the ego to consciousness as the stable pole in the play of psychic phenomena, is extraordinarily more lively within a large circle than it is for life in a narrower group. Stimulations of sensation, which are especially important for subjective ego consciousness, occur most where a highly differentiated individual stands amid other highly differentiated individuals, and where comparisons, frictions, and specialized relations release a profusion of reactions that remain latent in a narrower undifferentiated circle, but which in the larger circle, by virtue of their abundance and diversity, elicit the sensation of the ego as that which is absolutely "one's own."

Personal Autonomy and the Elaboration of Social Organs

A more indirect route by which the relatively large circle gains a special intrapersonal freedom and autonomy of being for its members is the elaboration of functional organs. This elaboration—which was investigated above—permits the originally direct interaction of individuals to crystallize and to be transferred to particular persons and complex structures. The more purely and completely this division of labor occurs—visible in the magnitude of the group's enlargement—the more the individual is emancipated from the interactions and coalescences that it replaces, and the more he is left to his own centripetal concerns and tendencies. The generation of functional organs is the means whereby the cohesion of the group is united with the greatest freedom of individuals.

To be sure, the organs bind each group element to themselves and thus to one another; but the decisive point is that the direct interactions that preceded this system drew the totality of a human being into special achievements that required disproportionate expenditures of energy. He who is not a judge for his whole life long, but only when the community is called together, not only is inhibited in his actual functioning, but is also encumbered in the execution of the judicial office by inappropriate conceptions and interests, in a manner entirely different from the professional judge. In contrast, he is only involved with the court in an advanced situation when his whole interest is really engaged in it. As long as each head of a household is a priest, he must function in that capacity whether he feels like it or not; but once there is a church with a professional priest, he enters it only when he feels the urge and thus really has his heart in it. As long as there is no diversification of production, the individual has to consume whatever happens to have been produced, even if very different needs and wishes have arisen in the meantime; but as soon as there are special producers for each need, he can search out whatever he might like so that he need not consume with mixed feelings.

Thus, the differentiation of social organs does not mean that individuals are detached from their connections with the whole, but rather means that they devote only the substantively relevant parts of their personalities to those bonds. The point at which the individual momentarily touches the totality or the structure of the whole no longer pulls parts of his personality into the relationship that do not belong there. It is with social organs—the consequences and distinguishing characteristics of the growth of the group—that the involvements become dissolved wherein the individual has to convey and yield into situations and activities elements of himself that do not belong to what he wants of himself.[4]

[4]   The remainder of this chapter consists of three sections: a "Note on the Analogy between Psychological and Social Patterns," a discussion of comparable analogies with intellectual patterns, and an analysis of the basic categories for organizing the data of human experience. The last of these appears in this volume as chapter 4.—Ed.

19

FASHION

1904

I

THE WHOLE HISTORY of society is reflected in the striking conflicts, the compromises, slowly won and quickly lost, between socialistic adaptation to society and individual departure from its demands. We have here the provincial forms, as it were, of those great antagonistic forces which represent the foundations of our individual destiny, and in which our outer as well as our inner life, our intellectual as well as our spiritual being, find the poles of their oscillations. Whether these forces be expressed philosophically in the contrast between cosmotheism and the doctrine of inherent differentiation and separate existence of every cosmic element, or whether they be grounded in practical conflict representing socialism on the one hand or individualism on the other, we have always to deal with the same fundamental form of duality which is manifested biologically in the contrast between heredity and variation. Of these the former represents the idea of generalization, of uniformity, of inactive similarity of the forms and contents of life; the latter stands for motion, for differentiation of separate elements, producing the restless changing of an individual life. The essential forms of life in the history of our race invariably show the effec-

---

Reprinted from "Fashion," *American Journal of Sociology* 62 (May 1957) ; originally published in *International Quarterly* (New York), 10 (1904). Translator unknown. Published in German as *Philosophie der Mode* (Berlin: Pan-Verlag, 1905), and in slightly revised and enlarged form in *Philosophische Kultur* (Leipzig: W. Klinkhardt, 1911).

tiveness of the two antagonistic principles. Each in its sphere attempts to combine the interest in duration, unity, and similarity with that in change, specialization, and peculiarity. It becomes self-evident that there is no institution, no law, no estate of life, which can uniformly satisfy the full demands of the two opposing principles. The only realization of this condition possible for humanity finds expression in constantly changing approximation, in ever retracted attempts and ever revived hopes. It is this that constitutes the whole wealth of our development, the whole incentive to advancement, the possibility of grasping a vast proportion of all the infinite combinations of the elements of human character, a proportion that is approaching the unlimited itself.

Within the social embodiments of these contrasts, one side is generally maintained by the psychological tendency towards imitation. The charm of imitation in the first place is to be found in the fact that it makes possible an expedient test of power, which, however, requires no great personal and creative application, but is displayed easily and smoothly, because its content is a given quantity. We might define it as the child of thought and thoughtlessness. It affords the pregnant possibility of continually extending the greatest creations of the human spirit, without the aid of the forces which were originally the very condition of their birth. Imitation, furthermore, gives to the individual the satisfaction of not standing alone in his actions. Whenever we imitate, we transfer not only the demand for creative activity, but also the responsibility for the action from ourselves to another. Thus the individual is freed from the worry of choosing and appears simply as a creature of the group, as a vessel of the social contents. . . .

Thus we see that imitation in all the instances where it is a productive factor represents one of the fundamental tendencies of our character, namely, that which contents itself with similarity, with uniformity, with the adaptation of the special to the general, and accentuates the constant element in change. Conversely, whereever prominence is given to change, wherever individual differentiation, independence, and relief from generality are sought, there imitation is the negative and obstructive principle. The principle of adherence to given formulas, of being and of acting like others, is irreconcilably opposed to the striving to advance to ever new and individual forms of life; for this very reason social life represents a battle-ground, of which every inch is stubbornly contested, and social institutions may be looked upon as the peace-treaties, in which the constant antagonism of both principles has been reduced externally to a form of coöperation.

II

The vital conditions of fashion as a universal phenomenon in the history of our race are circumscribed by these conceptions. Fashion is the imitation of a given example and satisfies the demand for social adaptation; it leads the individual upon the road which all travel, it furnishes a general condition, which resolves the conduct of every individual into a mere example. At the same time it satisfies in no less degree the need of differentiation, the tendency towards dissimilarity, the desire for change and contrast, on the one hand by a constant change of contents, which gives to the fashion of today an individual stamp as opposed to that of yesterday and of to-morrow, on the other hand because fashions differ for different classes—the fashions of the upper stratum of society are never identical with those of the lower; in fact, they are abandoned by the former as soon as the latter prepares to appropriate them. Thus fashion represents nothing more than one of the many forms of life by the aid of which we seek to combine in uniform spheres of activity the tendency towards social equalization with the desire for individual differentiation and change. Every phase of the conflicting pair strives visibly beyond the degree of satisfaction that any fashion offers to an absolute control of the sphere of life in question. If we should study the history of fashions (which hitherto have been examined only from the view-point of the development of their contents) in connection with their importance for the form of the social process, we should find that it reflects the history of the attempts to adjust the satisfaction of the two counter-tendencies more and more perfectly to the condition of the existing individual and social culture. The various psychological elements in fashion all conform to this fundamental principle.

Fashion, as noted above, is a product of class distinction and operates like a number of other forms, honor especially, the double function of which consists in revolving within a given circle and at the same time emphasizing it as separate from others. Just as the frame of a picture characterizes the work of art inwardly as a coherent, homogeneous, independent entity and at the same time outwardly severs all direct relations with the surrounding space, just as the uniform energy of such forms cannot be expressed unless we determine the double effect, both inward and outward, so honor owes its character, and above all its moral rights, to the fact that the individual in his personal honor at the same time represents and maintains that of his social circle and his class. These moral rights, however, are frequently considered unjust by those without the pale. Thus fashion on the one hand signifies union with those in the same class, the uniformity of a circle characterized by it, and, *uno actu*, the exclusion of all other groups.

Union and segregation are the two fundamental functions which are here inseparably united, and one of which, although or because it forms a logical contrast to the other, becomes the condition of its realization. Fashion is merely a product of social demands, even though the individual object which it creates or recreates may represent a more or less individual need. This is clearly proved by the fact that very frequently not the slightest reason can be found for the creations of fashion from the standpoint of an objective, aesthetic, or other expediency. While in general our wearing apparel is really adapted to our needs, there is not a trace of expediency in the method by which fashion dictates, for example, whether wide or narrow trousers, colored or black scarfs shall be worn. As a rule the material justification for an action coincides with its general adoption, but in the case of fashion there is a complete separation of the two elements, and there remains for the individual only this general acceptance as the deciding motive to appropriate it. Judging from the ugly and repugnant things that are sometimes in vogue, it would seem as though fashion were desirous of exhibiting its power by getting us to adopt the most atrocious things for its sake alone. The absolute indifference of fashion to the material standards of life is well illustrated by the way in which it recommends something appropriate in one instance, something abstruse in another, and something materially and aesthetically quite indifferent in a third. The only motivations with which fashion is concerned are formal social ones. The reason why even aesthetically impossible styles seem *distingué*, elegant, and artistically tolerable when affected by persons who carry them to the extreme, is that the persons who do this are generally the most elegant and pay the greatest attention to their personal appearance, so that under any circumstances we would get the impression of something *distingué* and aesthetically cultivated. This impression we credit to the questionable element of fashion, the latter appealing to our consciousness as the new and consequently most conspicuous feature of the *tout ensemble*.

Fashion occasionally will affect objectively determined subjects such as religious faith, scientific interests, even socialism and individualism; but it does not become operative as fashion until these subjects can be considered independent of the deeper human motives from which they have risen. For this reason the rule of fashion becomes in such fields unendurable. We therefore see that there is good reason why externals—clothing, social conduct, amusements—constitute the specific field of fashion, for here no dependence is placed on really vital motives of human action. It is the field which we can most easily relinquish to the bent towards imitation, which it would be a sin to follow in important questions. We encounter here a close connection between the consciousness of personality and that of the material forms of life, a connection that runs all through history. The more objective our view of life has become in the last centuries, the more it has stripped the picture of nature of all subjective and anthropomorphic elements, and the more sharply has the conception of individual personality become defined. The social regulation of our inner and outer life is a sort of embryo condition, in which the contrasts of the purely personal and the purely objective are differentiated, the action being synchronous and reciprocal. Therefore wherever man appears essentially as a social being we observe neither strict objectivity in the view of life nor absorption and independence in the consciousness of personality.

Social forms, apparel, aesthetic judgment, the whole style of human expression, are constantly transformed by fashion, in such a way, however, that fashion—*i.e.*, the latest fashion—in all these things affects only the upper classes. Just as soon as the lower classes begin to copy their style, thereby crossing the line of demarcation the upper classes have drawn and destroying the uniformity of their coherence, the upper classes turn away from this style and adopt a new one, which in its turn differentiates them from the masses; and thus the game goes merrily on. Naturally the lower classes look and strive towards the upper, and they encounter the least resistance in those fields which are subject to the whims of fashion; for it is here that mere external imitation is most readily applied. The same process is at work as between the different sets within the upper classes, although it is not always as visible here as it is, for example, between mistress and maid. Indeed, we may often observe that the more nearly one set has approached another, the more frantic becomes the desire for imitation from below and the seeking for the new from above. The increase of wealth is bound to hasten the process considerably and render it visible, because the objects of fashion, embracing as they do the externals of life, are most accessible to the mere call of money, and conformity to the higher set is more easily acquired here than in fields which demand an individual test that gold and silver cannot affect.

We see, therefore, that in addition to the element of imitation the element of demarcation constitutes an important factor of fashion. This is especially noticeable wherever the social structure does not include any superimposed groups, in which case fashion asserts itself in neighboring groups. Among primitive peoples we often find that closely connected groups living under exactly similar conditions develop sharply differentiated fashions, by means of which each group establishes uniformity within, as well as difference without, the prescribed set. On the other hand, there exists a wide-spread predilection for importing fashions from without, and such foreign fashions assume a greater value within the circle, simply because they did not originate there. The prophet Zephaniah expressed his indignation at the aristocrats who affected imported apparel. As a matter of fact the exotic origin of fashions seems strongly to favor the exclusiveness of the groups which adopt them. Because of their external origin, these imported fashions create a special and significant form of socialization, which arises through mutual relation to a point without the circle. It sometimes appears as though social elements, just like the axes of vision, converge best at a point that is not too near. The currency, or more precisely the medium of exchange among primitive races, often consists of objects that are brought in from without. On the Solomon Islands, and at Ibo on the Niger, for example, there exists a regular industry for the manufacture of money from shells, etc., which are not employed as a medium of exchange in the place itself, but in neighboring districts, to which they are exported. Paris modes are frequently created with the sole intention of setting a fashion elsewhere.

This motive of foreignness, which fashion employs in its socializing endeavors, is restricted to higher civilization, because novelty, which foreign origin guarantees in extreme form, is often regarded by primitive races as an evil. This is certainly one of the reasons why primitive conditions of life favor a correspondingly infrequent change of fashions. The savage is afraid of strange appearances; the difficulties and dangers that beset his career cause him to scent danger in anything new which he does not understand and which he cannot assign to a familiar category. Civilization, however, transforms this affectation into its very opposite. Whatever is exceptional, bizarre, or conspicuous, or whatever departs from the customary norm, exercises a peculiar charm upon the man of culture, entirely independent of its material justification. The removal of the feeling of insecurity with reference to all things new was accomplished by the progress of civilization. At the same time it may be the old inherited prejudice, although it has become purely formal and unconscious, which, in connection with the present feeling of security, produces this piquant interest in exceptional and odd things. For this reason the fashions of the upper classes develop their power of exclusion against the lower in proportion as general culture advances, at least until the mingling of the classes and the leveling effect of democracy exert a counter-influence.

Fashion plays a more conspicuous *rôle* in modern times, because the differences in our standards of life have become so much more strongly accentuated, for the more numerous and the more sharply drawn these differences are, the greater the opportunities for emphasizing them at every turn. In innumerable instances this cannot be accomplished by passive inactivity, but only by the development of forms established by fashion; and this has become all the more pronounced since legal restrictions prescribing various forms of apparel and modes of life for different classes have been removed.

III

Two social tendencies are essential to the establishment of fashion, namely, the need of union on the one hand and the need of isolation on the other. Should one of these be absent, fashion will not be formed—its sway will abruptly end. Consequently the lower classes possess very few modes and those they have are seldom specific; for this reason the modes of primitive races are much more stable than ours. Among primitive races the socializing impulse is much more powerfully developed than the differentiating impulse. For, no matter how decisively the groups may be separated from one another, separation is for the most part hostile in such a way that the very relation the rejection of which within the classes of civilized races makes fashion reasonable, is absolutely lacking. Segregation by means of differences in clothing, manners, taste, etc., is expedient only where the danger of absorption and obliteration exists, as is the case among highly civilized nations. Where these differences do not exist, where we have an absolute antagonism, as for example between not directly friendly groups of primitive races, the development of fashion has no sense at all.

It is interesting to observe how the prevalence of the socializing impulse in primitive peoples affects various institutions, such as the dance. It has been noted quite generally that the dances of primitive races exhibit a remarkable uniformity in arrangement and rhythm. The dancing group feels and acts like a uniform organism; the dance forces and accustoms a number of individuals, who are usually driven to and fro without rime or reason by vacillating conditions and needs of life, to be guided by a common impulse and a single common motive. Even making allowances for the tremendous difference in the outward appearance of the dance, we are dealing here with the same element that appears in the socializing force of fashion. Movement, time, rhythm of the gestures, are all undoubtedly influenced largely by what is worn: similarly dressed persons exhibit relative similarity in their actions. This is of especial value in modern life with its individualistic diffusion, while in the case of primitive races the effect produced is directed within and is therefore not dependent upon changes of fashion. Among primitive races fashions will be less numerous and more stable because the need of new impressions and forms of life, quite apart from their social effect, is far less pressing. Changes in fashion reflect the dulness of nervous impulses: the more nervous the age, the more rapidly its fashions change, simply because the desire for differentiation, one of the most important elements of all fashion, goes hand in hand with the weakening of nervous energy. This fact in itself is one of the reasons why the real seat of fashion is found among the upper classes. . . .

The very character of fashion demands that it should be exercised at one time only by a portion of the given group, the great majority being merely on the road to adopting it. As soon as an example has been universally adopted, that is, as soon as anything that was originally done only by a few has really come to be practiced by all—as is the case in certain portions of our apparel and in various forms of social conduct—we no longer speak of fashion. As fashion spreads, it gradually goes to its doom. The distinctiveness which in the early stages of a set fashion assures for it a certain distribution is destroyed as the fashion spreads, and as this element wanes, the fashion also is bound to die. By reason of this peculiar play between the tendency towards universal acceptation and the destruction of its very purpose to which this general adoption leads, fashion includes a peculiar attraction of limitation, the attraction of a simultaneous beginning and end, the charm of novelty coupled to that of transitoriness. The attractions of both poles of the phenomena meet in fashion, and show also here that they belong together unconditionally, although, or rather because, they are contradictory in their very nature. Fashion always occupies the dividing-line between the past and the future, and consequently conveys a stronger feeling of the present, at least while it is at its height, than most other phenomena. What we call the present is usually nothing more than a combination of a fragment of the past with a fragment of the future. Attention is called to the present less often than colloquial usage, which is rather liberal in its employment of the word, would lead us to believe.

Few phenomena of social life possess such a pointed curve of consciousness as does fashion. As soon as the social consciousness attains to the highest point designated by fashion, it marks the beginning of the end for the latter. This transitory character of fashion, however, does not on the whole degrade it, but adds a new element of attraction. At all events an object does not suffer degradation by being called fashionable, unless we reject it with disgust or wish to debase it for other, material reasons, in which case, of course, fashion becomes an idea of value. In the practice of life anything else similarly new and suddenly disseminated is not called fashion, when we are convinced of its continuance and its material jutification. If, on the other hand, we feel certain that the fact will vanish as rapidly as it came, then we call it fashion. We can discover one of the reasons why in these latter days fashion exercises such a powerful influence on our consciousness in the circumstance that the great, permanent, unquestionable convictions are continually losing strength, as a consequence of which the transitory and vacillating elements of life acquire more room for the display of their activity. The break with the past, which, for more than a century, civilized mankind has been laboring unceasingly to bring about, makes the consciousness turn more and more to the present. This accentuation of the present evidently at the same time emphasizes the element of change, and a class will turn to fashion in all fields, by no means only in that of apparel, in proportion to the degree in which it supports the given civilizing tendency. It may almost be considered a sign of the increased power of fashion, that it has overstepped the bounds of its original domain, which comprised only personal externals, and has acquired an increasing influence over taste, over theoretical convictions, and even over the moral foundations of life.

IV

From the fact that fashion as such can never be generally in vogue, the individual derives the satisfaction of knowing that as adopted by him it still represents something special and striking, while at the same time he feels inwardly supported by a set of persons who are striving for the same thing, not as in the case of other social satisfactions, by a set actually doing the same thing. The fashionable person is regarded with mingled feelings of approval and envy; we envy him as an individual, but approve of him as a member of a set or group. Yet even this envy has a peculiar coloring. There is a shade of envy which includes a species of ideal participation in the envied object itself. An instructive example of this is furnished by the conduct of the poor man who gets a glimpse of the feast of his rich neighbor. The moment we envy an object or a person, we are no longer absolutely excluded from it; some relation or other has been established—between both the same psychic content now exists—although in entirely different categories and forms of sensations. This quiet personal usurpation of the envied property contains a kind of antidote, which occasionally counter-acts the evil effects of this feeling of envy. The contents of fashion afford an especially good chance of the development of this conciliatory shade of envy, which also gives to the envied person a better conscience because of his satisfaction over his good fortune. This is due to the fact that these contents are not, as many other psychic contents are, denied absolutely to any one, for a change of fortune, which is never entirely out of the question, may play them into the hands of an individual who had previously been confined to the state of envy.

From all this we see that fashion furnishes an ideal field for individuals with dependent natures, whose self-consciousness, however, requires a certain amount of prominence, attention, and singularity. Fashion raises even the unimportant individual by making him the representative of a class, the embodiment of a joint spirit. And here again we observe the curious intermixture of antagonistic values. Speaking broadly, it is characteristic of a standard set by a general body, that its acceptance by any one individual does not call attention to him; in other words, a positive adoption of a given norm signifies nothing. Whoever keeps the laws the breaking of which is punished by the penal code, whoever lives up to the social forms prescribed by his class, gains no conspicuousness or notoriety. The slightest infraction or opposition, however, is immediately noticed and places the individual in an exceptional position by calling the attention of the public to his action. All such norms do not assume positive importance for the individual until he begins to depart from them. It is peculiarly characteristic of fashion that it renders possible a social obedience, which at the same time is a form of individual differentiation. Fashion does this because in its very nature it represents a standard that can never be accepted by all. While fashion postulates a certain amount of general acceptance, it nevertheless is not without significance in the characterization of the individual, for it emphasizes his personality not only through omission but also through observance. In the dude the social demands of fashion appear exaggerated to such a degree that they completely assume an individualistic and peculiar character. It is characteristic of the dude that he carries the elements of a particular fashion to an extreme; when pointed shoes are in style, he wears shoes that resemble the prow of a ship; when high collars are all the rage, he wears collars that come up to his ears; when scientific lectures are fashionable, you cannot find him anywhere else, etc., etc. Thus he represents something distinctly individual, which consists in the quantitative intensification of such elements as are qualitatively common property of the given set of class. He leads the way, but all travel the same road. Representing as he does the most recently conquered heights of public taste, he seems to be marching at the head of the general procession. In reality, however, what is so frequently true of the relation between individuals and groups applies also to him: as a matter of fact, the leader allows himself to be led.

Democratic times unquestionably favor such a condition to a

remarkable degree, so much so that even Bismarck and other very prominent party leaders in constitutional governments have emphasized the fact that inasmuch as they are leaders of a group, they are bound to follow it. The spirit of democracy causes persons to seek the dignity and sensation of command in this manner; it tends to a confusion and ambiguity of sensations, which fail to distinguish between ruling the mass and being ruled by it. The conceit of the dude is thus the caricature of a confused understanding, fostered by democracy, of the relation between the individual and the public. Undeniably, however, the dude, through the conspicuousness gained in a purely quantitative way, but expressed in a difference of quality, represents a state of equilibrium between the social and the individualizing impulses which is really original. This explains the extreme to which otherwise thoroughly intelligent and prominent persons frequently resort in matters of fashion, an extreme that outwardly appears so abstruse. It furnishes a combination of relations to things and men, which under ordinary circumstances appear more divided. It is not only the mixture of individual peculiarity with social equality, but, in a more practical vein, as it were, it is the mingling of the sensation of rulership with submission, the influence of which is here at work. In other words, we have here the mixing of a masculine and a feminine principle. The very fact that this process goes on in the field of fashion only in an ideal attenuation, as it were, the fact that only the form of both elements is embodied in a content indifferent in itself, may lend to fashion a special attraction, especially for sensitive natures that do not care to concern themselves with robust reality. From an objective standpoint, life according to fashion consists of a balancing of destruction and upbuilding; its content acquires characteristics by destruction of an earlier form; it possesses a peculiar uniformity, in which the satisfying of the love of destruction and of the demand for positive elements can no longer be separated from each other.

Inasmuch as we are dealing here not with the importance of a single fact or a single satisfaction, but rather with the play between two contents and their mutual distinction, it becomes evident that the same combination which extreme obedience to fashion acquires can be won also by opposition to it. Whoever consciously avoids following the fashion does not attain the consequent sensation of individualization through any real individual qualification, but rather through mere negation of the social example. If obedience to fashion consists in imitation of such an example, conscious neglect of fashion represents similar imitation, but under an inverse sign. The latter, however, furnishes just as fair testimony of the power of the social tendency, which demands our dependence in some positive or negative manner. The man who consciously pays no heed to fashion accepts its forms just as much as the dude does, only he embodies it in another category, the former in that of exaggeration, the latter in that of negation. Indeed, it occasionally happens that it becomes fashionable in whole bodies of a large class to depart altogether from the standards set by fashion. This constitutes a most curious social-psychological complication, in which the tendency towards individual conspicuousness primarily rests content with a mere inversion of the social imitation and secondly draws in strength from approximation to a similarly characterized narrower circle. If the club-haters organized themselves into a club, it would not be logically more impossible and psychologically more possible than the above case. Similarly atheism has been made into a religion, embodying the same fanaticism, the same intolerance, the same satisfying of the needs of the soul that are embraced in religion proper. Freedom, likewise, after having put a stop to tyranny, frequently becomes no less tyrannical and arbitrary. So the phenomenon of conscious departure from fashion illustrates how ready the fundamental forms of human character are to accept the total antithesis of contents and to show their strength and their attraction in the negation of the very thing to whose acceptance they seemed a moment before irrevocably committed. It is often absolutely impossible to tell whether the elements of personal strength or of personal weakness preponderate in the group of causes that lead to such a departure from fashion. It may result from a desire not to make common cause with the mass, a desire that has at its basis not independence of the mass, to be sure, but yet an inherently sovereign position with respect to the latter. However, it may be due to a delicate sensibility, which causes the individual to fear that he will be unable to maintain his individuality in case he adopts the forms, the tastes, and the customs of the general public. Such opposition is by no means always a sign of personal strength.

V

The fact that fashion expresses and at the same time emphasizes the tendency towards equalization and individualization, and the desire for imitation and conspicuousness, perhaps explains why it is that women, broadly speaking, are its staunchest adherents. Scientific discretion should caution us against forming judgments about woman "in the plural." At the same time it may be said of woman in a general way, whether the statements be justified in every case or not, that her psychological characteristic in so far as it differs from that of man, consists in a lack of differentiation, in a greater similarity among the different members of her sex, in a stricter adherence to the social average. Whether on the final heights of modern culture, the facts of which have not yet furnished a contribution to the formation of this general conviction, there will be a change in the relation between men and women, a change that may result in a complete reversal of the above distinction, I do not care to discuss, inasmuch as we are concerned here with more comprehensive historical averages. The relation and the weakness of her social position, to which woman has been doomed during the far greater portion of history, however, explains her strict regard for custom, for the generally accepted and approved forms of life, for all that is proper. A weak person steers clear of individualization; he avoids dependence upon self with its responsibilities and the necessity of defending himself unaided. He finds protection only in the typical form of life, which prevents the strong from exercising his exceptional powers. But resting on the firm foundation of custom, of what is generally accepted, woman strives anxiously for all the relative individualization and personal conspicuousness that remains.

Fashion furnishes this very combination in the happiest manner, for we have here on the one hand a field of general imitation, the individual floating in the broadest social current, relieved of responsibility for his tastes and his actions, yet on the other hand we have a certain conspicuousness, an emphasis, an individual accentuation of the personality. It seems that there exists for each class of human beings, probably for each individual, a definite quantitative relation between the tendency towards individualization and the desire to be merged in the group, so that when the satisfying of one tendency is denied in a certain field of life, he seeks another, in which he then fulfills the measure which he requires. Thus it seems as though fashion were the valve through which woman's craving for some measure of conspicuousness and individual prominence finds vent, when its satisfaction is denied her in other fields.

During the fourteenth and fifteenth centuries Germany exhibits an unusually strong development of individuality. Great inroads were made upon the collectivistic regulations of the Middle Ages by the freedom of the individual. Woman, however, took no part in this individualistic development: the freedom of personal action and self-improvement were still denied her. She sought redress by adopting the most extravagant and hypertrophic styles in dress. On the other hand, in Italy during the same epoch woman was given full play for the exercise of individuality. The woman of the Renaissance possessed opportunities of culture, of external activity, of personal differentiation such as were not offered her for many centuries thereafter. In the upper classes of society, especially, education and freedom of action were almost identical for both sexes. It is not astonishing, therefore, that no particularly extravagant Italian female fashions should have come down to us from that period. The need of exercising individuality in this field was absent, because the tendency embodied therein found sufficient vent in other spheres. In general the history of woman in the outer as well as the inner life, individually as well as collectively, exhibits such a comparatively great uniformity, leveling and similarity, that she requires a more lively activity at least in the sphere of fashion, which is nothing more nor less than change, in order to add an attraction to herself and her life for her own feeling as well as for others. Just as in the case of individualism and collectivism, there exists between the uniformity and the change of the contents of life a definite proportion of needs, which is tossed to and fro in the different fields and seeks to balance refusal in one by consent, however acquired, in another. On the whole, we may say that woman is a more faithful creature than man. Now fidelity, expressing as it does the uniformity and regularity of one's nature only in the direction of the feelings, demands a more lively change in the outward surrounding spheres in order to establish the balance in the tendencies of life referred to above. Man, on the other hand, a rather unfaithful being, who does not ordinarily restrict dependence to a relation of the feelings with the same implicitness and concentration of all interests of life to a single one, is consequently less in need of an outward form of change. Non-acceptance of changes in external fields, and indifference toward fashions in outward appearance are specifically a male quality, not because man is the more uniform but because he is the more many-sided creature and for that reason can get along better without such outward changes. Therefore, the emancipated woman of the present, who seeks to imitate in the good as well as perhaps also in the bad sense the whole differentiation, personality and activity of the male sex, lays particular stress on her indifference to fashion.

In a certain sense fashion gives woman a compensation for her lack of position in a class based on a calling or profession. The man who has become absorbed in a calling has entered a relatively uniform class, within which he resembles many others, and is thus often only an illustration of the conception of this class or calling. On the other hand, as though to compensate him for this absorption, he is invested with the full importance and the objective as well as social power of this class. To his individual importance is added that of his class, which often covers the defects and deficiencies of his purely personal character. The individuality of the class often supplements or replaces that of the member. This identical thing fashion accomplishes with other means. Fashion also supplements a person's lack of importance, his inability to individualize his existence purely by his own unaided efforts, by enabling him to join a set characterized and singled out in the public consciousness by fashion alone. Here also, to be sure, the personality as such is reduced to a general formula, yet this formula itself, from a social standpoint, posssesses an individual tinge, and thus makes up through the social way what is denied to the personality in a purely individual way. The fact that the demi-monde is so frequently a pioneer in matters of fashion is due to its peculiarly uprooted form of life. The pariah existence to which society condemns the demi-monde produces an open or latent hatred against everything that has the sanction of law, of every permanent institution, a hatred that finds its relatively most innocent and aesthetic expression in the striving for ever new forms of appearance. In this continual striving for new, previously unheard-of fashions, in the regardlessness with which the one that is most diametrically opposed to the existing one is passionately adopted, there lurks an aesthetic expression of the desire for destruction, which seems to be an element peculiar to all that lead this pariah-like existence, so long as they are not completely enslaved within.

When we examine the final and most subtle impulses of the soul, which it is difficult to express in words, we find that they also exhibit this antagonistic play of the fundamental human tendencies. These latter seek to regain their continually lost balance by means of ever new proportions, and they succeed here through the reflection which fashion occasionally throws into the most delicate and tender spiritual processes. Fashion insists, to be sure, on treating all individualities alike, yet it is always done in such a way that one's whole nature is never affected. Fashion always continues to be regarded as something external, even in spheres outside of mere styles of apparel, for the form of mutability in which it is presented to the individual is under all circumstances a contrast to the stability of the ego-feeling. Indeed, the latter, through this contrast, must become conscious of its relative duration. The changeableness of those contents can express itself as mutability and develop its attraction only through this enduring element. But for this very reason fashion always stands, as I have pointed out, at the periphery of personality, which regards itself as a *pièce de résistance* for fashion, or at least can do so when called upon.

It is this phase of fashion that is received by sensitive and peculiar persons, who use it as a sort of mask. They consider blind obedience to the standards of the general public in all externals as the conscious and desired means of reserving their personal feeling and their taste, which they are eager to reserve for themselves alone, in such a way that they do not care to enter in an appearance that is visible to all. It is therefore a feeling of modesty and reserve which causes many a delicate nature to seek refuge in the leveling cloak of fashion; such individuals do not care to resort to a peculiarity in externals for fear of perhaps betraying a peculiarity of their innermost soul. We have here a triumph of the soul over the actual circumstances of existence, which must be considered one of the highest and finest victories, at least as far as form is concerned, for the reasons that the enemy himself is transformed into a servant, and that the very thing the personality seemed to suppress is voluntarily seized, because the leveling suppression is here transferred to the external spheres of life in such a way that it furnishes a veil and a protection for everything spiritual and now all the more free. This corresponds exactly to the triviality of expression and conversation through which very sensitive and retiring people, especially women, often deceive one about the individual depth of the soul. It is one of the pleasures of the judge of human nature, although somewhat cruel withal, to feel the anxiousness with which woman clings to the commonplace contents and forms of social intercourse. The impossibility of enticing her beyond the most banal and trite forms of expression, which often drives one to despair, in innumerable instances signifies nothing more than a barricade of the soul, an iron mask that conceals the real features and can furnish this service only by means of a wholly uncompromising separation of the feelings and the externals of life.

VI

All feeling of shame rests upon isolation of the individual; it arises whenever stress is laid upon the *ego*, whenever the attention of a circle is drawn to such an individual—in reality or only in his imagination—which at the same time is felt to be in some way incongruous. For that reason retiring and weak natures particularly incline to feelings of shame. The moment they step into the centre of general attention, the moment they make themselves conspicuous in any way, a painful oscillation between emphasis and withdrawal of the *ego* becomes manifest. Inasmuch as the individual departure from a generality as the source of the feeling of shame is quite independent of the particular content upon the basis of which it occurs, one is frequently ashamed of good and noble things. The fact that the commonplace is good form in society, in the narrower sense of the term, is due not only to a mutual regard, which causes it to be considered bad taste to make one's self conspicuous through some individual, singular expression that not every one can repeat, but also to the fear of that feeling of shame which as it were forms a self-inflicted punishment for the departure from the form and activity similar for all and equally accessible to all. By reason of its peculiar inner structure, fashion furnishes a departure of the individual, which is always looked upon as proper. No matter how extravagant the form of appearance or manner of expression, as long as it is fashionable, it is protected against those painful reflections which the individual otherwise experiences when he becomes the object of attention. All concerned actions are characterized by the loss of this feeling of shame. As a member of a mass the individual will do many things which would have aroused unconquerable repugnance in his soul had they been suggested to him alone. It is one of the strangest social-psychological phenomena, in which this characteristic of concerted action is well exemplified, that many fashions tolerate breaches of modesty which, if suggested to the individual alone, would be angrily repudiated. But as dictates of fashion they find ready acceptance. The feeling of shame is eradicated in matters of fashion, because it represents a united action, in the same way that the feeling of responsibility is extinguished in the participants of a crime committed by a mob, each member of which, if left to himself, would shrink from violence.

Fashion also is only one of the forms by the aid of which men seek to save their inner freedom all the more completely by sacrificing externals to enslavement by the general public. Freedom and dependence also belong to those antagonistic pairs, whose ever

renewed strife and endless mobility give to life much more pi-
quancy and permit of a much greater breadth and development,
than a permanent, unchangeable balance of the two could give.
Schopenhauer held that each person's cup of life is filled with a
certain quantity of joy and woe, and that this measure can neither
remain empty nor be filled to overflowing, but only changes its
form in all the differentiations and vacillations of internal and external relations. In the same way and much less mystically we may
observe in each period, in each class, and in each individual, either
a really permanent proportion of dependence and freedom, or at
least the longing for it, whereas we can only change the fields over
which they are distributed. It is the task of the higher life, to be
sure, to arrange this distribution in such a way that the other values
of existence require thereby the possibility of the most favorable
development. The same quantity of dependence and freedom may
at one time help to increase the moral, intellectual, and aesthetic
values to the highest point and at another time, without any change
in quantity but merely in distribution, it may bring about the exact
opposite of this success. Speaking broadly, we may say that the
most favorable result for the aggregate value of life will be obtained when all unavoidable dependence is transferred more and
more to the periphery, to the externals of life. Perhaps Goethe, in
his later period, is the most eloquent example of a wholly great life,
for by means of his adaptability in all externals, his strict regard
for form, his willing obedience to the conventions of society, he
attained a maximum of inner freedom, a complete saving of the
centres of life from the touch of the unavoidable quantity of dependence. In this respect fashion is also a social form of marvelous
expediency, because, like the law, it affects only the externals of
life, only those sides of life which are turned to society. It provides
us with a formula by means of which we can unequivocally attest
our dependence upon what is generally adopted, our obedience to
the standards established by our time, our class, and our narrower
circle, and enables us to withdraw the freedom given us in life from
externals and concentrate it more and more in our innermost
natures.

Within the individual soul the relations of equalizing unification and individual demarcation are to a certain extent repeated. The antagonism of the tendencies which produces fashion is transferred as far as form is concerned in an entirely similar manner also to those inner relations of many individuals, who have nothing whatever to do with social obligations. The instances to which I have just referred exhibit the oft-mentioned parallelism with which the relations between individuals are repeated in the correlation between the psychic elements of the individual himself. With more or less intention the individual often establishes a mode of conduct or a style for himself, which by reason of the rhythm of its rise, sway, and decline becomes characterized in fashion. Young people especially often exhibit a sudden strangeness in behavior; an unexpected, objectively unfounded interest arises and governs their whole sphere of consciousness, only to disappear in the same irrational manner. We might call this a personal fashion, which forms an analogy to social fashion. The former is supported on the one hand by the individual demand for differentiation and thereby attests to the same impulse that is active in the formation of social fashion. The need of imitation, of similarity, of the blending of the individual in the mass, are here satisfied purely within the individual himself, namely through the concentration of the personal consciousness upon this one form or content, as well as through the imitation of his own self, as it were, which here takes the place of imitation of others. Indeed, we might say that we attain in this case an even more pronounced concentration, an even more intimate support of the individual contents of life by a central uniformity than we do where the fashion is common property.

A certain intermediate stage is often realized within narrow circles between individual mode and personal fashion. Ordinary persons frequently adopt some expression, which they apply at every opportunity—in common with as many as possible in the same set—to all manner of suitable or unsuitable objects. In one respect this is a group fashion, yet in another respect it is really individual, for its express purpose consists in having the individual make the totality of his circle of ideas subject to this formula. Brutal violence is hereby committed against the individuality of things; all variation is destroyed by the curious supremacy of this one category of expressions, for example, when we designate all things that happen to please us for any reason whatsoever as "*chic*," or "smart," even though the objects in question may bear no relation whatsoever to the fields to which these expressions belong. In this manner the inner world of the individual is made subject to fashion, and thus reflects the aspects of the external group governed by fashion, chiefly by reason of the objective absurdity of such individual manners, which illustrate the power of the formal, unifying element over the objective rational element. In the same way many persons and circles only ask that they be uniformly governed, without thinking to inquire into the nature or value of the authority. It cannot be denied that inasmuch as violence is done to objects treated in this way, and inasmuch as they are all transformed uniformly to a category of our own making, the individual really renders an arbitrary decision with respect to these objects, he acquires an individual feeling of power, and thus the *ego* is strongly emphasized.

The fact that appears here in the light of a caricature is everywhere noticeable to a less pronounced degree in the relation of persons to things. Only the noblest persons seek the greatest depth and power of their *ego* by respecting the individuality inherent in things. The hostility which the soul bears to the supremacy, independence, and indifference of the universe gives rise—beside the loftiest and most valuable strivings of humanity—to attempts to oppress things externally; the *ego* offers violence to them not by absorbing and molding their powers, not by recognizing their individuality only to make it serviceable, but by forcing it to bow outwardly to some subjective formula. To be sure the *ego* has not in reality gained control of the things, but only of its own false and fanciful conception of them. The feeling of power, however, which originates thus, betrays its lack of foundation and its fanciful origin by the rapidity with which such expressions pass by. It is just as illusionary as the feeling of the uniformity of being, which springs for the moment from this formulating of all expressions. As a matter of fact the man who carries out a schematic similarity of conduct under all circumstances is by no means the most consistent, the one asserting the *ego* most regularly against the universe.

On account of the difference in the given factors of life, a difference of conduct will be essential whenever the same germ of the *ego* is to prevail uniformly over all, just as identical answers in a calculation into which two factors enter, of which one continually varies, cannot be secured if the other remains unchanged, but only if the latter undergoes variations corresponding to the changes of the former.

VII

We have seen that in fashion the different dimensions of life, so to speak, acquire a peculiar convergence, that fashion is a complex structure in which all the leading antithetical tendencies of the soul are represented in one way or another. This will make clear that the total rhythm in which the individuals and the groups move will exert an important influence also upon their relation to fashion, that the various strata of a group, altogether aside from their different contents of life and external possibilities, will bear different relations to fashion simply because their contents of life are evolved either in conservative or in rapidly varying form. On the one hand the lower classes are difficult to put in motion and they develop slowly. A very clear and instructive example of this may be found in the attitude of the lower classes in England towards the Danish and the Norman conquests. On the whole the changes brought about affected the upper classes only; in the lower classes we find such a degree of fidelity to arrangements and forms of life that the whole continuity of English life which was retained through all those national vicissitudes rests entirely upon the persistence and immovable conservatism of the lower classes. The upper classes, however, were most intensely affected and transformed by new influences, just as the upper branches of a tree are most responsive to the movements of the air. The highest classes, as everyone knows, are the most conservative, and frequently enough they are even archaic. They dread every motion and change, not because they have an antipathy for the contents or because the latter are injurious to them, but simply because it is change and because they regard every modification of the whole as suspicious and dangerous. No change can bring them additional power, and every change can give them something to fear, but nothing to hope for. The real variability of historical life is therefore vested in the middle classes, and for this reason the history of social and cultural movements has fallen into an entirely different pace since the *tiers état* assumed control. For this reason fashion, which represents the variable and contrasting forms of life, has since then become much broader and more animated, and also because of the transformation in the immediate political life, for man requires an ephemeral tyrant the moment he has rid himself of the absolute and permanent one. The frequent change of fashion represents a tremendous subjugation of the individual and in that respect forms one of the essential complements of the increased social and political freedom. A form of life, for the contents of which the moment of acquired height marks the beginning of decline, belongs to a class which is inherently much more variable, much more restless in its rhythms than the lowest classes with their dull, unconscious conservatism, and the highest classes with their consciously desired conservatism. Classes and individuals who demand constant change, because the rapidity of their development gives them the advantage over others, find in fashion something that keeps pace with their own soul-movements. Social advance above all is favorable to the rapid change of fashion, for it capacitates lower classes so much for imitation of upper ones, and thus the process characterized above, according to which every higher set throws aside a fashion the moment a lower set adopts it, has acquired a breadth and activity never dreamed of before.

This fact has important bearing on the content of fashion. Above all else it brings in its train a reduction in the cost and extravagance of fashions. In earlier times there was a compensation for the costliness of the first acquisition or the difficulties in transforming conduct and taste in the longer duration of their sway. The more an article becomes subject to rapid changes of fashion, the greater the demand for *cheap* products of its kind, not only because the larger and therefore poorer classes nevertheless have enough purchasing power to regulate industry and demand objects, which at least bear the outward semblance of style, but also because even the higher circles of society could not afford to adopt the rapid changes in fashion forced upon them by the imitation of the lower circles, if the objects were not relatively cheap. The rapidity of the development is of such importance in actual articles of fashion that it even withdraws them from certain advances of economy gradually won in other fields. It has been noticed, especially in the older branches of modern productive industry, that the speculative element gradually ceases to play an influential *rôle*. The movements of the market can be better overlooked, requirements can be better foreseen and production can be more accurately regulated than before, so that the rationalization of production makes greater and greater inroads on chance conjunctures, on the aimless vacillation of supply and demand. Only pure articles of fashion seem to prove an exception. The polar oscillations, which modern economics in many instances knows how to avoid and from which it is visibly striving towards entirely new economic orders and forms, still hold sway in the field immediately subject to fashion. The element of feverish change is so essential here that fashion stands, as it were, in a logical contrast to the tendencies for development in modern economics.

In contrast to this characteristic, however, fashion possesses this peculiar quality, that every individual type to a certain extent makes its appearance as though it intended to live forever. When we furnish a house these days, intending the articles to last a quarter of a century, we invariably invest in furniture designed according to the very latest patterns and do not even consider articles in vogue two years before. Yet it is evident that the attraction of fashion will desert the present article just as it left the earlier one, and satisfaction or dissatisfaction with both forms is determined by other material criterions. A peculiar psychological process seems to be at work here in addition to the mere bias of the moment. Some fashion always exists and fashion *per se* is indeed immortal, which fact seems to affect in some manner or other each of its manifestations, although the very nature of each individual fashion stamps it as being transitory. The fact that change itself does not change in this instance endows each of the objects which it affects with a psychological appearance of duration.

This apparent duration becomes real for the different fashion-contents within the change itself in the following special manner. Fashion, to be sure, is concerned only with change, yet like all phenomena it tends to conserve energy; it endeavors to attain its objects as completely as possible, but nevertheless with the relatively most economical means. For this very reason, fashion repeatedly returns to old forms, as is illustrated particularly in wearing-apparel; and the course of fashion has been likened to a circle. As soon as an earlier fashion has partially been forgotten there is no reason why it should not be allowed to return to favor and why the charm of difference, which constitutes its very essence, should not be permitted to exercise an influence similar to that which it exerted conversely some time before.

VIII

The power of the moving form upon which fashion lives is not strong enough to subject every fact uniformly. Even in the fields governed by fashion, all forms are not equally suited to become fashion, for the peculiar character of many of them furnishes a certain resistance. This may be compared with the unequal relation that the objects of external perception bear to the possibility of their being transformed into works of art. It is a very enticing opinion, but one that cannot hold water, that every object is equally suited to become the object of a work of art. The forms of art, as they have developed historically—constantly determined by chance, frequently one-sided and affected by technical perfections and imperfections—by no means occupy a neutral height above all world objects. On the contrary, the forms of art bear a closer relation to some facts than they do to others. Many objects assume artistic form without apparent effort, as though nature had created them for that very purpose, while others, as though wilful and supported by nature, avoid all transformation into the given forms of art. The sovereignty of art over reality by no means implies, as naturalism and many theories of idealism so steadfastly maintain, the ability to draw all the contents of existence uniformly into its sphere. None of the forms by which the human mind masters the material of existence and adapts it to its purpose is so general and neutral that all objects, indifferent as they are to their own structure, should uniformly conform to it.

Thus fashion can to all appearances and *in abstracto* absorb any chosen content: any given form of clothing, of art, of conduct, of opinion may become fashionable. And yet many forms in their deeper nature show a special disposition to live themselves out in fashion, just as others offer inward resistance. Thus, for example, everything that may be termed "classic" is comparatively far removed from fashion and alien to it, although occasionally, of course, the classic also falls under the sway of fashion. The nature of the classic is determined by a concentration of the parts around a fixed centre; classic objects possess an air of composure, which does not offer so many points of attack, as it were, from which modification, disturbance, destruction of the equilibrium might emanate. Concentration of the limbs is characteristic of classic plastics: the *tout ensemble* is absolutely governed from within, the spirit and the feeling of life governing the whole embrace uniformly every single part, because of the perceptible unity of the object. That is the reason we speak of the classic repose of Greek art. It is due exclusively to the concentration of the object, which concentration permits no part to bear any relation to any extraneous powers and fortunes and thereby incites the feeling that this formation is exempt from the changing influences of general life. In contrast to this everything odd, extreme and unusual will be drawn to fashion from within: fashion does not take hold of such characteristic things as an external fate, but rather as the historical expression of their material peculiarities. The widely projecting limbs in baroque statues seem to be in perpetual danger of being broken off, the inner life of the figure does not exercise complete control over them, but turns them over a prey to the chance influences of external life. Baroque forms in themselves lack repose, they seem ruled by chance and subjected to the momentary impulse, which fashion expresses as a form of social life. But still another factor confronts us here, namely, that we soon grow tired of eccentric, bizarre or fanciful forms and from a purely physiological standpoint long for the change that fashion outlines for us.

I have had occasion to point out above that the *tempo* of fashion depends upon the loss of sensibility to nervous incitements which are formed by the individual disposition. The latter changes with the ages, and combines with the form of the objects in an inextricable mutual influence. We find here also one of the deep relations which we thought to have discovered between the classical and the "natural" composition of things. The conception of what is included in the term natural is rather vague and misleading, for as a rule it is merely an expression of value, which is employed to grace values prized for different reasons, and which has therefore been uniformly supported by the most antagonistic elements. At the same time, we may limit the term "natural" from a negative standpoint by a process of exclusion, inasmuch as certain forms, impulses and conceptions can certainly lay no claim to the term; and these are the forms that succumb most rapidly to the changes of fashion, because they lack that relation to the fixed centre of things and of life which justifies the claim of permanent existence. Thus Elizabeth Charlotte of the Palatinate, a sister-in-law of Louis XIV, exceedingly masculine in her ways, inspired the fashion at the French Court of women acting like men and being addressed as such, whereas the men conducted themselves like women. It is self-evident that such behavior can be countenanced by fashion only because it is far removed from that never-absent substance of human relations to which the form of life must eventually return in some way, shape, or manner. We cannot claim that all fashion is unnatural, because the existence of fashion itself seems perfectly natural to us as social beings, yet we can say, conversely, that absolutely unnatural forms may at least for a time bear the stamp of fashion.

To sum up, the peculiarly piquant and suggestive attraction of fashion lies in the contrast between its extensive, all-embracing distribution and its rapid and complete disintegration; and with the latter of these characteristics the apparent claim to permanent acceptance again stands in contrast. Furthermore, fashion depends no less upon the narrow distinctions it draws for a given circle, the intimate connection of which it expresses in the terms of both cause and effect, than it does upon the decisiveness with which it separates the given circle from others. And, finally, fashion is based on adoption by a social set, which demands mutual imitation from its members and thereby releases the individual of all responsibility—ethical and aesthetic—as well as of the possibility of producing within these limits individual accentuation and original shading of the elements of fashion. Thus fashion is shown to be an objective characteristic grouping upon equal terms by social expediency of the antagonistic tendencies of life.

20

THE METROPOLIS
AND MENTAL LIFE
1903

THE DEEPEST PROBLEMS of modern life flow from the attempt of the individual to maintain the independence and individuality of his existence against the sovereign powers of society, against the weight of the historical heritage and the external culture and technique of life. This antagonism represents the most modern form of the conflict which primitive man must carry on with nature for his own bodily existence. The eighteenth century may have called for liberation from all the ties which grew up historically in politics, in religion, in morality and in economics in order to permit the original natural virtue of man, which is equal in everyone, to develop without inhibition; the nineteenth century may have sought to promote, in addition to man's freedom, his individuality (which is connected with the division of labor) and his achievements which make him unique and indispensable but which at the same time make him so much the more dependent on the complementary activity of others; Nietzsche may have seen the relentless struggle of the individual as the prerequisite for his full development, while Socialism found the same thing in the suppression of all competition—but in each of these the same fundamental motive was at work, namely the resistance of the individual to being levelled, swallowed up in the social-technological mechanism.

Reprinted from *Social Sciences III Selections and Selected Readings*, vol. 2, 14th ed. (University of Chicago, 1948). Translated by Edward A. Shils. Originally published as "Die Grosstadt und das Geistesleben," in *Die Grosstadt. Jahrbuch der Gehe-Stiftung* 9 (1903).

When one inquires about the products of the specifically modern aspects of contemporary life with reference to their inner meaning —when, so to speak, one examines the body of culture with reference to the soul, as I am to do concerning the metropolis today— the answer will require the investigation of the relationship which such a social structure promotes between the individual aspects of life and those which transcend the existence of single individuals. It will require the investigation of the adaptations made by the personality in its adjustment to the forces that lie outside of it.

The psychological foundation, upon which the metropolitan individuality is erected, is the intensification of emotional life due to the swift and continuous shift of external and internal stimuli. Man is a creature whose existence is dependent on differences, i.e., his mind is stimulated by the difference between present impressions and those which have preceded. Lasting impressions, the slightness in their differences, the habituated regularity of their course and contrasts between them, consume, so to speak, less mental energy than the rapid telescoping of changing images, pronounced differences within what is grasped at a single glance, and the unexpectedness of violent stimuli. To the extent that the metropolis creates these psychological conditions—with every crossing of the street, with the tempo and multiplicity of economic, occupational and social life—it creates in the sensory foundations of mental life, and in the degree of awareness necessitated by our organization as creatures dependent on differences, a deep contrast with the slower, more habitual, more smoothly flowing rhythm of the sensory-mental phase of small town and rural existence. Thereby the essentially intellectualistic character of the mental life of the metropolis becomes intelligible as over against that of the small town which rests more on feelings and emotional relationships. These latter are rooted in the unconscious levels of the mind and develop most readily in the steady equilibrium of unbroken customs. The locus of reason, on the other hand, is in the lucid, conscious upper strata of the mind and it is the most adaptable of our inner forces. In order to adjust itself to the shifts and contradictions in events, it does not require the disturbances and inner upheavals which are the only means whereby more conservative personalities are able to adapt themselves to the same rhythm of events. Thus the metropolitan type—which naturally takes on a thousand individual modifications—creates a protective organ for itself against the profound disruption with which the fluctuations and discontinuities of the external milieu threaten it. Instead of reacting emotionally, the metropolitan type reacts primarily in a rational manner, thus creating a mental predominance through the intensification of consciousness, which in turn is caused by it. Thus the reaction of the metropolitan person to those events is moved to a sphere of mental activity which is least sensitive and which is furthest removed from the depths of the personality.

This intellectualistic quality which is thus recognized as a protection of the inner life against the domination of the metropolis, becomes ramified into numerous specific phenomena. The metropolis has always been the seat of money economy because the many-sidedness and concentration of commercial activity have given the medium of exchange an importance which it could not have acquired in the commercial aspects of rural life. But money economy and the domination of the intellect stand in the closest relationship to one another. They have in common a purely matter-of-fact attitude in the treatment of persons and things in which a formal justice is often combined with an unrelenting hardness. The purely intellectualistic person is indifferent to all things personal because, out of them, relationships and reactions develop which are not to be completely understood by purely rational methods— just as the unique element in events never enters into the principle of money. Money is concerned only with what is common to all, i.e., with the exchange value which reduces all quality and individuality to a purely quantitative level. All emotional relationships between persons rest on their individuality, whereas intellectual relationships deal with persons as with numbers, that is, as with elements which, in themselves, are indifferent, but which are of interest only insofar as they offer something objectively perceivable. It is in this very manner that the inhabitant of the metropolis reckons with his merchant, his customer, and with his servant, and frequently with the persons with whom he is thrown into obligatory association. These relationships stand in distinct contrast with the nature of the smaller circle in which the inevitable knowledge of individual characteristics produces, with an equal inevitability, an emotional tone in conduct, a sphere which is beyond the mere objective weighting of tasks performed and payments made. What is essential here as regards the economic-psychological aspect of the problem is that in less advanced cultures production was for the customer who ordered the product so that the producer and the purchaser knew one another. The modern city, however, is supplied almost exclusively by production for the market, that is, for entirely unknown purchasers who never appear in the actual field of vision of the producers themselves. Thereby, the interests of each party acquire a relentless matter-of-factness, and its rationally calculated economic egoism need not fear any divergence from its set path because of the imponderability of personal relationships. This is all the more the case in the money economy which dominates the metropolis in which the last remnants of domestic production and direct barter of goods have been eradicated and in which the amount of production on direct personal order is reduced daily. Furthermore, this psychological intellectualistic attitude and the money economy are in such close integration that no one is able to say whether it was the former that effected the latter or *vice versa*. What is certain is only that the form of life in the metropolis is the soil which nourishes this interaction most fruitfully, a point which I shall attempt to demonstrate only with the statement of the most outstanding English constitutional historian to the effect that through the entire course of English history London has never acted as the heart of England but often as its intellect and always as its money bag.

In certain apparently insignificant characters or traits of the most external aspects of life are to be found a number of characteristic mental tendencies. The modern mind has become more and more a calculating one. The calculating exactness of practical life which has resulted from a money economy corresponds to the ideal of natural science, namely that of transforming the world into an arithmetical problem and of fixing every one of its parts in a mathematical formula. It has been money economy which has thus filled the daily life of so many people with weighing, calculating, enumerating and the reduction of qualitative values to quantitative terms. Because of the character of calculability which money has there has come into the relationships of the elements of life a precision and a degree of certainty in the definition of the equalities and inequalities and an unambiguousness in agreements and arrangements, just as externally this precision has been brought about through the general diffusion of pocket watches. It is, however, the conditions of the metropolis which are cause as well as effect for this essential characteristic. The relationships and concerns of the typical metropolitan resident are so manifold and complex that, especially as a result of the agglomeration of so many persons with such differentiated interests, their relationships and activities intertwine with one another into a many-membered organism. In view of this fact, the lack of the most exact punctuality in promises and performances would cause the whole to break down into an inextricable chaos. If all the watches in Berlin suddenly went wrong in different ways even only as much as an hour, its entire economic and commercial life would be derailed for some time. Even though this may seem more superficial in its significance, it transpires that the magnitude of distances results in making all waiting and the breaking of appointments an ill-afforded waste of time. For this reason the technique of metropolitan life in general is not conceivable without all of its activities and reciprocal relationships being organized and coordinated in the most punctual way into a firmly fixed framework of time which transcends all subjective elements. But here too there emerge those conclusions which are in general the whole task of this discussion, namely, that every event, however restricted to this superficial level it may appear, comes immediately into contact with the depths of the soul, and that the most banal externalities are, in the last analysis, bound up with the final decisions concerning the meaning and the style of life. Punctuality, calculability, and exactness, which are required by the complications and extensiveness of metropolitan life are not only most intimately connected with its capitalistic and intellectualistic character but also color the content of life and are conducive to the exclusion of those irrational, instinctive, sovereign human traits and impulses which originally seek to determine the form of life from within instead of receiving it from the outside in a general, schematically precise form. Even though those lives which are autonomous and characterised by these vital impulses are not entirely impossible in the city, they are, none the less, opposed to it *in abstracto*. It is in the light of this that we can explain the passionate hatred of personalities like Ruskin and Nietzsche for the metropolis—personalities who found the value of life only in unschematized individual expressions which cannot be reduced to exact equivalents and in whom, on that account, there flowed from the same source as did that hatred, the hatred of the money economy and of the intellectualism of existence.

The same factors which, in the exactness and the minute precision of the form of life, have coalesced into a structure of the highest impersonality, have, on the other hand, an influence in a highly personal direction. There is perhaps no psychic phenomenon which is so unconditionally reserved to the city as the blasé outlook. It is at first the consequence of those rapidly shifting stimulations of the nerves which are thrown together in all their contrasts and from which it seems to us the intensification of metropolitan intellectuality seems to be derived. On that account it is not likely that stupid persons who have been hitherto intellectually dead will be blasé. Just as an immoderately sensuous life makes one blasé because it stimulates the nerves to their utmost reactivity until they finally can no longer produce any reaction at all, so, less harmful stimuli, through the rapidity and the contradictoriness of their shifts, force the nerves to make such violent responses, tear them about so brutally that they exhaust their last reserves of strength and, remaining in the same milieu, do not have time for new reserves to form. This incapacity to react to new stimulations with the required amount of energy constitutes in fact that blasé attitude which every child of a large city evinces when compared with the products of the more peaceful and more stable milieu.

Combined with this physiological source of the blasé metropolitan attitude there is another which derives from a money economy. The essence of the blasé attitude is an indifference toward the distinctions between things. Not in the sense that they are not perceived, as is the case of mental dullness, but rather that the meaning and the value of the distinctions between things, and therewith of the things themselves, are experienced as meaningless. They appear to the blasé person in a homogeneous, flat and gray color with no one of them worthy of being preferred to another. This psychic mood is the correct subjective reflection of a complete money economy to the extent that money takes the place of all the manifoldness of things and expresses all qualitative distinctions between them in the distinction of "how much." To the extent that money, with its colorlessness and its indifferent quality, can become a common denominator of all values it becomes the frightful leveler—it hollows out the core of things, their peculiarities, their specific values and their uniqueness and incomparability in a way which is beyond repair. They all float with the same specific gravity in the constantly moving stream of money. They all rest on the same level and are distinguished only by their amounts. In individual cases this coloring, or rather this de-coloring of things, through their equation with money, may be imperceptibly small. In the relationship, however, which the wealthy person has to objects which can be bought for money, perhaps indeed in the total character which, for this reason, public opinion now recognizes in these objects, it takes on very considerable proportions. This is why the metropolis is the seat of commerce and it is in it that the purchasability of things appears in quite a different aspect than in simpler economies. It is also the peculiar seat of the blasé attitude. In it is brought to a peak, in a certain way, that achievement in the concentration of purchasable things which stimulates the individual to the highest degree of nervous energy. Through the mere quantitative intensification of the same conditions this achievement is transformed into its opposite, into this peculiar adaptive phenomenon—the blasé attitude—in which the nerves reveal their final possibility of adjusting themselves to the content and the form of metropolitan life by renouncing the response to them. We see that the self-preservation of certain types of personalities is obtained at the cost of devaluing the entire objective world, ending inevitably in dragging the personality downward into a feeling of its own valuelessness.

Whereas the subject of this form of existence must come to terms with it for himself, his self-preservation in the face of the great city requires of him a no less negative type of social conduct. The mental attitude of the people of the metropolis to one another may be designated formally as one of reserve. If the unceasing external contact of numbers of persons in the city should be met by the same number of inner reactions as in the small town, in which one knows almost every person he meets and to each of whom he has a positive relationship, one would be completely atomized internally and would fall into an unthinkable mental condition. Partly this psychological circumstance and partly the privilege of suspicion which we have in the face of the elements of metropolitan life (which are constantly touching one another in fleeting contact) necessitates in us that reserve, in consequence of which we do not know by sight neighbors of years standing and which permits us to appear to small-town folk so often as cold and uncongenial. Indeed, if I am not mistaken, the inner side of this external reserve is not only indifference but more frequently than we believe, it is a slight aversion, a mutual strangeness and repulsion which, in a close contact which has arisen any way whatever, can break out into hatred and conflict. The entire inner organization of such a type of extended commercial life rests on an extremely varied structure of sympathies, indifferences and aversions of the briefest as well as of the most enduring sort. This sphere of indifference is, for this reason, not as great as it seems superficially. Our minds respond, with some definite feeling, to almost every impression emanating from another person. The unconsciousness, the transitoriness and the shift of these feelings seem to raise them only into indifference. Actually this latter would be as unnatural to us as immersion into a chaos of unwished-for suggestions would be unbearable. From these two typical dangers of metropolitan life we are saved by antipathy which is the latent adumbration of actual antagonism since it brings about the sort of distanciation and deflection without which this type of life could not be carried on at all. Its extent and its mixture, the rhythm of its emergence and disappearance, the forms in which it is adequate—these constitute, with the simplified motives (in the narrower sense) an inseparable totality of the form of metropolitan life. What appears here directly as dissociation is in reality only one of the elementary forms of socialization.

This reserve with its overtone of concealed aversion appears once more, however, as the form or the wrappings of a much more general psychic trait of the metropolis. It assures the individual of a type and degree of personal freedom to which there is no analogy in other circumstances. It has its roots in one of the great developmental tendencies of social life as a whole; in one of the few for which an approximately exhaustive formula can be discovered. The most elementary stage of social organization which is to be found historically, as well as in the present, is this: a relatively small circle almost entirely closed against neighboring foreign or otherwise antagonistic groups but which has however within itself such a narrow cohesion that the individual member has only a very slight area for the development of his own qualities and for free activity for which he himself is responsible. Political and familial groups began in this way as do political and religious communities; the self-preservation of very young associations requires a rigorous setting of boundaries and a centripetal unity and for that reason it cannot give room to freedom and the peculiarities of inner and external development of the individual. From this stage social evolution proceeds simultaneously in two divergent but none the less corresponding directions. In the measure that the group grows numerically, spatially, and in the meaningful content of life, its immediate inner unity and the definiteness of its original demarcation against others are weakened and rendered mild by reciprocal interactions and interconnections. And at the same time the individual gains a freedom of movement far beyond the first jealous delimitation, and gains also a peculiarity and individuality to which the division of labor in groups, which have become larger, gives both occasion and necessity. However much the particular conditions and forces of the individual situation might modify the general scheme, the state and Christianity, guilds and political parties and innumerable other groups have developed in accord with this formula. This tendency seems, to me, however to be quite clearly recognizable also in the development of individuality within the framework of city life. Small town life in antiquity as well as in the Middle Ages imposed such limits upon the movements of the individual in his relationships with the outside world and on his inner independence and differentiation that the modern person could not even breathe under such conditions. Even today the city dweller who is placed in a small town feels a type of narrowness which is very similar. The smaller the circle which forms our environment and the more limited the relationships which have the possibility of transcending the boundaries, the more anxiously the narrow community watches over the deeds, the conduct of life and the attitudes of the individual and the more will a quantitative and qualitative individuality tend to pass beyond the boundaries of such a community.

The ancient *polis* seems in this regard to have had a character of a small town. The incessant threat against its existence by enemies from near and far brought about that stern cohesion in political and military matters, that supervision of the citizen by other citizens, and that jealousy of the whole toward the individual whose own private life was repressed to such an extent that he could compensate himself only by acting as a despot in his own household. The tremendous agitation and excitement, and the unique colorfulness of Athenian life is perhaps explained by the fact that a people of incomparably individualized personalities were in constant struggle against the incessant inner and external oppression of a de-individualizing small town. This created an atmosphere of tension in which the weaker were held down and the stronger were impelled to the most passionate type of self-protection. And with this there blossomed in Athens, what, without being able to define it exactly, must be designated as "the general human character" in the intellectual development of our species. For the correlation, the factual as well as the historical validity of which we are here maintaining, is that the broadest and the most general contents and forms of life are intimately bound up with the most individual ones. Both have a common prehistory and also common enemies in the narrow formations and groupings, whose striving for self-preservation set them in conflict with the broad and general on the outside, as well as the freely mobile and individual on the inside. Just as in feudal times the "free" man was he who stood under the law of the land, that is, under the law of the largest social unit, but he was unfree who derived his legal rights only from the narrow circle of a feudal community—so today in an intellectualized and refined sense the citizen of the metropolis is "free" in contrast with the trivialities and prejudices which bind the small town person. The mutual reserve and indifference, and the intellectual conditions of life in large social units are never more sharply appreciated in their significance for the independence of the individual than in the dense crowds of the metropolis because the bodily closeness and lack of space make intellectual distance really perceivable for the first time. It is obviously only the obverse of this freedom that, under certain circumstances, one never feels as lonely and as deserted as in this metropolitan crush of persons. For here, as elsewhere, it is by no means necessary that the freedom of man reflect itself in his emotional life only as a pleasant experience.

It is not only the immediate size of the area and population which, on the basis of world-historical correlation between the increase in the size of the social unit and the degree of personal inner and outer freedom, makes the metropolis the locus of this condition. It is rather in transcending this purely tangible extensiveness that the metropolis also becomes the seat of cosmopolitanism. Comparable with the form of the development of wealth—(beyond a certain point property increases in ever more rapid progression as out of its own inner being)—the individual's horizon is enlarged. In the same way, economic, personal and intellectual relations in the city (which are its ideal reflection), grow in a geometrical progression as soon as, for the first time, a certain limit has been passed. Every dynamic extension becomes a preparation not only for a similar extension but rather for a larger one and from every thread which is spun out of it there continue, growing as out of themselves, an endless number of others. This may be illustrated by the fact that within the city the "unearned increment" of ground rent, through a mere increase in traffic, brings to the owner profits which are self-generating. At this point the quantitative aspects of life are transformed qualitatively. The sphere of life of the small town is, in the main, enclosed within itself. For the metropolis it is decisive that its inner life is extended in a wave-like motion over a broader national or international area. Weimar was no exception because its significance was dependent upon individual personalities and died with them, whereas the metropolis is characterised by its essential independence even of the most significant individual personalities; this is rather its antithesis and it is the price of independence which the individual living in it enjoys. The most significant aspect of the metropolis lies in this functional magnitude beyond its actual physical boundaries and this effectiveness reacts upon the latter and gives to it life, weight, importance and responsibility. A person does not end with limits of his physical body or with the area to which his physical activity is immediately confined but embraces, rather, the totality of meaningful effects which emanates from him temporally and spatially. In the same way the city exists only in the totality of the effects which transcend their immediate sphere. These really are the actual extent in which their existence is expressed. This is already expressed in the fact that individual freedom, which is the logical historical complement of such extension, is not only to be understood in the negative sense as mere freedom of movement and emancipation from prejudices and philistinism. Its essential characteristic is rather to be found in the fact that the particularity and incomparability which ultimately every person possesses in some way is actually expressed, giving form to life. That we follow the laws of our inner nature— and this is what freedom is—becomes perceptible and convincing to us and to others only when the expressions of this nature distinguish themselves from others; it is our irreplaceability by others which shows that our mode of existence is not imposed upon us from the outside.

Cities are above all the seat of the most advanced economic division of labor. They produce such extreme phenomena as the lucrative vocation of the *quatorzieme* in Paris. These are persons who may be recognized by shields on their houses and who hold themselves ready at the dinner hour in appropriate costumes so they can be called upon on short notice in case thirteen persons find themselves at the table. Exactly in the measure of its exten-

sion the city offers to an increasing degree the determining conditions for the division of labor. It is a unit which, because of its
large size, is receptive to a highly diversified plurality of achievements while at the same time the agglomeration of individuals and
their struggle for the customer forces the individual to a type of
specialized accomplishment in which he cannot be so easily ex-
terminated by the other. The decisive fact here is that in the life
of a city, struggle with nature for the means of life is transformed
into a conflict with human beings and the gain which is fought for
is granted, not by nature, but by man. For here we find not only
the previously mentioned source of specialization but rather the
deeper one in which the seller must seek to produce in the person
to whom he wishes to sell ever new and unique needs. The necessity
to specialize one's product in order to find a source of income
which is not yet exhausted and also to specialize a function which
cannot be easily supplanted is conducive to differentiation, refinement and enrichment of the needs of the public which obviously
must lead to increasing personal variation within this public.

All this leads to the narrower type of intellectual individuation
of mental qualities to which the city gives rise in proportion to its
size. There is a whole series of causes for this. First of all there
is the difficulty of giving one's own personality a certain status
within the framework of metropolitan life. Where quantitative increase of value and energy has reached its limits, one seizes on
qualitative distinctions, so that, through taking advantage of the
existing sensitivity to differences, the attention of the social world
can, in some way, be won for oneself. This leads ultimately to the
strangest eccentricities, to specifically metropolitan extravagances
of self-distanciation, of caprice, of fastidiousness, the meaning of
which is no longer to be found in the content of such activity itself
but rather in its being a form of "being different"—of making
oneself noticeable. For many types of persons these are still the
only means of saving for oneself, through the attention gained
from others, some sort of self-esteem and the sense of filling a position. In the same sense there operates an apparently insignificant
factor which in its effects however is perceptibly cumulative,
namely, the brevity and rarity of meetings which are allotted to

each individual as compared with social intercourse in a small city. For here we find the attempt to appear to-the-point, clear-cut and individual with extraordinarily greater frequency than where frequent and long association assures to each person an unambiguous conception of the other's personality.

This appears to me to be the most profound cause of the fact that the metropolis places emphasis on striving for the most individual forms of personal existence—regardless of whether it is always correct or always successful. The development of modern culture is characterised by the predominance of what one can call, the objective spirit over the subjective; that is, in language as well as in law, in the technique of production as well as in art, in science as well as in the objects of domestic environment, there is embodied a sort of spirit [*Geist*], the daily growth of which is followed only imperfectly and with an even greater lag by the intellectual development of the individual. If we survey for instance the vast culture which during the last century has been embodied in things and in knowledge, in institutions and comforts, and if we compare them with the cultural progress of the individual during the same period—at least in the upper classes—we would see a frightful difference in rate of growth between the two which represents, in many points, rather a regression of the culture of the individual with reference to spirituality, delicacy and idealism. This discrepancy is in essence the result of the success of the growing division of labor. For it is this which requires from the individual an ever more one-sided type of achievement which, at its highest point, often permits his personality as a whole to fall into neglect. In any case this overgrowth of objective culture has been less and less satisfactory for the individual. Perhaps less conscious than in practical activity and in the obscure complex of feelings which flow from him, he is reduced to a negligible quantity. He becomes a single cog as over against the vast overwhelming organization of things and forces which gradually take out of his hands everything connected with progress, spirituality and value. The operation of these forces results in the transformation of the latter from a subjective form into one of purely objective existence. It need only be pointed out that the metropolis is the proper arena for this type of culture which has outgrown every personal element. Here in buildings and in educational institutions, in the wonders and comforts of space-conquering technique, in the formations of social life and in the concrete institutions of the State is to be found such a tremendous richness of crystallizing, depersonalized cultural accomplishments that the personality can, so to speak, scarcely maintain itself in the face of it. From one angle life is made infinitely more easy in the sense that stimulations, interests, and the taking up of time and attention, present themselves from all sides and carry it in a stream which scarcely requires any individual efforts for its ongoing. But from another angle, life is composed more and more of these impersonal cultural elements and existing goods and values which seek to suppress peculiar personal interests and incomparabilities. As a result, in order that this most personal element be saved, extremities and peculiarities and individualizations must be produced and they must be over-exaggerated merely to be brought into the awareness even of the individual himself. The atrophy of individual culture through the hypertrophy of objective culture lies at the root of the bitter hatred which the preachers of the most extreme individualism, in the footsteps of Nietzsche, directed against the metropolis. But it is also the explanation of why indeed they are so passionately loved in the metropolis and indeed appear to its residents as the saviors of their unsatisfied yearnings.

When both of these forms of individualism which are nourished by the quantitative relationships of the metropolis, i.e., individual independence and the elaboration of personal peculiarities, are examined with reference to their historical position, the metropolis attains an entirely new value and meaning in the world history of the spirit. The eighteenth century found the individual in the grip of powerful bonds which had become meaningless—bonds of a political, agrarian, guild and religious nature—delimitations which imposed upon the human being at the same time an unnatural form and for a long time an unjust inequality. In this situation arose the cry for freedom and equality—the belief in the full freedom of movement of the individual in all his social and intellectual relationships which would then permit the same noble essence to emerge equally from all individuals as Nature had placed it in them and as it had been distorted by social life and historical development. Alongside of this liberalistic ideal there grew up in the nineteenth century from Goethe and the Romantics, on the one hand, and from the economic division of labor on the other, the further tendency, namely, that individuals who had been liberated from their historical bonds sought now to distinguish themselves from one another. No longer was it the "general human quality" in every individual but rather his qualitative uniqueness and irreplaceability that now became the criteria of his value. In the conflict and shifting interpretations of these two ways of defining the position of the individual within the totality is to be found the external as well as the internal history of our time. It is the function of the metropolis to make a place for the conflict and for the attempts at unification of both of these in the sense that its own peculiar conditions have been revealed to us as the occasion and the stimulus for the development of both. Thereby they attain a quite unique place, fruitful with an inexhaustible richness of meaning in the development of the mental life. They reveal themselves as one of those great historical structures in which conflicting life-embracing currents find themselves with equal legitimacy. Because of this, however, regardless of whether we are sympathetic or antipathetic with their individual expressions, they transcend the sphere in which a judge-like attitude on our part is appropriate. To the extent that such forces have been integrated, with the fleeting existence of a single cell, into the root as well as the crown of the totality of historical life to which we belong—it is our task not to complain or to condone but only to understand.

21

SUBORDINATION AND

PERSONAL FULFILLMENT

1908

THE MOTIVATION of the endeavor [to abolish super-subordination] lies exclusively in the feeling-states of individuals, in the consciousness of degradation and oppression, in the descent of the whole ego to the lowness of the social stratum, and, on the other hand, in the personal haughtiness into which self-feelings are transformed by externally leading positions. If some kind of social organization could avoid these psychological consequences of social inequality, social inequality could continue to exist without difficulties. . . . The rational organization of society and the elimination of command and subjection appear as values not questioned beyond themselves, values claiming realization irrespective of those personal, eudaemonistic results. And yet, in these [values] lies that real psychological power which socialism has at its disposal to inject into the movement of history. As a mere *means*, however, socialism succumbs to the fate of every means, namely of never being, in principle, the *only* one. Since different causes may have the same effect, it is never impossible that the same purpose may be reached by different means. Insofar as socialism is considered an institution depending on the will of people, it is only the first proposal for eliminating those eudaemonistic imperfections which derive from historical inequality. For this reason, it is

Reprinted from *The Sociology of Georg Simmel* (Glencoe, Ill.: Free Press, 1950), pp. 283–85, 299–303. Translated by Kurt H. Wolff. Originally published in *Soziologie* (Munich and Leipzig: Duncker & Humblot, 1908).

so closely associated with the need for abolishing these inequalities that it appears synonymous with it.

Super-Subordination without Degradation

But if it were possible to dissolve the association between super-subordination and the feeling of personal devaluation and oppression, there is no logical reason why the all-decisive feeling of dignity and of a life which is its own master should stand and fall only with socialism. Maybe this aim will be achieved if the individual feeling of life grows more psychologically independent of external activity in general and, in particular, of the position which the individual occupies within the sphere of this external activity. It could be imagined that, in the course of civilization, work in behalf of production becomes more and more a mere technique, more and more losing its consequences for the personality and its intimate concerns. As a matter of fact, we do find as the sociological type which underlies various developments, an approximation to this separation of personality and work. While originally the two were fused, division of labor and production for the market, that is, for completely unknown and indifferent consumers, have later permitted the personality increasingly to withdraw from work and to become based upon itself. No matter how unconditional the expected obedience may be, at this later stage it at least no longer penetrates into the layers that are decisive for life-feeling and personality-value. Obedience is merely a technical necessity, a form of organization which remains in the separate sphere of external matters, in the same way as manual labor itself.

This differentiation of objective and subjective life-elements, whereby subordination is preserved as a technical-organizational value which has no personally and internally depressing and degrading consequences, is, of course, no panacea for all the difficulties and suffering that are everywhere produced by domination and obedience. In the present context, the differentiation is merely the principal expression of a tendency which is only par-

342 INDIVIDUALITY AND SOCIAL STRUCTURE

tially effective and which in actuality never yields an undistorted and conclusive result. Voluntary military service, however, is one of its purest examples in our time. The intellectually and socially highest person may subordinate himself to a non-commissioned officer and actually tolerate a treatment which, if it really concerned his ego and feeling of honor, would move him to the most desperate reactions. But he is aware that he must bow before an objective technique, not as an individual personality, but only as an impersonal link requiring such discipline. This awareness, at least in many cases, prevents a feeling of degradation and oppression from arising. In the field of economics, it is particularly the transition from job work to machine work and from compensation in kind to compensation in wage which promote this objectification of super-subordination—as compared with the situation of the journeyman where the supervision and domination of the master extend to all aspects of the journeyman's life, quite beyond the prerogative which accrues to the master from the journeyman's role as a worker.

The same goal of development might be served by a further important type of sociological formation. It will be recalled that Proudhon wished to eliminate super-subordination by dissolving all dominating structures which, as the vehicles of social forces, have become differentiated out of individual interaction, and by once more founding all order and cohesion upon the direct interaction of free, coordinate individuals. But this coordination can perhaps be reached even if superordination and subordination continue to exist—provided they are reciprocal. We would then have an ideal organization, in which A is superordinate to B in one respect or at one time, but in which, in another respect or at another time, B is superordinate to A. This arrangement would preserve the organizational value of super-subordination, while removing its oppressiveness, one-sidedness, and injustice. As a matter of fact, there are a great many phenomena of social life in which this form-type is realized, even though only in an embryonic, mutilated, and covert way. A small-scale example might be the production association of workers for an enterprise for which they elect a master and foreman. While they are subordinate to him in regard to the technique of the enterprise, they yet are his superordinates with respect to its general direction and results. All groups in which the leader changes either through frequent elections or according to a rule of succession—down to the presidents of social clubs—transform the synchronous combination of superordination and subordination into their temporal alternation. In doing so, they gain the technical advantages of super-subordination while avoiding its personal disadvantages. All outspoken democracies try to attain this by means of brief office terms or by the prohibition of re-election, or both. In this fashion, the ideal of everybody having his turn is realized as far as possible. Simultaneous superordination and subordination is one of the most powerful forms of interaction. In its correct distribution over numerous fields, it can constitute a very strong bond between individuals, merely by the close interaction entailed by it. . . .

Coercion

[The conviction is quite generally held that] coercion is necessary for social organization. The idea is that human nature simply needs coercion lest human actions become completely purposeless and formless. For the general character of this postulate, it is irrelevant whether subordination be under a person and his arbitrariness, or under a law. There are, admittedly, certain extreme cases where the formal value of subordination no longer makes up for the senselessness of its content; but, aside from these, it is of only secondary interest whether the content of the law be a little better or a little worse—exactly, it will be remembered, as was the case concerning the quality of the ruling personality. Here one could refer to the advantages of hereditary despotism—a despotism which, obviously, is to a certain extent independent of the qualities of the person—particularly where it dominates the overall political and cultural life of large territories, and has certain advantages over a free federation.

These advantages are similar to the prerogative of marriage over free love. Nobody can deny that the coercion of law and custom holds innumerable marriages together which, from the moral standpoint, ought to break apart. In these instances, the persons concerned subordinate themselves to a law which simply does not fit their case. But in other instances, this same coercion—however hard, momentarily and subjectively, it may be felt to be—is an irreplaceable value, because it keeps together those who, from the moral standpoint, ought to stay together but, for some momentary ill-temper, irritation, or vacillation of feeling, would separate if they only could, and thus would impoverish or destroy their lives irreparably. The content of marriage laws may be good or bad, may be or may not be applicable to a given case: the mere coercion of the law to stay together develops individual values of an eudae-monistic and ethical nature (not to mention values of social ex-pediency) which, according to the pessimistic, perhaps one-sided standpoint presupposed here, could never be realized in the ab-sense of all coercion. The mere consciousness of everyone that he is bound to the other by coercion may, in some cases, make the common life utterly unbearable. But in other cases, this conscious-ness will bring about a tolerance, self-discipline, and thorough psy-chological training which nobody would feel inclined to undergo if separation were possible at all times. These traits are produced, rather, only by the desire to make the unavoidable life in common at least as bearable as possible.

Occasionally, the consciousness of being under coercion, of being subject to a superordinate authority, is revolting or oppres-sive—whether the authority be an ideal or social law, an arbitrarily decreeing personality or an executor of higher norms. But, for the majority of men, coercion probably is an irreplaceable support and cohesion of the inner and outer life. In the inevitably symbolic language of all psychology: our soul seems to live in two layers, one of which is deeper, hard or impossible to move, carrying the real sense or substance of our life, while the other is composed of momentary impulses and isolated irritabilities. This second layer would be victorious over the first and even more often than it actually is; and, because of the onslaught and quick alternation of its elements, the second layer would give the first no opportunity to come to the surface, if the feeling of a coercion interfering from somewhere did not dam its torrent, break its vacillations and caprices, and thus, again and again, give room and supremacy to the persistent undercurrent.

In comparison with this functional significance of coercion as such, its particular content is of only secondary importance. Senseless coercion may be replaced by sensible coercion, but even the latter has its significance, which is relevant here, only in that which it shares with the former. Moreover, not only the toleration of coercion, but also opposition to it—both to unjust and to justified coercion—has for the rhythm of our surface life this same function of inhibition and interruption: to make conscious and effective the deeper currents of the most intimate and substantial life, which cannot be inhibited by any external means. Insofar as coercion is associated with some form of domination, the association reveals that element in domination which is, as it were, indifferent to the quality of the ruler and to any individual right to dominate, and which thus shows the deeper sense of the claim to authority as such.

The Inevitably Disproportionate Distribution of Qualifications and Positions

It is, in fact, impossible in principle that, in the scale of super-subordination, personal qualification and social position correspond to one another throughout and without remainder—no matter which organization might be proposed for attaining such a correspondence. The reason is that there are always more people qualified for superordinate positions than there are such positions. Among the ordinary workers in a factory, there certainly are very many who could equally well be foremen or entrepreneurs; among common soldiers, many who are fully capable of being officers; among the millions of subjects of a prince, doubtless many who would be equally good or better princes. Rule "by the grace of God" gives expression to the fact that not any subjective quality, but a super-human criterion, decides who shall rule.

Moreover, the fraction of those who have attained leading positions among those who are qualified for them, must not be assumed to be greater than it is, merely on the recognition of the fact that (surely) there also are a great many persons in superordinate positions who are not qualified for them. For, this sort of disproportion between person and position appears, for several reasons, more considerable than it actually is. In the first place, incompetence in a given position of control is especially visible; it is obviously more difficult to conceal than very many other human inadequacies— particularly *because* so many other men, thoroughly qualified for this same position, stand aside as subordinates. Furthermore, this disproportion often results not from individual shortcomings at all, but from contradictory requirements of the office; nevertheless, the inevitable consequences of these requirements are easily ascribed to the office occupant as his subjective faults. The idea of modern "state government," for instance, connotes an infallibility which is the expression of its (in principle) absolute objectivity. Measured by this ideal infallibility, it is natural that its actual executives should often appear inadequate.

In reality, purely individual shortcomings of leading personalities are relatively rare. If one considers the senseless and uncontrollable accidents through which men obtain their positions in all fields, the fact that not a very much greater sum of incapabilities manifests itself in their occupancies would be an incomprehensible miracle, if one did not have to assume that the latent qualifications for the positions exist in very great diffusion. This very assumption underlies the phenomenon that, under republican constitutions, the candidate for office is sometimes investigated only for negative traits; that is, it is merely asked whether he has, in some way, made himself unworthy of the office. Thus, in Athens, appointment was by lot, and the only questions examined were whether the candidate treated his parents well, paid his taxes, etc., in other words, whether there was anything against him—the assumption being that everybody was *a priori* worthy of the office. This is the deeper justification of the proverb: "If God gives somebody an office, he also gives him the mind necessary for it." For, precisely, the "mind" required for the occupancy of higher positions exists in many men, but it proves, develops, reveals itself only once they occupy the position.

This incommensurability between the quantity of qualifications for superordination and the quantity of their possible applications can perhaps be explained in terms of the difference between the character of man as a group member and as an individual. The group as such is low and in need of guidance. It develops qualities which all members have in common. But they are only those qualities which are securely inherited, that is, more primitive and undifferentiated traits or traits easily suggested—in short, "subordinate" qualities. Once a group of any size is formed, therefore, it is expedient that the whole mass organize itself in the form of subordination to a few. This, evidently, does not prevent any given individual member from having higher and finer qualities. But these are individual. They transcend in various respects what all have in common, and thus do not raise the low level of the qualities in which they coincide. From all this, it follows that the group as a whole needs a leader, and that, therefore, there can be many subordinates but only few superordinates—but that, on the other hand, every individual member of the group is more highly qualified than he is as a group element, that is, as a subordinate.

All social formations thus involve this contradiction between the just claim to a superordinate position and the technical impossibility of satisfying this claim. The arrangement by estates and the contemporary order come to terms with this contradiction by building the classes one on top of the other, with an ever smaller number of members in the upward direction, in the form of a pyramid, thereby limiting from the beginning the number of those "qualified" for leading positions. This selection is not based on the individuals available, but inversely, it prejudges these individuals. Out of a mass of equals, not everyone can be brought into the position he deserves. For this reason, the arrangements just mentioned may be considered as the attempt at training the individuals for predetermined positions, from the standpoint of these positions.

But instead of the slowness with which heredity and education, that is commensurate with rank, may succeed in this training, there also are acute procedures, so to speak. They serve, by means of authoritative or mystical edict, to equip the personality with the capability of leading and ruling, irrespective of his previous quality. For the tutelary state of the seventeeth and eighteenth centuries, the subject was incapable of any participation in public affairs; in political respects, he remained permanently in need of guidance. But the moment he occupied a state office, he at once attained the higher insights and the public spirit which enabled him to direct the collectivity—as if, by the sheer occupancy of office, there had emerged out of the immature person, through an inexplicable birth, not only the mature individual, but the leader equipped with all the prerequisites of intellect and character. This tension between everyone's *a priori* lack of qualification for a certain superiority and the absolute qualification which he acquires *a posteriori* through the interference of a higher authority, reaches its peak in Catholic clergy. Here, family tradition, or education from childhood on, play no role. Even the personal quality of the candidate is unimportant in comparison to the spirit which exists in mystical objectivity and which is bestowed upon him through consecration to priesthood. The superior position is not given to him because he alone is naturally predestined for it—although this may, of course, be of some importance and does form the basis for a certain differentiation among those admitted. Nor is it given to him on the greater chance of his being "called" rather than not. No, the consecration *creates* the special qualification for the position to which it calls the individual, because it transfers the *spirit* to him. The principle of God giving an office and the required competence along with it is here realized in the most radical fashion, in both of its two dimensions—unfitness prior to the occupancy, and subsequent fitness created by the "office" itself.

VI. Forms versus Life Process: The Dialectics of Change

22

SOCIAL FORMS AND INNER NEEDS

1908

A BASIC DUALISM . . . pervades the fundamental form of all sociation. The dualism consists in the fact that a relation, which is a fluctuating, constantly developing life-process, nevertheless receives a relatively stable external form. The sociological forms of reciprocal behavior, of unification, of presentation toward the outside, cannot follow, with any precise adaptation, the changes of their inside, that is, of the processes that occur in the individual in regard to the other. These two layers, relation and form, have different tempi of development; or it often is the nature of the external form not to develop properly at all.

Evidently, the strongest external measure for fixing internally variable relations is law. Examples are the marital form, which unyieldingly confronts changes in personal relationship; the contract between two associates, which continues to divide business profit evenly between them, although one of them does all the work, and the other none; membership in an urban religious community that has become completely alien or antipathetic to the member. But even beyond these obvious cases, inter-individual as well as inter-group relations, which have hardly begun, can constantly be observed to have an immediate tendency toward solidifying their form. The form thus comes to constitute a more or less rigid handicap for the relation in its further course, while the form itself is

---

Reprinted from *The Sociology of Georg Simmel* (Glencoe, Ill.: Free Press, 1950), pp. 385–86. Translated by Kurt H. Wolff. Originally published in *Soziologie* (Munich and Leipzig: Duncker & Humblot, 1908), chap. 8.

incapable of adapting to the vibrating life and the more or less profound changes of this concrete, reciprocal relation.

But this is only the repetition of a discrepancy within the individual himself. Our inner life, which we perceive as a stream, as an incessant process, as an up and down of thoughts and moods, becomes crystallized, even for ourselves, in formulas and fixed directions often merely by the fact that we verbalize this life. Even if this leads only rarely to specific inadequacies; even if, in fortunate cases, the fixed external form constitutes the center of gravity or indifference above and below which our life evenly oscillates; there still remains the fundamental, formal contrast between the essential flux and movement of the subjective psychic life and the limitations of its forms. These forms, after all, do not express or shape an ideal, a contrast with life's reality, but this life itself.

Whether they are the forms of individual or social life, they do not flow as our inner development does, but always remain fixed over a certain period of time. For this reason, it is their nature sometimes to be ahead of the inner reality and sometimes to lag behind it. More specifically, when the life, which pulsates beneath outlived forms, breaks these forms, it swings into the opposite extreme, so to speak, and creates forms ahead of itself, forms which are not yet completely filled out by it. To take an instance from the field of personal relations: among friends, the *Sie* [polite form of address] is often felt to be a stiffness that is incommensurate with the warmth of the relation; but when it finally comes to the *Du* [intimate form of address], this too, at least in the beginning, strikes them just as often as something slightly "too much," as the anticipation of full intimacy which has yet to be achieved. Another example is the change of a political constitution, by which obsolete forms that have become unbearably oppressive are replaced by freer and larger ones, while the reality of the political and economic forces is not always ripe for them: an overly narrow frame is replaced by one which, for the time being, is still too wide.

23

THE TRANSCENDENT CHARACTER OF LIFE

1918

I

MAN'S POSITION in the world is defined by the fact that in
every dimension of his being and his behavior he stands at every
moment *between two boundaries*. This condition constitutes the
formal structure of our existence, manifesting itself in countless
ways in the diverse provinces, activities, and destinies of human
life. We feel that the content and value of each hour stand between
a higher and a lower; every thought between a wiser and a more
foolish; every possession between a more extended and a more limited; every deed between a greater and a lesser measure of meaning, adequacy, and morality. We are constantly orienting ourselves, even when we do not employ abstract concepts, to an
"over us" and an "under us," to a right and a left, to a more or
less, a tighter or looser, a better or worse. The boundary, above
and below, is our means for finding direction in the infinite space
of our worlds.

By virtue of the fact that we *have* boundaries everywhere and
always, so accordingly we *are* boundaries. For insofar as every content of life—every feeling, experience, deed, or thought—possesses a given intensity, a specific hue, a certain quantity, and a
certain position in some order of things, there proceeds *from* each
content a continuum in two directions, toward its two poles. Every

---

From *Lebensanschauung: Vier Metaphysische Kapitel* (Munich and Leipzig: Duncker & Humblot, 1918), chap. 1. Translated by Donald N. Levine.

content thus participates in two continua, which meet in it, and which it bounds. This participation in realities, tendencies, and ideas which involve a plus and a minus, a this side and a that side of our here and now, may well be obscure and fragmentary; but it gives life two complementary, if often also contradictory, values: richness and determinacy. For these continua, by which we are bounded and whose segments we ourselves bound, form a sort of coordinate system, through which, as it were, the locus of every part and content of our life may be identified.

For grasping the full significance of "boundaries" in our existence, however, this property of determinacy forms only the point of departure. For, although the boundary as such is necessary, every single determinate boundary can be stepped over, every enclosure can be blasted, and every such act, of course, finds or creates a new boundary. The pair of statements—that the boundary is unconditional, in that its existence is constitutive of our given position in the world, but that no boundary is unconditional, since every one can on principle be altered, reached over, gotten around—this pair of statements appears as the explication of the inner unity of vital action.

Out of countless cases I name one which is very characteristic of the agitation of this process and of the persistence of our life through it: knowing and not knowing about the consequences of our actions. We are all like the chess player in this regard. If he did not know, to a certain extent, what the consequences of a certain move would be, the game would be impossible; but it would also be impossible if this foresight extended indefinitely. Plato's definition of the philosopher as he who stands between knowing and not-knowing holds for man in general. The slightest consideration shows how every single step of our life is determined and rendered possible by the fact that we perceive its consequences, and likewise because we perceive them only up to a certain point, beyond which they become confused and finally escape our vision altogether.

It is not only our standing on this border between knowledge and ignorance, moreover, which makes our life what we know it to be. Life would be completely different if every boundary were definitive, if with advancing life (both in general and in regard to every individual undertaking) the uncertain did not become more certain, the surely believed more problematic. As a result of the inherent flexibility and dislocation of our boundaries, we are able to express our essence with a paradox: we are bounded in every direction, and we are bounded in no direction.

This essential fluidity of our boundaries further implies that we also *know* our boundaries as such—first the individual and then in general. For only whoever stands outside his boundary in some sense knows that he stands within it, that is, knows it as a boundary. Kaspar Hauser did not know that he was in prison until he came into the open and could see the walls from without.

With regard to the designation of things which occur in gradations, our direct experience and our imagination are limited to definite magnitudes. Speed and slowness beyond a certain degree are not actually conceivable. We have no real picture of the speed of light or of the slowness with which a stalactite grows: we cannot project ourselves into such tempi. We cannot effectively imagine temperatures of 1,000 degrees or absolute zero; what lies beyond red and violet in the solar spectrum is not accessible to our vision; and so forth. Our imagination and *primary* apprehension stake out areas from the infinite fullness of reality and the infinite modes of apprehending it, probably to the end that whatever magnitude is thereby delimited provides an adequate basis for our practical conduct.

II

This very reference to such boundaries, however, shows that we can somehow step over them—indeed, that we *have* stepped over them. Speculation and calculation induce us to move beyond the world of sensible reality; they reveal to us that this world is bounded by enabling us to look at its boundaries from the outside. Our concrete, immediate life posits an area that lies between an upper and a lower boundary. But consciousness makes life become more abstract and advanced, transcending the boundary, and thereby confirming its reality as a boundary. Life holds the boundary fast, stands on this side of it—and in the same act stands on the other side of it; the boundary is viewed simultaneously from within and from without. The two aspects belong equally to its confirmation. Just as the boundary itself partakes both of "this side" and of "that side," so the unified act of life includes both the state of being bounded and the transcending of the boundary, despite the fact that this seems to present a logical contradiction.

This process by which the mind transcends itself occurs not only in individual episodes, when we extend the limits of some quantitative boundary in order, by springing beyond it, to recognize it for the first time as a boundary. This process also governs the most all-embracing principles of consciousness. One of the most enormous steps beyond a boundary, which at the same time results in an otherwise unattainable knowledge about our boundedness, lies in the expansion of our sensible world by means of the telescope and the microscope. Formerly, the natural use of the senses gave man a world whose circumscription was consistent with his total organization. But since we have built eyes which see at millions of kilometers what we normally observe only at very short distances, and others which disclose the finest structures of objects at an enlargement that would have no place in our natural perception of space, this harmony has been disrupted. A most thoughtful biologist expressed himself in this regard as follows:

A being with eyes the strength of a giant telescope would be formed quite different from us in other regards, too. It would possess completely different faculties for ultilizing what it would see. It would fashion new objects, and above all would have a vastly longer life-span than ours. Perhaps even its conception of time would be fundamentally different. As soon as we become aware of the disproportion between the space and time relations in such worlds and those of our own existence, we need only to remind ourselves that we could not walk on stilts a half kilometer long. But whether we enlarge our sense organs or our locomotive organs beyond their due is in principle the same: in both cases we break through the natural fitness of our organism.

We have thus transcended the compass of our natural being in certain directions, that is, the adjustment between our total organization and our world of perception. We are now surrounded by a world which, if we consider man a unified being whose several parts are in appropriate relations one to another, is no longer "ours." Looking back from this world, however, which was won by transcending our being through its own powers, we perceive ourselves in a hitherto unheard of cosmic diminution. In pushing out our boundaries to the realm of the measureless, our consciousness is reduced to diminutive proportions by relations to such vast spaces and times.

A similar situation obtains with respect to the forms of cognition. If we assume that the ascertainment of fact depends on a priori categories of knowledge which transform the given material of the world into objects, what is "given" must nevertheless be susceptible to being informed by these categories. Now it is either the case that the human mind is so set up that nothing at all can be "given" to it which does not fit these categories, or else they may determine from the outset the way in which a "givenness" can take place. Whether this determination of fact takes place one way or another, there exists no guarantee that the given (be it given in the sensible or the metaphysical manner) will actually enter *completely* into the forms of our cognition. Just as little as everything that is given us from the world enters into the forms of art, just as little as religion can possess itself of *every* content of life, so little perhaps is the totality of the given accommodated by these forms or categories of cognition.

However, the fact that we, as knowing beings, and within the possibilities of cognition itself, can even conceive the idea that the world might not wholly enter the forms of our cognition, the fact that even in a purely problematical way we can think of something given in the world which we just cannot think of—this represents a movement of the mental life over itself. It is a breaking through and attaining the beyond, not only of a single boundary, but of mind's limits altogether; an act of self-transcendence, which alone sets the immanent limits of cognition, no matter whether these limits are actual or only possible.

This formula holds no less for the content of knowledge than for the forms of cognition. The one-sidedness of the great philosophies brings to most unambiguous expression the relation between the infinite ambiguity of the world and our limited capacities for interpretation. The fact that we know this one-sidedness as such, however—and not only individual instances of it, but one-sidedness as a necessity in principle—this places us above it. We deny it the moment we know it as one-sidedness, without thereby ceasing to stand in it. That we do not simply stand within these boundaries, but by virtue of our awareness of them have passed beyond them—this is the sole consideration which can save us from despair over them, over our limitations and finitude. That we are cognizant of our knowing and our not-knowing, and are likewise aware of this broader cognizance, and so forth into the potentially endless—this is the real infinity of vital movement on the level of intellect. Every limit is herewith transcended but of course only as a result of the fact that it is set, that is, that there exists something to transcend.

It is only with this self-transcending movement that the mind shows itself to be something absolutely vital. This carries over into the realm of ethics in the idea, arising ever again in numerous forms, that the moral task of man is to overcome himself. This notion appears all the way from a completely individualistic form:

> Von der Gewalt, die alle Wesen bindet,
> Befreit der Mensch sich, der sich überwindet
>
> [From the force all creatures heed
> He who transcends himself is freed]

to that of the philosophy of history:

> Der Mensch ist etwas, das überwunden werden soll.
>
> [Man is something that is to be overcome.]

Logically considered, this, too, presents a contradiction. Who overcomes himself is to be sure the victor, but he is also the defeated. The ego succumbs to itself, when winning; it achieves victory, when suffering defeat. Yet the contradiction only arises when one hardens the two aspects of this unity into opposed, mutually exclusive conceptions. It is precisely the fully unified process of the moral life which surpasses every lower state through a higher one, and again this latter state through a still higher. That man overcomes himself means that he reaches out beyond the bounds which the moment sets for him. There must be something at hand to be overcome, but it is only there for the purpose of being overcome. So, also as an ethical agent, man is the limited being that has no limit.

III

This hasty sketch of a very general and not especially profound aspect of life may serve to prepare the way for that conception of life which is to be developed here. I take as point of departure for this discussion a consideration of time.

The present, in the strict logical sense of the term, does not encompass more than the absolute "unextendedness" of a moment. It is as little time as the point is space. It denotes merely the collision of past and future, which two alone make up time of any magnitude, that is, real time. But since the one is no longer, and the other not yet, reality adheres to the present alone. This means that reality is not at all something temporal. The concept of time can be applied to the contents of reality only if the atemporality, which they possess as *present*, has become a "no more" or a "not yet," at any rate a nothing. Time is not in reality, and reality is not time.

We acknowledge the force of this paradox, however, only for the logically observed object. The subjectively *lived* life will not adjust to it. The latter feels itself, no matter whether logically justified or not, as something real in a temporal dimension. Common usage indicates this, if in an inexact and superficial way, by understanding under "present" never the bare punctuality of its conceptual sense, but always including a bit of the past and a somewhat smaller bit of the future. (These "bits" vary in size according to whether it is a question of the personal or political, cultural or geological "present.")

Considered now more deeply, the reality of life at any moment is related to its past in a very different way from a mechanical phenomenon. The latter is so indifferent toward its past, out of which it has emerged as an effect, that the same condition can on principle be produced by a number of different causal complexes. On the other hand, the hereditary material out of which an organism develops contains countless *individual* elements, such that the past sequence leading to *its* individuality can by no means be replaced by another. Previous effects do not vanish without a trace into the current effect, as do mechanical effects, which can result from different combinations of causes.

The protrusion [*Hineinleben*] of the past into the present first appears in full purity, however, when life has reached the stage of intellectual activity. At this level it has two forms at its disposal: *objectification in concepts and pictures* which, from the moment of their creation, become the reproducible possession of countless succeeding generations, and *memory*, through which the past of the subjective life not only becomes the cause of that of the present but also continues over into the present with its contents relatively unchanged.

Insofar as previous experience lives in us as memory, not as a content without association to some point in time, but bound up in our consciousness with its temporal position, it is not entirely transformed into effect (as the mechanistic and causal mode of observation would suggest). The sphere of actual, present life stretches all the way back to it. This of course does not mean that the past as such thereby rises from the grave. It does mean, however—since we know the experience is not in the present, but rather is attached to some moment in the past—that our present does not remain at one point, as does that of a mechanical existence. It is, so to speak, extended backward. At such moments we live out of the moment back into the past.

Our relation to the future parallels our relation to the past. The future is most inadequately characterized by defining man as the "goal-setting being." The somehow remote "goal" appears as a fixed point, discontinuous with the present, whereas what is decisive is the immediate carryover of present will, feeling, and thought into the future. The living present exists in the fact that it transcends the present. With every exertion of the will, here and now, we demonstrate that a threshold between now and the future is just not real; that as soon as we assume such a threshold, we stand at once on this side and on that side of it. The concept of "goal" permits the continuous movement of life to coagulate about one point (whereby it manages to satisfy most of the demands of rationalism and of practise). It swallows up the stretch of uninterrupted temporal life between "now" and "later" and creates thereby a gap marked on one side by the firm point of the present, on the other by the rigidly located "goal."

Insofar as the future, like the past, is localized at some point, however indefinite, and the process of life is disrupted and crystallized into the terms of logical differentiation among three grammatically separate tenses, the immediate continuous stretching of itself into the future, which every living present signifies, gets concealed. The future does not lie ahead of us like some unexplored land, separated from the present by a sharp boundary line, but rather we live continually in a border region which belongs as much to the future as to the present. All theories which locate the essence of human spirit in the will simply say that spiritual existence projects out beyond its narrow present, so to speak, that the future is already reality within it. A mere wish may well be aimed toward the distant, not yet alive future, but the actual will stands directly outside the contrast between present and future. At the very moment of willing we are already beyond it, for the unextended state to which logic would restrict the will's activity could not accommodate the establishment of the *direction* in which the living will must move further. Life *is* truly past and future; these are not just appended to it by thought, as they are to inorganic reality.

Even below the level of intellect one will have to recognize the same form at work both in procreation and in growth: that life at any given moment transcends itself, that its present forms a unity with the "not-yet" of the future. As long as one separates past, present, and future with analytical sharpness, time is unreal, because by this separation only the temporal unextended, that is, the atemporal moment of the present tense, is real. Life, however, is the unique mode of existence for whose reality this distinction does not hold. The three tenses in their logical separateness are applicable to it only through subsequent dissection, following the mechanistic model. For life alone is time real. (The whole ideality of time in Kant is possibly bound up deeply with the mechanistic element in his world view.) Time is the—perhaps abstract—form in our consciousness of life itself, as experienced in unformulable, immediate concreteness. Time is life seen apart from its contents, because life alone transcends the atemporal present of every other kind of reality in both directions and thereby realizes, all by itself, the temporal dimension, that is, time.

IV

If we retain the concept and fact of the present at all, as we are justified and indeed compelled to do, the essential structure of life thus signifies a continual reaching out beyond itself as something in the present. The process whereby actual life reaches out into that which is not its actuality, such that this reaching out nevertheless constitutes its actuality, is not something which has been tagged on to life. This process, realizing itself in procreation, growth, and the intellectual activities, is the very essence of life itself. *The mode of existence which does not restrict its reality to the present moment, thereby placing past and future in the realm of the unreal, is what we call life.* Its unique continuity is rather sustained outside of this separation, so that its past actually exists into its present, its present actually exists out into its future.

The statement that life realizes itself in the form which I have characterized as a "reaching out over itself" [*Hinausgreifen uber sich selbst*] is grounded in an antinomial relation. We conceive of life as a continuous stream proceeding through sequences of generations. Yet the bearers of this process, those who make it up, are *individuals*, that is, closed, self-centered, unambiguously distinct beings. While the stream of life flows through those individuals (more accurately: flows *as* these individuals), it dams up in each one of them and becomes a sharply outlined form. Each individual then asserts itself as something complete against other individuals of its kind as well as against the total environment, and does not tolerate any blurring of its boundary. Here lies an ultimate, metaphysically problematic condition of life: that it is boundless continuity and at the same time boundary-determined ego.

Vital movement is somehow held still not only in the "I" as a total existence, but also in all experienced contents and objectivities. Wherever something with a definite form is experienced, life is caught up as it were in a blind alley. Life feels its streaming crystallized into that something and given form by that form; it is bounded. But since its further flowing is not to be stopped, since the persisting centrality of the total organism, of the "I," or of its respective contents, cannot nullify the essential continuity of the flowing, there arises the idea that life pushes out beyond the given organic, or spiritual, or objective form; that it overflows that dam. A purely continuous, Heraclitic flux lacking a definite, persisting something, would not contain the boundary over which a reaching out is to occur, nor the subject *which* reaches out. But as soon as something exists as a unity unto itself, gravitating toward its own center, then all the flow from this side to that side of its boundaries is no longer agitation without a subject. Rather, the flux remains somehow bound up with the center. Even the movement outside its boundary belongs to the center; it represents a reaching out in which the form always remains subject and yet which goes out beyond this subject.

Life is at once flux without pause and yet something enclosed in bearers and contents, formed about midpoints, individualized, and therefore always a bounded form which continually jumps its bounds. That is its essence. Certainly the category which I here name "the reaching out of life over itself" is meant only symbolically, only with an indication that it is to be improved. Taken in its essence, however, I hold it to be basic, primary. It has been described here only in a schematic and abstract way. I have presented only the bare pattern of the concretely filled life, insofar as its essence (not something that might be added to its being, but rather directly constitutive of its being) may be expressed by the formula that *transcendence is immanent in life*.

V

The simplest and most fundamental instance of what is meant here is self-awareness, which is also the original phenomenon of the mind as something humanly alive. The "I" not only confronts itself, making itself as knower the object of its own knowing; but it even judges itself as a third party, esteems or deprecates itself, and so is put above itself. It moves beyond itself constantly, and yet remains in itself, since its subject and object are here identical. The self articulates this identity in the intellectual process of knowing itself without thereby mutilating it.

The process by which consciousness towers over itself as something known approaches the unlimited: I know not only that I know, but I also know that I know this; writing down this sentence I lift myself yet again above the previous stages of this process; and so on. A difficulty in thinking appears here. It is as if the "I" were always chasing after itself, without ever being able to overtake itself. The difficulty disappears, however, as soon as one recognizes the process of "reaching beyond itself" as the primary phenomenon of life, occurring here in its most sublimated form, detached from all accidental content.

By virtue of our highest, self-transcending consciousness at any moment we are absolute above our relativity. But as the further advance of this process again relativizes that absolute, the transcendence of life appears as the true absoluteness, in which the contrast between the absolute and the relative is collapsed. Through such elevation above the contrasts which inhere in the basic fact that transcendence is immanent in life, the eternally felt conflicts in life come to rest. That life is at once fixed and variable; of finished shape, and developing further; formed, and ever breaking through its forms; persisting, yet rushing onward; circling around in subjectivity, yet standing objectively over things and over itself—all these contrasts are but instances of that metaphysical fact: the innermost essence of life is its capacity to go out beyond itself, to set its limits by reaching out beyond them, that is, beyond itself.

The ethical problem of will involves the same form as that manifested by the intellectual self-transcendence of life in its consciousness of self-awareness. We can conceive of the activity of human will only through the image that a plurality of strivings is typically alive within us, from which a higher will selects one to develop further and culminate in action. It is not in those desires for whose emergence we generally do not feel responsible but in this ulti-

mate, decision-making will that we experience what we call freedom and what establishes our responsibility. It is naturally one
and the same will which discloses itself in this process of self-
transcendence, just as it is one and the same "I" which distinguishes in self-awareness between object and subject. For the former, however, the multiplicity of contents precipitates a *choice*,
something which does not come into question for the theoretical
self-awareness.

Even the infinite regress of this latter has a certain analogy in
the nature of human will. We often find that a decision made by
exerting the will against itself does not correspond to what we
really desire. There remains a still higher will within us which
could quash that very decision. On the other hand, one may say
that the course of practical self-appraisal, no matter how high it
climbs, never finds a check, or, paradoxically, the will also really
wills our will. Everyone is familiar with the peculiar malaise of
situations where we have chosen to do something which we do not
regard as our ultimate will. Perhaps many difficulties in the problem of freedom, like the problem of the self, result from imparting
substance to the processes just referred to, something which language can scarcely avoid. When this happens, such stages appear
as closed, autonomous parties among which only mechanical interplay is possible. This would not be so if one saw in all of that the
primary phenomenon in which life reveals itself as a continuous
process of self-transcendence, and in which (difficult to grasp by
logic) this stress of itself and constant abandonment of itself is precisely the mode of its unity, of its remaining in itself.

VI

A deep contradiction exists between continuity and form as
ultimate world-shaping principles. Form means limits, contrast
against what is neighboring, cohesion of a boundary by way of a
real or ideal center to which, as it were, the ever flowing sequences
of contents or processes bend back, and which provides every cir-
cumference with a source of resistance against dissolution in the
flux. If one takes seriously the concept of continuity, the extensive

representation of the absolute unity of being, such autonomy of an enclave of being is not admissible. One cannot even speak then about continual destruction of forms, for something that could be destroyed would not be able to arise in the first place. For this reason Spinoza was unable to derive any positive *determinatio* from the conception of absolute, unified being. Form, on the other hand, cannot be altered. It is eternally invariable. The form of an obtuse-angled triangle remains forever just that. If shifting the side makes it acute-angled, its form, in whatever moment I catch it, is absolutely fixed and absolutely different from that of any other moment, no matter how slight the deviation. The expression—the triangle has changed "itself"—imparts to it, in anthropomorphic fashion, a lifelike subjectivity which alone is capable of self-change. Form, however, is individuality. It can be identically reproduced in countless bits of matter; but that it should exist twice as pure form makes no sense. That would be as if the sentence—two times two equals four—could, as ideal truth, exist twice, although it can of course be realized by countless centers of consciousness. Equipped with this metaphysical uniqueness, form impresses on its bit of matter an individual shape, makes it peculiar to itself and distinguished from differently formed items. Form tears the bit of matter away from the continuity of the next-to-one-another and the after-one-another and gives it a meaning of its own, a meaning whose determinateness is incompatible with the streaming of total being, if the latter is truly not to be dammed.

If now life—as a cosmic, generic, singular phenomenon—is such a continuous stream, there is good reason for its profound opposition against form. This opposition appears as the unceasing, usually unnoticed (but also often revolutionary) battle of ongoing life against the historical pattern and formal unflexibility of any given cultural content, thereby becoming the innermost impulse toward culture change. On the other hand, individuality as distinct form seems to have to withdraw from the continuity of life's flux, which admits no closed structures. Empirical indications of this are close at hand. The highest peaks of individuality, the greatest geniuses, almost consistently produce few or no offspring. Women, during periods of emancipation, in striving to advance from their status as "women in general" to a stronger expression and justification of their individuality, seem to show a declining fertility. Through numerous indications and disguises among strongly individualized men of higher cultures one feels a hostility toward their function, a hostility against being a wave in the ongoing stream of life which surges through them. That is by no means only a presumptuous exaggeration of their personal significance, a desire to distinguish themselves qualitatively from the masses. It represents a feeling for the unreconcilable opposition between life and form, or, in other words, between continuity and individuality. The content of the latter, its characteristic peculiarity or uniqueness, is not important here. What is decisive is the for-itself, in-itself character of individual form in its contrast to the all-embracing continuous stream of life, which not only dissolves all form-giving boundaries but even prevents them from coming into being.

Nevertheless, individuality is everywhere something alive, and life is everywhere individual. So one might suppose that the whole problem of incompatibility of the two principles is just one of those conceptual antinomies which appear whenever immediately lived reality is projected onto the plane of intellectuality. There it inevitably breaks up into a plurality of elements which did not exist at all in its primary objective unity, and which now, hardened and logically independent, show discrepancies among themselves. The intellect may try subsequently to reconcile them, but seldom with full success; for its intrinsically analytic character prevents it from creating pure syntheses.

Such, however, is not completely the case. That dualism lies embedded in the very depths of the feeling of life, only there it is of course surrounded by a living unity. It is known as a dualism only where it steps over the edge of that unity (which happens only in certain culture-historical situations). Only at this border does it deliver itself up as a problem to the intellect, which cannot help projecting it as an antinomy back to that ultimate stratum of life. That stratum is dominated by something which intellect can only call the overcoming of the dualism by unity, but which is actually a third principle, beyond dualism and unity: the essence of life as the transcendence of itself. In *one* act, it creates something more than the vital stream itself—individual structure—and then breaks through this product of a blockage in that stream, lets the stream surge out over the bounds and submerge itself again in the ongoing flux. We are not divided into life free from limits and form made secure by them. We do not live partly in continuity, partly in individuality, the two asserting themselves against each other. Rather, the fundamental character of life resides precisely in that internally unified function which I, albeit symbolically and inadequately, have termed the transcendence of itself. This function actualizes as *one* life what is then split through feelings, destinies, and conceptualization into the dualism of continuous life flux and individual closed form.

Should one prefer to characterize the one side of this dualism as life pure and simple, the other as individual structure and a simple contrast to the former, then it is valid to seek an absolute concept of life which subsumes within itself that dichotomous characterization. Just as there is an ultimate concept of the good which includes both good and bad in their relative sense, and an ultimate concept of beauty which contains within itself the contrast of the beautiful and the ugly, so life in the absolute sense is something which includes life in the relative sense and its respective opposite, or discloses itself to them as to its empirical phenomena. Self-transcendence thus appears as the unified act of building up and breaking through life's bounds, its *alter*, as the character of life's absoluteness, which makes its analysis into reified opposites quite intelligible.

Schopenhauer's will to life and Nietzsche's will to power doubtless lie in the direction of concrete fulfillment of this idea of life; though Schopenhauer feels boundless continuity to be more decisive, Nietzsche stresses more individuality encased in form. What is decisive, however, what constitutes life, is the absolute unity of both. This insight has escaped them, perhaps because they restrict the process of self-transcendence to the activity of the will. Actually, it holds for all dimensions of vital movement.

VII

So viewed, life has two mutually complementary definitions. It is *more-life*, and it is *more-than-life*. The "more" does not arrive by accident to augment a life already stable in its quantity, but life is the movement which at every moment draws something into itself—for each of its parts, even when these are comparatively pitiful—in order to transform it into its life. No matter what its absolute measure, life can only exist by virtue of its being more-life. So long as life is present at all, it gives birth to living things, since sheer physiological self-maintenance involves continual regeneration. This is no function which it exercises among others, but insofar as it does this it is life.

If, furthermore, as I am convinced, death is immanent in life from the outset, this, too, involves a stepping out of life beyond itself. From its center, life stretches out toward the absolute of life, as it were, and becomes in this direction more-life; but it stretches out toward nothingness as well. As life persists and yet increases itself in one action, so also it persists and declines in one action, *as* a single action. We encounter here again that *absolute* concept of life, of more-life, that includes the more and the less as relativities and is genus proximum to both. The deep relationship between birth and death, which man has always perceived, as if some formal relation existed between them as life catastrophes, finds here its metaphysical pivot. Both events are attached to the subjective life and transcend it, toward above and toward below, so to speak. The life beyond which they extend is nevertheless not conceivable without them. To climb beyond oneself in growth and reproduction, to sink below oneself in old age and death—these are not additions to life, but such rising up and spilling over the boundaries of the individual condition constitutes life itself. Perhaps the whole idea of the immortality of man simply signifies the accumulated feeling, heightened for once into a huge symbol, for this self-transcendence of life.

The logical difficulty raised by the statement that life is at once itself and more than itself is only a problem of expression. If we wish to express the unified character of life in abstract terms, our intellect has no alternative but to divide it into two such parts, which appear as mutually exclusive and only subsequently merge to form that unity. Naturally a contradiction arises once these parts are fixed in mutual opposition. It is obviously an *ex post facto* reconstruction of immediately lived life to characterize it as a unity of boundary-setting and boundary-transcending, of individual centeredness and reaching out beyond its own periphery, for the very act of designating this point of unity necessarily breaks it up. According to abstract formulation, the constitution of life in its quantity and quality and the transcendence of this quantity and quality can only touch each other at this point whereas the life which goes on there includes within itself both sides, constitution and transcendence, as a real unity. As I indicated above, intellectual life cannot but present itself in forms: whether words or deeds, pictures or any sort of contents in which psychic energy currently realizes itself. But these forms enjoy in the very moment of their emergence an objective significance of their own, a fixity and inner logic, with which they confront the life which created them. The latter is a restless flux that not only streams beyond this and that definite form, but overflows *every* form because it is *form*. Because of this contrast in essence, life cannot lose itself in form. The achievement of every structure is at once a signal to seek out another one, in which the play—necessary structure, and necessary dissatisfaction with the structure as such—is repeated. As life it needs form; as life, it needs more than the form.

Life is thus caught up in a contradiction, that it can only be accommodated in forms and yet cannot be accommodated in forms, that it passes beyond and destroys everything which it has formed. This, of course, appears as a contradiction only in logical reflection, which conceives the individual form as an intrinsically valid, real or ideal fixed structure, discontinuous with other forms, and in logical contrast to movement, streaming, reaching further. Life as immediately experienced is precisely the unity of being formed and that reaching out beyond form which manifests itself at any single moment as destruction of the given current form. Life is always more life than there is room for in the form allotted by and grown out of it.

Insofar as psychic life is perceived in terms of its contents, it is finite. It consists then of these ideal contents, which now have the form of life. But the process reaches beyond them. We conceive, feel, desire this and that—such are clearly defined contents, something logical realized only now, something in principle completely definite and definable. Yet as we experience it, we feel something else to be present, something unformulable, indefinable: we feel of every life as such that it is more than every assignable content. It swings out beyond every content, regarding it at once from within (as is the nature of logical description of content) and from without. We are in this content and at the same time outside of it. In taking up this content into the form of *life*, we have by that very fact more than the content.

VIII

Thereby is the dimension suggested in which life transcends, not only as more-life, but as more-than-life. This is everywhere the case where we call ourselves creative, not just in the specific sense of a rare, individual power, but in that obvious for all imagination: imagination produces content that has its own sense, a logical coherency, a certain validity or permanency that is independent of its being produced and borne by life. This independent character of any product of the imagination speaks as little against its origin out of the pure, exclusive creativity of the individual life as the origin of physical offspring from no other potency than that of the parents is called into question by the fact that an offspring is a fully independent being. And just as the creation of this being who becomes independent of the creator is immanent to physiological life and in fact characterizes life as such, so the creation of an independently meaningful content is immanent to life at the stage of intellect. The fact that our ideas and cognitions, our values and judgments stand completely apart from the creative life in their meaning, their objective intelligibility and historical effectiveness—exactly this is the characteristic of human life. Just as transcending its current, limiting form within the plane of life itself constitutes more-life, which is nevertheless the immediate, inescapable essence of life itself, so does transcendence into the level of objective content, of meaning that is logically autonomous and no longer vital, constitute the more-than-life, inseparable from life, and the very essence of mental life. This signifies nothing other than that life is not just life alone, although it is nothing but life. We must employ a further, the furthest concept, that of absolute life, which includes the relative contrast between life in the narrower sense and content independent of life.

One can even pronounce as definition of the intellectual life that it produces something with a meaning and law unto itself. This self-alienation of life, this confronting itself in an autonomous form, appears as contradiction only when one constructs a sharp boundary between its within and its without, as though they were two self-centered substances. Life is to be conceived of rather as a continuous movement, whose unity at every point is divided into those opposing directions only by the space symbolism of our expression. Having made this assumption, however, we are able to look at life only as the continual reaching out of the subject into what is foreign to him, or as the creation of something foreign to him. The latter is by no means subjectivized thereby, but it persists in its independence, in its being more-than-life. The absoluteness of its otherness is much too watered down, mediated, or made problematic by the idealistic notion that "the world is my idea," which has the further consequence of making the actual full transcendence appear impracticable, illusory. No, the absoluteness of this other, of this more, which life creates or into which it penetrates, is precisely the formula and condition of life as it is lived. Life is from the outset nothing other than a reaching-out-beyond-itself.

This dualism, sustained in full sharpness, not only fails to contradict the unity of life, but is indeed the very way in which its unity exists. This finds extreme expression in the prayer: "Lord, Thy will be done, and not mine." Logically taken, it appears dumbfounding that I wish something and in the same act wish that it does *not* come to be. This paradox disappears with the insight that life here, just as in the theoretical and productive spheres, has raised itself in the form of an autonomous structure above itself, and in this development has so remained with itself that it knows the will attributed to *that* structure as its own. It is thus of no matter whether or not the lower level (which is still retained as "my" will) corresponds in content with the higher (which is nevertheless one's own also, since the "I" *wishes* its fulfillment). Transcendence reveals itself as the immanent condition of life perhaps most strikingly of all here, where the process knows itself from the start as transcendent and feels the will of the transcendent object to be its ultimate own.

IX

One of the ultimate concerns of the modern world view can be thus characterized. Man has always been aware of certain realities and values, certain objects of belief and validities for which there is no room in the strictly circumscribed life space filled up by his immediate own, self-centered substance. He expresses the certainty of this awareness at first by imparting to all such the character of separate existences outside of life. He sets them in the sharply separated beyond and lets them react back from there onto life (though, to be sure, one does not know just how this happens).

Critical enlightenment, which recognizes nothing "beyond" the subject, rises to oppose this naivete. It throws back within the bounds of subjective immediacy everything located in the beyond, and thus declares as illusion whatever wishes to persist as independent confrontation of man. This is the first step of the great tendency in intellectual history: everything which had been established outside of life with its own existence and which came to life from beyond is placed back in life itself by means of a mighty revolution. But since life is conceived at this point as absolute immanence, everything remains in a subjectivization (albeit with manifold nuances), a denial of the form of the beyond. One fails to notice that this delimitation of the subject has even made him dependent on the idea of the beyond, that only in relation to this beyond did the boundary take shape in which life was caught and chased itself around in the unbreakable circle of the self.

Now here the attempt is made to conceive of life as something which constantly reaches beyond limits toward its beyond and which finds its essence in this reaching beyond. It is an attempt to define life in general by way of this transcendence, where by the closure of its individuality form is maintained, but only in order to be broken through by the continuous process. Life finds its essence, its process, in being more-life and more-than-life. Its positive is as such already its comparative.

I am well aware of the logical difficulties involved in the conceptual expression of this way of viewing life. I have tried to formulate it, in full presence of the logical danger, because perchance the level is here attained in which logical difficulties by themselves are insufficient to impel silence—because it is here that the metaphysical root of logic itself draws nourishment.

THE CONFLICT IN

MODERN CULTURE

1918

WHENEVER LIFE progresses beyond the animal level to that of the spirit, and spirit progresses to the level of culture, an internal contradiction appears. The whole history of culture is the working out of this contradiction. We speak of culture whenever life produces certain forms in which it expresses and realizes itself; works of art, religions, sciences, technologies, laws, and innumerable others. These forms encompass the flow of life and provide it with content and form, freedom and order. But although these forms arise out of the life process, because of their unique constellation they do not share the restless rhythm of life, its ascent and descent, its constant renewal, its incessant divisions and reunifications. These forms are frameworks for the creative life which, however, soon transcends them. They should also house the imitative life, for which, in the final analysis, there is no space left. They acquire fixed identities, a logic and lawfulness of their own; this new rigidity inevitably places them at a distance from the spiritual dynamic which created them and which makes them independent.

Herein lies the ultimate reason why culture has a history. Insofar as life, having become spirit, ceaselessly creates such forms which become self-enclosed and demand permanence, these forms are inseparable from life; without them it cannot be itself. Left to

Reprinted with the permission of the publisher from Georg Simmel, *The Conflict in Modern Culture and Other Essays*, translated by K. Peter Etzkorn (New York: Teachers College Press, 1968). Originally published in German as *Der Konflikt der modernen Kultur* (Munich and Leipzig: Duncker & Humblot, 1918).

itself, however, life streams on without interruption; its restless rhythm opposes the fixed duration of any particular form. Each cultural form, once it is created, is gnawed at varying rates by the forces of life. As soon as one is fully developed, the next begins to form; after a struggle that may be long or short, it will inevitably succeed its predecessor.

History, as an empirical science, concerns itself with changes in the forms of culture, and aims to discover the real carriers and causes of change in each particular case. But we can also discern a deeper process at work. Life, as we have said, can manifest itself only in particular forms; yet, owing to its essential restlessness, life constantly struggles against its own products, which have become fixed and do not move along with it. This process manifests itself as the displacement of an old form by a new one. This constant change in the content of culture, even of whole cultural styles, is the sign of the infinite fruitfulness of life. At the same time, it marks the deep contradiction between life's eternal flux and the objective validity and authenticity of the forms through which it proceeds. It moves constantly between death and resurrection— between resurrection and death.

This characteristic of cultural processes was first noted in economic change. The economic forces of every epoch develop forms of production which are appropriate to their nature. Slave economies, guild constitutions, agrarian modes of soil labor—all these, when they were formed, expressed adequately the wishes and capacities of their times. Within their own norms and boundaries, however, there grew economic forces whose extension and development these systems obstructed. In time, through gradual explosive revolutions, they burst the oppressive bonds of their respective forms and replaced them with modes of production more appropriate. A new mode of production, however, need not have overwhelming energy of its own. Life itself, in its economic dimension—with its drive and its desire for advancement, its internal changes and differentiation—provides the dynamics for this whole movement. Life as such is formless, yet incessantly generates forms for itself. As soon as each form appears, however, it demands a validity which transcends the moment and is emancipated from the pulse of life. For this reason, life is always in a latent opposition to the form. This tension soon expresses itself in this sphere and in that; eventually it develops into a comprehensive cultural necessity. Thus life perceives "the form as such" as something which has been forced upon it. It would like to puncture not only this or that form, but form *as such*, and to absorb the form in its immediacy, to let its own power and fullness stream forth just as if it emanated from life's own source, until all cognition, values, and forms are reduced to direct manifestations of life.

At present, we are experiencing a new phase of the old struggle —no longer a struggle of a contemporary form, filled with life, against an old, lifeless one, but a struggle of life against the form *as such*, against the *principle* of form. Moralists, reactionaries, and people with strict feelings for style are perfectly correct when they complain about the increasing "lack of form" in modern life. They fail to understand, however, that what is happening is not only a negative, passive dying out of traditional forms, but simultaneously a fully positive drive towards life which is actively repressing these forms. Since this struggle, in extent and intensity, does not permit concentration on the creation of new forms, it makes a virtue of necessity and insists on a fight against forms simply because they are forms. This is probably only possible in an epoch where cultural forms are conceived of as an exhausted soil which has yielded all that it could grow, which, however, is still completely covered by products of its former fertility.

Similar events certainly took place during the eighteenth century. Then, however, they occurred over a longer period, from the English Enlightenment of the seventeenth century to the French Revolution. Moreover, there was an almost completely new ideal standing behind these revolutions: the liberation of the individual, the application of reason to life, the progress of mankind towards happiness and perfection. New cultural forms developed easily in this milieu—almost as if they had somehow been prepared—and provided inner security to mankind. The conflict of the new forms against the old did not generate the cultural pressure we know today, when life in all possible manifestations agitates against being directed into any fixed forms whatever.

The concepts of *life*, which several decades ago became dominant in the philosophical interpretation of the world, prepared the way for our situation. In order to place this phenomenon within the arena of the history of ideas, I will have to range a little further afield. In every important cultural epoch, one can perceive a central idea from which spiritual movements originate and towards which they seem to be oriented. Each central idea is modified, obscured and opposed in innumerable ways. Nevertheless, it represents the "secret being" of the epoch. In every single epoch, the central idea resides wherever the most perfect being, the most absolute and metaphysical phase of reality join with the highest values, with the most absolute demands on ourselves and on the world. Certainly, there follow logical contradictions. Whatever is unconditionally real does not require to be realized, nor can one evidently say that an existing most unquestioned being is only supposed to come into being. *Weltanschauungen* in their ultimate perfections do not concern themselves with such conceptual difficulties. Wherever they commit one, where otherwise opposing series of existence and ethical obligation are joined, one can be assured to locate a really central idea of the respective world view.

I will indicate with greatest brevity a few of these central ideas. For Greek classicism, it was the idea of *being*, of the uniform, the substantial, the divine. This divinity was not presented pantheistically without form, but was molded into meaningfully plastic forms. The Christian Middle Ages placed in its stead the concept of *God* as at once the source and goal of all reality, unquestioned lord over our existence and yet demanding free obedience and devotion from us. Since the Renaissance, this place has come to be occupied gradually by the concept of *nature*. It appeared as the only being and truth, yet also as an ideal, as something which first had to be represented and insisted upon. At first this occurred among artists, for whom the final kernel of reality embodied the highest value. The seventeenth century built its ideas around the concept of *natural law*, which alone it saw as essentially valid. The century of Rousseau enshrined *nature* as its ideal, its absolute value, the goal of its longing. Toward the end of this epoch, *ego*, the spiritual personality, emerged as a new central concept. Some thinkers represented the totality of being as a creation of the ego; others saw personal identity as a *task*, the essential task for man. Thus the ego, human individuality, appeared either as an absolute moral demand or as the metaphysical purpose of the world. Despite the colorful variety of its intellectual movements, the nineteenth century did not develop a comprehensive central idea—unless, perhaps, we give this title to the idea of *society*, which for many nineteenth-century thinkers epitomized the reality of life. Thus the individual was often seen as a mere point of intersection for social series, or even as a fiction like the atom. Alternately, complete submergence of the self in society was demanded; to devote oneself completely to society was viewed as an absolute obligation, which included morality and everything else. Only at the very end of the century did a new idea appear: the concept of *life* was raised to a central place, in which perceptions of reality were united with metaphysical, psychological, moral, and aesthetic values.

The expansion and development of the concept of life is confirmed by the fact that it brought together two important philisophical antagonists, Schopenhauer and Nietzsche. Schopenhauer is the first modern philosopher who does not inquire for some *contents* of life, for ideas or states of being [*Seinsbeständen*] within the deepest and most decisive strata. Instead, he asks exclusively: What is life, what is its meaning, purely *as* life? One must not be misled by the fact that he does not use the term "life," but speaks only about the *will* toward life, of the will itself. The will represents his answer concerning the question about the meaning of life which transcends all his speculative extrapolations beyond life. This means that life cannot obtain any meaning and purpose from beyond itself. It will always grasp its own will though it be disguised in a thousand forms. Since it can only remain within itself, because of its metaphysical reality, it can find only unbounded illusion and ultimate disappointment in each apparent goal. Nietzsche, on the other hand, who also starts from life as the singular determination of itself and the sole substance of all its contents, finds in life itself the purpose of life which it is denied from the outside. This life by its nature is increment, enrichment, development towards fulfillment and power, towards a force and beauty flowing from itself. It gains greater value not through reaching a designated goal, but through its own development by becoming *more* alive and thus gaining a value which increases towards the infinite. Although Schopenhauer's desperation about life is radically opposed to Nietzsche's jubilation because of deep, essential contrasts which deride any intellectual mediation or decision, these two thinkers share a basic question which separates them from all earlier philosophers. This basic question is: What is the meaning of life, what is its value merely as life? One can only inquire into knowledge and morality, self and reason, art and God, happiness and suffering, once this first puzzle has been solved. Its solution decides everything else. It is only the original fact of life which provides meaning and measure, positive or negative value. The concept of life is the point of intersection for these two opposed lines of thought which provide the framework for the fundamental decisions of modern life.

I will now illustrate through several contemporary examples the uniqueness of the cultural situation we are [in 1914] undergoing, in which the longing for a new form always overturns the old one, in particular, the opposition against the principle of form as such. We find this opposition even when consciousness appears to progress towards new structures. The Middle Ages had their ecclesiastical Christian ideals, and the Renaissance had its rediscovery of secular nature. The Enlightenment embraced the ideal of reason, and German idealism embellished science by artistic fantasies and provided for art a foundation of cosmic width through scientific knowledge. But the basic impulse behind contemporary culture is a negative one, and this is why, unlike men in all these earlier epochs, we have been for some time now living without any shared ideal, even perhaps without any ideals at all.

If you were to ask educated people today by what ideals they live, most would give a specialized answer derived from their occupational experience. Only rarely would they speak of a cultural ideal which rules them as total human beings. There is a good reason for this. Not only is there a lack of material for a comprehensive cultural ideal, but the fields which it would have to circumscribe are too numerous and heterogeneous to permit such intellectual simplification. Moving to individual cases, I will address myself first to art.

Of the various endeavors which collectively are designated as *Futurism*, only the movement which calls itself *Expressionism* seems to have a sharply delineated identity of its own. If I am not mistaken, the meaning of Expressionism is that the inner emotions of the artist are manifest in his work exactly as he experiences them; his emotions are continued, extended in the work. Human emotions cannot be reified in artistic convention, or moulded by a form which is forced on them from without. For this reason Expressionism has nothing in common with that imitation of a being or of an event which is the intention of Impressionism. Impressions, after all, are not purely individual products of the artist, exclusively determined from within, but passive and dependent on a world outside. The work of art which reflects them is a sort of mixture between the artistic life and the peculiarity of a given object. Any artistic form must reach the artist from somewhere: from tradition, from a previous example, from a fixed principle. But all these sources of form are restraints on life, which wishes to flow creatively from within itself. If life yields to such forms, it only finds itself bent, rigidified, and distorted in the work of art.

Let us consider, in its purest form, the expressionistic model of the creative process. The movements of the pointer's spirit, according to this model, extend without any interference to the hand which holds the brush. The painting expresses them, just as a gesture expresses inner emotions or a shout expresses pain: the movements of the brush follow those of the spirit without resistance; hence the image on the canvas represents an immediate condensation of inner life, which did not permit anything superficial or alien to enter into its unfolding. Expressionistic paintings have often been named after some object with which they seem to have nothing in common, and many people consider this strange and irrational. In fact, however, it is not as meaningless as it would appear according to previous artistic preconceptions. The inner emotions of the artist, which flow forth in an expressionistic work, may originate in secret or unknown sources within the soul. But they can also originate in stimuli from objects in the external world. Until recently it was assumed that a successful artistic response must be morphologically similar to the stimulus that evoked it; indeed the whole impressionistic school was based on this conception. It was one of the great achievements of Expressionism to dispel this idea. Instead it demonstrated that there is no need for the identity between the form of the cause and that of its effect. Thus, the perception of a violin or a human face can evoke in a painter emotional responses which his art metamorphoses into a completely different form. One might say that the expressionistic artist replaces his model with the impulse lying behind the model that stimulates his life, which obeys only itself, towards movement. Expressed in an abstract manner, which nevertheless traces the realistic line of the wall, the creative act represents the struggle of life for self-identity. Whenever life expresses itself, it desires to express only itself; thus it breaks through any form which would be superimposed on it by some other reality.

The established phenomenon, the painting, does of course have a form. But according to the artist's intention, the form represents only a necessary evil. Unlike all previous artistic forms, it does not have a meaning by itself. For this reason, abstract art is also indifferent to the traditional standards of beauty or ugliness, which are connected with the primacy of form. Life, in its flow, is not determined by a goal but driven by a force: hence it has its significance beyond beauty and ugliness. Once the product exists, it becomes evident that it does not possess the kind of meaning and value which one expects from an objectified datum that has become independent of its creator. This value, however, has been withheld from the painting—we might say, almost jealously—by a life which gives expression only to itself. Our peculiar preference for the late works of major artists may be based on this fact. Creative life has here become so sovereign in these works, so self-sufficient and rich, that it rejects any other form which is traditional or shared with others. Its expression in a work of art is nothing but its natural fate. As connected and meaningful as the work may appear from this perspective, it may appear fragmented, unbalanced, as if composed of pieces, when viewed from the point of view of traditional forms. This is not an example of a senile incapacity for making a form, no weakness of age, but rather strength of age. In this epoch of his perfection, the great artist is so pure that his work will reveal through its form what has been autonomously generated through the drive of his life. The unique right of the form has been lost to the artist.

In principle it is completely possible that a form which is perfect and meaningful purely as a form will represent a fully adequate expression of immediate life, clinging to it as if it were an organically grown skin. This is undoubtedly so in the case of the great classical works of art. Disregarding them, however, we find a peculiar property of the spiritual realm which has implications far beyond its consequences for the arts. We might say that the arts express something which is alive beyond the scope of perfected and available artistic forms. Every major artist and each great work of art contain more breadth and depth which flow from hidden sources than art is able to express. Men try incessantly to shape and interpret this life. In classical examples the attempt is successful, and life fuses completely with art. However, life attains a more highly differentiated and more self-conscious expression in those cases where it contradicts and even destroys artistic forms. There is, for example, the inner fate which Beethoven intends to express in his last compositions. The old artistic form is not broken up; rather, it is overpowered by something else, something which breaks forth from another dimension.

It is similar in the case of metaphysics. Its goal is the search of truth; yet something more is often expressed through it. This something becomes unrecognizable, since it overpowers the truth as such, since what it asserts is full of contradictions and can be easily disproven. It can be counted among the typical paradoxes of the spirit—that only some systems of metaphysics would be given the status of truth if they were measured by the standard of actual experience. Perhaps, similarly, there is also some element in religion which is not religious; when this element comes to the surface, all concretized religious forms, in which there is true religion, may be destroyed. This is the inner dynamic of heresy and apostasy.

There is more in human products, perhaps in every single one which derives fully from the creative power of the spirit, than is contained in its forms. This marks off everything that has soul from all that is produced merely mechanically. Here, perhaps, may be found the motivation for the contemporary interest in the art of Van Gogh. In him more than any other painter, one senses a passionate life which swings far beyond the limits of pictorial art. It flows from a unique breadth and depth; that it finds in the painter's talent a channel for its expression seems only accidental, as if it could just as well have given life to practical or religious, to poetic or musical activities. It is primarily this burning life, which can be felt in its immediacy—and which sometimes enters into a destructive contrast with its obvious form—that makes Van Gogh so fascinating.

The desire for completely abstract art among some sectors of modern youth may stem from passion for an immediate and unrestrained [*nackten*] expression of self. The frenetic pace of the lives of our youth carries this tendency to its absolute extreme, and it is youth above all which represents this movement. In general, historical changes of an internal or external revolutionary impact have been carried by youth. In the special nature of the present change, we have a particular reference to it. Whereas adults because of their weakening vitality, concentrate their attention more and more on the objective *contents* of life, which in the present meaning could as well be designated as its forms, youth is more concerned with the process of life. Youth only wishes to express its power and its surplus of power, regardless of the objects involved. Thus cultural movement toward life and its expression alone, which disdains almost everything formal, objectifies the meaning of youthful life.

A fundamental observation must be made here which also applies outside the art world. What are we to make of the widespread *search for originality* among contemporary youth? Often it is only a form of vanity, the attempt to become a "sensation" both for oneself and others. The motive in better cases is a passion for giving expression to the truly individual life. The certainty that life is really only its expression seems to take hold of youth only in times such as ours, when nothing traditional is accepted. To accept any objective form, it is felt, would drain away human individuality: moreover it would dilute one's vitality by freezing it into the mold of something already dead. Originality reassures us that life is pure, that it has not diluted itself by absorbing extrinsic, objectified, rigid forms into its flow. This is perhaps a subliminal motive, not explicit but powerful, which underlies modern individualism.

We can find this same basic desire in one of the most recent philosophical movements which turns its back most decisively against traditional expressions of philosophy. I will designate it as *Pragmatism*, since the best known branch of this theory, the American, has thus been named. I consider this particular branch as most superficial and limited. We can construct an ideal type of Pragmatism independent of any existing fixed version, which will illuminate its relation to our present inquiry. Let us first understand what Pragmatism is attacking. Of all areas of culture, there is none which we consider more independent of life, none so autonomous in its isolation from the motives, needs, and fates of individuals than cognition. That two times two equals four, or that material masses are attracted to one another inversely to the square of their distances, is valid whether or not living minds know it, regardless of any changes of mind which mankind might undergo. Even technical knowledge, which is directly interwoven with life and plays a large role in the history of mankind, remains essentially untouched by the ups and downs of life's flow. So-called "practical" knowledge, after all, is only "theoretical" knowledge which has been applied to practical purposes. As a form of knowledge it belongs to an order with laws of its own, an idealized empire of truth.

It is this independence of truth, which has been presupposed throughout history, that Pragmatism most avidly denies. Our external life no less than our internal life, the pragmatist claims, is based on some imagination of knowledge. If it is true it will preserve and support our life; if it is an error, it will lead us into ruin. Our imaginations are formed by purely psychic influences. In no way are they mechanical reflections of the reality in which our real lives are intertwined. Hence it would be a most remarkable coincidence if they were to lead to desirable and predictable consequences within the realm of the real. It is probable, however, that among the numerous impressions and ideas which determine our active life, there are those which obtain the title of truth because they support and sustain life, while others with opposing consequences are called erroneous. Hence there is no originally independent truth which is subsequently drawn into the stream of life in order to guide it appropriately. On the contrary, among the infinite number of images and ideas which are borne along on the stream of our consciousness, there are some which correspond with our will to live. One might say that this is an accident; without this accident, however, we could not exist. It is precisely these supportive ideas which we recognize as right and true. Thus it is neither the objects by themselves, nor sovereign reason, which determine the truth-value of our thoughts. Rather, it is life—which expresses itself sometimes through the stark necessities of survival, sometimes through the deepest spiritual needs—that forces us to classify our ideas, one pole of which we designate as the full truth and the other as full error.

I cannot give a full exposition of this theory or criticize it here. Nor am I here concerned with its truth or falsity. I want simply to observe that it has been developed at a particular stage in history. Pragmatism, as we have seen, deprives truth [*Erkennen*] of its old claim to be a free-floating domain ruled by independent and ideal laws. Truth has now become interwoven with life, nourished by this source, guided by the totality of its directions and purposes, legitimized through its basic values. Life has thus reclaimed its sovereignty over a previously autonomous province. This can be reformulated in a more ideological way: The form of truth [*Erkennen*] in the past provided a fixed frame or an indestructible canvas for the total world of our thoughts and feelings, which it claimed to infuse with an inner consistency and a self-sufficient meaning. Now, however, thought and feeling are being dissolved in and by the stream of life; they yield to its growing and changing forces and directions, without providing them with any resistance based on an independent right or a timeless validity. The purest expression of Life as a central idea is reached when it is viewed as the metaphysical basic fact, as the essence of all being. This goes far beyond the transformation of the problem of knowledge: now every object becomes a pulse beat of absolute life, or one manner of its presentation, or a developmental stage. In the total unfolding of the world toward the spirit, life rises as spirit. As matter, it sinks below. When this theory resolves the problem of knowledge through an intuition which, beyond all logic and rational intelligibility, immediately grasps the intrinsic truth of things, it means to say that only life is capable of understanding life. From this perspective all objectivity, the object of all knowledge, must be transformed into life. Thus the process of cognition, now interpreted as a function of life, is confronted with an object which it can completely penetrate since it is equal in its essence. While original pragmatism resolved the image of the world into life from the point of view of the subject only, it [*Lebensphilosophie*] did this for the object as well. Nothing is retained here of form as a principle independent of life, as a mode of being with meaning and power of its own. What might still be designated form, when staying within the terms of this imagery, could only exist because of reprieve given by this life.

This movement away from formal principles reaches a zenith not only in the pragmatists, but in all thinkers who are filled with the modern feeling against closed systems. Earlier epochs, ruled by classical and formal considerations, had raised these systems to a level of sanctity. The closed system aims to unite all truths, in their most general concepts, into a structure of higher and lower elements which extend from a basic theme, arranged symmetrically and balanced in all directions. The decisive point is that it sees the proof of its substantive validity in its architectural and aesthetic completion, in the successful closure and solidity of its edifice. This represents the most extreme culmination of the formal principle: perfection of form as the ultimate criterion of truth. This is the view against which life, which is continuously creating and destroying forms, must defend itself.

The philosophy that exalts and glorifies life insists firmly on two things. On one hand it rejects mechanics as a universal principle: it views mechanics as, at best, a technique in life, more likely a symptom of its decay. On the other hand it rejects the claim of ideas to a metaphysical independence and primacy. Life does not wish to be dominated by what is below it; indeed, it does not wish to be dominated at all, not even by ideas which claim for themselves a rank above it. Although no higher form of life is capable of knowing itself without the guidance of ideas this now seems to be possible only because ideas themselves derive from life. It is the essence of life to generate its guidance, salvation, opposition, victories, and victims. It sustains and elevates itself, as it were, by an indirect route, through products of its own. That they confront it independently represents its own achievement, expresses its own distinctive style of life. This internal opposition is the tragic conflict of life as spirit. It gets more noticeable the more self-conscious life becomes.

Viewed in the most general cultural perspective, this movement implies a turn away from classicism as the absolute ideal for human culture. Classicism, after all, is the ideology of form, which regards itself as the ultimate norm for life and creation. Certainly nothing more adequate or refined has taken the place of the old ideal. The attack against classicism is not concerned with the introduction of new cultural forms. Instead self-assured life wishes to liberate itelf from the yoke of form as such, of which classicism is a historical representation.

I can report briefly on an identical trend within a specialized area of ethics. A systematic critique of existing sexual relationships has been named "the new morality." It is propagated by a small group, but its aims are shared by a large one. Its criticism is directed mainly against two elements of the contemporary scene: marriage and prostitution. Its basic theme can be expressed as follows: the most personal and intimate meaning of erotic life is destroyed by the forms in which our culture has reified and trapped it. Marriage, which is entered for a thousand nonerotic reasons, is destroyed from within by a thousand unyielding traditions and legalized cruelties; where it is not wrecked, it loses all individuality and leads to stagnation. Prostitution has almost turned into a legal institution which forces the erotic life of young people into a dishonorable direction which contradicts and caricatures its innermost nature. Marriage and prostitution alike appear as oppressive forms which thwart immediate and genuine life. Under different cultural circumstances, these forms may not have been so inappropriate. Now, however, they call forth forces of opposition which sprung from the ultimate sources of life. We can see here how large a shadow falls between the will to destroy old forms and the desire to build new ones. These reformers are not really interested in working out an adequate replacement for the forms which they condemn. The destructive force of their criticism impedes the cultural process of obsolescence and reconstruction which would normally take place. The force acting in the guise of new forms is temporarily and as it were without disguise directed against those old forms emptied of genuine erotic life. Now, however, it is confronted with the previously mentioned contradiction since erotic life, as soon as it is expressed in cultural contexts, necessarily requires some form. Nevertheless, it is only a superficial observer who sees here nothing but unbounded and anarchic lust. Genuine erotic life in fact flows naturally in individual channels. Opposition is directed against forms because they force it into generalized schemata and thereby overpower its uniqueness. The struggle between life and form is fought here less abstractly and less metaphysically as a struggle between individuality and generalization.

We can find the same tendency in contemporary religion. Observe, for instance, the fact that quite a few intellectually advanced individuals employ mysticism to satisfy their religious needs. This has been noticed since around the turn of the century. On the whole it can be assumed that these people were socialized into the ideologies of one or another of the existing churches. A double motivation for their mysticism is unmistakable. First of all, the forms which objectify and direct religious feeling are felt to be inadequate for contemporary life. On the other hand, these mystical tendencies suggest that life's longing may be frustrated by objective forms in themselves, that the religious impulse must search for different goals and ways. It seems clear that a firm determination and delimitation of the boundaries of religious experience has been replaced. Mysticism aspires toward a deity which transcends every personal and particular form; it seeks an undetermined expanse of religious feeling which does not conflict with any dogmatic barrier, a deepening into formless infinity, a mode of expression based only on the powerful longing of the soul. Mysticism appears as the last refuge for religious individuals who cannot as yet free themselves from all transcendental guidance, but only, as it were preliminarily, from that which is determined and fixed in content.

The most decisive instance of this development—even though it may be full of contradictions and be eternally separated from its objective—is a tendency for forms of religious *belief* to dissolve into modes of religious *life*, into religiosity as a purely *functional* justification of religion. Until recently, changes of religious culture have always proceeded in the following way: a certain form of religious life, originally fully adequate in its strengths and essential characteristics, gradually rigidifies in superficialties and narrow specialization. It is displaced by a newly rising form in which religious impulses can flow, dynamically and without impediment. In other words, a new religious form, a new series of beliefs took the place of an outmoded one. For a relatively large number of people today, the supernatural objects of religious belief have been radically excised; their religious impulse, however, has not thereby been eliminated. Its effective force, which formerly manifested itself through the development of more adequate dogmatic contents, can no longer express itself through the polarity of a believing subject and a believed object. In the ultimate state of affairs towards which this new tendency is aiming, religion would function as a medium for the direct expression of life. It would be analogous not to a single melody within the symphony of life, but to the tonality within which the whole work is performed. The space of life, filled entirely by secular contents, actions and fate, thoughts and feelings, would be permeated with that unique inner unity between humility and authority, tension and peace, danger and consecration, which can only be called religious. Life spent in this fashion would demonstrate its absolute value—a value which, under other circumstances, was given to it only through the singular forms in which it appeared and through the individual contents of belief towards which it had crystallized. Angelus Silesius gives us a foretaste of it, when he separates religious values from all fixed connections with something specific and recognizes their place as lived life.

> The Saint when he is drinking
> Is also pleasing God
> As if he were praying and singing.

He is not concerned, however, with the so-called "secular religion." The latter still clings to determinate contents, which are empirical instead of transcendental. It also channels religious life into specific forms of beauty and greatness, distinction, and lyrical motion. Here, however, religiosity is in question whether it is a direct process of life which encompasses every pulse beat: Is it a being, not a having, is it a form of piousness which is called belief whenever it deals with objects? Now, however, religiosity is similar to life itself. It does not aim to satisfy extrinsic needs, but searches instead for continuous life in a deeper sphere in which it is not yet torn between needs and satisfactions. In this sphere of religious perfection, it does not require an object which prescribes for it a certain form—just as an expressionistic painter does not satisfy his artistic needs by clinging to an exterior subject. Life wishes to express itself directly as religion, not through a language with a given lexicon and prescribed syntax. One could use an apparently paradoxical expression and say: The soul can find faith only by losing it. To preserve the integrity of religious feeling, it must shake off all determined and predetermined religious form.

This desire is often exposed to a form of purely negative criticism which doesn't even understand itself. Nevertheless, it encounters a profound difficulty: life can express itself and realize its freedom only through forms; yet forms must also necessarily suffocate life and obstruct freedom. Piety, or the power of believing, is part of the constitution of the soul, integral to its life: it would influence the soul even in the absence of a religious object—just as an erotic individual must conserve and prove his powers even though he might never meet an object worthy of his love. Nevertheless, I wonder whether the fundamental will of religious life does not require an object, whether a merely functional character and its unformed dynamics which color and bless the mere ups and downs of life—which appear to represent the definitive meaning of so many religious movements—can ever really satisfy it. Perhaps this new religiosity is only a casual interlude. It can be counted among the deepest inner difficulties of numerous modern people that it is impossible to further protect the religions of church tradition, while at the same time the religious drives continue to persist in spite of all "enlightenment." This is so since religion can be robbed only of its clothing but not its life. There is a tempting way out of this dilemma in the cultivation of the religious life as a thing in itself, the transformation of the verb "to believe" from a transitive "I believe that . . ." to a purely intransitive "I believe." In the long run, perhaps, this might become no less entangled in contradictions. Here again we see the basic conflict inherent in the nature of cultural life. Life must either produce forms or proceed through forms. But forms belong to a completely different order of being. They demand some content above and beyond life; they contradict the essence of life itself, with its weaving dynamics, its temporal fates, the unceasing differentiation of each of its parts. Life is inseparably charged with contradiction. It can enter reality only in the form of its antithesis, that is, only in the form of *form*. This contradiction becomes more urgent and appears more irreconcilable the more life makes itself felt.[1] The forms themselves, however, deny this contradiction: in their rigidly individual shapes, in the demands of their imprescriptible rights, they boldly present themselve as the true meaning and value of our existence. This audacity varies with the degree to which culture has grown.

1   Since life is the antithesis of form, and since that which is somehow formed can be conceptually described, the concept of life cannot be freed from logical imprecision. The essence of life would be denied if one tried to form an exhaustive conceptual definition. In order for conscious life to be fully self-conscious, it would have to do without concepts altogether, for conceptualization inevitably brings on the reign of forms; yet concepts are essential to self-consciousness. The fact that the possibilities of expression are so limited by the essence of life does not diminish its momentum as an idea.

Life wishes here to obtain something which it cannot reach. It desires to transcend all forms and to appear in its naked immediacy. Yet the processes of thinking, wishing, and forming can only substitute one form for another. They can never replace the form as such by life which as such transcends the form. All these attacks against the forms of our culture, which align against them the forces of life "in itself," embody the deepest internal contradictions of the spirit. Although this chronic conflict between form and life has become acute in many historical epochs, none but ours has revealed it so clearly as its basic theme.

It is a philistine prejudice that conflicts and problems are dreamt up merely for the sake of their solution. Both in fact have additional tasks in the economy and history of life, tasks which they fulfill independently of their own solutions. Thus they exist in their own right, even if the future does not replace conflicts with their resolutions, but only replaces their forms and contents with others. In short, the present is too full of contradictions to stand still. This itself is a more fundamental change than the reformations of times past. The bridge between the past and the future of cultural forms seems to be demolished; we gaze into an abyss of unformed life beneath our feet. But perhaps this formlessness is itself the appropriate form for contemporary life. Thus the blueprint of life is obliquely fulfilled. Life is a struggle in the absolute sense of the term which encompasses the relative contrast between war and peace: that absolute peace which might encompass this contrast remains an eternal [*göttlich*] secret to us.

Bibliographical Note

THE MOST COMPLETE bibliography of writings by and about Simmel is that prepared by Kurt Gassen in *Buch des Dankes an Georg Simmel*, edited by Gassen and Landmann (Berlin: Duncker & Humblot, 1958), pp. 309–65. Earlier bibliographies published in the United States are to be found in Nicholas J. Spykman, *The Social Theory of Georg Simmel* (Chicago: University of Chicago Press, 1925); Erich Rosenthal and Kurt Oberlander, "Books, Papers, and Essays by Georg Simmel," *American Journal of Sociology* 51 (1945): 238–47; Kurt H. Wolff, *The Sociology of Georg Simmel* (Glencoe, Ill.: Free Press, 1950), pp. liv–lxi; and Kurt H. Wolff, *Georg Simmel, 1858–1918* (Columbus: Ohio State University Press, 1959), pp. 357–82.

All the existing books of English translations of Simmel have been referred to in the notes to the introduction of this volume.